Government and Politics of France

COMPARATIVE GOVERNMENT AND POLITICS
Founding Series Editor: The late **Vincent Wright**

Published

Rudy Andeweg and Galen A. Irwin
Governance and Politics of the Netherlands

Nigel Bowles
Government and Politics of the United States (2nd edition)

Paul Brooker
Non-Democratic Regimes: Theory, Government and Politics

Robert Elgie
Political Leadership in Liberal Democracies

Rod Hague and Martin Harrop
Comparative Government and Politics (5th edition)

Paul Heywood
The Government and Politics of Spain

B. Guy Peters
Comparative Politics: Theories and Methods
[Rights: World excluding North America]

Tony Saich
Governance and Politics of China

Anne Stevens
Government and Politics of France (3rd edition)

Ramesh Thakur
The Government and Politics of India

Forthcoming

Judy Batt
Government and Politics in Eastern Europe

Robert Leonardi
Government and Politics in Italy

Comparative Government and Politics
Series Standing Order
ISBN 0–333–71693–0 hardback
ISBN 0–333–69335–3 paperback
(*outside North America only*)

You can receive future titles in this series as they are published by placing a standing order. Please contact your bookseller or, in the case of difficulty, write to us at the address below with your name and address, the title of the series and an ISBN quoted above.

Customer Services Department, Macmillan Distribution Ltd
Houndmills, Basingstoke, Hampshire RG21 6XS, England

Government and Politics of France

Third Edition

Anne Stevens

First edition 1992
Reprinted twice
Second edition 1996
Reprinted four times
Third edition 2003

Published by PALGRAVE MACMILLAN
Houndmills, Basingstoke, Hampshire RG21 6XS and
175 Fifth Avenue, New York, N.Y. 10010
Companies and representative throughout the world

PALGRAVE MACMILLAN is the global academic imprint of the Palgrave
Macmillan division of St. Martin's Press, LLC and of Palgrave Macmillan Ltd.
Macmillan® is a registered trademark in the United States, United Kingdom
and other countries. Palgrave is a registered trademark in the European
Union and other countries.

ISBN 0–333–99440–X hardback
ISBN 0–333–99441–8 paperback

This book is printed on paper suitable for recycling and made from fully
managed and sustained forest sources.

A catalogue record for this book is available from the British Library.

Library of Congress Cataloging-in-Publication Data
Stevens, Anne, 1942–
   Government and politics of France / Ann Stevens. — 3rd ed.
     p. cm. — (Comparative government and politics)
   Includes bibliographical references and index.
   ISBN 0–333–99440–X (cloth) — ISBN 0–333–99441–8 (pbk)
   1. France—Politics and government—1789– I. Title. II. Series.
   JN2451.S74 2003
   320.944—dc21
                                             2003051444

10 9 8 7 6 5 4 3 2 1
12 11 10 09 08 07 06 05 04 03

Printed and bound in Great Britain by
Creative Print Design (Wales), Ebbw Vale

For Helen

Contents

List of Tables, Figures, Exhibits and Maps

Exhibits

Maps

Preface

Early in the 1950s my parents tired of summer holidays mostly spent on chilly wind-swept beaches and embarked, with hire car, tents and four young children, on what was, in the lingering climate of post-war austerity, a still unusual adventure – a tour through France. I still recall the vivid realization, as the ferry approached Calais, that France looked different, and the even sharper shock of discovering that it really did sound different too. That journey took us from Calais to the Spanish border, and back along the Mediterranean coast. When the family turned towards the Channel again my twin sister and I stayed behind, to spend a further few weeks near Nîmes, in the Ardèche and in Marseilles with the French family with whom we had been corresponding.

That summer left its mark on both my twin and me. It was for both of us the start of a continuing interest in and affection for the country and the first of many visits. For me it was a beginning that, twenty years later, led me, through many changes and chances, to the study of contemporary France. My sister came earlier to the subject, as an undergraduate in Philip Williams' lectures when the Fifth Republic was still quite young. She retains her connections with France and French people. This book is dedicated to her.

This book is a new version of the one first published in 1992 with a second edition in 1996. Like its predecessors it is intended as an introduction to the study of French government and politics for students and also as a guide for general readers with an interest in French affairs. I have been pleased to learn that readers found the previous edition helpful, and am grateful to those students and their teachers whose comments assisted the initial drafting and the revisions. This third edition has been very extensively rewritten and restructured. Chapter 1 now attempts to give a sense of the broad sweep of French social, economic and intellectual life up to the present day. Chapter 2 deals with the multiple revisions to the constitution since 1992. Chapters 3 and 4 now deal with the complex dynamics at the heart of the core executive in France, while Chapters 5, 6 and 7 have been recast and extensively up-dated. Chapter 8 is an almost entirely new attempt to provide a guide to the kaleidoscope of French political parties, and Chapter 9 has new emphases and case studies to illustrate the current shape of interest group and social movement activity. Chapter 10 is also largely new, to give some sense of the ongoing issues which currently provide the content and context for political conflict, debate and activity. Throughout, the European dimension of French politics today has been highlighted.

Research and teaching on aspects of French politics and administration have been at the centre of my working life for the past three decades, and I owe a great deal to the many colleagues at Sussex, Kent and Aston, and to acquaintances and friends who make this area of study so congenial and stimulating. I am especially grateful to the Association for the Study of Modern and Contemporary France, to the editors of *Modern and Contemporary France* and to the Maison Française at Oxford for all they do to make the study of contemporary France both pleasant and fruitful.

I have accumulated many debts over the years I have worked in this field; as I look back I am particularly conscious of those to Dr Howard Machin, Professor John Gaffney, Professor Siân Reynolds, Professor Robert Elgie, and Dr Peter Holmes. The writing and revision of the book have also been much assisted by Professor Clive Church, Professor Françoise Dreyfus, Dr Michael Sutton and Dr Georgios Varouxakis. My family, Handley, Hilary, Lucy and Mary Stevens all believed in me and in the book, even when progress seemed difficult. So did a patient and supportive publisher, Steven Kennedy. With great sorrow I record how much the first two editions of this book owed to Vincent Wright's care and meticulous help, and how sorely, since his death in 1999, I have missed him. Without him there would have been no research, no teaching and no book at all. For the weaknesses and errors it contains I am alone responsible.

March 2003

ANNE STEVENS

List of Abbreviations

BSE	Bovine Spongiform Encephalopathy
CAC	*Commission des Agents de Change* (CAC-40 index of share values on the Paris stock exchange)
CAP	Common Agricultural Policy
CDS	*Centre des Démocrates Sociaux*
CFDT	*Confédération Française Démocratique du Travail*
CFTC	*Confédération Française des Travailleurs Chrétiens*
CGPME	*Confédération Générale des Petites et Moyennes Entreprises*
CGT	*Confédération Générale du Travail*
CNIL	*Commission National de l'Informatique et des Libertés*
CNJA	*Centre National des Jeunes Agriculteurs*
CNPF	*Confédération Nationale du Patronat Française*
CPNT	*Chasse, Pêche, Nature, Tradition*
CODER	*Commission du Développement Economique Régional*
DATAR	*Délégation à l'Aménagement du Territoire et à l'Action Régionale*
DL	*Démocratie Libérale*
EC	Economic Community
ECB	European Central Bank
ECSC	European Coal and Steel Community
EDF	*Electricité de France*
EEC	European Economic Community
EMS	European Monetary System
EMU	Economic and Monetary Union
ENA	*Ecole Nationale d'Administration*
EP	European Parliament
EU	European Union
FD	*Force Démocrate*
FEN	*Fédération de l'Education Nationale*
FN	*Front National*
FNLC	*Front National pour la Libération de la Corse*
FNSEA	*Fédération Nationale des Syndicats d'Exploitants Agricoles*
FO	*Force Ouvrière*
G7	Group of Seven leading industrial countries
GATT	General Agreement on Tariffs and Trade
GDF	*Gaz de France*
GDP	Gross Domestic Product
GE	*Génération Ecologie*

xiv

LCR	*Ligue Communiste Révolutionnaire*
LO	*Lutte Ouvriére*
MDC	*Mouvement des Citoyens*
MEDEF	*Mouvement des Entreprises de France*
MEP	Member of the European Parliament
MNR	*Mouvement National Républicain*
MPF	*Mouvement pour la France*
MRAP	*Mouvement contre le Rascisme et pour l'Amitié entre les Peuples*
MRG	*Mouvement des Radicaux de Gauche*
MRP	*Mouvement Républicain Populaire*
MSI	*Movimento Sociale Italiano*
OAS	*Organisation de l'Armée Secrète*
OECD	Organisation for Economic Co-operation and Development
OEEC	Organisation for European Economic Co-operation
PACS	*Pacte Civile de Solidarité*
PCF	*Parti Communiste Français*
POS	*Plan d'Occupation des Sols*
PR	*Parti Républicain*
PREP	*Pôle Républicain*
PRG	*Parti Radical de Gauche*
PS	*Parti Socialiste*
PSU	*Parti Socialiste Unifié*
RI	*Républicains Indépendents*
RPF	*Rassemblement du Peuple Française*
RPF	*Rassemblement pour la France*
RPR	*Rassemblement pour la République*
SFIO	*Section Française de l'Internationale Ouvriére*
SGCI	*Secretariat General de la Comité Intérministerielle pour les Questions de Coopération Économique Européenne*
SIVOM	*Syndicat Intercommunale à Vocation Unitaire*
SIVU	*Syndicat Intercommunale à Vocation Multiple*
SNCF	*Societé Nationale des Chemins de Fer Français*
TGV	*Train à Grande Vitesse*
UDF	*Union pour la Démocratie Française*
UMP	*Union pour un Mouvement Populaire*
UMP	*Union pour une Majorité Presidentielle*
UNEDIC	*Union pour l'Emploi dans l'Industrie et le Commerce*
UNSA	*Union Nationale des Syndicats Autonomes*

●   Regional prefecture

──   Regional boundaries

The Regions of France

1

France: An Introduction

France is sometimes represented as a hexagon. The coasts of the Channel and then the Atlantic, the Pyrenees and the Mediterranean sea, the Alps and the Jura, the Vosges and the Rhine and the long land frontier with Luxembourg and Belgium seem to outline a regular pattern. The shape of France is not, however, the consequence of some long and rational process of geometrical neatness and indeed the hexagon omits the large Mediterranean island of Corsica. It emerged only slowly, as successive French kings extended their control from their heartland around Paris, conquering Normandy, driving the English out of the South West and the West (Calais, the last English outpost, fell to the French in January 1558) asserting their domination over Burgundy (1481) and Provence (1491), and incorporating Brittany into the kingdom (1532). At the beginning of the nineteenth century Napoleon extended the sphere of metropolitan French administration into the Low Countries and parts of Germany and Northern Italy. In 1815 the Treaty of Vienna redefined France's borders: Corsica, annexed in 1769, remained French but Savoy and the town of Nice, which had been annexed during the Revolution, were lost. They were to return in 1860. The bitter history of Alsace (mostly incorporated into France in 1648) and Lorraine (incorporated in 1766) which were conquered and attached to the German Empire in 1870, regained by the Treaty of Versailles in 1919, conquered again in 1940 and liberated in 1945 left a deep mark on French historical consciousness.

As a result, perhaps, of this chequered history and a certain obsession with French territorial integrity which derives from it, the French constitutions of both 1946 and 1958 proclaim France as a secular, democratic, social, but also indivisible republic. Like many constitutional pronouncements this is a statement of will and intention as much as of fact. The intention is to bring together a country of great diversity and a contested and conflict-ridden political history into a united nation state. This chapter attempts to outline some of the main elements of that diversity. An examination of the geographical and historical diversity of France is followed by a consideration of some of the factors which have contributed to political change and development. The impact of the Revolution, the legacy of Napoleon, the rise of the Republic, relationships between state and church and the period of Liberation and reconstruction all had their repercussions upon the political, economic and social structures of France today. The final section of the chapter provides a very brief overview of social, economic and intellectual developments since 1958.

Geographical Diversity

France, with a land area of 212 919 square miles (543 965 square kilometres) is the third largest country in Europe, exceeded only by Russia and the Ukraine. North and west of a line from the mouth of the Gironde to the Ardennes the land only occasionally rises as high as 250 metres above sea level. South and east of this line the Massif Central, which occupies about one sixth of the land area, rises gradually southeastward with summits of over 1700 metres along the southern escarpment of the Cevennes. Its now extinct volcanoes were thrown up by the tectonic movements that produced the Alps. These, to the east, include the highest mountain in Europe, Mont Blanc (4807 metres). To the south of the Massif Central lie the undulating plains of Languedoc, separated by the valley of the Rhône from Provence, and from Spain by the mountain wall of the Pyrenees. North of the Alps are the wooded hills of the Jura, the Vosges and the Ardennes. More than 23 per cent of the land area of France is forested. The basins of the main rivers – Seine, Loire, Saône, Rhône, Garonne – shape and delineate the various regions. The island of Corsica lies south of the gulf of Genoa, some 100 kilometers south and west of the Côte d'Azur.

Geographical and climatic conditions help to account for the diversity of French landscapes, from the scrubby *macquis* of Provence and Corsica to the mountainous and pastoral landscape of the Alps, the broad flat cereal fields of the plains of Northern France and the vineyards of Languedoc, themselves somewhat different in appearance from the greener, more hilly wine growing country of Burgundy. The coasts of Northern and Western Brittany are rocky and spectacular; further south the Atlantic coast is formed of dunes and marshes. 'Differing conditions of geology, morphology, climate, soil and vegetation are responsible for widely differing natural habitats. Out of these habitats man has made regions, accentuating natural diversity by differences of organisation and use' (Pinchemel, 1987, p. 13).

At the 1999 census the population of metropolitan France was 58 518 748 people. This is similar to the populations of Italy (57.4 million) and the United Kingdom (56.8 million). In the middle of the eighteenth century, it is reckoned, France was the most densely populated country in Europe. Nowadays it is amongst the least densely populated. If France had the same average number of people per square kilometre as the United Kingdom it would have a population of 126 million (Pinchemel, 1987, p. 125). Since the beginning of the nineteenth century the population of France has almost doubled – but growth has not been at a steady rate. Population growth during the nineteenth century was slow, and the population actually declined not only during the First and Second World Wars, but also during the 1930s. Since 1945 the population has increased much more rapidly, growing since 1946 by some 14 million, a greater increase than that which had occurred over the previous century and a half. This increase is largely due to a marked, but fairly short-lived, rise in the birthrate during the babyboom years of 1945–55, combined with sharp reductions in the death rate, and particularly in infant mortality. Immigration has long been an important cause of population growth notably in the nineteenth century and early twentieth centuries and again since the 1950s. Some 4.3 million residents in France (7.4 per cent) at the time of the 1999 census had not been born in France nor held French nationality at birth although 1.56 million had subsequently acquired French nationality as had 800 000 people born in France but without French nationality. Of the 4.3 million 1.3 million, approximately 30 per cent, had been born in North Africa and 45 per cent in Europe (Boëldieu and Borrel, 2000).

The population of France is far from being uniformly distributed within the country. The most striking feature is the concentration in and around Paris. The Ile-de-France region – Paris and the surrounding area – which contained less than 4 per cent of the national population at the beginning of the nineteenth century, 6.5 per cent at the beginning of the twentieth century, and just over 15 per cent at the end of the Second World War, was, at the 1999 census, inhabited by nearly 19 per cent of the population of France.

This concentration is an extreme example of a more general phenomenon of urban growth. Towards the end of the 1920s about half the inhabitants of France lived in areas categorized as rural; that is, in districts which contained no settlement of more than 2000 inhabitants. In 1962, 30 per cent did so, and at the 1999 census 23 per cent (Bessy-Pietri *et al.*, 2000). All types of towns have grown, but especially those which now have populations of between 100 000 and 1 million, of which there are now 38 in France. The largest towns are Lyons, Marseilles and Paris, which, with over 2 million within its city boundaries, far outstrips the other two.

The rhetoric of republican values in France resists attempts to map or define cultural diversity. The Republic is indivisible, and all citizens are to be regarded as equal and in that sense indistinguishable. 'Multiculturalism' as practised, for example, in the United Kingdom, which recognizes the existence of different communities within one country and their right (within general limits) to varied language use, religious customs, clothing and other cultural practices, is explicitly rejected as likely to lead to division and conflict. Nevertheless France is diverse. It is, for example, diverse in religious affiliation. While the majority of the population relate to the Roman Catholic tradition, it is estimated that the second largest group – probably some four to five million (about three million of whom are of North African origin or ancestry) – are culturally Muslims, and there are much smaller Jewish, Protestant and other groups.

France is also linguistically diverse. The arrival of residents speaking languages other than French has increased the diversity of languages spoken, even if, for the reasons suggested above, this is not officially recognized, and indeed the Constitutional Council ruled against ratification of the Council of Europe convention on the protection of minority languages. However, the regional diversity of 'indigenous' languages has diminished. In 1863 at least a quarter of the country's population lived in communes that did not speak French and nearly 450 000 out of just over four million schoolchildren between the ages of seven and thirteen spoke no French at all (Weber, 1979, p. 67). Breton and the Langue d'Oc of the south, being different languages rather than dialects, most effectively resisted the onslaught of Parisian French during the nineteenth and twentieth centuries and are now precariously maintained by bilingual speakers supported by vigorous regional cultural movements, as is the language of Corsica, a Tuscan dialect of Italian.

The regions are also economically diverse. In France the main force of the industrial revolution was not experienced until the second half of the nineteenth century. The economic geography of France that was established before the First World War and is the basis of the present-day pattern arose from several diverse factors. These included the presence of natural resources – coal in Central France and the Nord-Pas-de-Calais, iron ore in Lorraine – or of long established traditional industries – textiles in Lyons and in the North for example. The growth and shape of the railway system was another factor, as was the development of hydro-electric power. Between the wars and until the mid-1950s industrialization was centred in Paris and to the North and East; indeed at that period over 50 per cent of industrial employment was located within the four regions of the Ile-de-France, the Nord-Pas-de-Calais, Lorraine and the Rhône-Alpes. Outside the Paris region this industrialization was based upon long-standing textile, chemical, mining and iron and steel-based industries (Tuppen, 1983, p. 147).

Since the 1950s the areas of traditional industrialization have experienced the problems associated with decline whilst some formerly largely agricultural areas especially in the West, but also in the Alps, have seen the growth of advanced technology industries in a number of towns. Government policy in the 1950s and 1960s was aimed at encouraging industry to move out of Paris. This resulted in the movement out of some industrial activities, though many firms retained headquarters in Paris. Much of the movement was into the area immediately surrounding Paris – the Ile-de-France. From the early 1970s policy concentrated more on industrial reorganization, concentration and adjustment than on decentralization. Even today industrial activity is quite unevenly distributed across France and contrasts exist between regions in the level and nature of their industrial activity.

'At the micro level of *pays* or *arrondissement* France is almost certainly the most variegated [of European countries] in its landscapes and traditional ways of life. The mosaic of mountain, hill, scarpland or plain has been interpreted through a long history of rural and small town development. The late arrival of large scale industry and urbanisation has not had the effect of creating the greater uniformity in ways of life found, for example, in Britain' (House, 1978, p. 56). Distinctive landscapes, building styles, methods of farming, products, lifestyles, even cooking, from the butter, cream and cider of Normandy to the olives, tomatoes, herbs and wine of Provence, reinforce feelings of regional identity. The mobility of the population in the decades since the Second World War, commercial and industrial developments and the impact of genuinely mass media such as television have all helped to produce a greater uniformity of lifestyle and experience throughout

France. However, many French people still have strong feelings for their own or their family's origins and a sense of belonging not only to the nation but also to the locality – of being French but also, perhaps chiefly, Breton, Alsatian, Provençal or Corsican.

The Impact of the French Revolution

The impact of the French Revolution upon the history of modern Europe lies not only in its social, economic and political consequences, but also in the perceptions, even the myths, which surrounded it and the strength of the political traditions and analyses which looked back to it as a crucial point of reference. These competing and contradictory traditions formed the basis for many of the conflicts and cleavages discussed below. Historians debate the causes and conse- quences of the Revolution; from its turbulent events stem many of the political and administrative currents, forces and patterns that shape modern France. Although continuities can also be traced, linking people, behaviour and institu- tions across the watershed of the Revolution, it was nevertheless an abrupt break with the pattern of what had gone before, a pattern that was very soon described as the old order (the *ancien régime*). That pattern was based in principle upon an absolute monarchy, upheld by a theory of divine right and by a hierarchical society which emphasized the existence of three separate orders, or estates, within society – the clergy, the nobility and the remainder, the third estate. Government consisted of the attempt by the King to manage a diverse and imper- fectly unified country through a system of royal officials. This administration was chiefly concerned with the maintenance of public order, the levying of taxes and provision for military needs and also with the commerce and industry of the country. The name of Louis XIV's minister, Colbert, is particularly associated with attempts to encourage trade, foster economic development and introduce industries through governmental supervision and initiative.

The old pattern was swept away with great speed by the Revolution (see Exhibit 1.1), swept away, moreover, in the name of rational philosophical uniform principles. The representatives of the three estates, summoned for the first time since 1614 to meet as the Estates General, and transformed into a National Assembly, voted in August 1789 for what is described as the abolition of feudalism – the ending of the old patterns of privileges and rights and the abolition of the sale of offices. These measures implied the restructuring of the systems of local administration, of justice and of taxation. The principles upon which this restructuring was to occur were set out in the Declaration of the Rights of Man, passed on 26 August 1789. This Declaration, which forms an integral part of the present-day French constitution, asserts the right of all men (but not women, who did not achieve political rights until 1944) to liberty, property, secur- ity and resistance to oppression. It insists that the law is the same for everyone, all citizens being equally entitled to avail themselves of its protection and equally subject to its sanctions, and that all citizens should be eligible for position and public employment on the sole criterion of ability. Political authority stems, according to Article 3, from the nation. The Declaration also includes an assertion of freedom of religious belief and of speech and publication.

With the abolition of the monarchy in 1792, Republicanism became an essential component of the Revolutionary tradition. The broad moral principles of rationality, liberty and equality which are still widely felt to be central to France's identity are encompassed within the concept of Republicanism.

The Revolution, however, left France deeply divided. There were divisions even within the revolutionary tradition. In popular mythology these have come to be symbolized by the divisions between Girondins – a group of members of the national assembly grouped around the representative from the Gironde, the area around Bordeaux – and the Jacobins – the party of Robespierre, named after the former Jacobin monastery where the group met. The Girondins are held to symbolize a more moderate, more participatory, form of republicanism, with an emphasis on local rights. The adjective 'Jacobin' is applied to a tradition which insists firmly upon the power and the authority of the central institutions of the republic, upon the need for uniformity throughout the country and upon a strong and centralized direction of public affairs.

Opposed to the revolutionary republican tradition there was a monarchist tradition, seeking a return to a hierarchical and ordered society. The restoration of the monarchy in 1815 marked a brief ascendancy for this political tradition which was an important component of the 'Right' in French political life for much of the nineteenth century. In addition to this 'anti-revolutionary' current, it is possible, following David Thomson, to identify a 'counterrevolutionary' current. 'Common to all forms was the blunting of some consequences of the Revolution by accepting and turning against them some of its other consequences and implications' (Thomson, 1969, p. 80). The political manifestations of this current were liberal Orleanism, dominant during the constitutional monarchy of the Orleanist King Louis-Philippe between 1830 and 1848, and the Bonapartists, with their appeal to a strong leader supported by popular plebiscite. All these currents played important roles in the politics of the nineteenth century, and even when the dynasties to which they were attached died out or dwindled the political cleavages which they symbolized continued.

Church and State

The salience, and the bitterness, of the division between revolutionary and reactionary political traditions was enhanced by the fact that it was deeply entangled with another area of conflict, that over the place and role of the Roman Catholic church within society. Under the *ancien régime* the church held a particular place in society, for religious doctrine played an important role in legitimizing the power of the monarch.

The initial period of the Revolution (see Exhibit 1.1) saw the ending of the privileges which the clergy had enjoyed in their role as feudal landowners. Then,

EXHIBIT 1.1

Regimes in France since 1789

May–June 1789	Estates General meets at Versailles and declares itself a constituent national assembly.
August 1789	Adoption of the Declaration of the Rights of Man.
September 1789	New constitution; limited monarchy.
August 1792	Invasion of the Tuileries Palace; end of the monarchy.
September 1792	Meeting of the Convention.
January 1793	Execution of the King.
April 1793	Establishment of the Committee of Public Safety.
June 1793	Vote for 1793 Constitution; never implemented.
10 October 1793	Convention decides that government will be 'revolutionary' until peace is achieved.
April 1795	Directory constitution.
November 1799	(18 Brumaire an VIII) Coup d'état of Napoleon Bonaparte.
December 1799	Constitution of the Consulate.
May 1804	Establishment of the First Empire.
April 1814	Restoration of the monarchy; Constitutional Charter.
March 1815	Return of Napoleon. Imperial constitution amended by *Acte Additionnel*.
June 1815	Second abdication of Napoleon – return to monarchy and 1814 charter.
1830	Constitutional monarchy (July monarchy) under Louis-Philippe.
1848	Second Republic.
1852	Second Empire under Napoleon III.
1870	Provisional regime.
1875	'Wallon amendment' – consolidation of Third Republic.
1940	Occupation. 'Vichy' regime continued Third Republic constitution except where amended by Pétain's constitutional acts.
1944	Provisional Government.
1946	Fourth Republic.
1959	Fifth Republic.

in 1790, as the need for money grew pressing, the National Assembly voted the Civil Constitution of the Clergy, which deprived the church of its landed possessions and its right to levy tithes and made the clergy salaried officials. The Pope condemned this move. From this time on resistance to the Revolution was increasingly identified with support for the church.

Equally, revolutionary principles came to appear incompatible with traditional religion and in 1793 a revolutionary calendar was introduced abolishing Sundays – weeks were replaced by 10-day periods – and removing traditional associations with the Christian year. A cult of reason was invented and a campaign of de-christianization begun. This was short-lived, and Napoleon, facing a society in which Roman Catholicism was still deeply anchored, brought order and compromise through the conclusion, in 1801, of a Concordat with the papacy. This remained in force until 1905. The church's lands were not restored, the clergy were paid salaries by the government and the degree of religious toleration introduced by the Revolution through the recognition of Protestants and Jews was maintained. In 1905 the advocates of *laïcité* (secularism) achieved the formal separation of churches and state, which no longer recognizes any religion nor pays any clergy.

By the end of the nineteenth century, the church was clearly identified with the forces of the reactionary Right, with conservatives who hankered for a return to an ordered hierarchical society. It had great difficulty accepting the principle of a republican regime, with all its implications of democracy and popular sovereignty, and only did so at all, and then partially, slowly and reluctantly, in a movement known as *ralliement*, at the urging of Pope Leo XIII in the 1890s.

The clash between clerical and anti-clerical forces was dramatically demonstrated at the time of the Dreyfus affair (see Exhibit 1.2), which linked together a

---

EXHIBIT 1.2

The Dreyfus Affair

In 1894 a list, probably recovered from a waste-paper basket in the German Embassy, and detailing documents apparently handed over to the Germans by an officer of the French army acting as a spy for them, came into the hands of French counter-intelligence. Suspicion fell upon Captain Alfred Dreyfus, a Jewish officer from Alsace. The evidence was flimsy, but the military authorities were being harassed by the right-wing press who alleged that a traitor had been discovered, but would escape justice because he was Jewish and consequently had influential protectors. A secret court-martial was held, Dreyfus was found guilty and sentenced to life imprisonment in the tropical prison island, Devil's Island. Two years later, with information continuing to flow to the Germans, a new counter-intelligence chief re-examined the case. Although senior officers tried to suppress his opinions, and to bolster up the case against Dreyfus with additional forged evidence, the doubts became known. In the hope of quelling them another officer, to whom some evidence had pointed, was court-martialled, in 1898, and triumphantly acquitted. Two days later the novelist Emile Zola published his famous article *J'accuse* accusing the army of deliberate injustice.

France became very divided indeed. There were those who believed in the necessity of upholding the rights of every individual, and who called for justice. The League for the Defence of the Rights of Man was founded. Many of those arguing for Dreyfus were strongly anti-clerical and anti-militarist. They were supported by a number of left-wing politicians. On the other hand were those who were convinced that to question the army's proceedings was to undermine the state and subvert national strength. The church, the monarchists and the aristocracy came out in support of the army, and there were very strong currents of anti-Semitism.

Eventually Dreyfus was brought back from Devil's Island. In 1899 another court-martial found him guilty but with extenuating circumstances, the nearest the army would come to admitting a mistake. Dreyfus was promptly pardoned by the President, and later completely exonerated by a civilian appeal court. But the divisions and passions which this extraordinary and melodramatic affair had aroused, and the myths it created, were not quickly forgotten.

whole series of complex themes, involving a large number of social and political groupings in taking sides and hence ranging themselves in virulent opposition to the proponents of the alternative view.

The identification of the church with reactionary and conservative principles and forces within society aroused fierce hostility to it amongst those who professed democratic and Republican traditions and amongst Socialists who had good Marxist reasons for their hostility (Hanley, 2002, Chapters 1–3). The field of education was a particularly hotly contested one, since this is a major way in which the church can impinge upon society. This hostility, known as anti-clericalism, persisted as a major trend in French political life. It coexisted with an even more widespread, but not politicized, social trend to indifference, as the population, especially the male population, ceased church-going. Nevertheless, although often inextricably intertwined with other issues, the old conflict between clerical and anticlerical sentiments has not been entirely forgotten in France.

The Legacy of Napoleon

Napoleon Bonaparte, who came to power initially as one of three consuls in 1799, was crowned Emperor in 1804, and was finally defeated and exiled by the British in 1815, introduced a third strand of political tradition that evoked some of the aspects of the Revolution – chiefly the emphasis upon direct popular support – and allied them to administrative rationality, authoritarian institutions and an assertion of national grandeur. Bonapartism was not a return to the hierarchical privileged society of the *ancien régime*: nor was it a continuation of the democratic republican aspects of the period from 1791 to 1799.

In political terms the legacy of Bonapartism was a political tradition which supported the idea of popular sovereignty as embodied within an empire and confirmed by plebiscite. It 'looked to an authoritarian government rather than to religion or the habit of deference to maintain order and social stability' (Anderson, 1977, p. 101). It can also be linked with the idea that a strong and charismatic leader may, especially at times of crisis, be required to override the incurable divisions of French society.

Perhaps more important than the political aspects of Bonapartism has been Napoleon's administrative legacy. He inherited the work of the Jacobins and the Directory, whose aim had been to give France a uniform administrative system and to organize militarily in order to win in war. Napoleon required a civil administration that would permit him to mobilize the resources that his campaigns required. He wished to see a well-organized country. He set about developing a pattern of local government based upon the territorial unit of the *département*. To supervise and control this local government he placed the prefectoral system upon a firm footing. A prefect was posted in each *département* as the local representative of the central government. Despite much hostility, for the prefect was often seen as the unacceptable and oppressive emanation of an authoritarian central power, especially given the early linkage of the system with Napoleon's need for a steady of flow of conscripts to his armies, the system survived the many changes of regime of the nineteenth and twentieth centuries. The administration of the French educational system also looks back to the Napoleonic division of the country into *académies*, under the overall control of a senior official appointed from Paris, grouping together state educational institutions at all levels.

Amongst the key principles upon which Napoleonic administration operated was, first, an insistence upon territorial and functional uniformity. All local authorities, whether large or small, affluent or impoverished, enjoyed the same legal and administrative powers as their counterparts elsewhere and the structures and functioning of all the public services were shaped to a uniform pattern. Secondly, the administrative institutions were not to be subject to the control and jurisdiction of Parliament or the Civil Courts. Control was, however, required, since the image and legitimacy of the state would suffer if irregularities and abuses occurred. Hence, important and powerful control systems were created within the administration, including administrative courts and prestigious inspectorates. To staff the administration Napoleon looked to a civil service which would, at the highest levels, be endowed with prestige and status.

The Napoleonic system was in some senses a system of checks and balances. A powerful, prestigious, able, efficient administration operating through centralized and authoritarian institutions would act as a counterweight to the elected assemblies. This dual tradition, of authoritarian administrative institutions and participatory assemblies, combining something of both the old royal aspirations to a unified and centralized and well-administered state, and of the democratic principles of the Revolution, can be traced throughout the subsequent history of French government. In its ideal of a highly structured rationally organized system, acting within a clear and codified legal framework, the French administration continues today to look back to Napoleon.

The Evolution of the Republic

In 1870 Napoleon III was defeated and captured by the invading Prussian armies and on 4 September the Third Republic was proclaimed. It was set up and consolidated in stages, rather than by a single constitutional act. Indeed, many of those who drew up the initial drafts of the laws which, in 1875, provided the constitutional framework for the Republic hoped they would prove to be temporary measures within which a constitutional monarchy could be restored. This did not occur. On 16 May 1877 the President, Marshal MacMahon, backed by monarchists and bonapartists, finding himself unable to create a government that would respect what he felt to be the proper balance of powers between Parliament and presidency, dissolved the National Assembly, which had a Republican majority. The subsequent election returned a majority who were clearly opposed to his views. MacMahon gave in and chose an acceptable Prime Minister. No President of the Third or Fourth Republics ever again felt able to use the dissolution of Parliament as a political weapon. MacMahon's experience marked the end of any inclination on the part of presidents of the Third Republic to exercise executive powers independently of Parliament (Anderson, 1977, p. 10).

The Third Republic survived many crises – the threat of a coup d'état by General Boulanger, the Dreyfus Affair (Exhibit 1.2), the Panama scandal, the Stavisky affair and the riots of 1934 being only some of the most serious and notorious – and the First World War. It collapsed only in 1940 under the force of invading German tanks. The balance of power within the institutions had tipped decisively towards Parliament. Its members knew that there would be no dissolution, and hence governments could be allowed to fall and new combinations to emerge. Between 1870 and 1914, for example, France had no fewer than 60 governments. The multiplicity of loosely organized party groupings within Parliament meant that all governments were combinations of political forces, based upon compromise and negotiation. There were, moreover, important political forces which did not accept the republican regime at all. Those on the extreme Right called for a return to monarchy or for 'strong' leadership. On the Left Marxist Socialists, including, after 1920, the Communists, condemned the Republic as bourgeois. When it collapsed, in 1940, under the overwhelming weight of the German invasion, its shortcomings were seized upon to provide at least part of the explanation for the rapid defeat.

The Third Republic was based upon direct manhood suffrage. Women did not obtain the vote until 1944. However, the advent of male suffrage did not, under the Third Republic, entail the emergence of organized political parties. Local committees would be set up to support candidates at particular elections, but only gradually did they begin to have a continuous existence, and the labels adopted by particular candidates were not necessarily a very clear guide to how they would behave once within Parliament. Even by the end of the Third Republic the only broadly organized mass-based parties with a disciplined group of members of Parliament were on the Left.

The Rise of Socialism

The slow development of the industrial revolution in France was accompanied by a slow development of working-class politics. France throughout the nineteenth century produced highly influential socialist thinkers and leaders, and a tradition of participation in political life by working men that could look back to the Revolution. However, the event that marked the movement most deeply was the Paris Commune of 1871, both for its actual effects and for the powerful myths which it engendered.

The working-class Left as it emerged in France was marked by a number of features. First, although union developments and political developments often went together, there was no close institutional connection between the socialist political parties and the union movement. Moreover, within the trade union movement there were several varied and conflicting strands.

Secondly the mass-based socialist party, known from its formation in 1905 until 1971 as the French Section of the Workers' International (*Section Française de l'Internationale Ouvrière* – SFIO), contained various strands of socialist thought. Its first great leader, Jean Jaurès, brought it to accept the possibility of reform through parliamentary institutions, but it long retained its revolutionary rhetoric.

Thirdly, in 1920 a majority of the SFIO's rank and file membership accepted Lenin's 21 conditions, devised to ensure the defence of the revolution in the Soviet Union, split off from the SFIO and formed the French Communist Party. Thereafter two organized parties existed to represent the Left.

Fourthly, whilst both parties claimed to be working-class parties, they were not necessarily strong in all the areas of the industrial working class and, conversely, they both enjoyed support from groups outside the main areas of industrialization. For at least the first half century of its existence the SFIO drew much of its support from workers in small plants and secondary industries, and above all from public employees and minor civil servants. The Communist Party was strong not only in the industrial centres around Paris and in the Nord-Pas-de-Calais, but also in more rural areas, such as parts of the Massif Central and the Mediterranean coast, where it represented not so much the working-class struggle as the tradition of dissent from, and resistance to, domination and authority that derived from the Revolution (Williams, 1972, p. 79).

Occupation, Resistance, Liberation

Before the rapid advance of the German armies in 1940 the Third Republic crumbled and fell. Under Marshal Pétain, the military hero of the First World War, an armistice was concluded. France was initially split into a *zone annexée*, joined to Germany, a *zone occupée*, controlled by the German authorities, and a *zone libre*, within which a government was reconstituted at Vichy, in central France. It was effectively a dictatorship, for Pétain as head of the French State (not Republic) was given plenary powers pending a new constitution, which was never promulgated. Its orientation was authoritarian and traditionalist, symbolized by the slogan *Travail Famille Patrie* (work, family, country). In November 1942 German troops occupied the whole country. The Vichy government was increasingly subject to the demands of the German forces and identified with collaboration with the Germans.

Resistance in France was initially limited and spasmodic. It developed only slowly, growing particularly after the institution of a system of forced labour in Germany for many young men. Those involved in the Resistance represented many strands of political ideas – Socialist, Catholic and, after Hitler's invasion of the Soviet Union in 1941, Communist. In 1942 a National Council of the Resistance was set up in France, and General de Gaulle (see Exhibit 2.1) came to be recognized as its leader. By 1944 he was the head of the French Committee for National Liberation, supported by a provisional consultative assembly, in Algiers, on which the National Council of the Resistance was represented. He succeeded in imposing the authority of this Provisional Government on each part of France as it was liberated, and in June 1944 triumphantly entered Paris.

The legacy of Occupation and Liberation was a bitter one. For many French people the first reaction to the trauma of defeat and occupation was a need to restore something like normality to everyday life (Paxton, 1972, pp. 16–18). Nevertheless, as the occupation continued, choices were made. The dilemmas and tragedies of these choices have formed the subject matter of telling works of literature and film. Times were hard for everyone. Average consumption levels fell to about 45 per cent of their pre-war level. Many people experienced the Nazi occupation as harsh and repressive, for example in the system of compulsory forced labour. France did not escape the anti-semitism of the Nazis, which found some echoes in anti-semitic views that had long been present within some sections of French society. However, in Paxton's words, 'Even Frenchmen of the best intentions, faced with the harsh alternative of doing one's job, whose risks were moral and abstract, or practising civil disobedience, whose risks were material and immediate, went on doing the job' (Paxton, 1972, p. 383).

The period of Liberation inevitably brought disorder and retribution. Whilst de Gaulle's government attempted to impose a degree of control and legality, there were widespread purges of actual and supposed collaborators, no doubt accompanied in some places by a good deal of personal rancour. There were about 10 000 executions, three-quarters of them while the fighting was going on and less than a thousand of them after due legal process. About 100 000 people suffered lesser legal penalties (Rioux, 1980, pp. 54–6).

These divisive events continue at times to cast long shadows over French life. There has been a shifting balance between the extent to which politicians will or can use their connections and influence to protect themselves and their friends, and increasing concern to face the legacies and condemn wrongdoing. For example, in 1994 Paul Touvier, a collaborator of the Gestapo in Lyons who had been pardoned by President Pompidou, was sentenced for crimes against humanity. A subsequent President, François Mitterrand, had, during the war, after escape from a prisoner of war camp, been both a sufficiently assiduous servant of the Vichy government to be decorated by it, and courageously and dangerously active in the Resistance. After, or possibly even during, the war he befriended René Bousquet who was eventually, but not until 1991 and then after considerable delays, indicted for crimes against humanity committed while he was a senior police official under Vichy (Tournier, 1995, p. 257). Bousquet was murdered before he came to trial. However, Maurice Papon, who had been a prefect from 1947, and Prefect of Police in Paris at the time of the massacre of Algerian demonstrators in Paris in 1961 and subsequently a minister under President Giscard d'Estaing, was sent to prison in 1998 for his part in the deportation of Jews during the occupation, though controversially released on age grounds (he was 92) in 2002.

Division and Instability

This traumatic period had a number of political effects. One was the discrediting of the ideas of the Right, since so many of their adherents had supported Vichy and collaboration. For the first decades after the war no political movement was willing to admit to being situated on the Right in politics.

The Communist Party and the SFIO emerged from the war strengthened by an honourable record of resistance, so that the 1946 general election marked a high point of the Communist vote. More than one voter in every four voted for the PCF, some, no doubt, seeking to assert their anti-collaborationist credentials by voting conspicuously for a leading party of the Resistance. The strength of the PCF, which was attracting by far the largest vote of any single party, was a very marked feature of France in the post-war years. Real fears of a Communist takeover certainly help to explain the virulent anti-Communism of some groups in post-war French politics, fears which may have been magnified by the apparent political instability of the period from 1946 to 1958.

In the Provisional Government over which de Gaulle presided until early 1946 were representatives of the three parties which, in the elections held in 1945, proved to enjoy massive support; they were the Communists, the SFIO and the Christian Democrats. The Right disappeared almost completely and the centre Republican and Radical groups, too associated with what were felt to be the weaknesses of the Third Republic, also did poorly.

That the new regime should be a parliamentary republic was unquestioned. What the balance of power between the institutions should be was much more in dispute, and in early 1946 de Gaulle resigned over what he saw as the parties' insistence on returning to the bad old ways of the past and putting their own interests first. The Fourth Republic, based upon a constitution adopted in October 1946, lasted until 1958 (see Exhibit 1.3).

The Fourth Republic was dogged for most of its existence by the perception that it was an unstable and precarious regime. A number of features contributed to this. They included:

- the balance of power between the institutions that resulted from the 1946 constitution;
- the succession of coalition governments;
- the nature of the party system;
- the traumatic process of de-colonization.

The 1946 constitution was the outcome of a turbulent process. De Gaulle, the head of the Provisional Government in 1945, viewing the strong representation of the traditional parties of the Left in the Assembly elected in 1945 with the task of producing a constitution 'gloomily assumed', in Maurice Larkin's words, that the Constitution that would emerge would fail to fulfil the needs of the country as he perceived them (Larkin, 1997, p. 139). He resigned in January 1946, undoubtedly

---

EXHIBIT 1.3

Prime ministers of the Provisional Government and the Fourth Republic

Charles de Gaulle September 1944 – January 1946
Felix Gouin January 1946 – 23 June 1946
Georges Bidault June 1946 – December 1946
Léon Blum December 1946 – January 1947
Paul Ramadier January 1947 – November 1947
Robert Schuman November 1947 – July 1948
André Marie July 1948 – August 1948
Robert Schuman August 1948 – September 1948
Henri Queuille September 1948 – October 1949
Georges Bidault October 1949 – June 1950
Henri Queuille June 1950 – July 1950
René Pleven July 1950 – February 1951
Henri Queuille March 1951 – July 1951
René Pleven August 1951 – January 1952
Edgar Faure January 1952 – February 1952
Antoine Pinay March 1952 – December 1952
René Mayer January 1953 – May 1953
Joseph Laniel June 1953 – June 1954
Pierre Mendès France June 1954 – February 1955
Edgar Faure February 1955 – January 1956
Guy Mollet February 1956 – May 1957
Maurice Bourgès-Manoury June 1957 – September 1957
Félix Gaillard November 1957 – 15 April 1958
Pierre Pflimlin 13 May 1958 – 28 May 1958
Charles de Gaulle 1 June 1958 – January 1959

---

in the hope that by so doing he would bring everyone to their senses. In fact a tripartite government of Communists, Socialists and Christian Democrats was formed. The first proposed constitution was rejected by referendum in May 1946. A new Constituent Assembly was elected, another tripartite government formed, and in October 1946 a constitution was approved by referendum. It bore a 'depressing resemblance' (Larkin, 1997, p. 142) to the constitutional arrangements of the Third Republic.

Although attempts were made to limit the extent to which Parliament could control the government and force frequent changes, in fact earlier patterns of behaviour persisted (Williams, 1972, p. 428). The weakness of the prime minister in the face of the members of Parliament, and the fragmentation of political groups led to a constant succession of coalition governments, for no single party group was strong enough to dominate the Assembly. Prime ministers had to devote a great deal of energy to putting together deals and agreements between the various political groups to ensure support for their programmes, and when they were not certain of doing so would often prefer to resign rather than risk formal defeat. Parliament feared a strong leader, and even those prime ministers who wished to act firmly found themselves frustrated by the unwillingness of their fragmented following to support them, and by the likelihood that even if support could be called upon one time, it would not be forthcoming the next time it was needed (Williams, 1972, p. 207). Although in many respects the changes of government were akin to reshuffles, governmental authority suffered, for the position of prime minister was derived not from electoral choice but from political manoeuvres and seemed highly precarious. Continuity or legitimacy in the handling of contentious matters could not be assured.

The fragmented nature of the party system compounded these difficulties, which were exacerbated by the rejection of the whole nature of the regime by two of the major political groupings (see Table 1.1). The Communists never fully accepted the rules of the game in the Fourth Republic, although they were willing to work within it and to return members of Parliament. Likewise, the Gaullists echoed de Gaulle's own virulent denunciations of the weaknesses of the regime. Moreover, at the point in the mid-1950s when the Gaullist movement seemed to be fading an alternative challenge to the system grew rapidly, vociferously expressed by Pierre Poujade and the shopkeepers and tradesmen who followed him in protesting against technocracy and economic progress.

Whether any regime, let alone the contested arrangements of the Fourth Republic, could have withstood the traumas that decolonization inflicted upon France is debatable. French decolonization was frequently bloody and bitter. The independence of Indo-China was conceded after military defeat. The war for Algerian independence brought down the Fourth Republic in 1958, and caused

TABLE 1.1

Support for the Fourth Republic: votes cast in general elections, 1946–58, %

	June 1946	November 1946	June 1951	January 1956
Parties supporting the regime				
Socialists	21.1	17.8	14.6	15.2
Radicals and allies	11.6	11.1	10	15.2
Christian democrats	28.2	25.9	12.6	11.1
Total	60.9	54.8	36.2	41.5
Parties opposing the regime				
Communists	25.9	28.2	26.9	25.9
Gaullists and allies		3.0	21.6	3.9*
Poujadists				11.6
Extreme Right				1.2
Total	25.9	31.2	48.5	42.6
Others	12.9	13.7	14.1	15.7

Note:
* The Gaullists split their support between a left-wing Republican Front alliance including the Socialist Party and some Radicals, and a more right-wing alliance including Christian Democrats.

bitter division within politics and society. Violence in Algeria on the part of those who sought independence began in 1954. Successive governments of the Fourth Republic remained committed to the retention of Algeria as an integral part of France – *Algérie Française* – and to the suppression of violence and terrorism. The parties were divided on the question of concessions to Algerian nationalism. There were also divisions provoked by the methods of the French authorities and the army, especially the use of torture. In February 1958 a bombing raid on a village (Sakhiet) over the border in Tunisia demonstrated the inability of the government to enforce its policies upon the military authorities in Algeria, for the army had acted without the backing of the civilian authorities in Algiers or Paris (Horne, 1979, p. 267). It also provoked international intervention, and much-resented attempts at mediation by an American mission. In the spring of 1958 the prospect of the advent of a prime minister who might be tempted, in the face of international pressure, the rising economic cost of the war and war-weariness in metropolitan France, to negotiate with the Algerian independence movement provoked the events in Algiers that led to the return of de Gaulle to power.

It took all de Gaulle's personal authority and powers of survival (he was the object of at least a dozen assassination attempts: Lacouture, 1986, p. 272), combined with a weary but widely held view that a solution must be found, to achieve the agreement that resulted in an independent Algeria in 1962, and in the settlement of over 800 000 French former inhabitants of Algeria in mainland France. The other African colonies were given the right to choose independence by the Constitution of 1958, and by 1962 all of them had done so.

All these factors contributed to a perception of a country whose deep and bitter divisions made the construction of a regime that would be widely accepted as legitimate and the maintenance of a government that would be capable of sustained and coherent policy seem at best improbable.

Reconstruction and Modernization

Beneath the froth of governmental instability the period from 1944 to 1958 was in fact a period of immense recovery from the devastation of war time. There were many aspects to the economic and social transformation that France under-went in the three 'glorious' decades after the war (Fourastié, 1979). Underlying them were some broad areas of social and economic consensus that allowed many of the transformations to proceed more within the tradition of administrative action than that of political conflict.

In 1944 General de Gaulle's Provisional Government was faced with harsh choices about the nature of the reconstruction of the economy and the methods to be employed. Within the governmental team there was a degree of conflict about the aims and methods that would be desirable. The outcome of these conflicts had a good deal of influence upon the subsequent nature and development of the French economy. The French government opted for an approach that recognized the virtues of a liberal and market-oriented approach to reconstruction.

Capitalism should be allowed to work reasonably freely. This required the modernization of an economy that Jean Monnet diagnosed as 'appallingly backward' (Monnet, 1978, p. 233). Monnet's solution involved the creation of a framework which would permit, indeed encourage, the growth of private, entrepreneurial, competitive capitalism in France. There was a danger, past experience suggested, that France would be content with 'frugal mediocrity behind a protectionist shield' (Monnet, 1978, p. 238). The role of the state was, in effect, to create modern capitalism in France. He created and administered planning mechanisms as a political framework for a depoliticized, agreed pattern of industrial growth. These worked best in a period of reconstruction when priorities were clear and external funding available, in the form of American Marshall Aid. The broader general attitudes were, however, more widely important.

The transformations of the three post-war decades were backed by steady economic growth. From 1950 to 1960 the average annual rate of growth of the economy was 5 per cent and from 1960 to 1970, 5.8 per cent (Parodi, 1981, p. 48). These transformations included, first, a vast change in the employment structure of the country. Between 1946 and 1975 the proportion of the workforce employed in agriculture, forestry and fisheries declined from more than one in three workers (36.46 per cent) to less than one in ten (9.5 per cent) (Parodi, 1981, p. 80).

Another transformation was the development of the public sector in the economy. The first nationalizations took place under the Socialist Popular Front government of 1936, and in 1945–6 some of the main public utilities (electricity, gas, coal-mining) were nationalized, as were half the banking and insurance companies. The late 1940s was also the period of the consolidation of the institutions of the welfare state. Insurance schemes that provided old-age pensions and covered illness, disability and unemployment were set up, and the system of family allowances extended.

France was a founder member of the European Coal and Steel Community (ECSC), devised largely by Jean Monnet, and promulgated by a French minister, Robert Schuman, who originated from Luxembourg and had consequently fought on the German side in the First World War. It was intended to provide the basis for a peacable long-term relationship between France and Germany and to ensure that two of the major components required for the production of the weapons of war came under such supranational control that never again could they be used to equip a 'European civil war'(see Sutton, forthcoming, Chapter 2). France was also a founder member of the European Economic Community (EEC) in 1958.

State, Society and Economy under the Fifth Republic

The advent of the Fifth Republic had two immediate consequences. One was a rallying around the notion that a new system must be found that would avert threats of violent civil conflict and permit the resolution of long-standing problems. So the new constitution was accepted by a very substantial majority. The Algerian war was brought to an end, and violence reduced to sporadic terrorism.

De Gaulle's leadership (see Chapter 3) sustained support for the system after the ending of the crisis which had brought him to power. His priorities, approach, style and leadership set a tone for future presidencies which has provided a point of reference for his successors, even if the development of the institutions, political circumstances and personal predilections have resulted in evolution and variation. The period was one of considerable political stability, which saw the steady development of a clear left-right and government-opposition alignment of political parties (see Chapter 8). This meant that political competition increasingly became competition between policy stances, policy ideas and personalities, within an accepted framework. The compromise (Elgie, 2003, p. 35), between a role for representative democracy with parliamentary control of government (see Chapter 7) and scope for strong leadership has effectively eliminated contesting approaches to the rules of the game. The point at which the Fifth Republic has seemed most likely to collapse came in 1968 when a general strike spread rapidly, prompted by widespread student riots (see Exhibit 9.2): but the challenges then were essentially social rather than political.

A resilient regime

Domestically de Gaulle's strengthening of the executive allowed the introduction of a number of reforms which had previously been stalled by conflicting interests, for example in agricultural policy and in tackling alcoholism. Externally he ensured that his vision of France's place in the world was promulgated. Amongst the consequences were the European Community 'Luxembourg accord' of 1966 which entrenched the veto where national interests were at stake and the repeated blocking (1963 and 1967) of British membership of the European Community. The assertion of French autonomy and status also prompted the 1961 decision that France would develop its own independent nuclear deterrent and the 1966 withdrawal from the military structures of the North Atlantic Treaty Organization (NATO).

The theme of modernization runs through the history of the Fifth Republic. The contribution of de Gaulle and his successor Georges Pompidou was essentially to political modernization. Modernization in France implies neither an end to ideology nor a consensual governance system of mutual accommodation and shared power. As David Bell points out, such a system is exceptional outside wartime and politics is about division. Indeed de Gaulle failed in his aspiration to build a permanent basis of 'all embracing and..widespread' support (Bell, 2000, p.201) and his defeat in a referendum in 1969 showed that he was no longer the indispensable guarantor of stability. Presidents, from de Gaulle onwards, have depended upon partisan support, and partisan conflict in France is adversarial. The modernizing effect of the de Gaulle and Pompidou era was to produce the first stages of an ordered, organized system of party competition between governing and opposition coalitions within an agreed framework.

The presidency of centre-right Valéry Giscard d'Estaing, which followed, was at the outset self-consciously modernizing in both style and content. The style did not survive the pressures of status and deference. However, his initial legislation introduced a number of modernizing reforms. Some of the legal restrictions on women's rights contained in the Code Napoleon were removed. Contraception had been legalized in 1967, but was now made more readily reimbursable under the healthcare system, and in 1974 abortion was legalized. The divorce law was reformed. The age of majority was reduced to 18. His later legislation, on immigration and law and order, was less liberalizing.

Mitterrand to Chirac

The election of a Socialist, François Mitterrand, as president in 1981 seemed to signal a further leap forward. Having defeated President Giscard d'Estaing, and backed by a parliamentary majority from the general election he immediately called, he brought in a new government team of Socialists, Communists and their allies. The rejoicing crowds in Paris on the night of the presidential election, many of them young, felt that a 'choice of society' had been made which would spread economic prosperity more widely, reduce unemployment, and encourage fairness and justice, for example in relation to immigrants. Two massive programmes were quickly introduced: the decentralization programme to reshape local government and administration (see Chapter 6), and a nationalization programme which resulted in the taking into state ownership of eleven of the largest industrial companies or groups, and thirty eight banks and finance houses. Mitterrand's 'redistributive keynesianism' (Hall, 1994, p. 177) encompassed a raised minimum wage and 100 000 additional public sector jobs. Social modernization included the abolition of the death penalty.

The 'u-turn' of 1983 which reversed this approach was a crucial moment (see Chapter 10) not only in specifying an economic direction from which successive governments from both sides have since scarcely deviated, but also in marking a move away from an idealistic commitment to massive change towards an explicitly moderate, pragmatic social democracy fashioned by competivity and market discipline. The decision was as much political as economic. It was presented as a 'choice for Europe'. It was also a recognition that a radically left wing programme was not feasible within an interdependent modern economic and political system. The Socialist party had needed Communist support as it strengthened its position in the 1970s but was no longer so dependent on it and needed to assert its credentials as an effective manager of an interdependent modern economy and a credible party of government. Mitterrand's tactics, which included a short-lived experiment with proportional representation for the National Assembly, did not save the Socialists from defeat in the parliamentary election of 1986, but they did prevent a total rout (see Figure 8.2). They also permitted the fast-rising extreme right National Front (*Front National* – FN) to gain a brief foothold in the National Assembly (see Chapter 8).

Mitterrand took further crucial decisions at the time of the 1986 defeat. He did not resign as President but called on the leader of the largest party in the National Assembly, Gaullist Jacques Chirac, to become Prime Minister. The result was a two year period of *cohabitation* between a president of one political complexion and a prime minister of another (see Chapters 2, 3 and 4). The institutional framework proved flexible enough to accommodate this pattern, and the general public by and large supported it. Chirac's premiership was robust, with a neo-liberal tone similar to that then current in the United States of Ronald Reagan and the United Kingdom of Margaret Thatcher. His privatization involved the sale of no fewer than thirteen major enterprises, worth 120 billion francs (Hayward and Wright, 2002, p. 196). He 'made a virtue of the austerity reluctantly practised by the Socialists' after 1983 (Levy, 1999, p. 63) and introduced various deregulatory measures. But unemployment rose (see Table 1.3). Mitterrand had gained popularity by his 'democratic' interpretation of *cohabitation*, and avoided implication in economic failures. In 1988 he defeated Chirac. Despite his battle with cancer he survived to become the only president of the Fifth Republic to complete two full seven-year terms. A constitutional amendment (see Chapter 2) reduced Chirac's second term to five years.

By the 1990s the Fifth Republic had proved sufficiently resilient to accommodate, first, *alternance* – that is, a complete change of the governing team from the previous government to the previous opposition became not only possible but frequent, as control of the government swung from Left to Right in 1986, 1993 and 2002, and back again in 1988 and 1997. Second, *cohabitation* – that is, a president from one camp and a prime minister from the other – allowed electoral choices to be reflected in governments and their programmes. Power was to a certain extent shared, and partisan competition was either defined by a known, rather brief, duration before the next compulsory elections, or became institutionalized into what Wright (1993, p. 116) called *cohabitension*.

By the 1990s the French political system had, arguably, stabilized, and, whilst retaining a number of very distinctive features, such as the dual executive, was increasingly losing some of its exceptional characteristics (see Cole 1998, Chapter 16 for this argument). The regime is not static: the change after 2002 from a seven to a five year term for the presidency, so that it coincides with the maximum term for the National Assembly, will result in new and unforeseen political outcomes (see Chapters 2, 3, 4 and 7). But the changes are evolutionary, and the regime itself not under challenge.

Within this stable framework, however, shifts occurred. As the institutional framework settled, so its interpretation became more crucial. On the one hand the role of the Constitutional Council (see Chapter 2) in defining the constitutional parameters of action became more salient. On the other hand the personalities and choices of the protagonists, and the scope for action afforded them by the political context, played an important role in determining the balance of power within the regime. Presidents might, by choice (Mitterrand 1988–91) or necessity (Chirac 1997–2002), play a reduced role. The choice of ministerial team could, as under Socialist prime minister Edith Cresson in 1991 of Gaullist Alain Juppé 1995–7 be almost exclusively composed of those who were presidential loyalists, or might, as under Jean-Pierre Raffarin from 2002, have a rather broader base.

There were also shifts in the balance of political forces. The 1992 referendum on the ratification of the Maastricht Treaty, a treaty which extended the process of European integration, was only won by the narrow margin of 51 per cent in favour. This demonstrated the depth of the division between those who saw the forward movement of European integration as a modernization and an opportunity, and those who wanted at most to restrict it to the consolidation of the benefits it had already brought to France, and even to remove France from the constraints that 'Brussels' was perceived as imposing. The Communist Party dwindled sharply, while the National Front continued its oscillating progress, entrenching itself in a number of regions and municipalities.

France in the 1990s was also characterised by what some commentators have called *morosité*. The absence of strongly articulated but feasible vision – and Mitterrand was tired and cynical, Chirac tarnished by promises he could not keep, Juppé perceived as technocratic and arrogant and unpopular, and Lionel Jospin (Socialist prime minister 1997–2002) austere and practical – encouraged voter apathy. Law and order and the extent of the crime rate became a preoccupation. Unemployment remained stubbornly high, and the commitment to Europe could be perceived as involving principally a requirement to hold down spending, potential threats to a generous model of social protection and especially pensions (see Exhibit 9.4) and the influx of 'unfair' competition stemming from the 'globalisation' under whose pressures cherished values and lifestyles might disappear. All too frequent investigations and prosecutions of senior officials, ministers and business leaders close to the regime fostered an impression of sleaze. The gloom lifted somewhat at the end of the 1990s, undoubtedly influenced by France's victory in the football World Cup, played in France in the summer of 1998. Economic growth accelerated, unemployment began to diminish, the replacement of the Franc by the Euro, culminating in the introduction of Euro notes and coins in January 2002, went rather smoothly and public confidence grew. But after September 2001 the global economy turned down and anxiety and pessimism recurred.

The French presidential election system (see Chapter 3) requires a head-to-head run-off in the second round. It was widely forecast that in 2002, as in 1995, this would involve Jacques Chirac and Lionel Jospin. The presence of extreme right National Front leader Jean-Marie Le Pen rather than Jospin was a profound shock. The demonstrators in the streets – and there were many, especially young people – and the voters who, although opposed to Chirac, nevertheless gave him, on an increased turn-out, over 82 per cent of the second ballot vote, showed that they were prepared to act when fundamental values seemed to be threatened. Re-ensconced in the Elysée Chirac was soon presented with a further opportunity to act as spokesman for an overwhelming majority of the French population. In the early months of 2003 he roundly insisted that force was not the way to disarm Iraq. France would 'under any circumstances' use her UN Security Council veto against a resolution explicitly authorizing war. The stance was hugely popular in France, but equally (in contrast to the first Gulf War in 1991 where French troops were engaged) provoked a massive rift between France and the United States. The repercussions on the European Union (EU) were also potentially substantial. The French stance revealed a chasm in approaches to foreign and defence policy between Britain and Spain on the one hand and France and Germany, joining with Russia, on the other. Enlargement of the EU by ten new central and eastern European and Mediterranean countries was scheduled for 2004. The attitude of Chirac and his government to the enlargement, which carried risks of the further diminution of French influence in the EU, was equivocal. When some of the applicants supported the USA and the UK, Chirac's reaction implied that enlargement could be called into question.

The Economic Context

The French economy has in general been a successful one. The 'thirty glorious years' of steady, rather high growth and full employment in the period of post-war reconstruction and modernization were brought to an end by the oil shocks and recession of the mid 1970s. However, although growth slowed, it nevertheless continued, at levels which compared not unfavourably with the average for the 15 current members of the European Union (see Table 1.2). The greatest weakness in the economy has been the levels of unemployment. It had been negligible in the early 1960s, running at some 200 000, but was already beginning to rise in the late 1960s, to about 600 000 in 1973–4, before leaping up to over one million in 1976. The brief period of economic recovery in the late 1980s saw a pause in the apparently inexorable rise, but by 1992–3 record levels – over 3 million unemployed – had been reached. The figure dropped back at the turn of century before beginning to creep up again in 2002 (see Table 1.3). Unemployment seems stubbornly resistant to the plethora of initiatives thrown at it – early retirement schemes, work placement schemes for young people, and the 35 hour week. The attempts of successive French governments to ensure that the impact of monetary

TABLE 1.2

Average annual growth rates in percentages (growth in Gross Domestic Product at constant prices)

Country	1961–70	1971–80	1981–90	1991–2000	2003*
France	5.6	3.3	2.5	1.8	1.7
EU average	4.9	3.0	2.4	2.0	n.a
USA	4.2	3.2	3.2	3.4	2.9

* Year to March 2003.
Sources: *L'Etat de la France*, 2002, p. 377, from OECD and EU figures; *The Economist*.

TABLE 1.3

Unemployment rates in percentages (harmonised annual averages)

Country	1980	1985	1990	1995	1997	1998	1999	2000	2002*	2003*
France	6.3	10.1	9.0	11.7	12.3	11.8	11.3	9.7	8.8	9.1
Germany	3.2	8.0	6.2	8.2	9.9	9.4	8.8	8.3	8.7	9.6
UK	5.6	11.5	7.0	8.7	7.0	6.3	6.1	5.6	5.1	5.0
USA	7.2	7.2	5.5	5.6	4.9	4.5	4.2	4.0	5.8	5.6

* January or February: source: *The Economist.*
Source *1980–2000*:   *L'Etat de la France*, 2002, p. 447, from Eurostat and OECD figures.

policy upon employment is a concern of EU policies for Economic and Monetary Union, and of the European Central Bank, arise from these figures. It was estimated in 2000 that 15 per cent of French households contained at least one unemployed person, and one in four workers had experienced unemployment within the previous three years (Mermet, 2000, p. 276). Unemployment is particularly high amongst young people. About twenty per cent of those aged 20 to 24 available for work (just over 60 per cent of the total in 1990 and rather over 50 per cent in 2000 – the remainder are still studying or otherwise unavailable) were unemployed throughout the 1990s (*L'Etat de la France*, 2002, p. 447).

The role of the state in the French economy has always been substantial, and remains so. Many major projects are due to partnerships between state and industry. Examples include Concorde, the nuclear energy programme, the construction of motorways, digital telephone exchanges, high speed trains, the Channel Tunnel, the Ariane space rocket. Some of the long-standing features which caused the economic system in France to be described as *dirigiste* – state-directed – have diminished since 1983. These features included:

- The size of the public sector. Many of the industrial, commercial and public service undertakings which the state used to own have been privatised since 1983, and more may be. In 1986 the public sector employed 2.35 million people: by 2000 the number was only 1.1 million (Loiseau, 2002). But in 2002 electricity, gas and the railways were still in public hands and the state retains holdings in France Télécom and Air France.
- The influence of the state over finance and credit. This too has been reduced since the credit rationing system was abandoned at the end of the 1970s, and the banks mostly privatised.
- The prestige and acknowledged expertise of the top civil servants, their provision, for example, of dynamic leadership in the post-war reconstruction, and their championing of a number of major projects.
- A general wariness of equity investment, even though the impact of deregulation of the stock exchange in the 1980s and of privatisation has been to produce an 'explosion' of shareholding (Ferrandon, 2002, p. 42).

TABLE 1.4

Distribution of employment by major sectors

	1960	1970	1980	1990	2000
Primary (agriculture, forestry, fishing)	22	13.3	8.4	5.6	4.3
Secondary (manufacturing, energy, construction)	36	37.9	34.8	28.8	22.7
Tertiary (services)	42	48.8	56.8	65.5	74

Source: adapted from Gadrey 2002, based on figures from INSEE.

The structures of the French economy have in some respects changed markedly during the Fifth Republic. As in many western economies the service sector has grown most sharply. Whereas in 1960 it contributed only just over half the Gross National Product, in 2000 (at constant prices) the contribution was over 70 per cent. This is reflected in employment, see Table 1.4. One consequence has been the shift in the balance of the population noted on p. 3.

The rise of the service sector also helps to explain the very large number of small and medium sized companies in the French economy. Many service companies are much smaller than manufacturing companies; 98 per cent of French companies employ fewer that 50 people. However, the place of truly independent companies has steadily diminished, as small companies are increasingly incorporated into holding groups: there were in 2000 some 9551 groups (up from 1306 in 1980) which between them employ nearly seven million people (Ferrandon, 2002, p. 40). In 1999 about a quarter of these worked for the approximately 2000 groups that were ultimately controlled by a foreign owner (up from just over 600 in 1989). With the growing influence of overseas shareholders (and especially British and American institutional investors), who in 2001 held over a third of the total capital of French companies, requirements for increased transparency of company financial information have grown. Equally the practice of protecting companies against hostile take-over by mutual holdings between two or more groups has diminished, and management has acquired a more American style. One feature remains unchanged: nearly a quarter of the top 50 non-financial companies in France are family-controlled (Ferrandon, 2002, p. 44).

During the 1990s French business became much more open to internationalisation. Despite a long tradition of caution about non-French investment, a caution which could in the post-war period be implemented through Finance Ministry control of credit and investment, the deregulation of the financial system combined with increasingly global business operations has resulted in total inward investment, essentially from other countries within the Eurozone, the United Kingdom and the United States, multiplying six-fold between 1985 and 2001 (Ferrandon, 2002, p. 41). Large French companies have also adopted energetic outward strategies. In some cases production has been transferred to lower cost locations, but equally there have been cross-frontier mergers and acquisitions. These have been notable, for example, in utilities, where French water companies (water companies have always been largely outside the public sector in France) and also public sector monopolies such as *Electricité de France* are now very active world wide. In 2002 there were 39 French groups in the *Fortune* magazine list of the top 500 world companies.

Social Changes

Alongside the evolution of the economy major social shifts have occurred in France under the Fifth Republic. First, the population has grown and become more ethnically mixed (see p. 13), an evolution that has produced tension and strain (see Chapter 10). Combined with the shifts in occupational structure (see p. 25) this resulted in a very rapid period of urban growth. A consequence of this growth, as also of failure to invest during the inter-war period and of slow post-war recovery, were poor housing conditions. In 1954 fewer than 60 per cent of all households had running water. Virtually all now do (Ardagh, 2000, p. 201). A massive programme of new building of state sponsored housing (*Habitations à loyer modéré* – HLMs), administered by specialised agencies, not local authorities, was undertaken especially in the first two decades of the Fifth Republic, accompanied by a boom in private development. At the end of the 1990s 17 per cent of households lived in social housing (Mermet, 2000, p. 177). The early 'new towns', on the outskirts of the big cities, tended to be high rise, poorly served by public amenities, including transport, and prone to social exclusion and problems. More recent developments, such as Evry or Cergy-Pontoise near Paris, have fared better. By the turn of the century French people were slightly more likely to be owner occupiers than tenants (54 per cent, up from 41 per cent in 1962) and to live in a house rather than a flat – 56 per cent lived in houses, up from 48 per cent at the end of the 1980s.

Family structures have also changed. The number of marriages each year in proportion to the size of the population has stabilised at around the average for the EU. But the average age of first marriage has risen, from 22 for women in 1970 to nearly 28 in 1998. Forty per cent of births are to unmarried mothers, and in a third of marriages the couple already has at least one child. The legal act of marriage has to be undertaken by the civil authorities (the local mayor or his or her deputy). In 1965 78 per cent of marriages were also celebrated in church; in 1999 the figure was only 44 per cent. The divorce rate has quadrupled during the Fifth Republic, so that four in ten marriages now end in divorce, up from one in ten in 1965 (Mermet, 2000, pp. 128–43). A new legal framework for unmarried couples, which offers recognition and inheritance rights (French law constrains the rights of any individual to leave property away from family members) the *Pacte Civile de Solidarité* (PACS), was introduced in 1999. A PACS can be concluded between any non-related same- or opposite-sex couple. The law was initially advocated by campaigners for rights for homosexual couples, but was extended to all unmarried couples to ensure its passage through parliament.

The changes in family structure are both a cause and a consequence of increasing secularisation in society. Just over 20 per cent of the French population in 2000 said they had no religious belief. About three quarters defined themselves as Roman Catholics, but only just over 30 per cent ever undertook formal catholic religious practices. Moreover, in the 15 to 24 age group 40 per cent said they had no religious affiliation. Islam is now the second largest religion in France, with about 2 per cent of the population (4 million people) claiming to adhere to it, not all of them practising. Protestantism, professed by only one per cent of the population, has produced two Socialist prime ministers of the 1990s, Michel Rocard and Lionel Jospin.

The economy has become more open and internationalised, but this is not equally true of French lifestyles. José Bové's battle against fast food (see Exhibit 9.3) symbolizes attachment to French style food, and although McDonalds has spread widely – and adapted some aspects of its offerings to French tastes – there are rather few Chinese, Indian or other foreign restaurants. Disneyland Paris survived a rocky start in the early 1990s, but only 40 per cent of its visitors are French (Ardagh, 2000, p. 629). France remains a country of inward tourism – with numbers of foreign visitors the highest of any country. But the French themselves spend their holidays in their own country. The relatively recent growth of urbanization means that many families still have a sense of roots in the countryside. This sentiment helps to explain French attachment to the preservation, if necessary through subsidies and if possible through the common agricultural policy of the EU (see Chapter 10), of what are seen as the important values embodied in rural lifestyles. Only one in ten French holidaymakers travels abroad, and there is no tradition equivalent to the British pre or post-university 'gap-year' with the wide travelling that implies.

A number of commentators have discerned an increasing 'social fracture' in the France of the 1990s. There seemed a growing gulf not only between those suffering from 'social exclusion' – the very poor, the homeless, the *sans papiers* (illegal immigrants and others without official status), the unemployed – and the rest of society, but also between those in dynamic, outward-looking competitive sectors and others. Fear – fear of loss of status, security, of acquired rights and established positions – underlay a number of protests and demonstrations, such as those in 1995 (see Exhibit 9.4). Direct action (see Chapter 9) has frequently provided a outlet for anxiety and frustration. Fear may also have motivated some of the voting patterns in the 2002 presidential elections (see Chapter 8).

Education, Culture and Intellectual life

One striking feature of Fifth Republic France has been the increase in the proportion of young people leaving school with qualifications. By the mid 1990s only some nine per cent left school with no qualification, while the proportion of the age cohort achieving the *baccalauréat*, entitling them to university entrance, is now over 60 per cent, compared with 11 per cent in 1960 (Mermet, 2002, p. 97). In

1999 over eighty per cent of those entitled to enter higher education did so. However, over 40 per cent of them fail to go beyond the first two years of the university course.

The relationship between state (secular) education and private (usually Roman Catholic) education was a focus for conflict in the early 1980s, when the Socialist government attempted to bring the systems even more closely into line. The agreement reached between government and church authorities was undermined by parliamentary amendments from the left 'still emotionally affected by the memory of...conflicting principles' (Duclaud-Williams, 1997). Catholic schools are very largely financed from public funds, so that fees for private education are minimal and, while they may appoint their teachers, they must apply the national curriculum. Despite the growing numbers of French citizens and inhabitants who profess Islam, there are no faith-based schools for Muslims. In 1989 three Muslim girls were excluded from school for wearing the Muslim headscarf, on the grounds that symbols of religious belief were not acceptable in secular state schools. In 1994, following a ministerial circular from the right-wing government aimed at preventing the wearing of the headscarf the highest administrative court, the *Conseil d'Etat*, ruled that only 'ostentatious' and 'proselytizing' signs of belief were not acceptable, but that has left open the way for varied interpretation. The outcome has been uneasy local compromises. The conflict highlighted an apparent conflict between the secular republican values of the state education system and a more pluralist approach. In general, however, 'multicultural' education is not favoured in France.

Despite the overall advance in the level of qualification some schools remain in conditions of considerable difficulty. These tend to be particularly those in the tower-block social housing quarters on the outskirts of the large towns – the areas known as '*la banlieue*', a word with very different connotations from its English translation 'suburb'. Here there are often heavy concentrations of ethnic minority families, many of them second generation and now French citizens, the so-called '*beurs*' – from the backwards teenage slang for *arabe*. With particularly high rates of unemployment amongst young people of North African origin – some 50 per cent as opposed to an average of about 20 per cent (Ardagh, 2000, p. 223) – and discrimination in employment, though illegal, reportedly common, school is not seen as offering hope for the future, and violence (including rape), drug-dealing and gangsterism are sometimes rife.

Media and culture

Some commentators, notably Henri Mendras (Mendras and Cole, 1991) have argued that French culture has become increasingly uniform, under the dual influence of education, and the mass media. Television and film are perceived by the French government as key elements in the shaping and preserving of a French national identity. For this reason French governments have defended the exclusion of TV and cinema (*l'exception culturelle*) from the world trade liberalisation agreements such as that in 1994 which set up the World Trade Organisation, and in subsequent negotiations in the OECD. The Fifth Republic in France has been the age of television. In 1965 there were only six million sets, but by 1982 over 90 per cent of households had a set, and between 1980 and the end of the century the proportion of households with a video recorder grew from almost none to over three quarters. About one fifth of households subscribe to the pay TV channel Canal Plus, and the same proportion to cable or satellite. The most frequently watched channel is TF1, originally a state channel, privatised in 1987, with on average 35 per cent of the audience (Mermet, 2002, p. 403). Film continues to play an important role. Urban young people are particularly likely to go to the cinema, the French in general do so more often than their European neighbours. The French film industry produces more films than any other European film industry, and a large amount of film is watched on TV. On the other hand the press plays a less striking national role. Few newspapers have a national circulation and those that do (*Le Monde, Le Figaro*) are unrelentingly serious. They are supplemented by a number of national news weeklies, but most of those who read newsmedia regularly read local papers.

The role of the intellectual
French cinema can be seen as playing an important part in French intellectual life, alongside the writing of books and articles for serious reviews and the elite press. French intellectual life can, with some justice, be perceived as being dominated by a number of leading figures, who set the tone and point the direction of much discussion. These intellectuals (the term came into common usage at the time of the Dreyfus affair – see Exhibit 1.2 – to denote prominent figures from the arts, literature or academia whose reputation legitimises their pronouncements on public affairs) are largely concentrated in Paris, and may often operate as teachers, editors of reviews, publishing editors, and commentators in the serious press and television (Howarth and Varouxakis, 2003, p. 139). In the post-war period, indeed until the 1970s, Marxism provided the key framework for intellectual discourse, with figures such as the philosophers Jean-Paul Sartre (1905–80 – a 'fellow-traveller', not a PCF member) and Louis Althusser dominating the scene, though there were also highly distinguished dissenting voices, such as the sceptical liberal Raymond Aron (1905–83). In the 1970s and 1980s, as the flaws in the Communist system became ever more obvious, the Marxist domination began to fall apart. The women's movement and psychoanalysts such as Jacques Lacan began to utilise and develop other frameworks such as Freudian psychoanalytic insights. Michel Foucault, who died in 1984, in his historical studies of power, aimed to demonstrate the mechanisms of repression, and directed his public activity towards human rights issues. Philosopher Jacques Derrida and others in turn attacked this structuralism, becoming known as post-structuralists. The sociologist Pierre Bourdieu (1930–2002), despite early denunciations of intellectuals' intervention in public affairs, became in the late 1990s not only perhaps the most high-profile academic in his field in France, but also a proponent of the view that understanding compelled action, and hence a vociferous critic of neo-liberal

orthodoxy and globalisation. French intellectual life today is more fragmented than it was at the beginning of the Fifth Republic, when there was a great gap between the anti-Communism of de Gaulle and the regime, and the Marxist frames of reference of many leading academics and writers. It is also more prone to the cult of the celebrity, bitterly attacked by Régis Debray as producing instant, but unserious, media pundits.

Culture remains crucial to French political life however: the state sees the promotion of culture as a key element of national policy, and ministers of culture – from novelist André Malraux under de Gaulle to flamboyant Jack Lang under Mitterrand – have been high profile figures. Presidents have favoured and spent lavishly on cultural *grands projets* – the cities of Science and Music at La Villette, the renewal of the Louvre Museum, the Pompidou Centre, the Opera House at La Bastille in Paris. Intellectual debates and controversies arise sharply, such as those over the novels of Michel Houllebecq in the late 1990s, or around the phenomenon of the new reactionaries in 2002 (Howarth and Varouxakis, 2003), and have clear political connotations. Equally, much political debate is deeply rooted in intellectual and philosophical terms of reference. These have changed, as the political, economic and social contexts have also changed. It is to the more specific details of the evolving governmental and political consequences that this book now turns.

2

The Constitutional Framework

The constitution of the Fifth Republic is of fundamental importance in shaping present-day political life and governmental activity in France. Written constitutions, within any particular political society, at least when they are the product of a genuinely indigenous movement rather than being imposed from without, perform a range of functions. They are likely to embody a critique of the situation that existed previously; they are a distillation of the broad political values of the ruling groups within society, and also, within democratic regimes, of as wide a spectrum of political opinion as possible; they incorporate aspirations about the way in which the future political life of the society should develop and progress; they contain specific rules which determine the balance of political power within society and legitimize political activity; and if they survive for a certain length of time they may become points of reference which shape and determine social and political values and policy-making as well as reflecting them.

The 'profound restlessness' (Thomson, 1969, p. 11) of French political life in the two centuries since the Revolution has over that period frequently prevented the emergence of values that were sufficiently stable to ensure the longevity of constitutions. When the values of the constitution are so widely contested that to many it appears more as the programme of the ruling party or coalition than a statement of legitimizing rules and a fair description of the balance of power, opposition is likely to take the form of a challenge to the whole constitutional regime as well as to the government of the day. One consequence is that the concept of a 'loyal opposition' with a recognized leader as part of the constitutional structure, remains unknown in France. During his periods in opposition it was Jacques Chirac's standing as Mayor of Paris that maintained his international and national visibility and gave him a certain advantage over other potential opposition candidates for the presidency. However, one of the main achievements of the current Fifth Republic constitution is its longevity. After 45 years all the major political parties and the massive majority of public opinion now accept the constitutional framework. It has been much amended but its replacement is not on the political agenda.

The constitution matters and shapes political life because it lays down the ground rules within which the shifting balance of power between political forces is accommodated. It determines who may legitimately wield power. In France the

31

political changes of the 1980s and 1990s brought the constitution into sharper focus after nearly two decades when its importance had been largely ignored and the balance of political forces had enabled presidents and governments to use and abuse it. Politicians now recognize that, so long as the constitution broadly reflects the national consensus about how power should, ultimately, be distributed, its framework cannot be ignored and bypassed. It is no coincidence that the same period has seen a steadily increasing role for the Constitutional Council, the main guardian of constitutionality.

The present French constitution came into force on 4 October 1958. It had been approved on 28 September by a referendum which produced, in metropolitan France, a turn out of 84.6 per cent of the voters, 79.3 per cent of whom voted for it. This chapter describes the constitutional precedents for the Fifth Republic and the demand for a new constitution in 1958. It outlines the objectives of its authors and the main constitutional provisions. It goes on to discuss the nature of the regime which the 1958 constitution instituted and the impact of two major developments. The first is the emergence of two competing interpretations, based upon the coexistence of the direct election of the president and the direct election of a parliamentary majority, and the possible resolution of this duality by the constitutional amendment installing a five-year presidential term (*quinquennat*). The second is the changing role of the Constitutional Council.

The Constitutions of the Third and Fourth Republics

The first republican regime in France began with the fall of the monarchy in 1792 and was embodied in the constitution of 1793, which was never implemented. The Second Republic followed the 1848 revolution that overthrew King Louis-Philippe and lasted until Louis-Napoleon's coup-d'état in 1851 and his installation as Emperor Napoleon III in 1852. It was based on the principle of universal male suffrage. Its constitution provided for a single-chamber legislature, elected for a three-year period, and a President, elected for four years. Both Parliament and President were seen as stemming from the expression of the popular will, and their relationship was unclear, until forcibly resolved by the actions of Louis-Napoleon who had been elected as the Second Republic's first President.

The Third Republic was the product of the defeat of France by the Prussians in 1870, of the Assembly (with a monarchist majority) that was hastily elected to fill the gap left by the collapse of the Empire, and of the constitutional laws passed in 1875 to provide a legal framework that might yet serve a constitutional monarchy. These laws provided for a two-chamber parliament, with a lower house directly elected by universal male suffrage for a maximum four-year term and an upper house (the Senate) elected by an electoral college that chiefly represented the local councils in a way which ensured the over-representation of the small and rural authorities. The President was elected for seven years by a joint meeting of the two houses, of which the Senators formed about one-third and the lower house (the Chamber of Deputies) constituted about two-thirds.

After the experience of Marshal MacMahon in 1877 (see p. 10 above) members of the Chamber of Deputies knew that they were safe in their seats for four years, and could afford to let governments fall, whilst the presidency quite rapidly ceased to exercise any real political functions. The power of the Chamber of Deputies was predominant, for the members controlled the agenda of the house, and had the right to call short debates and a vote on any subject whilst the Chamber's committees, which examined legislation before it came before the full house, could so alter the drafts that the government might have a major struggle in the full debates to get the proposals back to their original intention. 'These procedures reflected a conception of politics which preferred a ministry safely subordinate to the representatives of the people to one strong and independent enough to govern effectively' (Williams, 1972, p. 186).

Like most constitutions, the constitution of the Fourth Republic contained within it an element of criticism of the arrangements it replaced; for example, it sought to limit the blocking powers of the Senate. As Philip Williams (1972) points out, however, its authors were 'neither willing nor able to erect a new structure and tried only to repair the faults that the old one had revealed in its years of decline'. They hoped that the dominance – and alliance – of a few organized political parties would continue and ensure sound majorities for disciplined parties, which would underpin effective government (Chapsal and Lancelot, 1979, p. 142; Williams, 1972, p. 190). In fact the old habits of the Third Republic rapidly reasserted themselves, with all the consequent difficulties of governmental ineffectiveness and instability.

The Demand for a New Constitution in 1958

To tell the full, and in parts highly dramatic, story of the advent of the Fifth Republic would involve recounting much of the political history of France since the 1930s. A necessarily brief version of the story may perhaps begin where, in a sense, it also ends, with the personality and actions of General Charles de Gaulle (see Exhibit 2.1).

De Gaulle came into office as prime minister, for the second time, at the beginning of June 1958, at the height of the crisis caused by events in Algeria. France seemed to be on the brink of civil war, with the authorities in Paris incapable of exerting control over the army in Algiers, some of whose units had occupied Corsica and which was thought to be planning an invasion of metropolitan France. The National Assembly voted him into office and gave him, as he asked, authority to draw up a new constitution and submit it to a national referendum.

De Gaulle's insistence in 1958 that his return to office must involve the establishment of a new constitution was based on his repudiation of the principles underlying the arrangements of the Fourth Republic and his unrelenting hostility to the constitution which embodied them. He and his supporters were, however, not alone in their criticisms. Pressures for constitutional amendments had begun as

---

EXHIBIT 2.1

Charles de Gaulle 1890–1970

Born in 1890 to a bourgeois Catholic family in Lille, de Gaulle was, from 1909 to 1940, a professional soldier. His ability and intellectual force, as well as his astonishing sense of his own capacity, marked him out. On 1 June 1940 he was promoted Brigadier-General, and on 6 June left his active command on his appointment as Under-Secretary of State (junior minister) for War in Paul Reynaud's government. He was involved in the intense consultation between the French and British governments during the disastrous days of the fall of France and it was thus that, following Reynaud's resignation on 16 June, de Gaulle was able to avail himself of a British plane that had brought him to the government headquarters in Bordeaux to escape back to London on 17 June. He knew that Marshal Pétain, whom President Lebrun had appointed as prime minister, would seek armistice terms. On 18 June the BBC broadcast, from London, de Gaulle's appeal for the continuation of resistance to the enemy.

In the absence of more senior figures the British government, by the end of June, recognized de Gaulle as the leader of the Free French. By 1944 he had succeeded in becoming the recognized leader of the Resistance within France and of the Provisional Government, based at first in Algiers, which took over in France as Liberation proceeded. In October 1945 a general election and a referendum returned an Assembly with constituent powers, dominated by three large organized political parties. In January 1946 de Gaulle resigned, thus marking his rejection of what he saw as the resurgence of purely party politics. In 1948 he created the Rally of the French People (*Rassemblement du Peuple Français*), launching it with massive meetings, but when it failed to sweep him into power and became like other parties he abandoned it. He returned to his country home at Colombey-les-Deux-Eglises to write his memoirs. He re-emerged dramatically onto the political stage in 1958 as the last prime minister of the Fourth Republic and then, from 1959 to 1969, the first President of the Fifth Republic. He resigned the presidency in 1969 and died in 1970.

De Gaulle had a distant, reserved, arrogant personality, dominating both by the six feet four inches of his physical presence, and by his unshakeable confidence in his destiny and mission. He could, when he chose, be courteous and charming. He was a brilliant communicator, using, indeed manipulating, language and image in radio and television broadcasts and set-piece press conferences.

In 1921 de Gaulle married Yvonne Vendroux. She succeeded, separately, in escaping to England, with their children, in 1940. De Gaulle was devoted to her and his family, especially to his handicapped younger daughter, who died young.

In his book on the qualities of leadership, *Le fil de l'épée* (The Edge of the Sword) published before the war, de Gaulle evokes three features essential to a leader – a doctrine, character and prestige. All these he possessed or acquired, but perhaps his doctrine or, rather, his single-minded vision of the greatness that France does and must represent, in the end remains his most influential and powerful characteristic.

---

early as 1950 and amendments had actually been made in 1954. By 1958 a large majority of the National Assembly were in favour of reform. The initiation of the process of reform was approved by 408 votes to 165 in May 1958. Diagnoses of the disease and prescriptions for its remedy varied, but several found an echo within the new constitution.

There were few formal limitations upon the drafters of the new constitution: Parliament, in voting, by a law of 3 June 1958, for the powers on which de Gaulle insisted to enable him to undertake the formulation of a new constitution, laid down five basic principles. They were:

- that all power must proceed from a system of direct suffrage;
- that both organizationally and operationally legislative and executive powers must be separated;
- that the government must be responsible to Parliament;
- that the independence of the judiciary must be guaranteed
- that the constitution must define the relationship between metropolitan France and 'her associated peoples'; that is, at that period, her overseas colonies and territories.

The law also specified that the draft constitution must be submitted for comment to a constitutional consultative committee consisting of sixteen members of the National Assembly, ten members of the upper house and thirteen members nominated by the government, assisted by representatives of the prime minister, the four senior ministers, and the minister of justice. In addition the Council of State, the senior governmental legal advisory body, was to be consulted. Since a referendum would follow this drafting and consultative process it can be said that effectively the constitution was the product of joint action between government and people, effectively by-passing parliamentary structures (Dreyfus and D'Arcy, 1993, p. 153).

The writing of the Fifth Republic's constitution had three further distinctive features: first, it was very rapidly undertaken: work began in the middle of June and a completed working draft was ready on 15 July. The final version was published just over three weeks before the referendum, on 4 September. Secondly, the draft of the constitution was prepared, under the direction of Michel Debré, De Gaulle's minister of justice, who was to become the first prime minister of the new regime, by a small working party. This working party was supervised by a cabinet committee which included De Gaulle, Debré, and the four senior ministers, who represented some of the major political forces within the National Assembly. Thirdly, since most of the discussions which surrounded the drafting process remained confidential until the publication of the archives at the end of the 1980s, it was for a long period difficult, in some areas, to gauge with any certainty the real intentions of the authors.

The Objectives of the Authors of the Constitution

De Gaulle himself outlined his own views on the requirements of a constitution for France in a speech in Bayeux in June 1946, six months after his resignation (see Exhibit 2.2). He spoke there of an old Gallic propensity for quarrelling and division, and for partisan rivalries beneath which, he said, the main interests of the country too often disappeared. The solution was a clear separation of legislative,

---

EXHIBIT 2.2

Extracts from Charles de Gaulle's speech at Bayeux 16 June 1946

It is essential that our new democratic institutions themselves remedy the effects of our continual political effervescence. This is indeed, for us a question of life or death, given the world and the century in which we live, where the position, the independence and even the existence of our country and the French colonies is well and truly at stake. It is certainly central to democracy that opinions are expressed and that their proponents can try, through the vote, to achieve the policies and legislation they think right. But equally principles and experience all demand that the legislative, executive and judicial branches of government should be clearly separated and powerfully balanced, and that, over and above fleeting political circumstances, a national authority (*arbitrage*) should be established which can ensure continuity whatever happens.

Everyone agrees that the final voice on laws and budgets must be that of a directly elected Assembly. But the first instincts of such an Assembly are not always clear-sighted and untroubled. So a second Assembly, elected and constituted in a different way, needs to take on the task of publicly examining what the first house is doing...

Everything points to the creation of a second Chamber whose members would chiefly be elected by our local councils. It would be natural also to include representatives of the economic organizations, family associations and scholarly societies so that the voices of the principal interests of the country can be heard within the state institutions...

The executive branch cannot derive from this bicameral legislative Parliament. Otherwise there would be the risk of a confusion between the branches of government and the Government would soon be no more than a group of delegates...The unity, cohesion and internal discipline of the Government of France should be sacred, or the authority of the country rapidly becomes impotent and worthless. How could this unity...be maintained over time if the executive depended on another institution which it should balance and each of the members of the Government...was no more than a party's delegate?

The executive power must derive from the Head of State who is above the parties...In making appointments the Head of State must reconcile the general interest with the political tendency evident in Parliament. He must appoint ministers, and especially the Prime Minister who will direct the Government's policies and work. The Head of State must promulgate laws and enact regulations...He must preside over cabinet meetings...It should be his task to act as umpire (*arbitre*) over and above day-to-day politics, usually through his advice, and sometimes, in difficult periods, by inviting the country to exercise its sovereignty through a general election. Should it ever happen that our country is in danger, the Head of State should be the guarantor of national independence and of the treaties into which we have entered.

Source: de Gaulle (1959) pp. 649–52 (author's translation).

---

executive and judicial powers. He argued for a bicameral legislature, whose upper house should consist of members elected by local councils but which might also include representatives of other organized groups. More importantly, he outlined a role for the head of state, who would be indirectly elected by a large electoral college. De Gaulle's elevated concept of the role of the President owed much, in Nicholas Wahl's words:

> to all of de Gaulle's experience since 1940, not to mention his monarchist youth...his peculiarly symbolic role as leader of the Free French; his almost absolute monarchic powers as President of the Provisional Government in 1944–1946; his frustration at seeing the customary weakness of the Third Republic's Presidency emerge again in the constitution of the Fourth Republic; his continuing expectation after 1945 that a continuing World War would again bring a catastrophe like that of 1940; his dismay at the liquidation of an overseas empire, the first to rally to Free France and then lost because no institution bound the territories to the Republic affectively as well as effectively; and finally his consideration of himself as 'national capital' to be drawn on as an ultimate recourse in time of crisis. (Wahl, 1959, p. 376)

The application of de Gaulle's ideas to the circumstances of 1958 produced the important constitutional provisions which define the role of the Head of State – the President of the Republic. The constitution attributes to the President all the powers traditionally enjoyed by French presidents, but substantially increases them (see Chapter 3).

De Gaulle's ideas about the shape that the constitution should take were elaborated during the 1940s and 1950s by some of his supporters, notably Michel Debré. As early as 1943 Debré had begun, on behalf of the National Council of the Resistance, to develop constitutional ideas. He did so from a background as a civil servant with a legal training and outlook, having been a member of the Council of State since 1935 and closely involved with proposals for reforms in governmental structures. Debré's analysis of France's constitutional problems stemmed from a conviction that the roles of the legislature and the executive were insufficiently separated. The parliamentary system as it developed under the Third and Fourth Republics had, he thought, produced weak and short-lived governments, insensitive to the responsibilities of the state, devoid of a sense of the general interest, and lacking coherence, continuity and stability. Nor could the political system on its own, in his opinion, be relied on to produce the necessary qualities. An institutional framework was needed which would be a substitute for disciplined public behaviour and mechanistically enforce the required responses. It was in this light that he interpreted de Gaulle's views about the presidency, but he also brought to the 1958 constitution his support for a reform mooted some years previously, the idea that no one should be allowed to continue as a member of Parliament following appointment as a minister. Ministers would have the right to attend and speak in the National Assembly and the Senate, but not to vote.

Moreover he ensured that the separation of powers was further enforced by the specific delineation, in Article 34, of those areas in which Parliament might legislate. According to Article 37 'matters other than those regulated by laws fall within the field of rule-making' which is the domain of the government. Debré insisted that a Constitutional Council should be created to determine whether laws respected the constitution, a function which would include policing the boundary between the legislative area of Parliament and the regulatory and executive area of the government.

The currents of ideas that had already been advocating reform of the Fourth Republic's constitution were represented in the process of formulating the new constitution by the four ministers of state all of whom had been prominent in the political and parliamentary life of the Fourth Republic, including two former prime ministers, Mollet and Pflimlin, the independent Louis Jacquinot and Félix Houphouët Boigny, representing the parties of the French territories in Africa. Their concern, in the words of one of them, Socialist Party leader and former prime minister Guy Mollet, was 'to put into operation a parliamentary system that would escape those defects of the previous regime that had been universally denounced: excessive control by the legislature over the executive and the consequent governmental instability' (Mollet, 1973, p. 33). All of those involved in drafting the constitution were, if, as Mollet admits, for varied motives, concerned to reinforce governmental authority. However, he continues, most of them wished to see this combined with the assertion of continued parliamentary powers which would ensure that Parliament could insist on its role, but without threatening or harassing the government (Mollet, 1973, pp. 32, 35, 38).

For those for whom such concerns were uppermost, the constitutional provisions which related to the requirement that the prime minister must tender the resignation of the government if defeated by a motion of censure or the rejection of the government's programme or of a general statement of its policy, coupled with the precautions with which the procedures for votes of censure were surrounded, were of particular importance.

The Letter of the Constitution

The document that emerged from this complex drafting process has since undergone formal revisions on fifteen separate occasions (see below and Table 2.1). It initially consisted of 92 articles, of which 13 have been removed, two completely replaced, and 23 changed, two of them (both crucial articles – Article 6 on the election of the president and Article 28 on the sessions of parliament) twice. Ten completely new articles have been added, and two of these have already been amended. It now consists of 88 articles preceded by a preamble (see Exhibit 2.4), which makes it one of the shortest contemporary constitutions (Carcassonne, 2000, p. 346).

The preamble incorporates within the scope of the constitution both the 1789 Declaration of the Rights of Man and Citizen and the principles contained within the preamble to the 1946 constitution (see Exhibit 2.3). Thus it attributes at least some continued existence to a document that it also replaces. The preamble to the 1946 constitution contains a statement of what it calls political, economic and social principles. Some of these principles involve civic rights: equal rights for

EXHIBIT 2.3

The Declaration of the Rights of Man and Citizen 1789

1   Men are born and remain free and equal in rights; social distinction may be based only upon general usefulness.
2   The aim of every political association is the preservation of the natural and inalienable rights of man; these rights are liberty, property, security and resistance to oppression.
3   The source of all sovereignty resides essentially in the nation; no group, no individual may exercise authority not emanating expressly therefrom.
4   Liberty consists of the power to do what is not injurious to others...
5   The law has the right to forbid only actions which are injurious to society...
6   Law is the expression of the general will; all citizens have the right to concur personally, or through their representatives, in its formation; it must be the same for all, whether it protects or punishes. All citizens, being equal before it, are equally admissible to all public offices, positions and employments, according to their capacity, and without other distinction than that of virtues and talents.
7   No man may be accused, arrested or detained except in cases determined by law...
8   The law is to establish only penalties that are absolutely and obviously necessary; and no one may be punished except by virtue of a law established and promulgated prior to the offence and legally applied.
9   Since every man is presumed innocent until declared guilty, if arrest be deemed indispensable, all unnecessary severity for securing the person of the accused must be severely repressed by law.
10 No one is to be disquieted because of his opinions, even religious, provided their manifestation does not disturb the public order established by law.
11 Free communication of ideas and opinions is one of the most precious of the rights of man. Consequently, every citizen may speak, write and print freely, subject to responsibility for the abuse of such liberty in the cases determined by law.
12 The guarantee of the rights of man and citizen necessitates a public force; such a force, therefore, is instituted for the advantage of all and not for the particular benefit of those to whom it is entrusted.
13 For the maintenance of the public force and for the expenses of administration a common tax is indispensable; it must be assessed equally on all citizens in proportion to their means.
14 Citizens have a right to ascertain, by themselves or through their representatives, the necessity of the public tax, to consent to it freely, to supervise its use, and to determine its quota, assessment, payment and duration.
15 Society has the right to require of every public agent an accounting of his administration.
16 Every society in which the guarantee of rights is not assured or the separation of powers is not determined has no constitution at all.
17 Since property is a sacred and inviolable right, no one may be deprived thereof unless a legally established public necessity obviously requires it, and upon condition of a just and previous indemnity.

Translation source: Stewart (1951).

women 'in all spheres'; the rights to belong to a trade union and undertake collective bargaining; the right 'within the framework of the laws which govern it' to strike; the right of asylum for refugees. Other principles envisage a role for the state in economic and social life: the public ownership of firms which are or become 'national public services' or monopolies; guarantees of the provision of free and secular education and of social protection which amount to a commitment to a welfare state and indeed to full employment. The 'Resistance – Liberation discourse' (Ross, 1987, pp. 57–83) of the period, with its criticisms of the old elites and the failures of the 1930s, was clearly reflected in this 1946 preamble, but in 1958 it could still be accepted as compatible with de Gaulle's vision of an economically and socially modernized France, which could unite behind the goal of rebuilding international status and respect.

The constitutional entrenchment of such rights may seem broad and general. Indeed specific mechanisms for enforcing them are not clearly provided but, for example, in 1982 the Constitutional Council used the principles of the Declaration of the Rights of Man (see Exhibit 2.3) to defend the right of shareholders in companies that were to be nationalized to adequate compensation and in 1993 to insist on proportionality between the gravity of an offence and the penalty prescribed.

The constitution, in Article One, states, in a well-known phrase, that France is 'an indivisible, secular, democratic and social republic'. In Article Two it asserts the sovereignty of the French people and also reflects Abraham Lincoln's famous Gettysburg speech phrase, in asserting that the 'principle' of the Republic is 'government of the people, by the people, for the people'. Since 1992 it has also stated that 'the language of the Republic is French', an amendment inserted in the context of the debates around the Maastricht Treaty of European Union as a symbolic reaffirmation of French national identity and status within Europe (Wilcox, 1994).

The structure of the constitution is set out in Exhibit 2.4. Many of its provisions are discussed in subsequent chapters, but a number of general points may be made here. First, the constitution clearly assigns sovereignty to the French people but, in contrast, for example, to the constitutional conventions of the United Kingdom, does not go on to infer from this the absolute sovereignty of the representatives of the people in Parliament. Indeed Article 34 specifies those areas in which parliament may legislate, and specifically precludes it from action in any other spheres, which are the domain of the government. Moreover, Article 55 provides that treaties duly approved and ratified take precedence over laws as long as they are observed by the other contracting parties. For many years this provision enabled France in principle to assimilate the legislation of the European communities into French law without undue difficulty. However, it proved inadequate to handle the rather more far-reaching changes required to conform with developments in European integration in the 1990s, and the constitutional amendments of that decade (see Table 2.1) included the introduction of a new Title 'The European Communities and the European Union'.

EXHIBIT 2.4

The structure of the constitution of the Fifth Republic in 2002

Preamble	
Article One	The French Republic
Title One: Articles 2 to 4	Sovereignty
Title Two: Articles 5 to19	The President
Title Three: Articles 20 to 23	The Government
Title Four: Articles 24 to33	Parliament
Title Five: Articles 34 to 47, 47–1, 48 to 51	Parliament and Government
Title Six: Articles 52 to 53, 53–1, 53–2, 54 to 55	Treaties
Title Seven: Articles 56 to 63	The Constitutional Council
Title Eight: Articles 64 to 66	The Judicial Authority
Title Nine: Articles 67 to 68	The High Court of Justice
Title Ten: Articles 68–1, 68–2, 68–3	Criminal liability of members of the government
Title Eleven: Articles 69 to 71	The Economic and Social Council
Title Twelve: Articles 72 to 75	Local Government
Title Thirteen: Articles 76 to 77	Temporary Provisions for New Caledonia*
Title Fourteen: Article 88 **	Association Agreements
Title Fifteen: Articles 88–1 to 88–4	The European Communities and the European Union
Title Sixteen: Article 89	Constitutional Amendment***

Notes:

* An initial title of the 1958 constitution (originally Title Twelve, then Title Thirteen) was concerned with the relationship of France's then overseas possessions, the states which were to form the 'community'. The 1958 constitution was a dual document. Formulated as it was in a period when the European nation states were rapidly divesting themselves of their colonial inheritance and as the problems and tensions of decolonization, reflected internally, were producing a devastatingly acute internal crisis, the 1958 constitution not only outlined a new regime for France, but was intended to be the foundation 'charter' of a new set of relationships within her former empire. Special institutions for the 'community' were envisaged as, in Article 85, was a special method, used only once, for amending that part of the constitution which comprised the 'charter'. By 1962 all the territories concerned were fully independent, and the 'community' with its institutions, had ceased to exist. Having become completely obsolete Title Thirteen was removed in 1995 only to be revived in 1998 to accommodate two totally new articles, 76 and 77.
** The constitutional amendment of 1995 removed all the articles of Title 13 but did not renumber subsequent articles. The constitution consequently jumps from Article 77 to Article 88.
*** The 1958 constitution also contained a title (initially Fifteen, then Seventeen) which contained the temporary arrangements for the transition between the Fourth and the Fifth Republics. This too was removed by the amendment of 1995.

The constitution instituted two bodies new to the French system: the Constitutional Council, which is more fully discussed below, and the Economic and Social Council. De Gaulle favoured representation not only along conventional electoral lines but also through the representation in the functions of the state of groups with economic and social interests. He saw this as a way of

---

EXHIBIT 2.5

The Economic and Social Council

Title Ten of the 1958 constitution institutes an Economic and Social Council, whose opinion the government may seek on proposed legislation, and must ask for on any bills of 'an economic or social character'; the Council's composition is not specified by the constitution. It has, since 1984, consisted of 230 members including 69 representatives of workers and employees, 72 of employers, and three of the 'liberal professions'. A further 19 members represent co-operatives and friendly societies and 17 come from family associations, housing associations, the mutual savings banks and similar bodies. Eight members represent the economic and social activities of the overseas territories, and two French nationals living abroad. Some of these representatives are elected by specified bodies – trade union confederations, for example – and others are appointed by the government at the suggestion or on the advice of various organizations. In addition 40 members are directly appointed by the government on the basis of their expertise in economic, social, scientific or cultural areas.

The Economic and Social Council has remained a marginal body, having in fact been consulted only 200 times since 1958 (Carcassonne, 2000, p. 308). Although it has formally to be consulted on the five-year plans that have been drawn up regularly since 1946 it has no role in the formulation of the plans, itself an increasingly marginalized process. The Council's views have carried little weight, and although it has occasionally produced interesting reports, largely on its own initiative, their impact has always been limited.

---

associating with the legislative process groups outside what he considered to be the divisive and ideologically blinkered political parties (see Exhibit 2.5). His preference would probably have been, as he proposed at Bayeux and again in a reform put forward for referendum and defeated in 1969, the inclusion of such functional representation within the upper house of the legislature. However, the 1946 constitution had created a separate consultative economic committee, and an analogous solution was retained in 1958.

Amending the Constitution

The constitution contains within it a mechanism for its amendment, embodied in Title Sixteen, which has been utilized in an apparently accelerating rhythm. This Title consists of a single article, Article 89. President de Gaulle twice attempted to effect constitutional amendments by a procedure which bypassed Article 89, once successfully and once unsuccessfully (see Exhibit 2.6). Under Article 89 a bill to amend the constitution must be passed in both houses of Parliament in identical terms. A further stage is then required which may take one of two forms. If the government has proposed the amendment, it may be submitted to a joint meeting of both houses of Parliament, held in considerable splendour at Versailles and known as a Congress of Parliament, which must approve it unaltered by a three-fifths' majority. This mechanism for the revision of the constitution may be regarded as the normal one, and has been invoked for all but one of the

---

EXHIBIT 2.6

Constitutional amendments under de Gaulle

In 1962 the method of electing the President was changed from election by an electoral college to direct election by all voters. In 1969 a proposal to reform the Senate (the upper house of the legislatures) which would be combined with the Economic and Social Council and to introduce a measure of regional government was defeated. The mechanism used for both these attempts was hotly disputed, for its constitutionality was questioned. In both cases de Gaulle invoked two articles of the constitution, Article 3 which says 'national sovereignty belongs to the people, who exercise it through their representatives or by way of referendum' and Article 11 which permits the President, on the proposal of the government, to submit to referendum 'any government bill dealing with the organisation of the public authorities'. These articles were held to provide a mechanism for constitutional revision which bypassed Parliament. Almost all the leading constitutional lawyers of the time took the view that Article 89 sets out the only valid amendment procedure. The government in 1962 consulted its highest legal advisory body, the Council of State, as is required for all draft legislation. The Council of State's opinions are always confidential, but a leak revealed that all but one of its members regarded the procedure as unconstitutional.

The Constitutional Council was not formally able to give a view until after the referendum. At that point the President (Speaker) of the Senate, who had bitterly attacked de Gaulle for holding the referendum, referred the amendment to the Council. Although earlier unofficial soundings had shown the Council to be in agreement with the Council of State, once faced with a proposal approved by referendum it did not feel able to overturn the people's decision (Quermonne, 1980, p. 65). De Gaulle used a similar procedure in 1969, on the grounds that having approved his constitutional amendment in 1962 the people had also implicitly approved the procedure. The referendum resulted in the rejection of the proposed amendment and led directly to de Gaulle's resignation as President. No president since then has suggested bypassing parliament.

---

successful revisions between de Gaulle's referendum of 1962 and 2002 (see Exhibit 2.7). No amendment has ever been rejected at the Versailles stage. In the 1970s two proposals were withdrawn when the votes in the two houses made it clear that they would not achieve the three-fifths majority. In January 2000 a Congress of Parliament was cancelled at short notice by President Chirac, with the acquiescence of Prime Minister Jospin, when it became apparent that support for amendments to increase the independence of the judiciary, to alter the provisions for New Caledonia and to change the status of French Polynesia had dwindled since their passage through Parliament the previous November.

In the 1990s the pace of constitutional change accelerated. Several factors help to explain this acceleration:

- The impact of international treaties
- Constitutional reform as an arena for presidential action
- Pressure from evolving public opinion

EXHIBIT 2.7

Constitutional amendments

Year	Day	Principal provisions	Method
1960	4 June	Revision of article about relations with African territories and Madagascar	A.85*
1962	6 November	Direct election of the president	See Exhibit 2.6
1963	30 December	Altered dates for parliamentary sessions	A 89 – Congress
1974	29 October	Extension of right of referral to Constitutional Council	A 89 – Congress
1976	18 June	Procedures in the case of death or serious impediment of presidential election candidates during the election period	A 89 – Congress
1992	25 June	Added Title on the European Communities and the European Union. Specified that the language of the Republic is French	A 89 – Congress
1993	27 July	Created the Court of Justice of the Republic to try ministers accused of illegal actions in the exercise of their ministerial functions. Reformed the High Council of the Judiciary (*ConseilSupérieur de la Magistrature*)	A 89 – Congress
1993	25 November	Allowed for making of agreements with other European states on treatment of demands for asylum (permitted implementation of the Schengen agreement)	A 89 – Congress
1995	4 August	Extended period of Parliamentary sessions. Changed scope of parliamentary immunity. Extended scope of questions on which a referendum can be called. Deleted obsolete provisions	A 89 – Congress
1996	22 February	Brought the financing of the social security system into the domain of the law (Article 34)	A 89 – Congress
1998	20 July	Transitional arrangements for New Caledonia	A 89 – Congress
1999	25 January	Allowed for transfer of powers to European Union in relation to free movement of persons (visa policy) to permit implementation of the Treaty of Amsterdam and increased parliamentary scrutiny of EU legislative proposals	A 89 – Congress

⟶

⎯⎯⎯⎯→

1999	8 July	'parity' amendment – allowed law to 'favour' equal access of men and women to elected positions and stated that political parties should contribute to the implementation of this. Provided for implementation of the Treaty on the International Criminal Court	A 89 – Congress
2000	2 October	Reduced presidential term of office to five years (*quinquennat*)	A 89 – Referendum
2003	17 March	'Decentralisation' amendment specified that France is organised on a decentralised basis. Provided for the implementation of the European arrest warrant	A 89 – Congress

Note:

* Article 85, now deleted, provided a special procedure for amendment of the constitution in relation to the provisions for relationships with the French possessions in Africa and with Madagascar.

The first of these factors accounted for the first amendment since 1976. In 1992 President Mitterrand judged it prudent to ask the Constitutional Council (see below pp. 50–6) to verify whether the proposed Treaty of European Union (the Maastricht Treaty) was compatible with the constitution. The Council's response was that it was not: constitutional revision would be required to give all EU citizens the right to vote in local elections, and to permit economic and monetary union and a common visa policy. Since an amendment was essential the opportunity was taken to add provisions specifying French as the language of the Republic and making amendments to articles concerning the French overseas territories and the Constitutional Council. The amendment achieved a three-fifths vote with ease, in part because the Gaullist *Rassemblement pour la République* (see Chapter 8) chose to abstain. The extent of the political divisions that were emerging over the ratification of the Maastricht Treaty divisions were thus partially concealed, only emerging sharply in the closeness of the vote in the referendum on ratification three months later.

The impact of an international agreement was also incorporated into the constitution by the amendment in 1993, prompted by the Constitutional Council ruling unconstitutional a bill that had been introduced in order to give effect to one of the provisions of the Schengen agreement. Following this amendment the bill that had previously been overturned was passed. For the Treaty of Amsterdam and then for the Treaty instituting the International Criminal Court the president and prime minister acted pre-emptively and jointly, despite *cohabitation* (that is, they came from political parties which opposed each other – see Chapter 3) to refer the texts to the Constitutional Council, and the necessary revisions followed in January and July 1999.

The second factor emerged in the early 1990s as, during his second term of office (1988–95), and in the context of his increasing withdrawal from day to day politics, President Mitterrand commissioned a report by an expert committee on a number of reform proposals. He was perhaps seeking to pre-empt revived discussion of reducing the presidential term of office to five years (*quinquennat*), a suggestion first put to parliament by President Pompidou in 1973, which might have risked foreshortening his own tenure. No action had been taken before the general election of 1993 overturned the Socialist government. Nevertheless, the new government took up two of the ideas that had been mooted, and the result was the constitutional amendment of July 1993.

During his presidential campaign in 1995 Jacques Chirac did not show much interest in constitutional and institutional issues, marking himself out thereby from his second-round opponent, Lionel Jospin, who called for a five-year term for the president, more decentralization and a stronger Parliament. Nevertheless, constitutional reform (instituting a single nine-month annual session for Parliament (see Chapter 7) and extending the scope of the issues upon which a referendum may be called) was one of the first major measures he undertook, and his first term of office was marked by the most far-reaching amendments since the 1962 change in the method of electing the president.

A third explanatory factor for the acceleration of amendment was political and public pressure. The two major amendments of the late 1990s illustrated this. During the 1990s unfavourable comparison with other European countries arose from the persistent under-representation of women in elected or senior political positions in France and the hostility many faced if they did achieve office. Examples include Prime Minister Cresson, and the female ministers – the so-called *jupettes* (a punning and derisory diminutive deriving both from the French word *jupe* – a skirt – and the prime minister's name) – in Alain Juppé's first government in 1993. A campaign for 'parity' became increasingly vocal. The constitutional issues were substantial, and the debate considerable (see Exhibit 2.8). Since both president and prime minister supported the amendment, the debate was not polarized along party political lines, although the outcome represented some compromise between the views of the National Assembly and the Senate.

Political pressure – stemming principally from *cohabitation* (see Chapter 3) and the 1995 presidential election campaign, and stirred up by a former president of the Republic, although there was a longer history – also lay behind the amendment reducing the presidential term of office to five years. The traditional seven-year term for presidents of the Republic – instituted as a stop-gap alternative to the monarchy by the constitutional laws of 1875 (Duhamel, 2000, p. 21) – had suited de Gaulle well enough, despite the radically changed status of the president in the Fifth Republic (see Chapter 3), for it symbolized stability and a status 'above' politics. President Pompidou, exercising a more overtly political presidency, told parliament in 1973 that his experience had confirmed his long-held belief that the seven-year term did not suit the new institutions and proposed a reduction to five years. The initial votes in the two houses separately suggested

EXHIBIT 2.8

Parity

During the early 1990s the absence of women with electoral mandates was a subject for concern in France where the proportions were amongst the lowest in the European Union and neither the move to proportional representation in 1986 nor away from it in 1988 helped them (see Table 7.3). In the Senate the number of women rose from 19 to 35 out of 321 (11 per cent) following the 2001 partial elections.

In 1982 the Constitutional Council (ruling 82–146 DC of 18 November 1982) ruled against a bill proposing that in local elections, for which parties put up lists of candidates (see Exhibit 6.1), not more than 75 per cent of the candidates might be of the same sex. They said that if all citizens are constitutionally equal then the law cannot, in the absence of a change to the constitution, recognize or acknowledge any difference between them, even one so apparently evident as their sex.

Nevertheless the call for 'parity' – that is equal representation, not just the equality of lack of discrimination or equal treatment – continued. In 1988 *Les Verts*, the ecologist party, included a provision for equal representation into its party rules (Dauphin and Praud, 2002, p. 8). In 1994 Michel Rocard's Socialist Party list for the European Parliament election was equally balanced between men and women. In 1999, following intense debate amongst politicians, feminists and intellectuals (see Dauphin and Praud, 2002) the provision in Article 3 of the constitution that 'the law favours the equal access of men and women to elected mandates and positions' was enacted.

This amendment allowed the passage of the law of 6 June 2000, which requires the equal representation of men and women on the lists for elections to which proportional representation applies (see Exhibit 6.1). Nor can women be consigned to the bottom of the list so that they do not actually gain seats: for one-ballot elections such as the European Parliament elections, men and women must alternate on the lists (so-called 'zip' lists), and for two-ballot proportional elections they must be equally represented in each group of six. For general elections the law provides that parties which do not present equal numbers of men and women will be penalized by being refused a proportion of the state subventions to which they would otherwise have been entitled.

In the municipal elections of March 2001 the impact of the law was evident. In the communes to which the law applied, the number of female town councillors more than doubled from 21.9 per cent to 47.5 per cent. However, in simultaneous elections in the *départements* to which the law does not apply only 20 per cent of the candidates and less than 10 per cent of the councillors subsequently in office were women (Dauphin, 2002). The results of the general election of 2002, fought under the new law, were also not spectacular: 71 women were elected (12.3 per cent). The financial penalties, calculated with reference to the proportion by which a party's female candidates fell short of 50 per cent, were duly applied, and the Socialist Party, for example, found itself obliged to reduce its headquarters staff by four posts to accommodate its losses (*Le Nouvel Observateur*, 25–31 July 2002).

that the bill would not receive the necessary three-fifths' majority in the joint meeting and it was withdrawn. In the presidential election of 1995, Lionel Jospin, the unsuccessful second-round candidate, included such a reduction in his programme. Chirac did not. He remained opposed until 2000, when the issue was raised by former president Giscard d'Estaing, who put forward a private member's bill in the National Assembly. Chirac decided to promote the amendment which was supported not only by Jospin, who had been prime minister since 1997, but also by prominent supporters of his own such as former prime minister Alain Juppé. The simple reason in favour of the change was that it was likely to rule out the situation in which successive elections could result in the president and the prime minister coming from opposed political parties (*cohabitation*), since presidential and parliamentary terms would be likely to coincide. There could, however, be no guarantee that this would happen, for both parliamentary dissolutions and presidential demise or resignation could potentially intervene. Nor could it be certain that voters would, as in 1981 and 2002, though less convincingly in 1988, vote the same way at two elections within weeks of each other. A more coherent, though perhaps less publicly visible argument, was advanced by political scientist Olivier Duhamel, who pointed out that the coexistence of a five-year maximum for parliament and seven-year term for president had meant that the voters had been choosing governments for the changeable periods between two national level elections, whether legislative or presidential. Since the mid-1970s, a period which had seen no presidential death in office or resignation, the gaps had varied seemingly randomly from 2 to 5 years. Coincident terms should engender rather greater stability and enable voters to have a better idea of what they were doing (Duhamel, 2000). Since the change would affect the way the citizens choose those in power it was deemed appropriate, for the first time, to deploy the Article 89 provisions for a referendum on the text approved by both houses of parliament. However, it proved difficult to persuade the electorate that the outcome mattered. Only a quarter of the electorate bothered to vote, though nearly three-quarters of those who did approved the change.

The Constitutional Balance: What Type of Regime?

The principal author of the constitution of the Fifth Republic was adamant that the system which it installed was what he called a parliamentary system. This system he contrasted with two other possible republican forms. One of these he called a *régime d'assemblée* – government by assembly – and the other was a presidential system (Debré, 1958, p. 621). The system that he characterized as 'government by assembly' had, in his view, been exemplified by the Third and Fourth Republics. Prime ministers could not be appointed until the Assembly had approved them. Governments could relatively easily be overthrown by a hostile vote. The Assembly could control its own agenda. Initial discussion of proposed bills took place in committees of the Assembly, which could alter and reshape the proposals. The Assembly controlled the legality of elections and could thus to some extent determine its own membership. There was no system for determining whether laws were in conformity with the constitution. Debré saw the political stalemate that all too frequently arose from 'an assembly with the responsibility for choosing and sustaining a government, yet with a compulsion to check its action and a deep suspicion of its motives' (Williams, 1972, p. 438) as an inevitable consequence, at least in France, of the concentration of powers within one institution. The changes which the Fifth Republic's constitution introduced, above all in the role of Parliament, clearly marked a decisive departure from the previous model.

An answer to the question whether the Fifth Republic is a presidential regime depends partially upon the definition employed. Some commentators take the constitution of the United States of America as providing the 'ideal type' of a presidential regime, against which the French situation may be measured (Quermonne and Chagnollaud, 1996, Ch. IX). Using such a definition, a presidential regime would be characterized by the following major features:

- a President who is both head of state and head of the government;
- a ministerial team chosen solely by the President, and not, consequently, responsible to or dismissible by the legislature;
- a President who is not answerable to the legislature and who can be removed only by a process of impeachment;
- a fixed term legislature; this means that crises within the legislature cannot be used to undermine the President or challenge his legitimacy.

Debré, in rejecting in 1958 the notion of a presidential regime for France, also assumed a fifth condition – that a President under such a system would have to be directly elected by universal suffrage, a condition which does not apply in the United States.

From a purely legalistic point of view it can be argued that only one of the American characteristics listed above – that the President is not answerable to Parliament – is found in France. Moreover, in 1958 direct election of the President was not envisaged. At the time, the arguments which insisted that the new constitution would not impose a presidential regime had a specific political significance, even if they were couched in somewhat theoretical and legalistic terms. The circumstances in which de Gaulle had emerged as the 'providential' rescuer of France from crisis and even incipient civil war, combined with other traits evident in his political past – distrust of political parties, anti-communism, emphasis upon a strong state and international standing, the use of large and spectacular rallies and meetings as a means of political campaigning – all these gave rise to a degree of concern about possible fascist tendencies within his political approach. It was essential at the time to allay fears that the constitution necessarily involved an intolerable concentration of power in one person's hands.

A purely legalistic approach, however, does not give a clear picture of the way in which the political system under the constitution has evolved. Guy Mollet, who helped to persuade his own Socialist Party to support the constitution in 1958, wrote bitterly fifteen years later that it required an effort of the imagination to see how the constitution was intended to function; no effort had been made to apply it as it had been written: all that had happened was a succession of distortions

(Mollet, 1973, pp. 39, 137). A noted French scholar, Jean-Louis Quermonne (Quermonne and Chagnollaud, 1996), concludes that the regime falls halfway between a parliamentary and a presidential system and should not be regarded as analogous to other constitutional frameworks. Other commentators (Duhamel, 2000, pp. 40–2) argue that, at least between the 1962 direct election amendment and the 2000 five-year presidency amendment, what France, confusingly, possessed was two constitutions, parliamentary and presidential, and which was in force at any one time depended upon the political context. Yet the 1958 constitution has survived both substantially amended and largely unchallenged. The text expected, in the almost unanimous view of the political commentators of the time, to be strictly temporary, but embodying the aspirations of a broad spectrum of opinion, contained within it from the beginning potential for development and interpretation.

What becomes clear is that a written constitution, whilst it may provide a framework and a point of reference for political values in a particular society, is also, crucially, never neutral or external to political life in a country. Its application and interpretation depend upon the political values and the balance of political forces within the country at any time.

The Development of the Regime

In the period between 1958 and 1986 the balance of forces within the regime developed in a way which reinforced the power and position of the President to an extent which made it increasingly possible to speak of a 'presidential regime'. The crucial feature was the emergence, especially after the 1962 direct election amendment, of the President as not only head of state but also effectively as head of the government.

By the end of the 1970s three of the four characteristics which were, in 1958, held to indicate the absence of a presidential regime – the separation of the headship of state from the headship of government; the choice by prime minister, not president, of the ministerial team; indirect election – had in practice been substantially eroded or disappeared. Moreover, although there is a maximum, rather than fixed, term for the legislature the right of dissolution has been sparingly used (five times between 1958 and 2002) and always as an attempt to reinforce the legitimacy of the president. In two cases (1981 and 1988) the dissolution immediately followed the election of a president of a different persuasion from that of the parliamentary majority. Both times – once (1981) overwhelmingly, and once (1988) requiring a coalition of political forces – a majority supportive of the president was returned. In 1962 de Gaulle's dissolution was a response to a vote of censure which, whilst formally against the government, was clearly directly aimed at him. He appealed to the popular vote against the 'politicians' of Parliament, and was rewarded by the return of an increased number of Gaullist members committed to unconditional support for the president. Equally in 1968 the early dissolution was a response to the events of May of that year, when student riots and workers' strikes put the authority of the government, and especially the personal status of the president, under great pressure (see Exhibit 9.2). The outcome was increased representation for the Gaullists who gained an overall majority. President Chirac, in 1995, found a parliamentary majority of his persuasion already in place so no dissolution was required. However, that Parliament's term would terminate in 1998. Wishing to ensure an ongoing majority for the full remainder of his seven years, he called an early election in 1997, a manoeuvre which backfired disastrously, leaving him with a hostile majority for the subsequent five years.

From the beginning discussions raged around the role of the president. They did so for two reasons; first, the difficulty of identifying, from the language that was used about the role, precisely what was involved. Article 5 provided a broad description. In specifying the president's relationship to the 'public authorities' it used the phrase 'he provides, by his arbitration, for the regular functioning of the public authorities and the continuity of the State'. *Arbitrage* can mean both arbitration, in a judicial sense, and umpiring. Although, as André Philip pointed out at the time, the umpire should not also be a player (Emeri, 1985, p. 80), the phrase could also be taken to mean that the president should lay down the outlines and all the main directions of the governmental programme. And this, indeed, was what occurred.

The second reason for discussion about the role of the president arose from the difficulty of separating the constitutional definition of the president's scope and the personal impact of de Gaulle himself. This was recognized at the time. Guy Mollet, anxious to preserve his notion of a constitutional balance that would retain the domination of the prime minister, attempted to persuade de Gaulle that he should not be a candidate for the presidency once the new republic was installed, but instead continue as prime minister, thereby ensuring the continued pre-eminence of that role. De Gaulle was clear however that his own place was not to be absorbed in the day-to-day details of government, still less to be implicated in the conflicts and hassle of party politics. He picked as his prime minister Michel Debré, a man with a minimal personal power base, even within the small group of long-term Gaullists, but with an immense loyalty to the president himself. De Gaulle did not intend to risk any challenges from the prime minister to his own dominant position at the top.

The 1958 election results reinforced this status. The constitutional referendum was widely recognized as being less a vote on a legal text than a national vote of confidence in de Gaulle. In the general election of November a rapidly organized group of Gaullists took 206 out of 536 National Assembly seats; and in the presidential elections of December 1958, 78 per cent of the electoral college voted for de Gaulle. De Gaulle found himself, then, with a degree of popular and indeed organized political support that nothing in the history of the Fourth Republic foreshadowed. He owed it, initially, not to a broad political programme or to any kind of national organization, but to the perception of the French people that he, and only he, could find and impose a solution to the problem of the future of Algeria. This he duly succeeded in doing. True to his emphasis on the need for direct national assent and for an assertion of the French people's confidence in his measures, he organized two referenda. They provided the assurances he required; indeed, at the second referendum in April 1962, 91 per cent of those voting in metropolitan France approved the terms of his settlement which led to Algerian independence.

In some ways the early commentators were right; the political and constitutional balance instituted in 1958 was a provisional and temporary one. The degree of support enjoyed by de Gaulle had permitted the government, under his guidance coupled with the energetic action of Debré, to tackle a number of outstanding problems. But that support, while not limited to questions relating to Algeria, was nevertheless heavily dependent upon de Gaulle's indispensability as the peacemaker with Algeria. With that task accomplished he needed a new base and possibly a redefined status. Those members of Parliament who defined their political position in terms of their loyalty to him were already organized as a political group. But de Gaulle was never willing to envisage himself as a party leader, or as dependent upon a particular and limited political power base.

In September 1962 de Gaulle announced a proposal to move to direct election of the president (see Exhibit 2.6). The provisions put forward, and approved by referendum, resulted in a two-ballot electoral system for the presidency. Unless a candidate receives over 50 per cent of the vote at the first ballot, which has never occurred, the two candidates with highest number of votes go forward to the second ballot a fortnight later.

It may seem surprising that it was not envisaged from the start that the office would require the legitimacy and support that direct election would imply. Three factors apparently influenced the preference for an electoral college shown by the drafters of the text: they were alluded to by Debré in his speech to the Council of State. First, direct elections would have implied very specifically that the new regime was to be 'presidential', an implication that in the circumstances of the time would have been widely unacceptable. Secondly, the dual nature of the constitution meant that the president was also the head of the 'French Community'. It would have been difficult to exclude the inhabitants of the African states who belonged to that Community from the choice of their head of state, and even more difficult for the inhabitants of France to accept that they, on a 'one person one vote' system, might be outvoted in the choice of the head of state of France by people living outside metropolitan France. And finally, within metropolitan France the Communist Party, locked into a 'cold war' role and widely felt to owe its most fundamental loyalties to the Soviet Union – in Guy Mollet's famous gibe, 'not to the Left of the Socialist party but to its East' – nonetheless consistently polled the highest percentage of electoral votes of any party. On a simple plurality system of election a Communist candidate might win, a possibility which none of those involved in the formulation of the constitution was prepared to contemplate.

By 1962 these factors could all be differently perceived. De Gaulle's regime was widely supported and not generally regarded as fascist or intolerable. The 'Community' had disappeared and its institutions were obsolete. The Communist

Party had not prospered, and the double-ballot electoral system used for parliamentary elections had proved capable of ensuring that the proportion of votes it received was not reflected in actual electoral success. The 'spark' (Rudelle, 1985, p. 117) which set off the process which led to the referendum was the assassination attempt against de Gaulle at Petit Clamart in August 1962. It came very close to succeeding, and the President's mind was then rapidly concentrated upon the need to provide a mechanism for ensuring that any successor to him could rely on the same broad measure of legitimacy and support that he enjoyed.

The outcome of the vote – just under 62 per cent of the voters approved direct election – has often been seen as the most crucial single event in the evolution of the regime. In terms of the balance of power its effect was to confer upon all future presidents a large measure of popular legitimacy and hence political pre-eminence. It precluded, as its opponents from amongst the political parties and the parliamentarians in 1962 had realized that it would, any return to a more Fourth Republican system of parliamentary predominance. It gave a legal and democratic rationale to presidential practice and, precisely as de Gaulle intended, provided, at least in part, a mechanical institutional substitute for the particular circumstances which provided him with his initial legitimacy. He himself was then obliged to utilize this mechanism in 1965, when the election went into a second ballot, and it became apparent that the presidency would henceforth be as much political as charismatic. Indeed, the presidential election of 1965 may be seen as the consummation of the process begun in 1962. François Mitterrand, one of the most active and vocal opponents of the 1962 revision, was nonetheless prepared to campaign for the presidency in 1965 on the basis that the president should have a policy programme to offer. He said that if elected he would seek (as in fact he did in 1981 and 1988), through a general election, the parliamentary majority with which to implement it.

The authors of the constitution did not think in terms of a presidential majority. Their expectation of the working of the constitution, extrapolated from previous experience, seems to have involved governments formed from relatively unstable coalitions, held together by the institutional glue of reformed parliamentary procedure and strengthened executive powers, protected by a Constitutional Council and supervised benignly by a president whose role was to protect the country from the damage that instability might otherwise cause. However, as the discussion of presidential practice in Chapter 3 helps to illustrate, 'presidential', at least within normal common-sense usages, is the appropriate description for the regime during those periods when the president is supported by such a parliamentary 'presidential majority'. But the evolution of the regime did not rapidly provide an answer to the question of how the system would work in the absence of a majority. For 28 years it seemed as if the French electors had accepted and acted upon what might be called 'the logic of presidentialism'. Parliamentary elections as they fell due at the expiry of normal five-year terms in 1967, 1973 and 1978 returned majorities which supported the President in office. In 1962 and 1968 the election results reaffirmed support for the president. In 1981 a newly elected president caused the electorate to confirm their choice, and a majority supporting him was returned. But there was nothing inevitable about this process, as presidents at the time of general elections more or less explicitly pointed out.

Four possibilities are open to presidents who find themselves faced with a general election that returns their political opponents. First, they might ask the country to think again, by a rapid dissolution and a second general election. The risks in such a course, which might look like contempt for the judgement of the electorate, would obviously be high. Secondly, some commentators (Quermonne, 1980, p. 581) took the view that a disavowal by the electorate of the parliamentary majority that had been supporting the president would amount to a disavowal of the president himself, who ought therefore to resign and thereby bring about a new presidential election which might bring the two institutions into line again. This was not the view of President Giscard d'Estaing in 1978 faced with such a possibility, which did not in fact materialize, and nor was it of his two successors, Mitterrand and Chirac, both of whom did have to confront such choices. When the situation first arose, following the general election of 1986, President Mitterrand equally did not adopt a third possible strategy and attempt to impose some compromise government that he might dominate and which just might have maintained its position in Parliament. Instead he turned to the fourth of the possible strategies and called on Jacques Chirac, the leader of the party which had the largest number of seats in the National Assembly, to form a government. He did so again in 1993, on that occasion appointing, not Chirac himself, but Chirac's nominee, Edouard Balladur. In both cases he was insistent that he retained and had exercised the president's right to make a choice. With these precedents Chirac in 1997 had effectively no political option other than to call upon Lionel Jospin to form a government. It was this level of political constraint upon presidential choice and the pattern of working that evolved (see chapter 3) that underpinned the argument that, at least until the *quinquennat* amendment, the constitution contained two alternative frameworks, presidential and parliamentary.

The political history of the period since 1981 has thus encompassed:

- *alternance*: the replacement in 1981 of one government by another of a radically different political complexion. This had not occurred since the Second World War, not even in 1958. Until 1981 some coalition partners and hence ministers had always been carried forward from one government to the next;
- the first two year period of *cohabitation* (Socialist president, Gaullist prime minister) from 1986 to 1988;
- the re-election of President Mitterrand in 1988;
- the subsequent general election which produced a minority Socialist government;
- a return to *cohabitation* (Socialist president, Gaullist prime minister) in 1993;
- in 1995 the victory of Chirac, who retained the Parliament elected in 1993 in which he enjoyed a majority but with a new prime minister and ministerial team;

- in 1997 the 'surprise' dissolution, and the commencement of an extended period of *cohabitation* (Gaullist president, Socialist prime minister) lasting until 2002;
- in 2000 the *quinquennat* amendment, followed in 2002 by the re-election of President Chirac for a five-year term and his achievement of a presidential majority (potentially for the same term) in the general election. *Cohabitation*, it may be argued, is a thing of the past.

In constitutional terms the effects of this history have been as follows:

- To force president, government and parliamentarians to fall back upon the actual provisions of the constitution and to explore and exploit more fully the possibilities it offers; the consequence has been a long-term strengthening of the constitution within the regime which is likely to survive the probable disappearance of *cohabitation*.
- To demonstrate the extent to which the constitution provided an accepted, unchallenged, yet flexible framework for the institutions of government in France; major shifts in political orientation and in the balance of power within this framework were possible without the constitution itself being contested.

Even during the periods of *cohabitation* the president remained a key figure in French political life. The importance of the prospect of the impending presidential elections within much political life in 1986–8 and 1993–5, the nature of the contest and the sense of severe shock and outrage which followed the emergence of Le Pen (see Chapter 8) as a second-round contestant in 2002; all these demonstrate the extent to which 'normality' is defined in presidential terms.

The Constitutional Council

The creation of the Constitutional Council has come to be recognized as the second major innovation in constitutional structure introduced by the Fifth Republic. In the case of the role of the presidency the full implications of the constitutional change only became clear after the 1962 amendment. Similarly, in the case of the Constitutional Council, it was the amendment of 1974 which clarified, confirmed and enlarged the scope of the new institution. Like the presidency, the Constitutional Council has moved well beyond the role envisaged for it by its creators (Avril and Gicquel, 1993, p. 71). Much of the motivation for its creation was the desire for an independent body that would reinforce the reforms of the parliamentary system introduced by the new regime. The National Assembly was no longer to control its own membership. The Constitutional Council would decide upon the validity of elections. Nor was Parliament to have unfettered control of its conduct of business. The Constitutional Council must approve the standing orders of both houses of Parliament and any amendment made to them. And Parliament was to keep strictly to the limits prescribed for it (see Chapter 7).

The Constitutional Council can annul any bill referred to it which ventures into the domain reserved for governmental action.

The Constitutional Council consists of nine appointed members, three appointed personally by the president, three by the president (speaker) of the National Assembly, and three by the president of the Senate. Each appointed member serves for a non-renewable term of nine years, and one-third of the membership is replaced every three years. If a member's term is terminated prematurely by death or resignation the replacement will serve only the remaining portion of the original term. In addition any former President of the Republic has the right to sit as a member of the Council. Presidents Auriol and Coty exercised this right during the early years of the Fifth Republic but neither President de Gaulle nor President Mitterrand did so. Ex-President Giscard d'Estaing could have participated in the work of the Council during the period between 1981 and his election to parliament in 1984 but declined to do so since he was still pursuing an active political career. In 1984 the Constitutional Council ruled that for ex officio members, as for others, holding a parliamentary seat was incompatible with participation in the work of the Council.

Membership of the Council is not confined to those with a legal background. Many members have indeed been magistrates and lawyers, including one former president of the Court of Justice of the European Communities and one former president of the European Court of Human Rights. Rather over one-fifth of the members who have served since 1958 have been professors of law or of political science; others have been former senior officials. The first woman (Mme Noëlle Lenoir) was appointed in 1992. In 2002 there were three women members, one academic sociologist, Dominique Schnapper, and two politicians, Simone Weil and Monique Pelletier, both of them with distinguished careers as ministers. Indeed, well over half the total membership of the Council since its creation has comprised former members of Parliament and ministers (who may also have been lawyers or officials). All the presidents of the Council have been drawn from this group of members. Charlot (1994, p. 200) argues that this has rendered the Council's independence more acceptable to successive governments. It cannot be held to be ignorant of the day-to-day realities of political life. Nevertheless, the appointments have at times proved controversial, and it is possible to perceive the fact that presidents of the Republic have always appointed adherents of their own persuasion as presidents of the Constitutional Council as confirming the essentially political nature of the Council. Such appointees normally outlast their appointers, so that it may equally be argued that the Council tends to become a bastion of the defeated tendency. President Mitterrand found himself making such appointments two years before the end of each of his mandates, and was criticized for both the appointment of Robert Badinter in 1986 and of Roland Dumas in 1995. The controversy grew when a number of accusations relating to Roland Dumas came under judicial investigation and attracted particularly vivid press coverage. Dumas did not resign immediately, although from March 1999 he 'suspended himself' from his position as president of the Council. Only in March

2000 did he finally resign. It was convenient for Jacques Chirac that the interim presidency during Dumas's 'suspension' fell to the oldest member of the Council who in fact owed his appointment to the president of the Senate, the then 78 year-old Yves Guéna, a staunch and highly distinguished Gaullist. He was confirmed in the position when Dumas resigned.

The Constitutional Council's role can be described under two headings: legal and advisory. The former is the major and dominant role, and itself falls into two main parts (see Table 2.1). The Constitutional Council judges the legality and validity of presidential, senatorial and National Assembly elections, and of referendums. It can therefore rule on cases where, following an election, the successful candidate is alleged to have been ineligible to stand, and on cases where a sitting member is alleged to have made him or herself ineligible to continue as a result of taking up an incompatible post. More importantly, it rules on the validity of elections in cases where electoral malpractice or fraud is alleged. 172 cases were referred to it in 1997 and 162 in 2002. In addition, from 1993 onwards new legislation permitted the National Committee (*Commission nationale des comptes de campagne et des financements politiques*) overseeing political party finances and electoral expenses to ask the Constitutional Council to consider cases. In all, 648 cases were referred by the National Committee in 1993 and 272 in 1997. Only six elections were annulled in 1993, one of them being that of the Socialist former minister of culture, Jack Lang, and even fewer – four – in 1997.

The Council also rules on whether laws passed by the National Assembly are constitutional or not. The government may ask it to consider whether a bill under discussion falls within the scope of parliamentary law-making (see Chapter 6). Once a law which falls into the category of 'organic laws' – laws which provide for the detailed implementation of the constitution, for example by determining the electoral system – has been passed, the Council must rule on whether it is constitutional. Other laws may be referred to the Council for a ruling before they are promulgated. If they are found to be unconstitutional they cannot enter into force.

The second activity which the Constitutional Council undertakes is an advisory one. It must be consulted if the President wishes to declare a state of emergency under Article 16 of the constitution. It is also consulted on the arrangements for presidential elections, and on the conduct of referendums. Finally, proposed international treaties can be referred to it. If they are ruled incompatible with the constitution it must be amended before the treaty can be ratified.

The Council initially played a somewhat modest role but has now emerged as an important source of limitation and constraint upon the actions of the government. There are two main explanations for the nature of the Council's development. First, in its early years the Council, influenced by the extreme prudence of its first president (the Council was known to have held that the 1962 constitutional amendment was effected by unconstitutional means, but did not publicly say so), acted in ways which supported the new regime. Moreover, a major use to which the Council was put was to ensure that Parliament did not stray beyond the limits of its constitutionally ordained boundaries. The Council was seen at least

TABLE 2.1

The business of the Constitutional Council: number and type of decisions

Years	1958–1996	1997	1998	1999	2000	2001
Elections						
Referendums	14				8	
Presidential elections	75					
National Assembly — total	1740	124	195	6	6	2
of which annulled	44	3	9	1	1	9
Senate — total	137					14
of which annulled	3					
Other parliamentary business						
Status of members of Parliament	27	1		1	1	
of which						
Compatibility of parliamentary functions	16			1		
Removal of member						
National Assembly	8					
Senate	3	1				
already resigned (Senate)						
Amendments to Standing Orders	56	1	3	3		
Constitutionality of laws and treaties						
Ordinary laws						
constitutional	106	1	3	4	2	7
partially unconstitutional	93	2	5	6	12	4
totally unconstitutional	8					
no powers /referred too late	3	1				
Organic laws						
constitutional	67	1	2	1	2	4
partially unconstitutional	11			1		1
totally unconstitutional	4			1		
Division between regulatory and legislative areas						
under article 41	11					
under article 37	179	2	2	4	3	
Treaties	5	1		2		1

Source: compiled using Maus (1995) and http://www.conseil-constitutionnel.fr/general/decision.htm.

in part as an element of the Gaullist system serving Gaullist ends (Keeler, 1985). Consequently, the willingness it showed in a decision in 1971 to take account of fundamental principles to protect certain civil liberties was largely discounted. The decision was crucial for two reasons, however. First, it established the principle that the rights set out in the documents referred to in the preamble to the Constitution (the Declaration of the Rights of Man and the Citizen and the preamble to the 1946 Constitution) were an integral part of the 1958 constitution and the rights they conferred could be relied on. Secondly, the decision (Decision 71–44 DC of 16 July 1971 relating to the right to set up an association) clearly indicated that the Council was willing to overturn laws proposed by the government when it was given the opportunity to do so.

Such opportunities arose very infrequently. For the first fifteen years of its existence, bills could be referred for a ruling on their constitutionality only by the president of the Republic, the prime minister and the presidents of the two houses of parliament. In the fifteen years before 1974 there were, in addition to 20 obligatory references of organic laws, only nine references to the Constitutional Council (Favoureu, 1998) Since during this period the government did not raise the question of the constitutionality of its own bills, and the president of the National Assembly belonged to the governing majority, the only source from which 'political' referrals were likely to arise at all was the president of the Senate. After Gaston Monnerville's unsuccessful referral of the 1962 constitutional amendment, there was no further referral by the president of the Senate until the 1971 case described above. Alain Poher then waited until 1973 before making a further referral.

The second factor which explains the nature of the Constitutional Council's development is the impact of the 1974 reform which enlarged the circumstances under which the Constitutional Council can be asked to review the constitutionality of a law (see Table 2.1). The constitutional amendment initiated by President Giscard d'Estaing in 1974 extended this possibility to any 60 members of either the National Assembly or the Senate. In 1992 a constitutional amendment equally extended the right of referral of a Treaty before ratification to 60 *deputés* or senators.

The effect of the 1974 amendment was not expected to be very great (Avril and Gicquel, 1993, p. 59). However, the number of references to the Council increased fivefold during the Giscard d'Estaing presidency, rising from nine in the first fourteen years of its existence to 47 in the subsequent seven years, of which 45 emanated from members of Parliament. Of these 45 referrals all but two (the 1975 law on abortion and the 1976 finance bill which was referred simultaneously by president, prime minister and the opposition) arose from members of the opposition. During these years the Council began slowly to demonstrate that its potential powers could not be ignored and the political opposition began to realize that challenge to the constitutionality of laws could be a useful political weapon. Only twelve of the 45 referrals between 1974 and 1981 resulted in a proposed law being held to be unconstitutional and, as John Keeler points out, up to 1981 no decision by the Council represented a major defeat for presidential or governmental policy (Keeler, 1985). However, some of the decisions certainly caused embarrassment to a government, for example the 1977 annulment of a law which would have given the police a very wide-ranging right to search private vehicles. Fear of a reference to the Council might be enough to induce changes in certain proposals.

The complete change in the political orientation of President and government brought about a new situation in 1981. The members of the Constitutional Council had all been appointed under the previous political dispensation. It was possible that they might take a fairly rigorous line with the new government which was challenging a number of the ideological principles which had governed political life throughout the Fifth Republic. John Keeler notes that some opposition parliamentarians saw the Council as a last bulwark against revolutionary change. The number of references to the Council increased still further, to 66 in the period from 1981 to 1986, and the extent to which the Council could indeed hinder the implementation of presidential policy was demonstrated by an early decision over the bill to put into effect one of the major planks of Mitterrand's election platform, the nationalization programme. The decision did not reject the principle of the government's right to nationalize, but did strike down some of the conditions under which this was to be achieved. The result was a political storm, but the government could do nothing but place another bill before Parliament, embodying the changes required in order to satisfy the Council.

The discovery by the political parties of the possibility of constitutional challenge to laws as a way of prolonging the political debate and reversing defeat in Parliament has continued to result in a substantial number of challenges to proposed laws. Moreover, a substantial proportion of the ordinary laws referred – since 1981 just over half – have been found to be, at least in part, unconstitutional.

Faced with a decision that a proposed law is unconstitutional, a government has only three possible courses of action. It may abandon a bill altogether, an unusual but not unknown occurrence; it may, and usually does, revise the law in the light of the Constitutional Council's comments; or it may seek to revise the constitution itself in order subsequently to allow the implementation of the measures it was proposing. This has happened only once, and in relation to the Schengen agreements on immigration and the right of asylum. Since then, proposed treaties, where there is likely to be any question of constitutionality in their application, have been referred before ratification, and constitutional amendments, if necessary, have followed.

There is, and will continue to be, a debate about the role of the Constitutional Council. Oppositions of both Left and Right use it, and will certainly continue to do so, as a means of obtaining changes in proposed laws that they have not been able to secure in Parliament although the outcome of a referral can never be predetermined. Governments are dissuaded from actions they might otherwise have favoured if they feel that there is a substantial likelihood that they may be overruled. Even when a government enjoys a considerable majority in Parliament it cannot act unchecked. The jurisprudence of the Constitutional Council provides a framework outside which it cannot stray. Equally, it is sometimes possible for a government to turn such constraints to its advantage. In 1990 Prime Minister Rocard submitted his bill on the financing of political parties to the Constitutional Council, presumably seeking to ensure that the bill, with its important implications for all parties, could not be held to be a purely partisan measure (Maus, 1991, p. 108). These considerations have led some to argue that the Constitutional Council has become a 'third chamber of the legislature' both in terms of its purely formal procedures, since, unlike a court, it intervenes before, not after, a bill becomes law, and because it applies essentially political considerations to the amendment of proposed legislation. Such arguments are strengthened, first, by a growing tendency by the Constitutional Council, since its 1971 decision, to use not merely the letter of the articles of the constitution but also general principles outlined in its preamble to guide its decisions. These general principles are, as Prime Minister Edouard Balladur pointed out to the special Congress of the two houses of Parliament called to pass the constitutional revision relating to the right of asylum, philosophical and political precepts formulated in very different times. Put more positively, the point is that the application of some very general principles – the right to equality, for example – requires, and finds within the Constitutional Council, creative and carefully judged interpretations (Mény, 1993, pp. 151–2). Secondly, some of the Council's decisions are, as its jurisprudence develops, more detailed and more precise, and hence more constraining on the government. This is especially true when the Council recognizes, as it has increasingly done, that, in the words of the proverb, 'the devil is in the details' and qualifies its declarations that a law is constitutional with directions about how it is to be applied if its constitutionality is to be preserved. The line between purely juridical and political interpretation is a very fine one, and hard to discern. If the Constitutional Council is tending towards the political side, encouraged by the political provenance of its presidents and a proportion of its membership, then the hypothesis that the Council is a further stage in the political process becomes more plausible.

On the other side of the argument the following observations can be made:

- Only about a quarter of the Council's decisions on ordinary laws have been based on the general principles of the constitution (Charlot, 1994, pp. 203–10). The others have relied on the strict interpretation of the constitution's articles.
- The Council has not shown particular favour to either the political Left or Right, nor has there been a marked difference between periods when the Constitutional Council might be supposed to be broadly politically aligned with the government in power and those when, because of the differing time-tables of Council appointments and electoral changes, it might not.
- The Constitutional Council can declare a proposed law unconstitutional. It can neither prevent a change in the constitution nor determine whether or how a government may act within the constitution. It certainly has not prevented governments of either political complexion carrying forward the major elements of their programmes, some of which – decentralization, nationalization,

privatization, changes in the law on immigration and citizenship, introduction of the 35-hour working week – have major and far-reaching effects.

The development of the Constitutional Council since 1959 has given it a far greater role than was anticipated at its creation. It now plays a central role in restraining and constraining the legislative actions of French governments, both positively, by its decisions, and negatively, by inhibiting governments from advancing proposals that might not be sustained. The role of the Council might have become even more prominent had President Mitterrand's 1991 attempt to amend the constitution succeeded. The effect would have been to allow any citizen to plead the unconstitutionality of any law affecting human rights as a defence before a court of law. The Constitutional Council would then have had to rule whether or not the contested law was unconstitutional. The proposed amendment was unsuccessful.

Nevertheless, because it relies upon the constitution as the source of its decisions, the Constitutional Council has also played an important role in securing general acceptance of the constitution and anchoring it within political life. The development of its role is one of the factors which explains why the more recent decades of the Fifth Republic have seen an enhancement of the place of the constitution itself within political life. The constitution can be changed, though not lightly or easily. It can no longer be ignored or set aside.

3

President and Prime Minister: Executive Leadership

The constitutional mechanisms described in the previous chapter encompass an essentially hybrid system, and, in the last two decades of the Twentieth century, allowed for such divergent interpretations that it was possible to talk of a dual configuration. The nature of the regime, and hence the location of political leadership oscillated in an erratic rhythm. The five-year term (*quinquennat*) amendment seems likely to steady the rhythm and once again place overall leadership firmly where the practice of the first two decades of the Fifth Republic had established it, with the president. The Fifth Republic differs from its predecessors in 'the emergence of the presidency as the major focus of political decision-making in France' (Knapp and Wright, 2001, p. 416). The president is directly elected by all voters. However, all voters also vote directly for the members of the National Assembly (see Chapter 6). The head of the government is the prime minister, who depends on the confidence of parliament to survive. When the double system of direct elections produces a National Assembly majority from the president's coalition of parties, then the president's position is so powerful that it is sometimes described as a 'republican monarchy'. The synchronization of electoral terms reinforces the likelihood that this will be the normal pattern.

Because of the date of the dissolution and election in 1997, the National Assembly was due to accomplish its full term a few weeks before the date in 2002 when President Chirac's first term expired. Parliamentary agreement to legislation that ensured that the presidential election preceded a delayed parliamentary one, confirms that the politicians accepted that the key figure is the president. However, the experience of three periods of *cohabitation*, one of them lasting for a full parliamentary term (1997–2002) produced changes in the contours of the political landscape. An examination of the power, changing practices and limitations of both the president's and the prime minister's role (see Exhibits 3.1 and 3.2) is therefore essential to an understanding of the system. This chapter is concerned with the nature of the presidency, with the governmental role of the prime minister and with the resources that each draws from the formal definitions of their role. The political aspects of their role and relationships, the ways in which they have operated, and the constraints upon their freedom of action form the subject of Chapter 4. The two chapters taken together aim to provide an overall view of the complex relationships within France's two-headed executive.

The Nature of the Fifth Republican Presidency

As president, Charles de Gaulle (see Exhibit 2.2) created a particular image for the presidency, and set expectations and approaches which his successors have adopted – and adapted. His charisma, his appearance and the physical impression he made, his status as in some senses the double saviour of France, and the very personal and strong notions of the role of the president which he conveyed inevitably proved to be amongst the major factors fashioning the development of the office.

In considering the nature of the presidency, two factors seem important; first, the president's role is legitimized by election through direct suffrage. Incumbency in the office is the outcome of choice by French voters. Secondly, the relationship of the president to the political life of France, as expressed through political parties, is a complex and ambiguous one.

De Gaulle's actions, as president, were, as we have seen, initially legitimized by the high level of popular support for the constitution which he recommended, as demonstrated by the results of the referendum of September 1958 and the parliamentary elections of November 1958. Thereafter, the paramount need for the achievement of a settlement in Algeria fulfilled much the same purpose, so that the outcome of the January 1961 referendum on self-determination for Algeria was again clearly a renewal of de Gaulle's mandate which allowed him a very free hand. With the settlement in Algeria in the spring of 1962, that source of legitimacy disappeared, and the introduction of presidential election by direct suffrage was linked to the need to find a new way for the president to retain a mandate for the degree of freedom of action which he had come to enjoy. The 1962 constitutional amendment is the major support for the status of the president.

EXHIBIT 3.1

The presidents of the Fifth Republic

January 1959–December 1965	Charles de Gaulle
December 1965–April 1969	Charles de Gaulle
(interim – acting President	Alain Poher)
June 1969–April 1974	Georges Pompidou
(interim – acting President	Alain Poher)
May 1974–May 1981	Valéry Giscard d'Estaing
May 1981–May 1988	François Mitterrand
May 1988–May 1995	François Mitterrand
May 1995–May 2002	Jacques Chirac
May 2002–	Jacques Chirac

One of the most enduring aspects of de Gaulle's legacy which has so shaped the nature of the presidency has, however, been the relationship of the president to the party political life of the country. In a country where party political differences have all too often been the product of deep and bitter ideological conflict which has frequently found expression in the rejection of the entire political and constitutional settlement, rather than simply in disagreement about programmes of government, de Gaulle's rejection of the politics of party could seem plausible and welcome. The discrediting of the Fourth Republic, which de Gaulle had from the start condemned as too much under the influence of the political parties, strengthened acceptance of this attitude. De Gaulle himself, although greatly assisted throughout his term of office by the presence in parliament of a majority focused around members pledged to support him, did not accept that he was in any way beholden to a party. He resolutely refused to allow his name to be formally attached to the party that grew up around him, although the adjective Gaullist was from the start consistently applied to it. No party political programme could, in this view, ever reflect the interests of more than a particular fraction of the French people; only a president who is genuinely above party politics can care for the common interests of all.

The electoral system for the presidency supports this approach. Candidates for election to the presidency must be nominated by 500 sponsors, who must themselves be amongst the approximately 38 000 French people who hold electoral office and be drawn from at least 30 different *départements* or overseas territories, with no more than 50 coming from any single *département*. The intention is that the presidential candidates should neither necessarily depend upon organized party support nor be the candidates of irresponsible groups or strictly local interests. The requirement may seem demanding: it did indeed prevent any candidate from the extreme Right standing in the 1981 presidential election and anti-European Charles Pasqua, who fell short by 50 signatures, from doing so in 2002. But in 2002 the number of candidates reached a record level (16) prompting debate about whether the requirement should be further tightened. Rather few of the candidates ever have any realistic prospect of winning. However, participation in the first round provides a degree of prominence for individual candidates and for the groupings they represent. They gain a certain measure of publicity for their views, both through broadcasting time, albeit strictly limited and controlled, and through official reimbursement of campaign expenses, and, potentially, an opportunity to exercise some leverage on the stronger candidates.

The election process is a two-ballot one. Unless one candidate receives 50 per cent of the votes, the two front runners go forward to the second round a fortnight later. First-round votes are quite widely distributed, and even the leading candidates generally receive a rather small proportion. In 2002 the sense that the outcome was a foregone conclusion seems to have kept many voters away from the first ballot polls. In the event the extreme Right candidate, Jean-Marie le Pen, edged out Prime Minister Lionel Jospin by 16.86 per cent to 16.18 per cent. Incumbent President Chirac achieved 19.88 per cent. This caused real shock, and voters of many persuasions rallied behind Chirac in the second round. A system which had been devised in 1962 at least in part to keep out one brand of extremism (Communism) worked as intended, to keep out another.

All de Gaulle's successors have at one and the same time enjoyed, or sought to establish, a sound party base whilst equally seeking to distance themselves from too close an identification with that base. President Pompidou's base was within the Gaullist party; as Prime Minister he had been careful to nurture and oversee it. President Giscard d'Estaing's party basis was in a much smaller grouping, the Independent Republicans, the junior partner in the Gaullist governmental coalition. His own image and personality, and the support of a number of Gaullists, who preferred him to the Gaullist candidate, were sufficient to propel him into the second ballot and victory, albeit a narrow one, over François Mitterrand in 1974. Although he attempted, during his incumbency, to build himself a broader basis for political support, he did not campaign for re-election on the strength of a party programme or even overt party organization.

Both François Mitterrand, who defeated Giscard d'Estaing in 1981, and Jacques Chirac, had much more blatantly party political careers than the first three presidents of the Fifth Republic. Mitterrand had shaped the fortunes of the Socialist Party as its First Secretary for a decade before his election in 1981, although he found it prudent to resign from that position just before announcing his candidacy. Chirac created the RPR in 1976 by a profound remodelling of the Gaullist party and was its effective leader thereafter whatever the formal office he held within it. However, their programmes for their election campaigns were in no sense party manifestos, as their titles – Mitterrand's *Letter to all the French People* in 1988 and Chirac's *France for Everyone* in 1995 – were at pains to suggest. Lionel Jospin's unsuccessful campaign for the presidency in 2002 may have been damaged by his failure to resign as prime minister well in advance and distance himself from party. He declared that he was not a Socialist, a statement which no one was likely to take at face value.

To those accustomed to different styles of political competition, the insistence that people who are fundamentally politicians should, as president, become in some sense apolitical may seem disingenuous, even hypocritical. This insistence, however, reflects the curious balance which the president continues to maintain between his figurehead, representational role and his political and governmental functions, the importance of which fluctuates depending upon the outcome of the presidential and general elections.

The Head of Government: The Prime Minister

The office of prime minister in France might at first sight appear to have been one of the casualties of the Fifth Republic. In 1964, speaking in a debate in the National Assembly, François Mitterrand, then an opposition member attacking the balance of the institutions of the Fifth Republic, said to the prime minister, 'You are, I recognise, a victim of the system imposed on you' (quoted in

Quermonne, 1980, p. 637). Under the Fourth Republic the prime minister, then known as the president of the council of ministers, however brief his incumbency, was the pre-eminent political figure. The President of the Republic had a sometimes influential but more shadowy and ceremonial role and the ministers owed their offices to prime ministerial choice. Under the Fifth Republic, de Gaulle's choice of the presidency as his role marked it out from the start as a major focus of political power. The government at that time seemed to be 'his' government, and to some observers the prime minister seemed little more than a chief of staff, dealing with the humdrum domestic details whilst the president concerned himself with the major affairs of the nation. De Gaulle himself disliked the use of the term '*chef du gouvernement*' to designate the prime minister, who was rather to regard himself or herself, as the appellation under the new constitution suggested, as the first amongst the ministers.

This perception of diminished power for the prime minister is, however, in many ways misleading. The prime ministers of the Fourth Republic had operated within multiple constraints. The brevity of so many prime ministers' periods in office between 1946 and 1958 emphasizes the limitations within which they acted. The prime ministers of the Fifth Republic in fact reaped the benefit of the changes which resulted from the rejection of the previous pattern. The limitations on the power of Parliament (see Chapter 7) have freed them from the uncertainties provoked by shifting coalitions. The extension of executive power and the reinforcement of the role of the government have increased the scope and legitimacy of the prime minister as the leader of the government.The development of the party system (see Chapter 8) and the advent of governments based securely upon a dominant party have given some of the Fifth Republic's prime ministers a strong political base and have enhanced the standing of the office. In all these respects prime ministers of the Fifth Republic have been more secure, and more legitimate than their predecessors of the Fourth Republic, and even outside *cohabitation* they have enjoyed greater freedom of action and a stronger pre-eminence within the government.

The Prime Minister and the President

It is a particular feature of the French political system, however, that governmental and political power is characterized by a duality at the top. The constitution specifically provides for a sharing of power, and in effect forces president and prime minister to cooperate.

Countersignature

Article 19 of the Constitution specifies that with certain listed exceptions, presidential decisions must be countersigned by the prime minister. The exceptions relate to the appointment of the prime minister, the referendum procedure, the dissolution of Parliament, the assumption of special powers, the transmission of

---

EXHIBIT 3.2

The prime ministers of the Fifth Republic

Michel Debré	January 1959–April 1962
Georges Pompidou	April 1962–July 1968
Maurice Couve de Murville	July 1968–June 1969
Jacques Chaban-Delmas	June 1969–July 1972
Pierre Messmer	July 1972–May 1974
Jacques Chirac	May 1974–August 1976
Raymond Barre	August 1976–May 1981
Pierre Mauroy	May 1981–July 1984
Laurent Fabius	July 1984–March 1986
Jacques Chirac	March 1986–May 1988
Michel Rocard	May 1988–May 1991
Edith Cresson	May 1991–April 1992
Pierre Bérégovoy	April 1992–April 1993
Edouard Balladur	April 1993–May 1995
Alain Juppé	May 1995–June 1997
Lionel Jospin	June 1997–May 2002
Jean-Pierre Raffarin	June 2002–

---

presidential messages to parliament, the nomination of members of the supreme council for the judiciary and the president's relationship with the Constitutional Council. These decisions which the president undertakes on his responsibility alone are clearly those that de Gaulle regarded as crucial to the ultimate exercise of power within the state. Nevertheless, apart from the assumption of emergency powers, many of them are also enjoyed by heads of state elsewhere with much more limited roles than that of the president of France, and it is the potential involvement of the president with a much wider range of decision-making that constitutes the specificity of the French executive leadership. The exercise of all the president's other constitutional powers requires the countersignature of the prime minister and any other ministers involved in the application of the decision.

Countersignature in France is a procedural device which fulfils two functions. The requirement for countersignature maintains, within the French system, the democratic convention that the head of state acts in almost all matters on the advice of the government, since only the government can answer for any actions before Parliament. Secondly, the provision that governmental or presidential acts must be countersigned by all the ministers concerned is a formal process which provides for a measure of collective responsibility for policy and its implementation. Under *cohabitation* the impact of countersignature was to reverse the normal direction of relationship at the centre. The initiative now rested with the prime minister, although the president's right of countersignature provided him with some scope for negotiation (Charlot, 1994, p. 195). As with so many other constitutional provisions, the rules can compel behaviour only in the most formal and general ways: but behind the formal procedures is the expectation that they will both reflect and shape much more detailed behaviour.

The dynamics of shared power

The functioning of the Council of Ministers, the preparation of legislative texts, senior appointments, and the conduct of certain policy areas cannot proceed, if only because of the requirements of countersignature, unless president and prime minister manage to find methods of working together. In the periods when the presidential majority which had brought the president into power was broadly the same as the governmental majority resulting from the general election the pre-eminence of the president is evident. Then the sharing of power tends to be based largely on personality, practice and convenience, rather than on any strict interpretation of the constitutional texts. The periods of *cohabitation* prove that coexistence remains possible, even when based upon the assertion of the legal powers of the two parties and their independent spheres.

Nevertheless, the necessary coexistence between president and prime minister has not always been easy or without tensions. The relationships between presidents and their successive prime ministers have been marked by a shifting balance of prestige and influence, related both to the political circumstances of the time, and to the personalities and expectations of the incumbents (see Elgie and Machin, 1991, pp. 73–4). Constitutionally president and prime minister, once an initial choice has been made, are condemned to live together; the president appoints the prime minister, but has no formal right of dismissal. In practice prime ministers have been dismissed (Debré in 1962, Pompidou in 1968, Chaban-Delmas in 1972, Mauroy in 1984, Rocard in 1991 and Cresson in 1992), though not in periods of *cohabitation*. Usually it has been clear that the prime minister concerned has agreed from the outset that he would not stay in office if the president required his resignation (Massot, 1987, p. 233).

The relationship, between five presidents and seventeen prime ministers has been characterized by a number of factors:

- First, whenever political and electoral support for the president found its expression in an electoral majority in the country both for him and for a government that would broadly support his policies, the pre-eminence of the president was assured. All the prime ministers who operated under these conditions expressed the view that the confidence of the President was essential to them (Massot, 1987, p. 233). However, while some have been very clearly the president's lieutenants (Couve de Murville, by profession a technocrat and servant of politicians, and Alain Juppé, also a former official and long used to working with Chirac in the Paris Town Hall, for instance) others, including Debré, the first prime minister under the new constitution, and Rocard and Bérégovoy under Mitterrand, have developed a more distinctive approach.

- Secondly, however, prime ministers cannot dispense with the support of the National Assembly. Pierre Mauroy recognized this in 1982 when he said that without the double approval of the president and the National Assembly, 'which both benefit from the legitimacy conferred by universal suffrage', the prime minister would be unable to continue in office. It was this factor which President Mitterrand acknowledged in 1986, when he chose to ask Jacques Chirac, leader of the largest party in the Assembly, to become the prime minister, rather than seeking a prime minister who might have been politically closer to himself, and have been able to form a minority government, but who would not have represented the electorate's choice. This set the pattern for *cohabitation* and profoundly influenced the discussion leading up to the introduction of the five, rather than seven year term for the presidency (see Chapter 2).
- Thirdly, prime ministers have been chosen from a variety of backgrounds. There is no single prerequisite for office. Some have come into power from a clearly political base – Lionel Jospin was the leader of the Socialist Party and had been its candidate in the 1995 presidential election while Chaban-Delmas had deep roots within the Gaullist party, as did Pierre Mauroy within the Socialist Party, and both were very long-standing mayors of large towns, an office which involves a great deal of political and executive autonomy and management (see Chapter 6). Debré and Fabius were both close personal associates of the President. Some prime ministers, Pompidou, Couve de Murville, Barre, had never contested a parliamentary seat before they became prime minister, though both Couve de Murville and Barre had previous ministerial experience. Raffarin's political experience was in local and regional government, as a Member of the European Parliament and in the Senate, before he became a minister in the 1995 Juppé government. It is a striking fact that out of seventeen prime ministers only Barre, Mauroy, Cresson, Bérégovoy and Raffarin had not held a post as a top administrative civil servant at some point in their career, and Barre had been a university professor (which in France is a civil service post) and a Commissioner of the European Communities. Six of the prime ministers (Chirac, Fabius, Rocard, Balladur, Juppé, Jospin) are graduates of the elite civil service training school, the *Ecole Nationale d'Administration*, which their predecessor Michel Debré had founded in 1946.
- Fourthly, Elgie (1993, p. 166) classifies the relationships of prime ministers to presidents into three types: first, subordinate, a category in which he includes all of de Gaulle's prime ministers. Juppé could also be included in this group. The second category is rival, and finally opponent, this latter category covering the prime ministers of *cohabitation*. However, not only does each relationship have its own particular nuances – the opponent relationship between Mitterrand and Chirac was not the same as that between Mitterrand and Balladur – but the relationships may change during the period in office. Even when the president has sought to minimize any challenge to his own political pre-eminence by appointing a prime minister whose administrative qualifications and lack of a personal political power base seemed to designate him for

an essentially 'chief of staff' role, that prime minister may increasingly take on a political role. The two most telling examples of this evolution are Georges Pompidou and Raymond Barre. Both were appointed from essentially non-political backgrounds, and became major political leaders, building up party support, and emerging themselves as presidential candidates – one successful, one unsuccessful. Similarly, the post of prime minister proved the inspiration for Balladur's candidacy in the 1995 presidential elections; he moved from being Chirac's subordinate to becoming his rival.

The striking frequency with which prime ministers have developed presidential ambitions, even when they may not have harboured them at the outset, shows where not only status but also real power lies. From the moment when General de Gaulle opted for the role of president rather than prime minister there has been no doubt that under the Fifth Republic the presidency is the dominant and most desirable role. For many prime ministers the assets of their post, but also its limitations, as compared to the presidency, have provided a basis and a standing which are an excellent spur and support to higher ambitions. Presidents and political colleagues have had to reckon with this fact.

The Formal Resources of the Presidency

The way in which successive presidents have interpreted and carried out their role has highlighted the strengths and resources upon which they can draw. For the definition of the role two these resources seem particularly important and they are considered in this chapter: the formal powers he can deploy and the nature and role of his personal staff. The president's own personality and personal approach, the political relationships which he enjoys and the way in which he cultivates them, as well his use of, and relationship to, the mass media support the political aspects of his leadership and are considered in the next chapter.

Formal powers

The starting point for the development of the presidential role is the formal powers which the constitution gives the president (see Exhibit 3.3). These can be considered under two heads: there are the traditional powers inherent in the president's role as head of state, and in addition the new powers that differentiate the constitution of the Fifth Republic from its predecessors. The traditional powers may be grouped into four categories (Massot, 1987, pp. 93ff): those in the judicial, in the legislative and in the diplomatic spheres, and those related to appointments in the public and military services. Even in these areas the constitution of 1958 tended to extend the scope of presidential action compared with the previous system.

In the judicial sphere the president retains the power, granted to all heads of the French state since 1802, to grant pardons (Article 17). Articles 64 and 65 of the

EXHIBIT 3.3

Presidential powers in the Constitution of the Fifth Republic

Title Two

Article 5 The President of the Republic shall see that the Constitution is observed. He shall ensure, by his arbitration, the proper functioning of the public authorities and the continuity of the State.

He shall be the guarantor of national independence, territorial integrity and observance of treaties.

Article 8 The President of the Republic shall appoint the Prime Minister. He shall terminate the appointment of the Prime Minister when the latter tenders the resignation of the Government.

On the proposal of the Prime Minister he shall appoint the other members of the Government and shall terminate their appointments.

Article 9 The President of the Republic shall preside over the Council of Ministers.

Article 10 The President of the Republic shall promulgate Acts of Parliament...He may...ask Parliament to reconsider the Act or sections of the Act. Reconsideration shall not be refused.

Article 11 The President of the Republic may, on a proposal from the Government...or on a joint motion of the two Assemblies...submit to a referendum any government bill dealing with the organization of the public authorities, or with reforms relating to the economic or social policy of the Nation and to the public services contributing thereto, or which provides for authorization to ratify a treaty that, although not contrary to the Constitution, would affect the functioning of the institutions....

Article 12 The President of the Republic may, after consulting the Prime Minister and the Presidents of the assemblies, declare the National Assembly dissolved....

Article 13 The President of the Republic shall sign the ordinances and decrees deliberated upon in the Council of Ministers.

He shall make appointments to the civil and military posts of the State...

Article 14 The President of the Republic shall accredit ambassadors and envoys extraordinary to foreign powers; foreign ambassadors and envoys extraordinary shall be accredited to him.

Article 15 The President of the Republic shall be commander of the armed forces...

Article 16 When the institutions of the Republic, the independence of the nation, the integrity of its territory or the fulfilment of its international commitments are under serious and immediate threat, and where the proper functioning of the constitutional public authorities is interrupted, the President of the Republic shall take the measures required by these circumstances, after formal consultation with the Pime Minister, the Presidents of the assemblies as and the Constitutional Council...

Article 17 The President of the Republic has the right to grant pardon.

Article 18 The President of the Republic shall communicate with the two assemblies of Parliament by means of messages which he shall cause to be read and which shall not be the occasion for any debate...

Article 19 Acts of the President of the Republic, other than those provided for under Articles 8 (first paragraph), 11, 12, 16, 18, 54*, 56* and 61* shall be countersigned by the Prime Minister and, where required, by the appropriate ministers.

Note:
* These articles relate to appointment to the Constitutional Council and the referral of texts to it.

constitution specify moreover that the president guarantees judicial independence, and presides over the body which regulates judicial behaviour, the *Conseil National de la Magistrature.*

In the legislative sphere the president is, like his predecessors, not allowed to attend parliamentary sessions even for purely formal purposes. President Mitterrand, with his very lengthy experience of life as a member of the National Assembly, apparently regretted being unable to visit Parliament even as a guest (speech of 13 June 1990 quoted in Maus, 1991, p. 40). The President can, however, send a written message to Parliament. He retains the head of state's duty to promulgate laws within a fortnight once they have been passed, but he also retains a right, which has figured in French constitutions since 1848, to demand a further reading of a bill. This occurs only very rarely, but in 1985, for example, President Mitterrand referred back a clause in a bill relating to New Caledonia. Presidential decrees open and close special sessions of parliament, and the President has (and, as in 1997, uses) the right to dissolve Parliament, though not within a year of a previous dissolution.

In foreign relations the president fulfils the traditional function, for a head of state, of receiving the credentials of foreign ambassadors, and accrediting and recalling French ambassadors abroad (Article 14). Article 52 of the constitution retains phrases used in previous constitutions to provide that the president ratifies international treaties, and the 1958 constitution also specifies that he negotiates them. To these traditional concepts the Fifth Republic added the strength of the formula found in Article 5, which insists that the president is the guarantor of national independence, of territorial integrity and of the observance of treaties and agreements. This traditional power has acquired an additional significance in the context of the European Union. The president sits in the European Council, even during periods of *cohabitation.* When France holds the rotating presidency of the European Council and the Council of Ministers, the French president becomes particularly prominent upon the European and world scene. It was Chirac who personally conducted the closing stages of the negotiations for the Treaty of Nice. However, the president's role in European affairs does not just affect his image and standing. It obliges his staff and those of the prime minister to cooperate closely, whether or not political differences exist. Even under cohabitation such cooperation has usually been technically harmonious, with the staff of both government and president involved in the necessary preparatory meetings. With the advent of the common currency and the growing range of European Union policy-making, the traditional diplomatic powers of the president paradoxically give him potential influence over a wide range of domestic policies. Uncontested when the president enjoys a majority, the definition of what is 'European' and hence the scope and nature of presidential influence and intervention (patents for biotechnology were one point of debate between Chirac's and Jospin's staff) can be a cause of conflict under *cohabitation* (Schrameck, 2001, p. 102).

The president has the right to authorize the appointment of large numbers of senior officials: some 5000 appointments or promotions a year (Massot, 1987). The most senior appointments require consultation within the Council of Ministers. This power of appointment extends to the armed services. He is chief of the armed services (Article 15), and presides over the two most senior committees concerned respectively with the study of defence problems and the execution of defence policy (Quermonne, 1980, p. 188). In circumstances other than *cohabitation* the procedure allows the president, in consultation with the prime minister, extensive powers of patronage, even if the procedure is often relatively automatic. Under *cohabitation* an informal understanding shared out part of this patronage (appointments to senior post in the *grands corps* by *tour extérieur*, see Chapter 5) between president and prime minister, while appointments to the other posts, particularly the most prominent, gave rise to considerable friction, especially, it seems, in the case of senior state prosecutors (Schrameck, 2001, p. 111).

In addition to these powers, which were largely those fulfilled, if essentially in ways which did not constitute the exercise of any real power, by the presidents of the Third and Fourth Republics, the 1958 constitution conferred important new powers upon the president.

First, the constitution specifies that the president is responsible *par son arbitrage* – through his arbitration – for the proper functioning of the public authorities and the continuity of the state. This concept in itself extends the role of the president beyond that of his predecessors.

The role of the president as the guarantor of the state is emphasized in Article 16 which enables him, after consultation with the Prime Minister and the presidents of the Senate, the National Assembly and the Constitutional Council (though he is not obliged to follow the advice he receives), to take the measures required by the circumstances if there is a serious threat to the institutions of the Republic, the independence of the state, the integrity of its territory or the fulfilment of its international obligations. The president himself, unchecked, may thus decide when such a threat exists and what is to be done. These 'emergency' powers were certainly inspired by de Gaulle's conviction that, had President Lebrun possessed them in 1940, he would have been better able to resist capitulating to the enemy. Parliament automatically reassembles while these powers are in operation, and cannot be dissolved during that time. The powers are potentially immense. They have in fact been used once, between April and September 1961 at the time of an attempted military takeover in Algeria, then still a French colony. Whilst few disputed the need for their use, more controversy was aroused by the length of time they were in operation, which was far longer than the duration of any threat from Algeria.

These draconian, if most exceptional, powers are the clearest departure from the previous pattern. However, the president has other new powers, again linked to the notion of his overall responsibility for the functioning of the state. He appoints three members of the Constitutional Council, and may submit proposed legislation or a treaty to the Council for a ruling as to its constitutionality. He may grant or refuse a request that a referendum be held made by either the government or the two houses of Parliament. These powers constitute the formal basis for his authority. They are an important resource, but the nature of his political relationships also contributes to the definition of the role that the president will play at any particular time.

The presidential staff

The Elysée Palace (the president's official residence) is not the White House (Massot, 1987, p. 113, and 2002, p. 29). Nevertheless amongst the most important resources upon which the role and position of the president depend is the presidential staff although they do not constitute a large and administrative department. Many of the 900 or so people who work at the Elysée or the other official presidential residences form a household rather than a staff, and are concerned with maintaining the dignity and representational functions of the presidency like the household of any other head of state (Massot, 2002, p. 30). They do not necessarily change when the presidency changes hands. There is, however, a small staff who fulfil political and executive, rather than 'domestic' duties. De Gaulle never had more than 33 civilian and thirteen military staff. Under Mitterrand the combined civilian and military staff reached nearly 70. The number declined again under Chirac who had an initial team of eighteen civilians, but seems to have settled at around 60.

De Gaulle created a distinctive separation between that part of his civilian staff concerned with his relationship with 'the nation' – the private office (*cabinet*) that traditionally formed part of the presidential household – and that part which, in the light of the new role of the Fifth Republic's president, would maintain the president's communication with the state. That section is the general secretariat of the presidency, not to be confused with the secretary-general of the government, a very senior official based in the prime minister's office (see below). Such separation has now largely disappeared, and the general secretariat is the key element of the staff. Until 1974 there was also a separate secretariat for African and Madagascan affairs, which, under the shadowy, somewhat sinister Jacques Foccart, acted almost as if it were an autonomous ministry. Ever since 1974, African affairs have had a distinctive position within the Elysée.

The secretary-general of the Elysée plays a key role. He – the incumbents have all been male, though there has been a female deputy secretary-general – is the chief point of contact for the staff of the Prime Minister and of other ministerial private offices. With the brief exception of Pierre Bérégovoy at the start of Mitterrand's incumbency, all the secretaries general, his deputies, and the head of the *cabinet* have been serving senior officials (Massot, 2002, p. 29). Many of them (Bérégovoy, eventually prime minister, Hubert Védrine, Dominique de Villepin, ministers for Foreign Affairs in the Jospin and Raffarin governments respectively) have gone on to ministerial office. He is the channel through whom advice and information, warnings and suggestions reach the president. He is responsible for the smooth running of the office and often for the choice of those who will work within it. The secretary-general has seldom been the President's sole adviser, indeed often not even his most important confidante, but in terms of the functioning of the governmental machine in France his role is a central one.

In general, the general secretariat has been organized by the assignment of a staff member (*conseiller*) to each large area of activity, a system which has proved efficient and limited conflict between staff members (Debbasch *et al.*, 1985, p. 290). In 2002 there was an essentially pyramidal structure under five senior 'advisers' responsible respectively for foreign affairs, Africa, the economy, social affairs, and education and culture (Massot, 2002, p. 30).

However, the system has often been diluted and complicated by a proliferation of extra-hierarchical positions. Some presidents have appointed special personal advisers. Under de Gaulle, only one person, Jacques Foccart, came close to fulfilling that role. His connections within the Gaullist Party, and within the French security services ran deep, in addition to his official responsibilities for African and Madagascan affairs. Under President Pompidou, conflict arose between Michel Jobert, Pompidou's secretary-general and Pierre Juillet, his special adviser – Juillet retired indignantly to his sheep-raising activities in central France for months at a time when he felt his voice was not carrying enough weight. From 1981 to 1991, Jacques Attali, civil servant, writer, and member of the Socialist Party's executive committee, was *conseiller special auprès du President*, occupying as such, both literally and figuratively, a key position in the operations of the Elysée. Relationships between the then secretary-general (Jean-Louis Bianco) and Attali were notoriously poor. President Chirac, himself an *énarque* (see Chapter 5) and with his long experience in administering Paris, has preferred to encourage a more 'civil service' style, and during his first *septennat* introduced no rival to secretary-general Dominique de Villepin (a former diplomat) as his principal adviser. However, with the return to power of a presidential majority in 2002, former prime minister Alain Juppé assumed a central role as presidential adviser. His style and record, along with the unpopularity of his 1995–7 government, ruled him out as prime minister. But he assumed a key role as organizer of the presidential majority, general secretary of the new presidential party *Union pour un mouvement populaire* (see Chapter 8) and as *eminence grise*.

Mitterrand also relied upon a number of other old friends and cronies, and both he and Chirac have had one of their children on their staff: Mitterrand's son Jean-Christophe as his adviser on African affairs (a role which in 2002 led to his detention in gaol during investigations into illegal transactions in sub-Saharan Africa) and Chirac's daughter Claude as a *conseiller* on communications. Indeed all presidents have drawn support, in the complex web of political and administrative relationships which they sustain, from longstanding networks of family, colleagues and acquaintances, for example those who had come through the Fourth Republic and the early days of the Fifth Republic with Mitterrand, or who had served with Chirac at the Paris Town Hall.

The main functions of the presidential staff are, first, to ensure that the president is very fully informed of political and administrative developments in all areas. They do this by maintaining a very wide range of contacts within and outside the administration – extending, it is alleged (for example in *Le Nouvel Observateur*, 7–13 January 1999, p. 13), to the use of telephone tapping. When there is no *cohabitation* and the president is effectively the head of the government, they can supplement these networks by attendance as observers at governmental meetings which prepare policy and its implementation, and by close liaison with other parts of the administration. This enables them to warn the president if anything is going awry. The staff undertake the intense preparation for major events such as the European Council meetings, and provide the president with briefings and drafts for his speeches, interviews and other public utterances. A separate section of the office, employing some 100 people, deals with the daily flood of correspondence from a multitude of private citizens who write in with grievances, requests and suggestions.

Under de Gaulle and Pompidou the role of the military staff was largely confined to assistance with the inevitable military aspect of the representational duties of a Head of State and to liaison between the Elysée and the other institutions concerned with defence. Under Presidents Giscard d'Estaing and Mitterrand the head of the military staff gained a much higher profile. During the Gulf War in the winter of 1991 Mitterrand relied heavily on his military staff to assist him in taking decisions relating to the conduct of the war, during which he 'fully assumed his responsibilities as Commander in Chief' (Howorth, 1993).

Outside the periods of *cohabitation* the perception can arise that in a certain sense the 'real' government is to be found within the Elysée Palace. It is certainly true that the existence of the Elysée staff enables the president to keep a very close eye on governmental projects and initiatives, and, when ministers are conscious of loyalty to the president, to intervene effectively. In some cases, indeed, the presidential office may pursue a policy initiative to the exclusion of the ministry concerned, especially where there may be some opposition from that ministry. Nevertheless the staff is not a large one, and in the end the president can only rely upon his political weight and authority and the effectiveness of his networks. Overt presidentialism perhaps reached its apogee under President Giscard d'Estaing. Mitterrand preferred less obvious dominance, but some areas of policy – for example, relationships with the newly nationalized industries, or the crucial economic U-turn of 1983 – were managed from the Elysée.

However, the effectiveness of the presidential staff crucially depends upon the other factors which determine the president's relationships with the government. During the periods of *cohabitation* their effectiveness in executive terms is limited. The president and his staff are at their strongest within the governmental machine when they are successful in uniting all those concerned, especially the prime minister and the ministries, around the president's overall political line, approach and style. It is upon his political position and success that the staff rely to convert potential into actual power.

The Position of the Prime Minister

The role of the prime minister dovetails with and balances that of the president, and like the presidency, varies in scope and influence depending upon the political circumstances of the time. There are however three major aspects to the role which are always present, even if their relative weight may vary. All prime ministers have a governmental role, an administrative role and a political role. The first two of these are examined below and and the political aspects of the role are discussed in Chapter 4.

The prime minister's staff

The prime minister's principal resource for undertaking his or her governmental and administrative roles is the private office (*cabinet*). This normally consists of between 50 and 60 members (Oberdorff, 1997, p. 418, Bigaut, 1997, p. 75). In 2002 the Matignon website listed 53 official members. The head of Jospin's private office, *directeur de cabinet* Olivier Schrameck, reports that meetings of the full *cabinet* involved some 65 persons (Schrameck, 2001, p. 37). The prime minister's staff have been largely, but not exclusively, drawn from within the civil service. The *directeur de cabinet* is always a close personal associate of the prime minister. The staff will always share the prime minister's general political orientation, but will not necessarily have been political activists. Like the president the prime minister has a military staff. Under Jospin the prime minister's *cabinet* was organized under about 20 *conseillers principaux*, each concerned with a particular sector of governmental activity. 'The presumption is that what are generally required are not specialists (though there always are some) but generalists with a network of core executive contacts which will enable them to coordinate effectively' (Hayward and Wright, 2002, p. 45). Under Rocard the *directeur de cabinet* was 'virtually a vice-prime minister, able to speak with authority on his behalf' (Hayward and Wright, 2002, p. 47) while Schrameck a decade later was more reticent, trying to ensure strict adherence to the rule that no member of the staff should give instructions to the ministries on their own initiative (Schrameck, 2001, p. 38). The prime minister's administrative role results in the attachment to the prime minister of a number of operational units, so that altogether the prime minister has some 5000 staff working directly for him or her (Oberdorff, 1997).

The prime minister's governmental role

According to General de Gaulle, the role of the prime minister was to direct, coordinate and oversee (*orienter, coordonner, suivre*) (Claisse, 1972, p. 170) the actions of the other ministers. Although under *cohabitation* the prime minister clearly also assumes the political leadership of the government, for much of the first three decades of the Fifth Republic this direction and control took place within a framework laid down by the president. Indeed during the presidency of Giscard d'Estaing this function seemed more to resemble the carrying out of orders. Prime Minister Barre, presenting his political programme to Parliament in 1977, spoke of fulfilling the tasks which the president had set him: during his seven-year term of office the president sent 29 letters, 17 on specific questions and 12 on general policy orientations, specifying the programme of work which he expected the government to follow (Peters *et al.*, 1997, p. 388).

Under the Socialist governments, between 1981 and 1986 and after 1988, whilst the president did decide upon the governmental agenda and priorities in conjunction with the prime minister, the exact content of the programme was not made public, and the action lost its presidentialist symbolism. Prime Minister Juppé, between 1995 and 1997 was, in the mould of his first predecessor, Michel Debré, a very active prime minister, known, however, to share very closely the political priorities of the president.

Whether the main directions of governmental action are set by the president or the prime minister, his or her powers of direction and coordination are particularly important in a system which does not incorporate a strong notion of the collective responsibility of the government. French ministers come from varied political and career backgrounds; all governments have included ministers from a number of parties (see Table 5.1); they may be held together by a loyalty to the President or, as under *cohabitation*, to a government of a particular political conception, but there is no convention in the written constitution nor in constitutional practice that requires them to act in a unified way, and conflicts may be fierce and public, whether over policy issues or political stances. Jean-Pierre Raffarin, presiding over a diverse coalition government pledged essentially to the support of a president whose programme was necessarily unspecific, and in fact far from internally consistent, found himself, in the summer of 2002, faced with reconciling very divergent policy statements from his ministers, for example about the financing of the health service (*The Economist*, 27 July 2002).

For this reason the prime minister has a key role to play. He or she may try to minimize dissent. Michel Rocard, for example, tried to ensure the coherence and propriety of government action by issuing periodic general circulars to all ministers. Topics included the government's European policy, and the modernization of the civil service. Jean-Pierre Raffarin held an introductory seminar for his government in 2002, and admitted wryly some weeks later, after a number of well-publicized incoherences between his ministers, that the prime minister's role was to *rattraper les maladresses* (rectify gaffes) (*Le Point*, 5 July 2002, p. 33). However, the prime minister's role goes a very long way beyond exhortation and encouragement, The structure of the French governmental machine means that a great deal of policy is coordinated, settled and decided by *arbitrage*, a process of hierarchical decision-making which involves the ministers concerned bringing the matter to the prime minister, (or at least to his or her *cabinet*) and setting out their case for his or her decision. This occurs in many policy areas (see Elgie,

1993, p. 153), not only in the most institutionalized of the areas of conflict that is the preparation of the estimates of public spending, where the prime minister makes the final decisions wherever the Ministry of Finance has been unable to reach agreement with a spending ministry. Raffarin's minister of the economy, finance and industry, Francis Mer, contrasting governmental experience with practices in industry, said 'We all have to share the facts, our convictions, our constraints, and then, in the light of the prime minister's political views, there is an *arbitrage*. I am ready to accept the decisions' (*Le Point*, 5 July 2002, p. 33) An understanding of the mechanism of *arbitrage* – of the notion that policy-making may proceed by the confrontation of, and authoritative choice between, rationally argued and internally consistent but sharply different cases, rather than through a consultative and consensual search for a solution which all can support – is central to any understanding of French policy-making style.

The prime minister's administrative role

The prime minister has administrative functions attached to his office, and a number of junior ministers with special responsibilities form part of his department. The central role and the prestige of the prime minister's office have ensured that four types of administrative work are attached to it (Massot, 1979; and Fournier, 1987, p. 152):

- First, the central role of servicing the collective action of the government. This role is fulfilled by the General Secretariat of the Government. Although General de Gaulle set a pattern by ensuring that the General Secretariat worked with the president in setting the agenda for the weekly cabinet meetings and servicing them, the location of the General Secretariat means that the prime minister can never be ignored or bypassed. Equally crucially, the General Secretariat co-ordinates and services the multitude of meetings between the prime minister and other ministers, or of groups of ministers or staff from their *cabinets* (see Chapter 5) where policy is settled and *arbitrages* occur. As an exception to a general pattern, the secretary-general of the government has (with one exception, the removal in 1986 of Jacques Fournier, who had come to the post from the presidential staff) not been replaced when the government changes. Indeed, it was subsequently acknowledged that the then secretary-general, Marceau Long, who had served its Giscardian predecessor, had greatly assisted the incoming Mitterrand government in 1981 in handling the unprecedented problems of a complete hand-over of power.
- Secondly, there are co-ordinating functions which potentially concern almost all government departments; these are the co-ordination of government policy towards the European Community, and the co-ordination of national defence policy. The bodies responsible for these – the General Secretariat of the Interministerial Committee for questions of European Economic Cooperation

(SGCI) and the Secretariat general for national defence – are attached to the prime minister's office. Official printing and publication also come under the prime minister.

- Thirdly, administrative tasks have been embarked upon, at different periods, which have been deliberately designed to cut across existing administrative boundaries, and ensure rapid and fruitful action. The prime minister, wishing to give a high status and political encouragement to these activities, has attached them to his own office (Fournier, 1987, pp. 157–8).

In most cases this attachment has proved to be a transitional one, even if sometimes of quite lengthy duration, which has led on to more independent ministerial status. The subsequent fate of the administration concerned has depended upon the degree of political status and priority accorded to it at any period. The Economic Planning Commission, founded in 1946, has, for most of its existence, been attached to the prime minister's office. This continued central attachment for the Plan is due to its initial political importance as a symbol and motor of postwar reconstruction, and subsequently to the weight of tradition. It is now characterized as a research and advisory body, and its policy-making role has been much diminished.

In contrast to the Economic Planning Commission, the organization concerned with spatial planning and regional development, the *Délégation à l'Aménagement du Territoire et à l'Action Régionale* (DATAR), rose in status in the 1990s, reflecting perhaps the growing role of local and regional initiatives since the decentralization reforms of 1983. The promotion of scientific research and care for the environment were also both launched from the prime minister's office. These bodies oscillated between attachment for a period to another ministry and reversion to the prime minister's office before becoming central parts of the responsibilities of other ministries.

In general the collection of responsibilities which accrues around the prime minister in this way can be heterogeneous and unwieldy, reflecting as it does the specific political exigencies and the particular priorities of the government of the day. Thus the priority attached to the repression of alcoholism (in the 1950s) and drug addiction (in the 1980s), the promotion of road safety or the problems of urban deprivation, housing and homelessness (in the 1990s) has in each case resulted in the setting up of a body serviced within the prime minister's office. Periodic reorganizations result in the removal of some of these bodies from the prime minister's jurisdiction although others remain so clearly in disputed territory between ministries that there is no other home for them.

The fourth administrative activity attached to the prime minister's office is the provision of administrative support for a number of autonomous institutions. The staff of the *médiateur de la république* (ombudsman), of the committee for access to official documents (freedom of information) and the broadcasting authority are, for example, for organizational purposes carried on the budget of the prime minister's office.

Conclusion

The formal arrangements for the relationship between president and prime minister endow the centre of the core executive in France with a complexity unrivalled in other Western European country. All attempts to mark out a durable and clear division of labour have failed. Tidy-minded academics in the 1960s and 70s attempted to distinguish a presidential *domaine reservé* (reserved sector), attributing, for example defence, foreign and post-colonial affairs, Europe and major economic orientations to the presidency and the daily business of domestic policy to the prime minister. These attempts foundered in part on the awkward tendency of presidents to involve themselves in whatever seemed to them to matter. Moreover, it is equally possible to argue, as constitutional expert and former prime ministerial adviser Guy Carcassonne does (Carcassonne, 1997), that the prime minister has his or her own particular sector, especially financial policy, spending and taxation, and even some areas of external relations such as foreign trade. The difficulty which arises in deriving a clear picture from the more formal provisions stems from the importance within the equation of poliical relationships and roles, and it is to these that the next chapter turns.

4

President and Prime Minister: Political Roles and Evolving Relationships

Within the framework described in Chapter 3, the operation of the executive leadership has been shaped by the political situations of the moment and by the individual priorities and perceptions of the presidents. It has throughout been characterized by three major features – a high degree of autonomy on the part of the president, a substantial political role for the prime minister, and equally a high degree of flexibility in the way in which the demands and opportunities of executive leadership have been characterized. There are however, also important constraints on the exercise of power. These features are considered below.

Presidential Practice

The president has never been seen as part of a team. Nor has he been encompassed by any notion of collective responsibility. When the president has been effectively the head of a governmental majority, there is always the possibility of government business being conducted either directly by the president, or by the president in conjunction with an individual minister. In certain spheres where this presidential autonomy has been particularly marked it has sometimes been argued that the combination of constitutional powers and traditional expectations gave the president a particular sphere in which he could and should act quite alone: foreign affairs, relations with Francophone Africa and defence can be seen as major components of this *domaine réservé* – reserved sector. The exigencies of the period meant that in the early years of de Gaulle's presidency these areas were particularly high amongst his priorities. De Gaulle, however, later denied that he had entertained any notion of a protected area (Quermonne, 1980, p. 181). But the notion has persisted, both in perception and practice: in his 14 July interview in 2002 Chirac was specifically asked about his *domaine réservé*. He denied that there was one, despite having been reported (*Le Point*, 4 June 2002) as reminding the minister of finance that the EU stability and growth pact was presidential, not ministerial business.

Presidents come into office with more or less explicit platforms and policy preferences. Under *cohabitation* these tend to be eclipsed by prime ministerial programmes. However, presidents have never been completely absent from public policy-making. President Pompidou, for example, defined and sustained the industrial policy that furthered the development of large companies and the identification of 'national champions'. It was President Giscard d'Estaing's personal impetus that produced the abortion and divorce reforms of the mid-1970s. The buildings presidents commission – their *grands projets* – constitute particularly visibly of the scope of presidential action. President Pompidou set the construction of the Pompidou Centre under way. President Giscard d'Estaing initiated the conversion of the Gare d'Orsay from redundant railway station to stunning museum. President Mitterrand insisted upon the removal of the Ministry of Finance from the Louvre buildings, the extension of the museum and the construction of the great glass entrance pyramid in the courtyard, and the building of the Opera House at the Bastille as well as the highly controversial and expensive national library (Collard, 1992). Chirac, paradoxically, although as mayor he presided over a Paris where buildings were cleaned and fountains played, is likely to be better remembered for presiding over France's victory in the 1998 football World Cup. When his re-election in 2002 for five years with the largest ever proportion of the vote and an overall majority gave him unusually unconstrained potential, he responded to a question about *grands projets* by listing improved road safety, the combat against cancer, and action in favour of the disabled.

Presidents who enjoy a majority have can be active in a broader area which goes well beyond merely setting the general orientation of policy. It should not be forgotten that Presidents Chirac, Mitterrand, Giscard d'Estaing and Pompidou had all had considerable experience as ministers, and in the case of these last two this experience was recent and extensive. Both Pompidou and Chirac had been prime ministers. Presidents have intervened decisively in economic, industrial, social and cultural policies, and have always been willing to step in when a matter has been either highly contentious, or particularly close to their personal concerns – President Pompidou's intervention to protect the place of Latin in the school curriculum and the withdrawal by President Mitterrand of the Savary education bill in 1984, are examples of interventions of this kind in an area (education) which has not on the whole attracted much presidential attention.

In undertaking such intervention the president is able to exploit both the formal resources discussed in Chapter 3, including his chairmanship of the Council of Ministers which means that he is fully aware of the future agenda of the government, and the activities of his staff and meetings with small groups of ministers to discuss a particular issue – the co-called *conseils restreints*. Presidents hold regular meetings, normally at least once a week, with the prime minister. In the evolution of presidential practice, personal and political resources have been as important as the formal resources discussed in Chapter 3.

Personality and personal approach

De Gaulle, as we have seen, was no dictator, and the fears of those who saw him as some kind of latter-day Mussolini were evidently misplaced. He was nevertheless an austere and aloof man, regarded by many as colossally arrogant. He can be protected from that charge only by the observation that he was never self-seeking; his claims for himself, and they were always far-reaching, were based on an unshakeable conviction, which he managed, when it mattered, to impose upon others, that he represented and spoke for the true interests of France. He was constrained by the values he thought truly worthy of France – republicanism and democracy, for example – but was deeply distrustful of anything that seemed like special pleading, whether for capitalism, whose representatives had, in his view, so singularly failed France in the 1930s and 1940s, or for the forces of class conflict which could only shatter a country that he regarded as special and indivisible. He was certainly constrained neither by personal loyalties or obligations, nor by constitutional niceties.

By choosing to occupy the presidency, de Gaulle brought to the office status and prestige. It is tempting to conclude that he designed the office specifically for himself, and there is no doubt that the constitutional expression of its formal powers reflects some of his particular concerns. However, de Gaulle's effect upon the office was rather like that of an awkwardly-shaped foot upon a tight fitting shoe; stretching, cracking and reshaping.

President Pompidou's term of office as prime minister, from 1962 to 1968, established his credentials as a potential President. Dismissed in 1968, he was elected President after de Gaulle's resignation the following year. During his term of office he had established himself as a very astute and effective politician, a powerful organizer and, especially in the confusion of the events of May 1968, a determined government leader. Until his long-drawn-out fatal illness, he brought these same qualities to the presidency. President Valéry Giscard d'Estaing's carefully cultivated image, at the time of his election in 1974, was one of youthfulness, dynamism, change and modernization – change, however, as his election slogan proclaimed, without risks. His technocratic confidence and experience in one of the most powerful ministerial posts – that of minister of finance – ensured throughout his term of office a substantial involvement in all aspects of governmental and political life. His initial modernizing image was borne out by his achievements in social modernization (provisions for divorce, legalization of contraception and abortion, lowering the voting age to 18) and in European integration (the creation, in partnership with Chancellor Schmidt of West Germany, of the European Monetary System). But as his term advanced, his style became increasingly edified, distant and haughty, which certainly contributed to his defeat. He has remained politically active as a *député* and a member of the European Parliament, marking the arrival of the new century both by proposing the law which led to the *quinquennat* amendment, and by chairing the convention charged with attempting to draw up a constitution for an enlarged European Union.

President Mitterrand succeeded in turning what might have been a handicap into an advantage. He was associated with the discredited Fourth Republic – he had been a member of Parliament and eleven times a minister – and twice an unsuccessful presidential candidate. Yet his 1981 electoral campaign managed to present what might have been perceived as a career of failure as one of slowly advancing yet irresistible achievement. *La force tranquille* – the quiet strength – was his slogan. A complex, perceptive, calculating and clever politician, it was he who was obliged, between 1986 and 1988, to find a way to accommodate the presidential office to a parliamentary majority and government of a sharply different political persuasion. He did so with well-judged astuteness and his behaviour during the period of *cohabitation* undoubtedly contributed to his re-election for a second term in 1988.

Astuteness, however, grew, during Mitterrand's second term of office, to look more like deviousness, and cleverness seemed mere machination. Some of his gambles failed to pay off. The Maastricht referendum result was closely balanced, and in no sense a vote of confidence in his government. The Socialist candidate for the battle to succeed him in 1995 was not Emmanuelli, whose cause he had favoured, but Jospin. The party itself was at a low ebb, almost as fragile and improbable a basis for a bid for power as it had been when he took it over in 1971. Scandal and tragedy did not spare him. The closing years of his period of office encompassed the suicide of two close associates, one of them former Prime Minister Pierre Bérégovoy; the revelation of the right-wing activities of his youth and suspicion over some of his continued loyalties; allegations of financial impro-prieties by others close to him; and the discovery that he had housed his mistress and their daughter in official apartments. He became increasingly physically frail as his terminal illness (cancer of the prostate) gripped him, although he confronted it with dignity, and survived, against the expectations of many, to the end of his mandate and beyond. It has, perhaps justly, been said of President Mitterrand that he 'had all the conditions for greatness except greatness itself' (quoted in *The Guardian*, 6 May 1995). However, his mark on the presidency, not only as a consequence of longevity in office but also of his choices and personal style, was as profound as that of de Gaulle. It was not the least of the paradoxes of this complex man that, having opposed the Fifth Republic's constitution, he presided over a period where the role of that constitution in the working of the presidency and in political life was accentuated.

Jacques Chirac thus took over a presidency that had changed in shape and emphasis. He had fought for it since 1981, succeeding, like Mitterrand at his third attempt. Despite his depth of political experience, through two periods as prime minister, separated by a decade, and, from 1977 to 1995 as the first Mayor of Paris since the office was restored by the reforms introduced in 1977, his polit-ical touch proved to be far from sure. His campaign had been tough, vigorous, political and unashamedly populist, despite his tendency to appear stiff and blustering on television. He argued for social inclusion, for a combination of low taxes and a flexible labour market, and above all for a rapid decrease in unemployment. After several months his popularity in the opinion polls had fallen drastically. Taxes had risen, unemployment was only creeping down, proposals for reform in the social security system produced widespread protest and strikes and had to be withdrawn, and the government was already tainted by scandal inherited from the municipal administration in Paris from which many of the ministers and presidential staff had come. The inclusion in the government of a record number of female ministers, and the sacking of many of them in an early reshuffle looked like cynicism and poor judgment on the part of both president and prime minister. The old image of impetuousness and hot-headedness had not been lessened by his decision, in the face of massive international protest, to resume nuclear testing in the Pacific and by his abrasive and intransigent approach to his relationship with the German Chancellor Helmut Kohl.

In the tradition of Gaullism, Chirac regarded the presidency as the appropriate setting for a strong leader. In 1997 he took an enormous political gamble in the hope of confirming his leadership, and lost. A majority favourable to him had been in place in the National Assembly since 1993 when he took office in 1995. He had decided not to call a general election at his accession, but installed a 'subordinate' (Alain Juppé) as prime minister. Juppé had long been a close associate of Chirac, and their political priorities were identical. Hence Chirac was able to afford him a role in the party, the government and in policy-making that was almost as substantial as that of *cohabitation* prime ministers (Machin, 2001, p. 81). But a general election would have to be called in 1998, and Chirac and Prime Minister Juppé wished to ensure that their configuration of power would last to the end of the *septennat*. Public opinion had turned rapidly and steeply against Chirac and Juppé in the early months of their incumbency: In the spring of 1997 it seemed to be rising in his favour. Moreover, it was likely that thereafter public expenditure constraints, required by the criteria for membership of the common European currency, would be biting even harder, so Chirac dissolved the National Assembly a year ahead of the required date and called a general election for 1997.

The success of the Socialists, led by Jospin, condemned Chirac to a full five years of *cohabitation*, which he survived with his stature much diminished and his opportunities for leadership largely disintegrated. He was protected only by the privileges of his office from judicial investigation of some aspects of his time as mayor of Paris. However, his open manner and populist bonhomie helped to restore his rating in the opinion polls. He profited little from his leading role in the final negotiations for the Treaty of Nice, opened to him by the president's formal role in the negotiation of treaties, and traditional position in relation to European and foreign affairs (see below). In fact the conduct of business there was widely portrayed as shambolic and the outcome, despite France having largely achieved her aims, as an unsatisfactory interim compromise. The aftermath of the terrorist attack in New York in September 2001, when Chirac took a lead in articulating French responses, reversed the trend. At the age of 69 he campaigned vigorously for re-election in 2002, this time for five years.

His cheerful, gregarious manner stood him in good stead. He could, of course, largely dissociate himself from the actions of the Jospin government, which he had at times openly criticized, and he may also have benefited from a seemingly ingrained tendency in French politics for the incumbent government to lose – this occurred in all the presidential and parliamentary elections since 1981 except 1995. But it was certainly the widespread sense of shock and outrage at the emergence as one of the two front-runners, after the first ballot, of Jean-Marie le Pen, leader of the extreme-right National Front (see Chapter 8) that rallied a wide spectrum of opinion behind him at the second ballot and ensured his victory in 2002.

The president is the holder of a very exposed and public office; his (or her – but there have been few female candidates and none has reached the second round) experience, his astuteness, his ability to choose and present a style of behaviour, his own strengths of personality, are all important resources that he must deploy in interpreting and fulfilling the role of president.

Political relationships

The political relationships of the president are crucial resources; as the balance of these relationships has changed from time to time, so have some aspects of the president's role. If the president is to act as head of government as well as head of state, and in order to implement a policy programme, the president requires an electoral majority to vote him into office and, potentially, renew his mandate, a prime minister and government – as Pompidou, then prime minister, told the National Assembly in 1964, 'In the first place, in order to do anything, the President of the Republic needs a government' (quoted in Quermonne, 1980, p. 176) – and a Parliament that will vote through the legislative measures required.

None of these three resources is unproblematic. The first requires the careful balance, discussed above, between building a sound basis of political support, possibly on the foundation of an organized political party, and avoiding appearing to be so partisan that the president's status 'above politics' is compromised. A prime minister may turn out to be as much a rival as a subordinate (see Chapter 3) as Balladur did in 1993–5. The key features of the president's relationship to the prime minister are that he has the formal right of appointment (Article 8), and prime ministers have in practice also been dismissed by the president. He also appoints the members of the government on the prime minister's advice.

The president also chairs the weekly meetings of the Council of Ministers (Article 9), and consequently signs such regulations and appointments as have, under Article 13 for example, to be discussed by the Council of Ministers. He is responsible for other discussions within the Council of Ministers required by the constitution, on bills to be presented to Parliament for instance (Article 39). The president's chairmanship of the Council of Ministers has given him a source of personal political scope which has varied. That it has been perceived as import-ant – if only as a 'formal spectacle' (Machin, 2001, p. 80) – is evident from the unwillingness of presidents to allow others to deputize for them in the chair. No major act which the government plans can avoid the attention, indeed the potential veto, of the president. On 14 July 1997 Chirac said pointedly that the president has the last word, a statement which Prime Minister Jospin later contested (*Le Monde*, 18 July 1997). But the President's formal powers, especially under *cohabitation*, are essentially negative. At the limit he can block policy, as Mitterrand prevented the Balladur government from resuming nuclear tests between 1993 and 1995 (Massot, 2002, p. 31) This however is rare, and in general, Mitterrand and Chirac did not seek to impede measures upon which the government had previously decided; equally they did not hesitate to make doubts about them public: Chirac described the implementation of the 35-hour week as *une expérimentation hasardeuse* – a dangerous experiment. Even when the president does benefit from a presidential majority the limited size and scope of his staff makes him heavily dependent on the effort of prime minister and ministers for the formulation and carrying through of policy.

Governmental policy, whether inspired by the president or not, if it requires legislation, has to be voted through Parliament. For much of the Fifth Republic the presence of majorities that would vote the necessary legislation has been a major presidential resource. As we have seen, in the early years of the Fifth Republic, the Algerian War served as an effective substitute for a majority; as long as de Gaulle was desperately needed, his government's policies would be accepted, and the legislation voted through at this period included some major measures, for example on agricultural restructuring and on education, as well as introducing a number of minor but much needed reforms (a measure aimed at reducing alcoholism, for example) which had long been blocked by the power of vested interests within the Fourth Republic. The general election of 1962 assured a solid majority coalition in support of the president, which lasted broadly until 1981. President Giscard d'Estaing, as a member of a minority party within the coalition found, however, that he could not automatically rely upon unconditional support. Some of his social reform measures – the divorce and abortion law reform bills – were passed only with the support of members of the opposition parties in the National Assembly. President Mitterrand's dissolution of the National Assembly after his election in June 1981 resulted in the return of an overall majority of Socialists.

Many commentators during that period argued that the voters had recognized what was held to be the inescapable 'logic' of the Fifth Republic. The combination of formal powers and customary practice enshrined within the balance of the institutions ensured the primacy of the president, so it was argued, and the exercise of this primacy equally required that he should be provided with the necessary parliamentary majority. Subsequent elections have shown that this logic is reliable only when, firstly, the second election closely follows the first. Secondly, the president must actively ask and campaign for a majority. When he does not (Mitterrand was slow to do so in 1988) the result may be far from clear-cut.

The crushing defeat of the Left in the 1993 general election presaged the result of the presidential election in 1995. Chirac can be said to have misjudged his timing, for instead of taking steps to ensure at least a five-year majority by a dissolution at that point, he elected to gamble on a seven-year majority by the dissolution in 1997. His miscalculation ushered in a full-term period of *cohabitation* but also gave an added point to the *quinquennat* amendment to which he eventually unenthusiastically assented. However, it was undoubtedly the reversal of the electoral timetable for 2002, asserting the primacy of the choice of president and implying a duty on the voters to give him a majority, as they duly did, that most forcibly underlined the linkages between presidency and presidential majority, as the title chosen for the winning coalition of groups, *Union pour une majorité presidentielle* (UMP) – Union for a Presidential Majority, made abundantly clear.

The president and the media

De Gaulle, whose broadcasts to occupied France on 18 June 1940 had become part of national mythology, understood the importance of the use of broadcasting media as means of direct communication between himself and the citizens. His broadcast addresses were designed to express the President's position as the spokesman for all French people. They marked serious events, for example in Algeria at the start of his presidency or the student disturbances of 1968 which produced another seven broadcasts (*Le Monde*, 12 September 1991). Televised press conferences, dramatic, carefully staged and prepared, such as the one where he announced his veto on British membership of the European Communities, took place at regular intervals. In addition, his presidential travels throughout France – and all the presidents have made frequent 'royal progresses' through *départements* or regions – provided occasions for speeches to large audiences that might contain important policy announcements or political statements.

De Gaulle's successors have continued to use television to address the nation, sometimes, but not always, with considerable success. However, by the end of the 1990s, full-blown presidential press conferences had become almost extinct, partly, no doubt, because as a major event, they are inappropriate during periods of *cohabitation*. Although it can be argued (Laughland, 1994, p. 91) that this represents a decline in the accountability and accessibility of the President, styles of broadcasting have evolved since the 1960s, and the formal, stage-managed press conference looks anachronistic. Since the 1970s, presidents have made rather more relaxed and informal television appearances, for example in the context of the New Year or the Elysée garden parties on the 14 July, and through individual interviews. De Gaulle always refused individual interviews; all his successors have granted them, to both press and television, although a habit of deference remains.

The President's relationship with the media, which is such a potentially powerful means for him to present his personality, approach and priorities, is managed in three ways. First, the French government enjoyed, until the early 1980s, a very close control over the broadcast media; both radio and television were in the hands of people appointed by the government, and overseen through a Ministry of Information. Although steps have since been taken to detach broadcasting from direct governmental influence, connections remain close. Secondly, the presidential office has a presidential spokesperson and a press officer, who keep in touch with journalists, writers and broadcasters. Thirdly, the presidency now has a good and accessible website.

The Political Role of the Prime Minister

The president of France has developed a style of political leadership that has emphasized detachment from party. Only through presidential elections at first seven and now five year intervals can he formally be held to account for his actions and political programme and then he is accountable in the broadest way, to the citizens at large, and only if he chooses to stand for re-election. The president does not account to Parliament for his actions: he cannot be invited to attend debates, he does not speak in them, he cannot be questioned by members of Parliament. The prime minister has a crucial political role, whatever his or her relationship with the presidency, though clearly its balance and intensity alters during periods of *cohabitation*.

The political role of the prime minister has three aspects: in relation to the government, for whose political cohesion he or she is largely responsible; in relation to Parliament, where the government must carry its programme and to some degree account for its actions, and in relation to the party or parties that support the government.

In seeking to ensure the political cohesion of the government the prime minister may operate under a number of handicaps:

• He or she may not be solely responsible for the composition and nature of his team. General de Gaulle was in the habit of naming those whom he wished to see in the key posts – defence, foreign affairs, the interior – and ensured the continuation in office from 1959 to the end of his presidency of André Malraux as Minister of Culture. In 2002 it was reported that President Chirac had chosen all the ministers, (although Raffarin specifically asked for Luc Ferry, the philosopher, as minister of education) and they had in some cases already been informed of their appointment by the president some hours before the prime minister officially told them that he was, as the constitution requires, proposing them (*Le Point*, 17 May 2002, p. 32, and 24 June 2002, p. 35). Compromises may occur. In the governmental reshuffles of 1990, for example, two ministerial departures (including that of Edith Cresson who was appointed prime minister the following year) were attributed to the wishes of the prime minister, two new appointments to the wishes of the president, and one more was alleged to have served the (different) interests of both. As one commentator said, there could be no better demonstration of the need for agreement between president and prime minister (Massot, 1991). Even a prime minister hostile to the president proved not to have an entirely free choice of his own governmental team. In March 1986 President Mitterrand strongly and effectively opposed the appointment of certain leading figures to foreign affairs and defence, which are closely linked to the constitutional sphere of presidential action, and in 1997 President Chirac, though greatly weakened by the failure of his political gamble, had to be consulted on the appointments to those posts.

- He or she does not necessarily, or indeed usually, combine party leadership with the role of prime minister. He or she cannot, therefore, automatically count upon the party loyalty of his governmental team which may include members with powerful individual political power bases of their own. In the 1970s Jacques Chirac handled this problem by ensuring that he used his prime ministerial position to ensure dominance within his party and took over as secretary-general of the Gaullist party. Following his departure in 1976, Raymond Barre's experiment in containing and handling inter-party conflict within the government was not a happy one.It proved that a prime minister cannot with impunity simply abdicate the political leadership of the parliamentary majority. Three times under the Fifth Republic – in 1968, 1981 and 2002 – a single party has enjoyed an absolute majority in the National Assembly. Nevertheless in 1968 and 1981 the government team was a coalition. In 2002 it was formed largely from members of the political groups that, having come together to form that majority then, in the autumn of 2002, merged into a single party (the *Union pour un Mouvement Populaire*) but there were a number of ministers with no previous political experience or overt affiliation. The ministerial team has to be accommodated and managed. Contrary to some expectations the inclusion of four Communist ministers, who were not, however, chosen from amongst the very top ranks of the Communist Party leadership, in the Mauroy government of June 1981 produced few problems, although they would not serve when Laurent Fabius replaced Mauroy in 1984, given the new approach that this symbolized. Equally, Elgie's study (1993, p. 20) shows that Chirac's response to the 1986 education bill crisis was hampered by the need to hold his ministerial team together. Jean-Pierre Chevènement resigned in dissent from posts in three socialist governments – under Mauroy in 1983, Rocard in 1991 and Jospin in 2000. Whilst the way in which it presents itself may differ between periods of presidentialism and those of *cohabitation* – when the prime minister needs especially to look to the preservation of his majority and his own future and that of his party, and to 'lock in' the support of the various groups and factions (Knapp and Wright, 2001, p. 115) – in every government the problem exists.

- Certain administrative positions give some ministers administrative power-bases that enable them to exercise a considerable degree of autonomy that is not mitigated by a clear concept of collective responsibility. In 1993–5, for instance, Charles Pasqua, the tough right-wing minister of the interior, operated virtually independently and ensured that he was publicly seen to be doing so. This is particularly true of the minister of finances; in the early 1970s Chaban-Delmas, reflecting on his experiences as prime minister, with Giscard d'Estaing as finance minister, accused the finance ministry of running its own, alternative policy. In 1992 Finance Minister Pierre Bérégovoy was said to be 'waging war' on Prime Minister Cresson.

• Except during *cohabitation* a prime minister has always to reckon with the fact that certain ministers may be in a position to appeal over his or her head directly to the president. Under Mitterrand, Jack Lang, the long-serving minister of culture, was considered to be particularly close to the president, as was Charles Hernu, the defence minister who had to resign over the sinking of the *Rainbow Warrior*. Paradoxically it was the independence that he consequently enjoyed that shielded both Mitterrand and Laurent Fabius, who was then prime minister, from greater implication in the scandal. Fabius himself, when prime minister, described in an interview how, as a minister, he had been in the habit of 'short-circuiting' the prime minister; an action which he later regretted, for it undermined the prime minister's authority (Elgie and Machin, 1991, n. 18). Chirac reportedly, but unsurprisingly, told the members of the new government in 2002 that they should not attempt to deal directly with him. Time will tell.

The second aspect of the prime minister's political role is the responsibility for ensuring the passage of government measures through Parliament. Despite the extent to which the constitution allows the government to manage the National Assembly (see Chapter 7), this is by no means always straightforward. The French political system does not put a high premium on unwavering obedience to a party line within the parliamentary parties, and prime ministers have regularly needed to resort to various devices to mask or curtail dissent among their own supporters. The difficulties that the Barre government experienced in 1979 in getting its expenditure estimates passed, or the backbench pressures which forced amendments in a carefully calculated Education Bill in 1984 (with the ultimate effect of wrecking the Bill) were examples of the difficulties with which Prime Ministers may have to contend. Rocard, at the head of a minority government after 1988, had to devote a good deal of time and energy to putting together the necessary package of parliamentary support to ensure the passage of each of the measures his government wished to introduce.

Prime Ministers' relationships to parties have fluctuated. Nevertheless, elections are fought on governmental records amongst other factors, and no prime minister has been able to ignore the impact of governmental performance on the electorate at large. Before the 1978 general election Prime Minister Barre, despite his minimal party attachments, presented himself as the leader of the governing coalition in a televised debate with Mitterrand, then the First Secretary of the Socialist Party. Socialist prime ministers since 1981 have had a clear, if not always easy, relationship with the Socialist Party; in choosing Mauroy as his first prime minister, Mitterrand picked a leader who possessed a strong power base within the party and who was trusted by it. Successive Socialist prime ministers maintained a steady working relationship with the general secretary of the party. Chirac in 1986 came into office as the leader of the Gaullist party, and in the expectation that he would be their presidential candidate in 1988. His relationship with party and electorate was thus of crucial importance to him, and he certainly used his role as prime minister in an attempt to maximize his electoral chances, for example in taking credit for the release of French hostages from Lebanon in the days before the Presidential election in 1988. His lack of success in that election may have encouraged him, in 1993, to concentrate on his role as party leader rather than undertake the leadership of a government in what were undeniably difficult economic circumstances. He chose not to serve as prime minister. His nominee in that post, Edouard Balladur, nevertheless found himself increasingly assuming the role of both governmental and political leader. His public standing was high and he decided to become a candidate in the 1995 presidential election. His ministers were faced with a choice between support for Chirac or for Balladur. The result was a divided party and an increasingly querulous government team. When Chirac won his reaction was marked: '*Balladurien*' ministers were not reappointed. The resultant weakening of the unity of the mainstream right contributed to its defeat in 1997.

Cohabitation

Even if active presidential intervention in the day-to-day conduct of the government hardly accords with the intention of the constitutional definitions of the prime minister's role, when the president enjoys a presidential majority there is, because the government and the parliamentary majority acquiesce in the situation, no constitutional, institutional or political way of distinguishing between governmental and presidential decisions (Luchaire *et al.*, 1989, p. 143). *Cohabitation* requires a different type of presidentialism. The first crucial step was Mitterrand's decision to ask Jacques Chirac, as leader of the party which had gained the highest number of seats in the 1986 election, to form a government. Whilst it became clear that the president did retain some ability to veto the appointment by the new prime minister of certain individuals to certain governmental posts, the recognition by the president of a democratic imperative, and the renunciation of any attempt to continue presidential pre-eminence, through a minority government for example, marked a clear evolution. Mitterrand's strategy in this period and again in 1993–5, when the prime minister was the majority party leader's nominee, was to retain his status in those areas with which the President had traditionally been closely associated. Hence he continued to attend meetings of the heads of government of the seven major economic powers (G7), for instance in Tokyo soon after the election, and of the European Council. Some confusion in protocol resulted, from which the prime minister emerged the loser (Mény, 1993, p. 102). In foreign relations and in matters of defence, where it clearly remained the president whose finger would ultimately be 'on the button', he was not prepared to relinquish his standing. Equally, the major construction and cultural projects associated with the presidency – the pyramid of the Louvre and the Opera at the Bastille – went forward, if not without controversy. After the 1997 victory Chirac stated publicly that he intended to retain 'the last word'. This was firmly, if less publicly, rebutted by Jospin, and a reasonably harmonious level of working cooperation established (Schrameck, 2001, p. 95).

On day-to-day matters, however, both Chirac and Mitterrand carefully dissociated themselves from the actions of the government. The president continued to preside over the weekly Council of Ministers, under *cohabitation* a purely formal exercise, but which at least ensures some knowledge of the governmental agenda. Instead of the very direct relationships which presidential staff 'normally' cultivate with ministerial staff, relationships between presidency and government were essentially channelled through the prime minister's office, as had been the case in previous *cohabitations*. Under Chirac, *conseils restreints* continued in the areas of defence or, for example, in preparation for European Councils (Schrameck, 2001, pp. 93–102).

In defence, foreign and European affairs, presidents have, from the first experience of *cohabitation*, succeeded in ensuring that they cannot be sidelined. In domestic affairs, however, under two of the *cohabitation* periods the twin heads of the executive have also been the potentially front-running rivals for the next major election. Political conflict is inevitably very acute. President Mitterrand, between 1986 and 1988, openly criticized the government, either in speeches where he took pains to defend past achievements, or through actions such as his reception at the presidential palace of a deputation of striking railwaymen in the winter of 1987. He also emphasized his dissent by using the letter of the constitution to obstruct procedures. Thus in July 1986 he refused to sign the governmental decrees (*ordonnances*) launching a programme of privatization and economic liberalization. He did so again in October and in December 1986, on measures relating to electoral boundaries and to flexible working hours. In all three cases the effect was to oblige the government to take the issues back to parliament as specific laws, and once they had, not without some trouble, been duly passed there, the president had no option but to promulgate the laws. Equally he refused to allow discussion of a change in the status of the nationalized Renault car company in a special session of Parliament called in early 1988 specifically to consider a new law on the financing of political parties. In each case the president was careful to obstruct the government only in ways which the constitution legitimized: he depended upon legal exactitude to reinforce his personal stance. For Mitterrand personally the strategy worked. His popularity in the opinion polls rose sharply and stayed high: in 1988 he was re-elected, by an increased majority. Patience, a degree of detachment and immense political astuteness enabled him to emerge as the winner from the period.

Mitterrand's re-election and the return of a Socialist government in 1988, though not of an overall Socialist majority in the National Assembly, did not immediately much alter the president's stance. His electoral programme – the *Letter to All the French People* – was extremely vague as a policy programme, although under Prime Minister Rocard such policy proposals as it did contain were implemented (see Elgie, 1991, p. 18). The popularity of the prime minister equalled or exceeded that of the president for a good part of 1989 and early 1990. It seemed that a balance of power much closer to that envisaged by some of the authors of the constitution was emerging, and not only under *cohabitation*. At least under Mitterrand any return to the dominance of presidential policy direction such as had characterized the period of Giscard d'Estaing seemed improbable and it was possible to speculate that a new style had been set.

Such speculation was belied by two factors. First, the advent of the Gulf crisis and war highlighted the predominant position of the president in foreign and defence affairs. Mitterrand took the leading role in France in the conduct of the war, having undertaken a very high profile international diplomatic effort to try to avert its outbreak. Secondly, recession and rising unemployment, which had reached over 2.8 million by the end of the year, helped to explain the falling ratings of the Socialist Party in the opinion polls and the (accurate) predictions of disaster for the Socialists in the local elections in the Spring of 1992 and the general election of 1993. President Mitterrand's replacement of Michel Rocard as prime minister by Mme Edith Cresson who, unlike Rocard, was known to be politically close to the president, seemed to mark a return to a more active political role by the president. Mme Cresson laboured under quadruple handicaps: the economic situation, her image as the president's protegé, her own lack of a personal network or power base, and the rampant sexism of much political discourse. She was hastily replaced by Pierre Bérégovoy, but nothing could avert the rout of the Socialists in 1993.

In 1993 Mitterrand was not expected to be a candidate in 1995 and nor, at first, was Balladur. Balladur's stately personality, compared to Chirac's combative approach, as well as Mitterrand's encroaching illness, may also have contributed to the impression that *cohabitation* was becoming a calmer, more normal, aspect of French politics. In 1997 *cohabitation* could be expected not to be a two-year temporary aberration but to encompass a full five-year term. Previous experience had provided some lessons. Jospin did not risk *ordonnances* to which the president might not agree, and cooperated over constitutional reform. But the two would be rivals for the presidency in 2002. Chirac criticised the 35-hour week legislation and was clearly opposed to the law providing for civil partnerships between unmarried, including same-sex, couples (the so-called PACS: see p. 26). Jospin particularly resented Chirac's use of information, which came to him in the meeting minutes he regularly received, to call for action on animal feed to prevent the spread of BSE, action which the government was preparing to announce. The president looked as if he had taken the initiative (Schrameck, 2001, p. 103). Equally, the government did nothing to limit the damage from the ongoing investigations into allegations of corruption against the president, although he was constitutionally protected from any court proceedings.

Despite the varied circumstances and tones of these periods – Hayward and Wright distinguish between 'cohabitation' and 'cohabitension' (Hayward and

Wright, 2002) – Chirac's behaviour in 1995 and 2002 suggests that periods of *cohabitation* have been interludes which may inflect and shape the evolution of presidential practice, but do not fundamentally alter it, and the *quinquennat* may render the issues of no more than historical interest.

Presidential practice undoubtedly evolved and changed throughout the 1980s. De Gaulle was able to exploit his dominance to stamp his own interpretation indelibly upon the presidency. But it was the political conditions of the time that made this possible. After 1981 the possibility of real changes in the tenure of power at the centre became a feature to be reckoned with in French political life, and the constraints and limits upon governmental and presidential practice assumed a greater political importance. President Mitterrand's approach to the exercise of presidential power responded to the conditions in which he found himself. Even before the 1986 elections some observers detected the emergence of a less interventionist and more aloof presidency. Similarly, the development of a more parliamentary application of the constitution has been a longer-term process spanning the periods of *cohabitation*. In some senses *cohabitation* merely made the underlying changes in some of the assumptions upon which behaviour was based more obvious and explicit.

The style of the exercise of presidential power has certainly changed, though it is likely that future presidents will find that it still offers a great deal of scope for flexible, if politically hazardous, interpretation. Over the past decade the checks and balances inherent in the system that was created in 1958 have become more prominent.

Limitations and Constraints

'The most powerful leader of the Western World', 'An elected monarch' – journalists have used phrases like these to describe the French president. As we have seen, his position as both head of state and, for much of the Fifth Republic, in certain senses head of the government as well, combined with the absence of some of the formal checks and balances which apply to the other prominent leader with similar assessments, the president of the United States, support such characterizations. Nevertheless the president's power is limited by checks and balances. De Gaulle's dominant personality overrode many of them, but changing personalities and changing political circumstance mean that as the regime has matured, the nature of the balance which does exist within it has become clearer. This section examines the checks and constraints which shape and limit the president's ability to develop and impose his policies. They fall into three categories:

- the limitations imposed by France's position in Europe and the world: these limit all leaders and governments, though they may be differently perceived and experienced in France;
- the limitations imposed by the political environment and French political culture;
- structural and constitutional limitations.

The global and European environment

De Gaulle's principal preoccupation was the reinstatement and maintenance of France's status and standing in the world community. He was able for a time to impose a perception of *grandeur* which implied that France could to a very large extent choose her path and role and shape her environment to fit her choice. It is a key part of the political skills of the president to persuade the French population that he can and does make a difference (Bell, 2000b, p. 242). That difference must be conducive to the external security and internal prosperity and good order of the country. Presidential skills must therefore be devoted to enabling France to operate successfully in a very wide international environment. Their freedom of manoeuvre is limited by what is possible in this context. Examples from the economic sphere include de Gaulle's 1968 refusal to countenance the humiliation that would have accompanied the devaluation of the franc in 1968. In 1969 one of Pompidou's early actions was to allow the devaluation. More strikingly, in 1983 it became sharply apparent that Mitterrand's initial policy of economic expansion – a dash for growth – by increased social and public expenditure, nationalization and job creation was unsustainable. The outcome was the economic U-turn of 1983, with reductions in public expenditure, raised taxes and utility prices, and a policy and rhetoric of austerity and competitivity. The argument is not that the president had no choice: there were certainly those who argued for a protectionist policy and France's exit from the European Monetary System. It is the craft of leadership to make such choices. But their number and nature is constrained by the international context and by increasing needs to cooperate as the issues, whether economic or environmental or arising from security and defence or human rights, become too large and expensive to be soluble at national levels. French presidents spend a good deal of time and effort in preparing for, and participating in, the G7/G8, the European Council and similar meetings.

The European Union constitutes a specifically constraining element of the international context. De Gaulle had opposed France's membership of the European Communities before he returned to power in 1958. At that point, however, he was prepared to accept its benefits in providing France both with certain economic benefits and with a wider arena in which to stake her claim for status and leadership. However, he made determined efforts, with varied success, to shape the evolution of what was then the European Communities to his liking. No subsequent president has gone as far in provoking crises. All have wished and worked to be seen to be contributing to *la construction de l'Europe* (the building of Europe). France is a very active and often influential participant in shaping and assenting to European legislation. But once this legislation is agreed, it has to be adhered to, and this produces real difficulties and constraints for the leaderships – as for example in the case of the dates for the hunting season, the importation of British beef or the liberalization of the domestic energy market. These issues are further discussed later (see Chapter 10).

Both globalization *(mondialisation)* and the consequences of European integration are particularly sensitive points in French politics. Both seem to contain
within them powerful rhetorical and practical challenges to French formulations
of social and political values. Many parts of the French economy and society have
responded with notable dynamism to these challeges: the success of French
companies in investing abroad – for example the acqusition by French companies
of British utility suppliers – is marked. But there is also a great deal of reticence
and even active protest (see Chapter 9). French leaders cannot afford to ignore
either their external context or the potential internal reaction to it.

The political environment and political culture

Party backing

In many other western democracies, including Germany, Spain and the United
Kingdom, much of the political strength of the execuive leadership derives from
leadership of a majority or dominant party. The role of the president and the
prime minister in relation to the political parties has been discussed. Here it is
important to observe that the parties may act as a constraint upon the power of
the executive leaders. Many French parties tend (see Chapter 8) to be weak in
membership and organization, prone to internal faction and vulnerable to splits
and indiscipline. And this tendency is not alleviated by strong leadership from,
and allegiance to, the very top. Indeed the fragility and instability of the parties
may be exacerbated by the dual executive leadership. Not only is power divided
at the top, but presidents both need to dissociate themselves from party (see p. 6)
and yet may seek to hamper a prime minister who seems to be attracting personal
support as de Gaulle did Pompidou. Mitterrand's attitude to Rocard did the
Socialist party no good. The relationship between Prime Minister Rocard's staff
and the Socialist Party leaders, even though they met regularly, was one in which
there was no solidarity and 'sometimes an atmosphere of hatred' (Rocard's
directeur de cabinet Huchon, quoted in Hayward and Wright, 2002, p. 48). Chirac
and Balladur, members of the same party, campaigned against each other. In such
circumstances power is constrained.

Electoral pressure

The president is not directly answerable to Parliament, and there is no formal
political institution within which his record can be constantly challenged. The
septennat could potentially provide a degree of insulation from the operation of
political and electoral pressures. However, the *quinquennat* may cause future presidents to keep their eye even more closely throughout on their chances of re-election,
even if it is unlikely that Chirac, who will by 2007 be 75, will stand again. Moreover,
other election results act as indicators of the standing and legitimacy of the president.
Electoral campaigns in France – municipal, *départemental*, regional, national,
European – punctuate political life with sometimes bewildering frequency, though

seldom in quite such close order as in 1988–9, when presidential, general, local and European elections, and a referendum all occurred within the space of just over a year. Presidents may wish to be above politics, but the electorate will judge their political performance, as de Gaulle was forced to recognize when, to his chagrin and surprise, he found himself forced into a second round in the 1965 presidential election. It is perhaps salutary for presidents to ponder the fact that apart from the special circumstances of the Algerian conflict and the events of 1968, all those general elections which have fallen part-way through a presidential term of office (1967, 1973, 1978, 1986, 1993, 1997) have seen a fall in the number of seats held by the president's own party. Despite constitutional status and longevity office, the French president is subject to democratic and electoral constraints.

Public opinion: polls

Apart from the presidential contests, however, the electoral battles do not impinge very directly upon the president. His standing in public opinion polls is an even more indirect and informal means by which public pressure may act as a constraint. Nevertheless, public opinion polling in France is highly organized, well publicized and taken very seriously. The president's staff includes a staff member with a specific responsibility for interpreting the polls, and indeed commissioning opinion surveys specifically for the president. The institutes which carry out the polling are advised or directed by leading academic political scientists. Many of the political opinion polls are concerned with the standing of political leaders, and with the popularity of the political parties. One key question relates to the views expressed by those polled of the president, and it is possible to trace the evolution of opinions over the whole period of the Fifth Republic. In 1980, for the first time, a higher percentage of those questioned said that they were unhappy with the president than satisfied with him, a shift in opinion that presaged President Giscard d'Estaing's defeat at the polls in 1981. The fortunes of both President Mitterrand and President Chirac were more mercurial.

In 1995 President Chirac gained the unenviable record for the shortest post-election honeymoon. The proportion of those polled who expressed satisfaction with him dropped by over 20 percentage points, from 59 to 33 per cent, in the space of three months. His successful electoral campaign had been based on an academic analysis of his 1988 campaign and extensive surveys of popular expectations and wishes (Machin, 2001, p. 89) Great expectations had consequently been aroused, which had promised lower taxes, no constraints on wages and job creation; disappointment when increases in taxation, a very small fall in unemployment and a freeze on public sector pay ensued was correspondingly greater. Matters were not improved by proposals to reform the much cherished, but highly expensive, social security system (see Exhibit 9.4). While a seven-year term of office may seem to provide scope to ignore initially poor ratings, the president could not afford to forget the parliamentary elections, though he paid a high price for an attempting to gamble on an apparent upturn. Opinion polls can at best indicate rather broad trends.

Public opinion: referendums

The constitution has provided one mechanism by which the president can seek the opinion of the citizens very directly on a particular question: the referendum (see Table 4.1). Initially confined, under Article 11 of the constitution, to questions about the organization of public institutions or the ratification of treaties which would affect the operation of public institutions, the right to hold a referendum was, by the constitutional amendment of July 1995, extended to questions concerning economic and social policy and the services which implement these. De Gaulle treated referendums primarily as a plebiscitary confirmation of his own standing. In 1958 the referendum which approved the new constitution was essentially a vote of confidence in de Gaulle – discussion of the details of the constitution took a very minor place. The two referendums on Algeria, one, in January 1961, to approve the principle of self-determination, and the second, in April 1962, to accept the Evian agreement which ended the conflict, also clearly demonstrated the electorate's willingness to accept whatever would lead to peace in Algeria and their confidence in de Gaulle's powers to bring it about.

In 1962 a referendum was used to push through the amendment to the constitution that instituted direct elections to the presidency. This controversial referendum (see Exhibit 2.6) was also a plebiscite – a vote of confidence in de Gaulle that would legitimize his continuation in power although the immediate crisis he had been brought in to solve had ended. In a broadcast he said as much – if there were only a feeble or doubtful majority in favour of his proposals he would resign. In 1962 the French electorate was not prepared to take that risk.

TABLE 4.1

Referendums in the Fifth Republic

Year	Subject	Result	Yes*	No*	Abs**
1958	Proposed constitution	Approved	85.14	14.85	19.51
1961	Self-determination for Algeria	Approved	74.99	25.00	26.24
1962 (April)	Independence for Algeria	Approved	90.80	9.19	24.66
1962 (Oct.)	Direct election of the President	Approved	62.25	37.74	23.02
1969	Reform of the Senate and creation of regions	Rejected	47.58	52.41	19.86
1972	Enlargement of the European Community	Approved	63.81	31.68	39.75
1988	Future of New Caledonia	Approved	79.99	20.00	63.10
1992	Ratification of the Maastricht Treaty of European Union	Approved	51.05	48.95	29.49
2000	Five year term for the presidency	Approved	61.43	16.09	69.81

Source: Ministry of the Interior/Conseil Constitutionnel.
Notes:
* Percentage of votes cast.
** Percentage of registered electors.

By 1969 the situation was different. Faced with the enormous challenge to regime, government and his personal standing represented by the events of May 1968 (see Exhibit 9.2) de Gaulle's first instinct was again to reconfirm his legitimacy by a referendum. He was dissuaded from this and instead dissolved Parliament and called a general election. A landslide victory for the Right resulted, but the following year de Gaulle again called a referendum (see Table 4.1). His motives were undoubtedly complex. The issue on which the voters were invited to decide was the reform of the upper chamber of Parliament – the Senate. This was linked to a reform of local government that would have given a greater emphasis to regional structures. That de Gaulle attached great importance to these reforms was evident. Moreover he may have wished to enforce his own authority over a parliamentary majority created largely by Pompidou whom he had dismissed as prime minister (Portelli, 1987, pp. 114–15, Hamon, 1985, pp. 504–21, Bell, 2000b, p. 99). The proposals were defeated and de Gaulle resigned.

Since 1969 there have been four referendums (see Table 4.1). However, unlike the referendums of the 1960s, only one of them has attracted a turnout of more than 60 per cent of voters. In 1972 there was litle risk of defeat for the president, but neither could he draw a marked political success from the result. Thereafter, until the 1980s, presidents preferred to rely for confirmation of their policies and legitimacy upon the normal calendar of elections and the representative institutions.

The 1992 referendum on the ratification of the Maastricht Treaty produced a turnout close to the levels of the 1960s. The issue turned out to be politically contentious in a way that had probably not been expected. The constitutional amendments required to permit the application of the terms of the Treaty had passed with little difficulty, and the Treaty could have been ratified by a parliamentary vote. President Mitterrand took the decision to utilize the alternative method of ratification in the context of opinion polls showing a comfortable majority of French people in favour of greater European integration, combined with evident disarray amongst the parties of the opposition on the issue. However, public support for the Treaty declined rapidly during the campaign, and voters conspicuously failed to follow the advice of the party leaders. The result was approval by a bare majority (51 per cent) and the opening up of political cleavages had effects well beyond the scope of the referendum.

In the two other referendums the number of voters who bothered to register their opinion was so low that considerable doubt must be cast on the usefulness of the referendum as a political tool. In 1988 the issue was not a crucial one for the electorate. In 2000 the *quinquennat* was put to referendum, albeit legally following the necessary votes in the two houses of Parliament, on the analogy of the 1962 amendment. But unlike 1962, when the issue could be presented as a choice between a return to the politics of the Fourth Republic or the survival of the Fifth, in 2000 there was no serious contention. President Chirac's attitude was one of studied indifference: he could live with either outcome. Small wonder that the turnout reached a record low.

In these circumstances presidential government has come less and less to rely upon a direct dialogue between president and people through the plebiscitary mechanism of a referendum. For much of the Fifth Republic representative democracy and its expression through political parties has proved more stable, acceptable and legitimate. President Chirac's 1995 constitutional amendment extending the possible use of the referendum is thus the more surprising. It harks back, first, to the unsuccessful call by the then opposition for a referendum on schools policy in 1984. That policy issue returned to the centre of political debate under the Balladur government in 1993, and from then on Chirac campaigned on the promise of extended scope for referendums to achieve progress in areas where parliamentary processes had resulted in deadlock. It also revived a quite specifically Gaullist theme, within which an alliance of president and voters could potentially outweigh a parliament which has steadily been increasing its importance (see Chapter 7). But if voters respond by staying away the alliance will be a shaky one, and moreover, as 1992 proved, a referendum is always a gamble. The new provision has never been used.

Constitutionality and legality

The constitution gives the executive very wide powers. The president's powers may, in periods of crisis and emergency, be virtually dictatorial. However, the executive's powers can be exercised only within the framework of the constitution. No French president, even with a prime minister, government and parliamentary majority behind him, enjoys the same ability to get his own way as the British doctrine of the absolute sovereignty of parliament confers upon a British prime minister with a sizeable parliamentary majority. There are two bodies in particular which supervise the constitutionality and legality of the actions of the president and the government. They are the Council of State (Counsel d'Etat) and the Constitutional Council. The necessity of having regard to the views of these bodies constitutes a constraint on the president's ability, even in the most favourable political context, to use his position and powers in an unfettered way. The outlook and attitude of these bodies has shifted during the period of the Fifth Republic. The Constitutional Council was discussed in detail in Chapter 2.

With the growing maturity of the Fifth Republic and the development of varying ways in which the government's actions can be challenged, the role of the Council of State has become less prominent. However, since the end of the Second World War the Council has developed a doctrine which insists upon the respect of certain fundamental principles, and it has used these to test the validity, especially, of governmental regulations. This practice certainly constitutes a constraint upon the freedom of action of the state. In the early years of the Fifth Republic, when there was very little challenge to the political supremacy of de Gaulle, the Council of State constituted, it has sometimes been argued, one of the few places where a genuine and principled opposition was expressed.

Two episodes illustrate the stand of the Council. In 1962 the Council advised de Gaulle that the procedure he proposed to use for the amendment of the Constitution was itself unconstitutional. The government did not in fact pay any heed to this advice, which was given confidentially, but knowledge of it leaked out (see Exhibit 2.6). Earlier, in 1961, the Council had acted more rapidly and decisively to curb governmental excesses in the *Canal* case (see Exhibit 4.1).

Since the 1960s the Council of State has not found itself faced with such very highly charged cases although its advice may still be sought in difficult circumstances. In 1993, faced with a conflict between its international obligations undertaken in the Schengen agreement and the Constitutional Council's negative ruling on the constitutionality of a bill to implement them, the government asked the Council of State for advice before proceeding to amend the constitution. The Council of State remains crucial in regulating the day-to-day grievances of the citizen in his or her dealings with the state. However, the Constitutional Council (see Chapter 2), which initially played a somewhat modest role, has more

---

EXHIBIT 4.1

The *Canal* case

In April 1962 General de Gaulle put to a referendum, as the constitution provided, a bill that incorporated the peace agreement reached with the Algerian liberation movement. The bill included provisions allowing the President to make decrees relating to Algerian matters. Using these powers de Gaulle set up, by decree, a Military Court of Justice to judge cases related to the Algerian war and the associated terrorism. No appeal was allowed against the Court's decisions.

André Canal was an active member of the terrorist OAS (Organisation de l'armée secrète) which fought against the French Government's policy towards Algeria. He was responsible for a number of bombings. In the summer of 1962 he was arrested and charged with a bomb attack in which a young child had been injured. On 17 October the Military Court of Justice condemned him to death. He asked for a ruling from the Council of State, which, acting very speedily, since it was supposed that Canal's execution was imminent, on 19 October declared that the decree which had set up the Military Court of Justice was contrary to the general principles of the law, since it allowed for no appeal. It therefore annulled the decree instituting the Court.

De Gaulle was furious. A Committee was set up to 'consider the problems posed by the operation and activities of the Conseil d'Etat'.

In January 1963 the government passed a law through Parliament, giving the force of statute law retrospectively to the decree setting up the Military Court of Justice. However, the law replaced the Military Court of Justice with a State Security Court which contained civilian magistrates, and from which appeal was possible to the Court of Appeal. To that extent the Conseil d'Etat's point of view was vindicated.

Canal's sentence was commuted to life imprisonment, and he was subsequently amnestied as part of the general amnesty for those convicted of crimes related to the Algerian war.

recently emerged as an important source of limitation and constraint upon the actions of the government. If the impact of the Constitutional Council upon the president's abilities to implement his policy was, during the first fifteen years of the Fifth Republic, minimal, the Council subsequently demonstrated that its potential powers could not be ignored. No president, even when he enjoys the support of the governing majority at both national and local levels, can exercise power without keeping a wary eye upon the constitutional framework as the Constitutional Council has defined and applied it. The real importance of the role and activities of the Constitutional Council serves to emphasize the point that the president is a 'constitutional monarch', and the constraints as well as the opportunities which the constitution provides have become steadily more apparent during the lifetime of the Fifth Republic.

Conclusion

The nature of, and relationships within, the political leadership at the heart of French government are both complex and dynamic. The intention of the founders of the Fifth Republic was to establish a stable and powerful executive which would allow France to regain status in world affairs, to develop and modernize and to solve internal conflicts and problems. The habits and practices established by de Gaulle placed the president at the centre of this powerful executive. For the first two decades the operation of the the strong executive and the growth of presidentialism was the key feature of the history of the regime. The combination of constitutional foundations and the relative stability of presidential coalitions has given presidents an advantageous position which, by the exercise of leadership skill, they have used to protect and assert their authority (Bell, 2000b, p. 242). But authority can be challenged and executive power was always potentially limited, by public upheaval, as in 1968, by defeat by the electorate, as in the 1969 referendum, by judicial intervention, as in the *Canal* case, and by the structures of the evolving party system, as well as by growing interdependence with European and global systems. In the subsequent decades of the Fifth Republic the checks and balances have become more important. And within the system, relationships have evolved: from the first the prime minister could not be a mere chief of staff, and prime ministers discovered, in Guy Carcassonne's words that 'the president may mistreat the prime minister but cannot do without him [or her]. The prime minister must humour the president, but can do without him. The president can always give orders, the prime minister can fail to obey' (Carcassonne, 1997, p. 408). The prime minister's chief resource is the government which, according to Article 20 of the constitution, he or she directs. The next chapter considers the governmental machine.

5

The Governmental Machine: Ministers and Civil Servants

The president and the prime minister provide political and executive leadership. The day-to-day work of government is carried out by ministers and civil servants. The role and conduct of the government – prime minister and ministers – shapes and conditions large areas of political life within France. However dominant the president, the government machinery is indispensable if political initiatives are to be realized and policy to be implemented. This machinery has a life and dynamic of its own; the role of the prime minister is crucial, and has, over the period of the Fifth Republic, become more, rather than less, central within public policy. Other ministers, however, may enjoy a good deal of autonomy within their own spheres, and seem at times almost to challenge the pre-eminence of the prime minister. In the complex relationships at the centre of governmental business the personal staffs of president, prime minister and ministers play a key part. They are the links between the world of the politicians, and that of the administration. The civil service in France enjoys a mixed and paradoxical reputation. It is greatly esteemed at the top, especially for its technical competence, yet criticized for pretension, elitism and politicization, and equally castigated for its cumbersome bureaucracy at lower levels yet admired for what are seen as essential contributions to France's prosperity and well-being. This chapter examines the nature of the political tier of government formed by ministers and that of the more administrative levels which civil servants operate. It discusses their interrelationships and a number of specific aspects of French administrative style.

The Machinery of Government

The French government normally consists of between about 35 and 55 ministers (see Table 5.1) in sharp contrast to, for example, the United Kingdom, where the full ministerial team can amount to up to one hundred members. There is normally a division between full cabinet ministers and junior ministers, although the Balladur government of 1993 to 1995 contained only 29 ministers and no junior ministers. The normal distinction between full cabinet members and junior ministers is that the latter only attend cabinet meetings when their

TABLE 5.1

Party composition of selected Fifth Republic governments

President	De Gaulle	Pompidou			Giscard d'Estaing		Mitterrand			Chirac		
Prime minister	Debré	Pompidou		Chaban-Delmas	Chirac	Barre	Mauroy	Chirac	Rocard	Juppé	Jospin	Raffarin[10]
Political Party	January 1959	April 1962	April 1967	June 1969	June 1974	August 1976	June 1981	March 1986	June 1988	May 1995	April 2000	June 2002
Gaullists	6	9	21	29	12	9		20		22		15
Republicans/liberals		3	3	7	8	10		7	1	7		6
Centrists	3[1]	5[2]		3[3]	2	2[4]		7[5]	1	7		1
Radicals	1	1			6[6]	5		2	1	1		1
UDF									3	2		8
Left Radicals							2		3		2	
Socialists							37		25		23	
Communists							4				3	
Miscellaneous	7						1[7]			2[8]	3[11]	
Non-party	10	11	5		8	10[9]		6	15	2	2	8
Total (including PM)	27	29	29	39	36	36	44	42	49	43	33	39

Notes:

1. Christian Democrats (MRP).
2. Christian Democrats (MRP).
3. Centre for Democracy and Progress.
4. Social Democrat Centre (CDS).
5. CDS.
6. Reformers.
7. Michel Jobert, ex-Gaullist whose *Mouvement des Démocrates* supported Mitterrand in the presidential election.
8. One former ecologist, one Other Right.
9. Designated as presidential majority.
10. All other than non-party merged into *Union pour un Mouvement Populaire* October 2002.
11. Two from *Les Verts*, one *Mouvement des Citoyens*

Source: Adapted from Safran (1995) p. 174, updated from www.premier-ministre.gouv.fr and other internet sources.

own business is under discussion, though Jean Pierre Raffarin in 2002 announced that all 39 ministers could attend all meetings. The honorific title Minister of State (*ministre d'état*) may be given as a mark of status and prestige to the most politically senior, sensitive or important ministers – for example in 1991 to Jean-Pierre Soisson, the leading non-socialist minister, signalling no doubt Rocard's desire to open up his coalition to the centre. The title has not been used since 1995. Ministers without a full department of their own are given the title Delegated Minister (*ministre délégué*), which usually carries full cabinet status. Junior ministers are called Secretary of State (*secretaire d'état*), a nomenclature that contrasts with the British pattern, where the title Secretary of State is held by the cabinet ministers, and a minister of state ranks rather low in the hierarchy of junior ministers. In France ministers, including junior ministers, have a clearly defined array of responsibilities for specific subjects, and whilst most junior ministers are technically attached to the senior minister of the ministry, there is little concept of a ministerial team within a department. The division of responsibilities results from decisions by the prime minister (in consultation with the president) when ministers are appointed, rather than from internal decisions by the senior minister in each ministry. The precise definition of the scope of each minister's responsibilities is set out in a legal document (*décret*), nowadays published not only in the *journal officiel* but someimes (during the Jospin government, for example) also on the minister's website. If the structure remains unchanged from one government to another the *décret* can remain unchanged, but in practice the formation of a new or reshuffled government can give rise to disputes about the sharing out of responsibilities.

Over the course of the Fifth Republic there have been a number of modifications and changes in the structure of ministerial responsibilities – the machinery of government. The ministries of foreign affairs, interior, justice, defence, and agriculture have stayed broadly unaltered throughout the period (Elgie and Machin, 1991, p. 67). In general modifications, have resulted from the specific political circumstances of the period. Such circumstances have also affected the nomenclature of certain ministries which change to express political priorities and aspirations, rather than simply to describe basic functions. The term 'solidarity' entered ministerial nomenclature with the advent of the Socialists in 1981, but has continued to figure in titles under governments of all complexions since. In 2002 the term 'environment' disappeared, to be replaced by 'ecology and sustainable development'.

Changes which go beyond nomenclature arise from a wish to give particular salience to specific aspects of governmental action. For example, concern for the rights and conditions of women was one of the features of the social reform aspects of the early years of Giscard d'Estaing's presidency. The result was the creation of an administration which was placed for some of the period (initially against the wishes of the prime minister (Giroud, 1977, pp. 60–9)) under a minister, and in the later years under an administrative official. In 1981 these activities, became a fully fledged ministry under a minister (Yvette Roudy). Under Chirac the ministry was abolished, and its functions placed successively under a free-standing junior minister and then under the Ministry for Labour, Employment and Vocational Training, and it has remained a far from prominent part of that ministry's business. The parity amendment to the constitution was moved forward by the Ministry of Justice. Under Raffarin, the Ministry of Social Affairs encompassed a Delegated Minister for Parity and Professional Equality, with no explicit reference to women.

One influence on the shape of government may be a prime ministerial 'divide and rule' strategy. This seems to have been the motive in 1978 when Raymond Barre, seeking to reduce the influence of the Ministry of Finance, and to ensure his own overall control over economic policy, split the ministry into two parts – a Ministry of the National Economy and a Ministry of the Budget. This division lasted only until 1981. Under Balladur in the first period of *cohabitation* and Bérégovoy in 1991 the Minister of Finance again brought together a very wide range of financial and economic responsibilities. When these two former finance ministers each in their turn became prime minister they were notably wary of the power they had themselves exercised and ensured a much wider division of tasks between various ministers. Juppé adopted a solution midway between the two extremes but had ousted his first finance minister, Alain Madelin, from the government within four months. Both Jospin and Raffarin brought together economy, finance and industry, an exceptionally wide remit. Under the Mauroy government after 1981, transport, housing and town planning and the environment were all separate ministries. In 1986 Chirac brought transport, housing and the environment together under a single ministry, with junior ministers for transport and for the environment. His successors, as the political salience of ecological issues has increased, and, under the Jospin government, the Greens formed part of the governing coalition, have maintained a separate ministry of the environment, or, as in 2002, ecology. Similarly, large areas of social policy were combined by Balladur within one ministry under the popular Simone Weil. Juppé redivided them, and under Jospin Martine Aubry brought them back together, covering responsibilities which in the numerous first Juppé government had been ascribed to no fewer than four separate ministers (*The Economist*, 14 August 1999).

These movements do, of course, affect the political status of specific interests, such as transport, or small and medium sized business, represented in the cabinet, alongside trade, by future prime minister Jean-Pierre Raffarin from 1995 to 1997, while under Jospin and Raffarin himself, both small business and trade were consigned to junior ministers under the ministry of the economy and finance. A full minister carries greater political clout. For the staff of each ministry concerned they have relatively little effect. Each minister, including, junior ministers, has a great deal of autonomy within his or her own sphere of responsibility, and there is very little sense of collegiality, either within ministries or at central government level.

The Characteristics of Ministers

The ministers who have constituted the governments of the Fifth Republic (see Table 5.1) have a number of distinctive features:

- Ministers cannot be members of parliament. Many, though not all – numbers have varied greatly in different governments – have been members of parliament at the time of their appointment. But they are obliged to renounce their membership on appointment as a minister. They may and do attend and speak before meetings of both the National Assembly and the Senate, though they are confined to the governmental bench. Some newly appointed ministers with long parliamentary experience have been known to forget and stray onto forbidden territory to greet their former colleagues. They cannot vote. If they lose office and wish to return to parliament they will have to re-fight their seat, either waiting for the next general election, or persuading their replacement to resign, as former interior minister Jean-Pierre Chevènement did in October 2000, or standing elsewhere should another vacancy occur.
- However, if the experience of fighting elections has not been an essential prerequisite for gaining office (see below), any minister explicitly rejected by the electorate has normally been deemed unable to continue. This custom has been flexibly interpreted, however. Dominique Versini, junior minister in Raffarin's first government retained her post after defeat in the general election, on the grounds, the prime minister's office explained, that this was not a specific rejection by the electorate as she had not previously held the seat.
- For much of the Fifth Republic, ministers' links with local politics have been powerful (see Chapter 6). For a number – for example Jean-Pierre Raffarin – their main political experience has been in local government, and, of those ministers who have fought elections, some have only done so at local level. The law that limits the holding of multiple offices does not apply to the position of minister, which is not an elected post. Consequently until the mid-1990s leading ministers, including prime ministers, often combined the post with that of mayor, sometimes of a major town. Chirac in Paris, Defferre in Marseilles, Chaban-Delmas followed by Juppé in Bordeaux, and Mauroy in Lille are notable examples, but in the summer of 1995 after the municipal elections no fewer than 22 ministers then serving were also mayors and a further eight were members of municipal councils. Moreover, nine were presidents of the council of a region or *département*. After 1997 Jospin took the view that it was impossible to function correctly and honestly as both minister and local office holder, and obliged potential ministers to choose. This produced severe dilemmas for a number of ministers, including Elizabeth Guigou, Jack Lang and Dominique Voynet, at the time of the municipal elections in 2001. Should they seek to maintain their local power bases, possibly at the expense of their ministerial posts? In the event, the elections witnessed a surprising number of defeats for leading political figures and most of the ministers were thus able to stay in post (Bilger-Street and Milner, 2001, p. 507). Raffarin has maintained Jospin's policy, so that

18 out of the 39 ministers in his post-general election government (including himself) were obliged to abandon positions as president of the council of a region or *département* or as mayor. Two leading majority politicians (Jean-Louis Debré, mayor of Evreux, and Philippe Douste-Blazy, mayor of Toulouse) were reportedly unwilling to give up as mayors in order to participate in government. Despite these moves away from the formal combination of posts, ministers' footholds in local politics often remain very firm.

- A high proportion of the ministers have had previous experience of administrative life as officials.
- They have mostly been men. There was only one woman minister between 1958 and 1972; between 1972 and 1993 the numbers varied between two and seven. During the 1995 presidential election campaign the candidates were pressed to make commitments not only about equal representation for women in elected positions but also about the number of ministerial posts that would be given to women (see Exhibit 2.7). Perhaps as a consequence, in Prime Minister Alain Juppé's first government there were twelve female ministers (28.6 per cent), four of them with cabinet rank. This exceptional situation lasted only a few months. In the government reshuffle of early November 1995 eight out of the twelve lost their posts, and of the remaining four only one was of Cabinet rank. The Jospin government of June 1997, however, contained 8 women in its 27 members: the two ministers ranking highest in the order of precedence were both women, Martine Aubry and Elisabeth Guigou. The parity act does not apply to appointed posts, but its influence is visible in the presence of 10 women out of 39 members in the June 2002 government, the most senior of them, Michèle Alliot-Marie, at Defence, a function which has typically been considered a masculine domain.
- Despite the arrival in power of the Socialists in 1981, 90 per cent of all the ministers of the Fifth Republic have come from positions in the upper ranks of industry, the public services or the professions and 80 per cent of all ministers have a higher education qualification (Gaxie, 1986).

In the first governments of the Fifth Republic a rather high proportion of the members of the government did not hold a parliamentary seat at the time when they were appointed minister. In the Debré government of 1959–62, 15 out of the 40 ministers were not members of Parliament. The new regime was seeking to distinguish itself from the discredited system it had replaced and emphasize a depoliticized technical effectiveness. The proportion remained relatively high (an average of 27 per cent) until 1968, but then dropped sharply as would-be ministers and those who already held office sought election, even if their appointment or reappointment meant that they had immediately to abandon their seats. Between the mid-1970s and 1993 the proportion of non-parliamentary ministers rose again to around 30 per cent. It fell sharply under Balladur between 1993 and 1995 (Knapp and Wright, 2001, p. 121) and stayed low under Jospin before rising again to nearly one-third under Raffarin, 12 out 39 of whose ministers had never held a seat as a member of the National Assembly or Senate. Two of these had been members of the European Parliament.

In some cases, such non-parliamentary ministers were chosen because they are prominent within the parties of the governing coalition, but have chosen not to seek election, or been unable, perhaps because their party is small, to secure it – the Communist minister Charles Fiterman, appointed in 1981, was an example of the first sort, the leader of the small *Parti Socialiste Unifié*, Huguette Bouchardeau, of the second. Sometimes such ministers are leaders of other important organizations – for example the farmers' leader, Michel Debatisse, was appointed a minister under Giscard d'Estaing. Other ministers may have been closely linked to the President without having, before their first appointment, been involved in electoral politics – Pierre Bérégovoy, Jack Lang or Dominique de Villepin, for example. All these ministers had, however, in some way been linked to political life; other ministers have been appointed to posts linked to their previous professional experience. Whilst their political sympathies clearly lie with the government, it is their expertise which explains the appointment. Under Mitterrand, the first Minister of Industry was the former chairman and managing director of the vehicle manufacturers Renault (Pierre Dreyfus) and in the 1988 Rocard government the Minister of Industry was the former head of the huge glass-makers, St Gobain. The Juppé governments formed in May and December 1995 included a lawyer specializing in environmental law as Minister of the Environment, while Jospin's government included the prominent doctor and humanitarian, Bernard Kouchner. Raffarin's minister of the economy, finances and industry came from heading one of Europe's biggest steel companies, Arcilor; his minister of education was an academic philosopher and his minister of research a (female) astronaut. Such appointments may contribute to an image of competence and professionalism for the government. This 'depoliticization' and 'legitimation by competence' (Gaxie, 1986, p. 66) seems to be particularly important when politics are in transition (as in 1959) or when political circumstances are difficult. In the minority government of Michel Rocard in 1988, there was a higher proportion of 'non-political' appointments (eight out of 48) than had been the norm for the 1980s.

However, political inexperience amongst ministers may sometimes be a hazard; one of Rocard's ministers – a famous surgeon appointed as minister of health – lasted only a few days in office. Moreover, even if they are not 'professional politicians' at the outset of their ministerial career, most rapidly become so, and seek electoral legitimacy, either (like Pompidou and Barre) through general elections, or (like Simone Weil, a magistrate before she became minister of health) in the European elections, or, at the very least, at a local level. It was President Mitterrand's instruction that he expected all his ministers to present themselves to some electoral process that caused a very small town in the Pyrenees to have a government minister as mayor after the 1989 local elections.

A much-remarked characteristic of the governments of the Fifth Republic has been the extent of the connection between ministers and the civil service. There was a popular perception that the coming of the Fifth Republic had blurred the distinction between political functions and administrative functions, and that to an important extent officials were being appointed directly into ministerial posts – a tendency which, it was argued, extended into political life the worrying features of administrative domination already evident in other areas, especially economic and industrial life. The proponents of this view could point to the proportion of ministers who had spent some part of their career as senior government officials. Between 1959 and 1981 just under 40 per cent of all ministers came into the government with a background of this sort; under the Socialists the proportions dropped to 14 per cent but, despite Chirac's attacks on technocracy during his campaign, rose to 20 per cent in the first government of his presidency. Seven of the 27 ministers in Jospin's first governments were graduates of the *Ecole Nationale d'Administration*. Under Raffarin the proportion was lower – 7 out of 39 – plus one graduate of the Ecole Polytechnique, and Noelle Lenoir, a member of the Council of State and former member of the Constitutional Council.

Nevertheless, the argument that what has occurred is a takeover by the civil service (*la fonctionnarisation de la politique*) is too simplistic. In France, success within the top civil service may be seen as a starting point for a variety of careers. Since there are no restrictions upon the political activities of civil servants in their private capacities these include careers in politics. Indeed the prestige and reputation which senior civil posts bring with them may prove to be a distinct advantage (Gaxie, 1986, p. 78). Thus two former senior officials who enjoyed a rapid ascension through ministerial posts culminating with that of prime minister, Chirac on the Right and Fabius on the Left, both commenced their ministerial careers by fighting parliamentary elections, and Fabius indeed served from 1978 to 1981 as an opposition member of Parliament. But access to ministerial office may also come to former civil servants who have made careers in industry, as in the case of Rocard's industry minister Roger Fauroux or Raffarin's minister of the economy, finances and industry, Francis Mer. Nor have civil servants necessarily been appointed directly to ministerial posts. They may have come into political activity in a number of ways: through contact with politicians, for example in their private offices within ministries; through an invitation to be involved in the study of a particular problem; through membership of and activity within a party. For example, Anne-Marie Idrac, appointed junior minister for transport in Juppé's government directly from a senior official post in the ministry, was an active member of the CDS, while Elisabeth Guigou's political activity in the Socialist Party pre-dated her appointment from the Ministry of Finances to the SGCI and the presidential staff and thence as a minister (Guigou, 2000).

The Pathology of the Ministerial Role: Corruption and Scandal

Ministers are located, in France, at the intersection of politics and administration not only at national, but also, in many cases, at local level. These local connections are very important, since many of the scandals which have arisen around certain leading politicians have been linked to their involvement in local administrations at various levels. But the scandals achieve a wider resonance because of the national prominence of the protagonists. Ministers receive a good deal of social deference. Their offices, and those of their close administrative collaborators, tend to display a style and elegance appropriate to the greatness of the state which they serve and represent. They enjoy considerable autonomy and extensive powers of patronage. They are subject to little critical scrutiny. Parliament's control (see Chapter 6) is not intense. There is little tradition of a campaigning and investigative press, although some newspapers and periodicals (notably *Le Canard Enchaîné* and *Le Monde*) have conducted effective enquiries and published revelations. Private life is protected by fierce privacy laws, so what may be common knowledge in the gossip of *le tout Paris* is well concealed from the general public, which is in any case little interested in some of the peccadillos of the establishment. It is hard to believe that the existence of a president's mistress and daughter (Anne Pingeot and her daughter by President Mitterrand, Mazarine) housed for a while in official accommodation, could, in most western countries, have gone unreported through two election campaigns and 13 years in office. Television and broadcasting are no longer totally under the government's thumb, but the government usually ensures it has a friend at the head of the regulatory agency and, despite increasing professionalism, 'interviews with senior politicians remained deferential' (Harrison, 1993, p. 109).

This is a context in which the line between acceptable and scandalous behaviour may, for some, become very indistinct. Scandal, of various kinds, has long been a feature of French political life. Philip Williams in 1970 (p. 3) said that France was 'the classic land of political scandal' (see also Jenkins and Morris, 1993). Recent decades have seen a proliferation of financial and political scandals in France, most of them involving ministers or public bodies. Most of the scandals fall into one of three categories:

- The abuse of power leading to immoral or criminal policy decisions by ministers or civil servants motivated by national, administrative or sometimes political expediency. This category includes the planting of a bomb on the Greenpeace ship *Rainbow Warrior* in 1985 which killed a crew member, and the decision that the blood transfusion service should stock and distribute blood which had not been screened for HIV contamination, although the risks were known. Illegal surveillance and telephone tapping have also been undertaken, notoriously, for example, involving the satirical and investigative weekly, *Le Canard Enchaîné*. The *Rainbow Warrior* case led to the resignation of the minister of defence, but to little public indignation. The case of contaminated blood resulted in the imprisonment of the head of the transfusion service. Nine years later and after much press and television drama and associated political debate, the three ministers concerned were acquitted by the Court of Justice of the Republic, created by constitutional amendment in 1993, which is the only body constitutionally capable of impeaching ministers. Fear of subjecting ministers to such an ordeal again undoubtedly influenced subsequent French government decisions about the import of meat from countries badly afflicted by Bovine Spongiform Encephalopathy (BSE).

• The abuse of patronage or influence in order to raise funds for political parties or purposes. Given the rising cost of political campaigning and electioneering and the difficulties which French political parties have had in ensuring a legal flow of funds to finance their activities, a variety of means have been used to obtain funds. A long-standing and fairly systematized, if clandestine and illegal, method involves the raising of what amounts to a levy on contracts for public works and other services provided to local authorities through false invoices or 'dummy' consultancies. This was the method employed by the Urba group of companies to provide a flow of money into Socialist Party coffers. Other forms of 'kickback' are also said to have been practised. The Luchaire affair in the late 1980s allegedly involved both illegal decisions in relation to the supply of arms to Iran and subventions to the Socialist Party by the contractors. However, the acquisition of funds by means on the fringes or over the borders of illegality to support political and electoral activity has not been confined to the Socialist Party. All the major political parties have been implicated in such dealings (Leyrit, 1995, p. 57). For example, allegations about kickbacks arose in February 1995 against members of the RPR in the Paris region, and there were similar problems in the 1990s in Lyons. At the turn of the century there were prosecutions relating to commissions paid to the RPR by the contractors who gained very large contracts for social housing in Paris and to commissions for the contract for the renovation of secondary schools in the Ile de France which may have gone to both majority and opposition parties. The 2002 presidential election campaign was much influenced by mutual accusations and allegations, with Jean-Marie Le Pen making much of his claim to be the only uncontaminated candidate while Chirac's opponents coined the epithet *supermenteur* (superliar, by analogy with superman) for him.

• The third major category of scandal has concerned those in which position or influence has been used to acquire direct personal benefit, for example through insider trading. A major example of a scandal of this sort was the allegations that profits had been made by those closely associated with President Mitterrand and the then minister of finance, Pierre Bérégovoy, through insider trading associated with the takeover of an American company by the nationalized French company, Pechiney. Allegations of this kind have been linked, not only to Socialists, but also to ministers from governments of the Right. The charges against Alain Carignon, which led to his resignation from Balladur's government and a prison sentence in 1995 included allegations that he had received not only payments to cover his campaign expenses but also personal benefits and gifts worth more than 20 million francs (Leyrit, 1995, p. 65). Similar allegations and rumours, sometimes combined with the particularly damaging innuendo that investigations are being hampered by interference from the top, have had an impact upon the career of a number of politicians.

Cupidity and dishonesty are not confined to politicians: 'by early 1997 the heads of a nearly a quarter of the companies in the CAC 40 stock market index [the leading companies quoted on the French stock exchange] were being formally investigated for one or another infringement' (Knapp and Wright, 2001, p. 399). But the very tight interlocking of the French industrial, commercial and political elite and the extent of government implication in big contracts at all levels mean that commercial and industrial corruption and embezzlement are very closely intertwined.

A number of commentators (Bornstein, 1994, Jenkins and Morris, 1993) have argued that scandals have had only a limited public impact. It is true that there had until the end of the 1990s been little sustained and vocal public outcry. It is also true that Balladur was a credible presidential candidate and Chirac won the presidential election in 1995 despite being, respectively, prime minister and party leader associated with a government which saw three of its members (Longuet, Roussin and Carignon) resign under the cloud of suspicion of financial scandals within six months in 1994. It is, however, equally true that the Socialist Party was regarded as being tarnished and handicapped by the scandals with which it was associated. It may be, as Jenkins and Morris suggest, that 'the French public, by endorsing [the] concentration of power [in the presidency], have sacrificed "open government" for things they value more highly – continuity, stability and simplified political choices. Does this imply therefore that scandal has become an acceptable "trade-off" for these other advantages?' (p. 163).

By the early 2000s, two counter arguments had emerged to this point of view. First, an increasingly active and independent judiciary has been pursuing cases. Prosecutors have courageously resisted pressure to abandon politically sensitive cases, and much has been revealed by their efforts (Wright, 2000, pp. 95 and 110). Secondly, the marked disillusion of the electorate with the traditional political parties in the 1990s was certainly linked with repugnance at immoral, criminal or self-seeking behaviour. Some commentators (Mény, 1992, Laughland, 1994) have denounced the corrosive impact of corruption. Some investigating magistrates and journalists have pursued cases with tenacity and vigour. The extent to which the context within which ministers and leading politicians operate offers temptations and opportunities for corrupt practices cannot be ignored. Politicians, however, recognize that they can no longer continue to rely on previous levels of public tolerance and indulgence. Roland Dumas's refusal for some time to give up the presidency of the Constitutional Council when he came under suspicion was widely deplored. In contrast, the effective and rather successful finance minister Dominique Strauss-Kahn resigned instantly when faced with judicial investigation of allegations that legal advice for which he had invoiced the French students' social insurance fund was fictitious and the invoices a way of channelling funds either to himself or his party. He admitted no guilt, but said that his sense of responsibility would not allow him to stay in office when there was any hint of irregularity. Judicial investigations relating to political funding induced the resignation of Raffarin's first minister for European Affairs, Donnedieu de Vabres, at the time of the post-electoral reshuffle.

One source of possible suspicion arose from the uses to which cash from the secret funds is put. The government had legally, but unaccountably, been using them to top up the salaries of ministers and their close collaborators. Jospin confined the secret fund strictly to the genuine needs of the secret security services. He transferred the bonuses paid to members of ministerial *cabinets* (see below) to regular (but taxable) pay packets and abolished top-ups to ministerial salaries. Since these were low – lower even than the pay of members of the National Assembly or senior officials – Raffarin faced an outcry from his ministers when they took office, and the Appropriations Act that he put through parliament in its July 2002 special session included a 70 per cent rise in salary for ministers. This was embarrassing, but a sign that transparency and responsibility were increasingly being perceived as the only option in a political environment increasingly unwilling to accord deference or allegiance to a system perceived as corrupt.

The Coordination of the Work of the Government

French government ministers enjoy a striking degree of deference within France's political and administrative structures, and, legally, a good deal of autonomy within their own fields. They may be very closely subject to control by the president or the prime minister; they may be engaged in bitter conflict with their colleagues over the scope of their responsibilities or the nature of their policies; but they are not, and do not, on the whole, feel themselves to be, part of a collegial enterprise. The weekly meeting of the Council of Ministers, with its communiqué drafted well in advance (Schifres and Sarazin, 1985) is essentially a ritual – and never more so than under *cohabitation* – rather than an opportunity for major discussions or unanticipated decisions.

Policy coordination – within the ministries

Within the ministries, policy coordination is effectively the task of the minister's private office, his *cabinet*. The current shape and role of ministers' *cabinets* in France developed during the nineteenth century and has evolved since. Every minister has attached to him a personal staff with important political and administrative functions (see Chapter 4 for the prime minister's cabinet). A minister has a free choice of these staff members; in practice, ministers have almost invariably chosen, as the head of this staff (*directeur de cabinet*) a person to whom they are politically and personally close but who also has the experience (usually through previous membership of a *cabinet*) and the status (usually through a senior official position) to carry a good deal of weight within official structures. The composition of the rest of the team may then be largely left to the *directeur*. Membership of a minister's personal staff will imply sufficient attachment to the minister's political views to ensure a degree of loyalty, but does not require identity of views. When one of Raffarin's ministers, Noelle Lenoir, was attacked as a 'traitor' on the grounds that she had deserted the politics of which she had previously given evidence by service in the *cabinet* of a Socialist minister under Rocard, the former prime minister himself defended her. She had been chosen for her firm views and her competence, not for her political convictions which had never been socialist (*Le Monde*, 18 June 2002). Political activism is hence not a requirement, although Rouban's studies have shown that since the 1980s about a third of *cabinet* members had either been active members of political parties or been involved in associations, trade unions or think-thanks where political and social issues are discussed (Rouban, 1998b, p. 178). Two other qualities are also important: professional competence and knowledge of the workings of the governmental machine.

The size of a *cabinet* may vary. Regular, but usually unsuccessful, attempts have been made to control the numbers of members of ministerial *cabinets*. Alain Juppé, fulfilling one of Chirac's campaign promises, in June 1995 reduced them from twelve to five for cabinet ministers and from between three and five for junior ministers to three. However, six months later at the time of his first reshuffle the limits were raised again to twelve for cabinet ministers, eight for delegated ministers and six for junior ministers. The websites for Raffarin's ministers show cabinets of some 12 to 18 members, not always including secretarial staff. The limit has frequently been evaded by the attachment to the *cabinet* of 'unofficial' members, and Bigaut (1997) estimates that despite the regulations, *cabinets* normally consist of between 20 and 30 staff.

Ministers are allowed a rather small sum of money with which to pay for their *cabinet*. Ministers consequently need to seek official and unofficial members whose salaries can be met from other sources especially now they can no longer top them up from secret funds. If the *cabinet* member is a serving official, he or she will be seconded to the *cabinet* with salary costs met by their department of origin. Academics are usually serving officials, and hence covered by this provision. The practice by which other bodies, especially public enterprises or non-profit associations, employed staff whom they then seconded to cabinets has increasingly come under public criticism and legal scrutiny. The Jospin government insisted that in such cases the full salary costs should be reimbursed to the body concerned (Schrameck, 2001, pp. 84–6).

The need for staff members who are familiar with the working of the governmental machine and its networks is the second major reason, alongside funding, for the choice of officials. In the 1970s, some 80–90 per cent of *cabinet* members were serving civil servants. With the coming of the Socialist government in 1981, this proportion dropped to below 70 per cent, as an increased number of people who had been on the staff of the party or of one of the trade union federations or outsiders such as journalists were appointed. From 1986 onwards, the figure has remained at or above 80 per cent. At the senior level of *directeur de cabinet* the number of 'outsiders' has been very limited indeed, although one of the consequences of the first experience of *alternance* was that 'outsiders' constituted five out of the 84 people who were *directeurs de cabinet* in the period of the Mauroy government between 1981 and 1984 (Fournier, 1987, p. 109). Now it can be said that *directeurs de cabinet* are 'all' officials (Bigaut, 1997, p. 142).

The organization of the *cabinet* may vary according to the minister's personal predilections – some are loosely structured, others more formal and hierarchical (see Thuillier, 1982, pp. 27–30; and Bigaut, 1997, pp. 107–8). In some cases, the minister may have a special adviser (*chargé de mission auprès du ministre*) who stands outside the hierarchy and is actually more powerful and influential than the *directeur de cabinet*.

The *cabinet's* tasks almost invariably fall under four headings:

- First and most mundanely, the *cabinet* is responsible for looking after the minister – ensuring that he or she has an organized round of appointments, is at the right place at the right time with the right papers.
- Secondly, the *cabinet* has the task of assisting the minister with his or her political life and with the political exposition of his or her policies. This has three facets: relationships with the party and the minister's former constituency; relationships with Parliament – preparation for debates, questions and other business; and relationships with the press and the public. In all these fields the *cabinet* staff take an active role, drafting or preparing for speeches, appearances in the media, press articles and other aspects of the minister's political life. The *cabinet* may draw on the resources of the ministry to assist, but the administrative division will not normally expect to be actively involved in the defence of policy.
- Thirdly, the *cabinet* staff are deeply involved in watching over and coordinating the work of the ministry. French ministries do not have one single official at their apex – they have no 'permanent head'. Rather, they are confederations of functional units (divisions – *directions*) each under a *directeur* or *directeur général*. Usually a group of the ministry's functions is placed under the oversight of one of the *cabinet* staff. That person will keep an eye on all that is being done, ensure that the minister's wishes are being carried out, and transmit the proposals of the ministry through to the minister. Ministers do not necessarily meet their *directeurs* very often; instead they rely upon their personal staff to act as a channel of communication. In these circumstances the role of the *cabinet* in the initiation, formulation and coordination of ministerial policy is crucial. In undertaking this role, their understanding of the minister's political intentions is very important.
- Fourthly, *cabinets* are centrally involved in interministerial coordination. The *directeur* or another member of staff represents the ministry at a great many of the interministerial meetings where policy is discussed and the different views of the different ministries are expressed. Members of the *cabinet* staff will maintain relationships with contacts in the other ministries concerned with their policy area so as to ensure that as far as possible the way is smoothed for their policy approach. For this reason it is crucial for a minister to ensure the presence in his or her *cabinet* of people from the *grands corps* who will be able to bring into play their particularly close network of contacts.

Cabinets have recently come in for a good deal of criticism, and suggestions, in reports on administrative reform, that they should be, if not abolished, at least confined to a narrower, more specifically and overtly political role. This, it is argued, would underline their political advice function, and ensure that the policy functions of the directorates within the ministries were not usurped or bypassed thus improving the quality of policy formulation and decision-making. However, *cabinets* have both policy coordination and political exposition roles which, given the nature of the administration, could not easily be located elsewhere. The *cabinet* is well described as the flexible gangplank that links the solid and unmoving quay of the administrative structures to the minister who rises and falls upon the more shifting yet dynamic waters of political life.

Policy coordination – between the ministries

In France, ministers guard their autonomy, and there is no convention of collegiality to enforce collective review and coordination of policy formulation. However, there are two mechanisms that substitute for such a convention. First, any legislative text, whether it be a bill presented to Parliament for its approval, or a regulation made under the government's constitutional powers, must bear the signature of all the ministers concerned by the proposal. Secondly, the role of the prime minister in coordinating governmental action, discussed in Chapter 4, results in large numbers of meetings between the representatives of different ministries. These meetings are called and serviced by the general secretariat of the government, usually on an ad hoc basis. Sometimes the prime minister may wish to call one to ensure that governmental plans are progressing. In other cases a minister may seek the prime minister's decision to resolve a conflict between ministries.

In all these meetings the role of the prime minister's *cabinet* is crucial. The *directeur* of the prime minister's *cabinet* holds weekly meetings of his her counterparts to coordinate governmental work. Members of the prime minister's cabinet play a leading role at all the meetings, and have the preponderant influence on the outcome. This may be a decision, or it may be the definition of the nature, extent and grounds of disagreement. The matter will then be put to the prime minister for his or her *arbitrage*. The outcome is recorded by the Secretariat General of the Government in a record called a 'blue' (*bleu*). Olivier Schrameck, Jospin's *directeur de cabinet*, records his uneasy sense that any such record might – as in the case of decisions on contaminated blood – lead in the long-distant future to legal action, even imprisonment (Schrameck, 2001, pp. 79–80). His response was to be particularly careful about decisions and about ensuring that ministers themselves took responsability for them.

There is a very large number of meetings, up to 1500 in the course of a year (Fournier, 1987, p. 201, Bigaut, 1997, p. 78). The president's staff is informed of the meetings as they occur, and of the outcome, and this continues during the periods of *cohabitation*, but during this time, members of the president's personal

staff attended only those interministerial meetings that were specifically concerned with foreign and European affairs and defence, rather than being present at almost all interministerial meetings, as is otherwise the case (Schrameck, 2001, pp. 100–2).

Much of the routine of business is undertaken on ministers' behalf by their *cabinets*, but at a higher level of coordination, there are meetings not between officials but between ministers, which may be called either by the prime minister, or by the president. Such meetings may be regular, as were those called by Jospin to deal respectively with the financing of public services and social security and with internal security and law and order (Schrameck, 2001, p. 35). As at official level, however, ad hoc meetings are much more important. These may be more or less formal meetings, of which a record is kept and distributed, or they may be informal, indeed individual, meetings such as those which the prime minister has with each minister in relation to the forthcoming year's expenditure plans. The prime minister plays a much more active, though not necessarily more influential, role than the president and different prime ministers have varied in the use they have made of such meetings.

Much of the tone and style of French public policy decision-making is set by the practice of prime ministerial *arbitrage* – an almost judicial choice between the rights and wrongs of conflicting but strongly argued viewpoints. That such a style is quite typically French and not necessarily shared throughout Western Europe becomes particularly apparent when such decisions have to be taken in new contexts, particularly the more consensual and collegial decision-making structures of the European Commission in Brussels, to which French officials find 'great difficulty' in adapting (Pascal Lamy, cited in Muller, 1992, p. 23). However, the activities of impulsion and coordination at the top are based upon a strongly entrenched administrative system, to which the next section of this chapter now turns.

The French Administrative Tradition

It is impossible to understand French public and political life without some understanding of the role which the French administration plays within society. This section considers a number of ways in which the French administrative system is distinctive. This distinctiveness stems first from historical context. The kings of the seventeenth and eighteenth centuries sought to weld the recently unified country together under their unchallenged authority. Their policies, both abroad and at home, required resources – money and manpower – and this meant the development of an administrative structure that would extract and deploy these resources. Moreover, the prosperity of the country had a direct effect upon these resources, and the King and his ministers regarded this as their concern, and took steps to foster certain types of economic activity. This activity became known as Colbertism, from the name of Louis XIV's minister Colbert, who was particularly active in economic policy.

The coming of the Revolution altered some aspects of this system, but reinforced others. The possibility of discussing and questioning governmental actions, and the possibility of making appointments to official positions on a basis that did not depend on inherited rights or the King's personal whim and favour were both opened up. It took a well over a century for both these principles to become accepted and entrenched. Since the monarch was no longer the source of authority and direction, the idea of the state became important. Just as the King had been seen as holding an overall responsibility for internal peace and order and the smooth working of society, so now the state, which was considered to be the expression of the general will of the whole nation, took over this role. The idea that central government had a good deal of responsibility for the prosperity and economic well-being of the country persisted. The revolutionary concern for equality meant that local variations and customs, and also local resistance to the authority of the central government, were suppressed. Uniformity was imposed, through the exercise of centralizing power in the name of revolutionary principles. Of crucial importance to the later development of the administration was the emergence of a body of officials in salaried posts, not purchased offices, by whom this power was exercised.

Napoleon followed the Revolution, and much of the pattern of French administration today can be traced back to the system which he developed (see p. 9, above), memorably described as '[s]tatist, powerful, hierarchically structured, ubiquitous, uniform, depoliticised, instrumental, expert and tightly controlled... a model attractive to tidy minds in untidy countries' (Wright, 1994, p. 116) Napoleon saw the administration as a force which would embody the general interest of the nation and act as a check and restraint on the narrower, more local and individual pressures and vested interests which were represented through democratic and representative institutions.

After the Second World War some of the aspects of the Napoleonic administration which had become attenuated were strengthened again. The mood of the times was for reform and restoration and, in France as elsewhere, for social democratic programmes involving, for example, nationalization and the establishment of a welfare state, that considerably increased the scope for administrative intervention. The administration of the period was confident and active, clear that the restoration and rebuilding of the French economy and society depended upon them as much as, if not more than, upon the politicians. A comprehensive reform and codification of the legislation governing the structure, terms and conditions of the civil service was undertaken, and recruitment to senior administrative posts transformed by the setting up of a new recruiting and training establishment, the *Ecole Nationale d'Administration* (ENA).

One of de Gaulle's objectives in establishing the Fifth Republic was to strengthen the legitimacy and the standing of the state. Administrative scope increased, both because more matters were left to executive regulation rather than parliamentary legislation, and because the emergence of a stable governmental majority within Parliament facilitated the passage of the legislation that was required. Foreign observers remarked upon the competence and confidence of top-level French civil servants. One of the factors underlying this image was the high standing of the administration. In 1996, 86 per cent of respondents in an opinion poll said they would be happy for their child to become a civil servant (Rouban, 1998a, p. 196). Other factors included the policy stability implied by the continuation in power of governments from within one political coalition between 1958 and 1981 and the long-term effects of the 1945 reforms upon the esteem and confidence of those who were reaching senior positions.

At the same time, this system was increasingly challenged and contested. To the ordinary citizen it seemed remote, bureaucratic, complicated and uncaring. In the 1950s Pierre Poujade, a small businessman, led a political movement which took much of its force from protests against bureaucracy, especially tax collection, and such complaints from similar groups persist. Goscinny and Uderzo, creators of the cartoon character Asterix, caricatured the smooth, elitist products of the top civil-service training establishments and portrayed the task of extracting an official document from a government office as akin to one of the labours of Hercules. The movements that are leading to increased decentralization (see Chapter 6) have resulted from dissatisfaction with the centralized nature of much of French government. The strength of these criticisms reveals the strength of the administrative tradition.

The structure of the French civil service: who is a civil servant?

In 1945, a general law – the *Statut Général de la Fonction Publique* – laid down the outlines of the terms and conditions of service for civil servants. This law was completely overhauled in 1983–4, and its guarantees extended to local government officials and health service administrators. The number of persons subject to the *statut général* in the mid-1990s was some 4.8 million (Ministère de la Fonction Publique, 1999, Meininger, 2000, p. 198). Of the rather over 1.6 million central civil servants in 1997, some 920 000 were university or school teachers, and some 126 000 police or prison officers. The civil service is based on two fundamental principles: that access is equally open to all qualified people on the basis of public competitive examination, and that it is a career service, offering lifetime employment. The law describes, in general terms, the procedures through which a person may acquire the status of a civil servant – a *fonctionnaire*. Once this status has been acquired, it conveys certain legal rights and duties and can be lost only as a result of retirement, voluntary resignation, or serious disciplinary proceedings. Civil servants can, and do, enforce the rights which their status confers on them, before the courts. In addition to the rights which civil servants enjoy, the law also places them under a number of obligations – to obey their hierarchical superiors, to be moderate in their public statements about what they do (the *obligation de reserve*), and (since the 1983 reforms) to be as informative as possible towards members of the public.

The civil service encompasses differing tasks and functions. Ministries are organized into central administrative sections and field services (*services décon-centrés*). These field services are groups of officials who are attached to the central ministry and organized by them, but who are stationed throughout France. Customs officers and tax inspectors are attached to the Ministry of Finance, the police of the national police force are attached to the Ministry of the Interior and so, since the summer of 2002, are the *Gendarmerie* although they retain their military status. All teachers in state education, at every level from nursery school to university, are officials of the Ministry of Education. Social security in France, however, is organized through a network of agencies which employ their own staff, so those who deal with claims and benefits are not civil servants. The consequence of these structures, combined with the French notions of the role of the state and the public services, is a relatively high level of staffing, concentrated in the central ministries.

The key role of the state and the central administration is symbolized within each of the 96 *départements* (counties) of France by the presence of a central government official, the prefect, who is the local representative of the state, with an appropriately impressive uniform and ceremonial functions, but also with the task of overseeing the activities of the central government bodies within the area (see Chapter 6).

'Corps' and 'grands corps'

In both the central administrations and the field services, civil servants are organized into categories defined by the educational qualification required for entry. Each of these categories is made up of a number of different *corps*.

In English the word 'corps' is familiar from its use for the diplomatic corps, and also for certain groups within the armed services. In France the oldest civil service *corps* were originally formed of civilian technical specialists, the bridges and highways engineers (*corps des ponts et chaussées*) founded in 1747 and the mining engineers, whose *corps* dates from 1744. Nowadays all established civil servants are members of a *corps*, that is a group of officials engaged at different levels in the same task or group of tasks, all of whom enjoy the same specific terms and conditions of service, and who may expect to enjoy a career progression within the *corps*. The largest *corps* is the primary school teachers, a *corps* in Category B, that is to say that the basic entry level requirement is at the level of at least the *baccalauréat* (the school leaving examination taken at age 18) but below full degree level.

Members of a *corps* may start their career with a period of specialized training: thus tax inspectors (a category A *corps* requiring a degree level qualification for entry) start at the national taxation college (*école nationale des impôts*) and magistrates (a category A *corps* attached to the Ministry of Justice) at the national magistrates' training college (*école nationale de la magistrature*).

The *corps* system with its competitive entry examination system, a feature which is held to be essential in ensuring objectively equal chances to all qualified applicants, puts specific hurdles in the path of any career rising from the lowest to the highest position, and in fact very few are able to do so. It also puts clear limits on the extent to which promotion on the basis of performance on the job is possible. Equally, however, especially within the smaller *corps*, close connections and cooperation can develop. This may foster coordination, working together, even innovation, though it also fosters defence of common and vested interests and determination not to surrender acquired rights and status.

The most prominent *corps* are the so-called *grands corps* (see Table 5.2). They, with the recruitment and training establishments through which most of their members pass, have a special and distinctive place within the administration and within French social structure. All the *grands corps* were founded over 150 years ago. All are small, cohesive and influential. Although each has specific tasks formally assigned to it, and in some cases other areas of activity to which it has

TABLE 5.2

Grands Corps and Grandes Ecoles

Corps	Founded	Membership				Recruited through	Entry level
		Men	Women	Total	Active within corps		
Bridges and highway engineers [1]	1713/1716				1 320	*Ecole polytechnique* founded 1794	*Baccalauréat* plus preparatory classes
Mining engineers[2]	1793				562		
Prefects[3]	1800	109	7	116		*Ecole Nationale d'Administration,* founded 1945	University degree or period in service
Diplomatic Corps[4]	1589 (ministry) 1799 (*corps*)				1 106		
Council of State[3]	1800	244	60	302	208		
Court of Accounts[3]	1807	305	56	361	181		
Finance Inspectorate[3]	1831	181	18	199	67		

Notes:

1. in 2000 (http://www.imprimerie.polytechnique.fr/CenterView.cfm? Table = Enseignement&ID = 916).

2. 1 January 2002 (http://www.syndim.net/Public/Presentation_corps_mines.htm).

3. 31 December 2000 (Le Pors and Milowski, 2002, p. 77).

4. 31 December 1999 (http://www.ladocumentationfrancaise.fr/BRP/014000697/0001.pdf p.158).

staked a long-standing and by now irrefutable claim, the prestige and status which each enjoys allow its members to benefit, both individually and collectively, from a high degree of autonomy in the organization of their working life and careers.

There are reckoned to be three, or perhaps five, 'administrative' *grands corps* and two 'technical' *grands corps* (Table 5.2). The three leading administrative *grands corps* are all, formally, importantly concerned with controlling and checking the work of other civil servants. Indeed, in general within the French civil service, those who are concerned with checks and controls tend to enjoy a higher status than those whose chief task is the execution of policy. The administrative *corps* are the Council of State, which is the highest court in administrative law cases and also the government's chief legal advisory body (see below), the Court of Accounts, which is the audit authority for public funds, and the Finance Inspectorate, whose formal task is the checking and control of financial procedures in any body which disburses public funds. The prefectoral *corps* and the diplomatic service are also categorized as *grands corps* by some commentators. The technical *grands corps* are the bridges and highway engineers and the mining engineers.

The administrative *grands corps* are mainly, though not exclusively, recruited through the National Administrative College – the *Ecole Nationale d'Administration* (ENA). Students are entitled to choose their posts in the order of their final assessment results. The highest ranked invariably choose the *grands corps*. The ENA was set up in 1945 in order to reform and revitalize recruitment to the senior levels of the French civil service. Its founder and six former students have now served as prime minister, and two of its graduates have become president of the Republic. It has from the start admitted men and women, though women constituted only 4.6 per cent of those who attended the ENA in its first 30 years. From the mid-1970s the proportion of women has risen to around 15 per cent at the end of the 1980s to about 40 per cent by the early 2000s. In 2000 the first female director (Marie-Françoise Bechtel) was appointed. The number of places offered each year has varied. In the 1960s the annual intake was around 60 to 70. In the 1970s the intake was expanded, rising from about 130 to around 150 by the mid-1980s. It was cut back sharply in 1986, partly to preserve the ENA's high status and partly to emphasize the government's determination to reduce the scope and role of the state, and, in the early 2000s, runs at just over 100 plus about 40 long-course foreign students(www.ena.fr). Between a half and two-thirds of its places each year are offered, by competitive entry examination, to people with at least a university degree. Most of the remaining one-third to one-half of the places (the proportion has been varied over the years) are offered to those who have already served for a certain period within the public service without the formal requirement of any academic qualification, although in practice, success in the competitive examination for these places requires academic ability of a level comparable to degree standard, and many successful entrants from within the public service have been at least as well qualified academically as their colleagues from the other 'external' competition.

The ENA has been, and continues to be, much criticized. It is readily portrayed as favouring those who have benefited from a particular type of elite, bourgeois, Parisian culture, and as providing an abstract, detached, intellectually rigorous and very demanding, but essentially impractical training. In response to these views Socialist governments took two controversial decisions. In the early 1980s a highly controversial new form of entry was introduced, in an attempt to restimulate one of the original motives for the creation of the ENA, that of 'democratizing' the entry. This so-called 'third way' (*troisième voie*) was immediately denounced by the government's opponents as a back-door way of opening up civil service posts to Communist trade-union delegates. Although the Chirac government abolished this after 1986, the need to open up the ENA was acknowledged by all. In 1990 a modified and less controversial *troisième voie* was created. Secondly, following a much contested decision by Edith Cresson in the early 1990s, part of the training of each cohort of students now takes place, expensively and inconveniently, in Strasbourg so that its European dimension is more fully developed.

The ENA serves three main purposes: first it conducts the initial recruitment of potential top civil servants; secondly, through its own testing, examining and ranking processes it selects the members of the different *corps* and thus marks out those who are destined for truly high-flying careers, and thirdly it provides an initiation into various aspects of administrative life and a measure of work experience and training.

The technical *grands corps* are recruited through the *Ecole polytechnique*. This recruits all its students from outside the public service, taking in about 300 a year. Its competitive entry examinations require two or three years of preparation in the special classes attached to some secondary schools, at well above the level of the *baccalauréat*. The *Ecole Polytechnique*, founded in 1794, is a military establishment, not opened to women until the early 1970s, and its students always take a prominent place in the military parades of the 14 July, but they are not necessarily destined for military careers. Its curriculum is a broad one, in applied science and engineering science, with some economics and management, though ability in mathematics remains the key to success. As with the ENA, the final ranking of the students is perhaps its most important function. Those achieving the highest places go on to further technical and management training in the college of their particular *corps*, and then into the appropriate ministry.

The *grands corps* are not the only *corps* into which the ENA and the *Ecole Polytechnique* recruit – students from the ENA who do not achieve the *grands corps* go on, amongst other possibilities, to be general administrators (*administrateurs civils*) or judges in the administrative courts. They are, however, particularly prominent. There is no longer automatically a 20 per cent gap between the starting salary of an ENA graduate in the Council of State, the Finance Inspectorate or the Court of Accounts and all the others, but the *grands corps* undoubtedly offer more interesting career prospects. Their small size means that new members quickly build up useful contacts. Senior members of the *corps* attempt to aid the career prospects of their juniors. The reputation which the *grands corps* members enjoy of being the most able of an already highly selected group ensures that interesting offers are made to them. They are able to leave the work of their *corps* on a secondment basis to take up senior policy positions throughout the administration. Certain positions are virtually guaranteed to them. Thus many of the senior posts in the Ministry of Industry are occupied by mining engineers; the bridges and highway engineers are particularly concerned with public works and town planning, whilst members of the Finance Inspectorate are to be found in many senior economic and financial policy posts. At any one time between one-third and one-half of the members of any of the administrative *corps* are likely to be working away from the formal tasks of their *corps*. To these formal tasks they can, however, at any moment return, a 'safety net' which can be of considerable importance in the development of a career.

Civil service management

The provision of a distinctive legal framework for the structures of civil service employment has, since its inception in 1946, which followed long debates by reformers and the Trade Unions (Jones, 1993, p. 146; Thuillier and Tulard, 1984, p. 84; Bodiguel *et al.*, 2000, pp. 39–47), been seen as a crucial guarantee of the integrity and above all the independence of the civil service. Administrative law in France thus concerns itself not only with the relationship of the citizen to the state, but also with 'the state administration as inhabiting an autonomous domain apart from civil society' (Clark, 1998, p. 100). This in turn has had a profound influence on the deployment and management of human resources within the civil service and on expectations about, and the nature of, the careers it offers since 'many crucial aspects of public service management...fall within the jurisdiction of the administrative courts' (Clark, 1998, p. 100).

One consequence is that the management of the French civil service presents a number of striking contrasts. In much of the civil service, structures are formal and hierarchical. There is an emphasis on rank and a very precise definition of the scope and powers of each official. For example, the signature of letters, or contacts with other parts of the administration may be undertaken only at relatively senior levels, so activities pass up and down the hierarchy. Careers in much of the service are predictable, and promotion depends largely upon seniority. The notion that management, in the sense of the effective use of personnel and resources, is a task that might be crucial is permeating the civil service only rather slowly under the influence of Anglo-American models.

There have been reform programmes. One was launched under the heading 'the renewal of the state' by Rocard in 1989, another by Juppé in 1995, and Jospin extended the process with ongoing attempts to ensure that the role of the centre was reduced. Chirac's decentralization proposals, set out in his message to Parliament in July 2002 will, if implemented, result in further reshaping. But reforms have seldom challenged the essential shape of civil service structures and operations, and in particular have not affected the status and conditions of *fonctionnaires*. In so far as they have done so, these have required extremely careful negotiation and have not infrequently failed. It did prove possible to change the status of the Post Office from a ministry to a public body. But attempts in 2000 by the then minister of the economy and finances, Christian Sautter, to co-locate the tax assessment and collection services caused such an uproar that Prime Minister Jospin required the withdrawal of the plans and Sautter lost his job.

The rigidity and regulation of the lower levels of the civil service forms a marked contrast to the flexibility and autonomy at the higher levels. At the highest levels, hierarchies can be overruled, for example by the device of attaching a young high-flier directly to the head of a section of the ministry to write a report or develop a particular policy. Members of the *grands corps* and other high-fliers can to a certain extent direct their own careers, helped by the assistance and patronage of senior members of their *corps* who will be anxious to 'send the lift back down' to bring up the junior members of their own *corps*, and will seek to ensure that they have positions that reflect well upon the status of the *corps*.

Some very senior French civil servants are able to act with a degree of authority and a public profile that resembles that of some ministers. The reasons that account for this autonomy include French notions that officials serve the state and the general interest rather than being entirely subordinate to a minister; the centuries-old acceptance that officials properly intervene in wide areas of economic and social life; and the legitimacy that civil servants owe to their reputation for technical and academic competence. In such circumstances the balance between politicians and administrators becomes a key factor and the question of the politicization of the upper levels of the civil service assumes particular importance.

Political administrative relationships

The French administration in general continues to be suffused by an ethos of bureaucratic order, of hierarchy and of the necessity for neutral and universal rules and legally regulated procedures. This derives from a Republican notion of democracy, requiring predictable decisions, and an absence of abitrary discretion (Wright, 1997). 'Independence' is taken to be an integral part of the French concept of the public service. This enables officials to insist ideologically on a clear distinction between the political and administrative spheres. Their guaranteed career is seen as a necessary safeguard of their obligation of neutrality. This obligation is understood to imply that a civil servant must deal in an even-handed way with all members of the public, regardless of their political or other opinions or actions. The concept of 'neutrality' is applied to the ways that civil servants look outwards towards the public, not to the ways in which they look upwards to their minister. In practice – and paradoxically – however, this autonomy, while its impact on most officials is limited to providing a security which continues to render public employment attractive, provides a great deal of scope for the administrative elite to play proactive roles.

Indeed, as Michel Crozier asserted as long ago as 1963 (Crozier, 1963, p. 364) the role of the members of the *grands corps* and other members of the administrative elite as agents of change and of mediation between the bureaucracy and the outside world is crucial (Quermonne, 1991, p. 152).

If ministers cannot depend upon a civil service culture which emphasizes subservience to the minister's wishes as a first priority, other methods are needed to ensure that policy congenial to the minister and the government is proposed, prepared and in due course implemented. The *cabinets* discussed above play an important role, but equally important is the freedom which the civil service law gives to the government to make appointments to senior posts within the civil service (*postes à discretion*) from any source. For a certain defined number of top posts, the law allows the government to make appointments which take into account the political affiliations of the person appointed. These affiliations will be known, since the personal political activities of civil servants are not restricted, beyond the requirement to be discreet about their actual work and avoid direct criticism of their minister. A study of the people who held posts as heads of central ministry directorates between 1984 and 1995 found that 36 per cent of them were actively politically committed (Rouban, 1998b, p. 180). Some 400 posts are affected by this provision, all of them at the most senior levels – prefects, heads of regional educational administration (*recteurs d'académie*), heads of directorates within the ministries. Many of these posts are not particularly politically prominent or sensitive, and ministers will usually fill them with competent people from within the career, with little attention to their political orientation. Almost all prefects are thus appointed from within the prefectoral *corps*.

The government's ability to fill prominent posts with people in whose attachment to their approach ministers can feel a degree of confidence can, at certain times, result in substantial changes (see Table 5.3). Not all the changes result from politically motivated considerations. Of the 1988 changes, about half seemed to have been undertaken for specifically political motives, nearly half of these in just two ministries: Education and the Interior, which, with the Interior and Foreign Affairs, regularly see the largest number of changes (Rouban, 1998b, p. 179). Administrative restructuring and natural career progression are also factors but the figures are striking.

TABLE 5.3

Proportion of Director posts in the central administration where the incumbent changed

1958–9	1962–3	1981–3	1986–7	1988–9	1993–4	1995–6
33.9	35.5	68	82.5	45.6	55.6	42.5

Source: Rouban, 1998b, p. 180.

This is possible in part because honourable outlets for those displaced can be found. A number of them move fairly directly into private sector posts but removal from a sensitive post does not necessarily mean departure from the public service. It may be possible for those concerned to take up posts of similar status but less prominence: for members of the *grands corps* a return to their *corps* of origin is a possibility; many senior positions within nationalized industries and public enterprises are filled by former civil servants whose formal position is one of long-term secondment; the new regional authorities have recruited senior staff from the central civil service. Those who replace them almost always – between 1984 and 1995 to the extent of 96 per cent – come from within the civil service themselves, although there is no formal requirement that they should do so.

There is a range of devices, from the fully legal – *postes à discretion*, the distribution of pay bonuses – to the probably illegal (Rouban, 1998b, p. 181), which ministers can employ to ameliorate the rigid specifications of pay and conditions and ensure they have a team that suits them. Edith Cresson's *cri de coeur* against accusations of nepotism within the European Commission 'are we supposed only to work with people we do not know?' reflects a situation with which she was familiar in France.

Control of the Administration

The French civil service is subject to four main types of oversight and scrutiny. They are: ministerial and parliamentary oversight, internal administrative oversight, legal oversight, and oversight by the *médiateur de la République* (ombudsman). The minister is legally the hierarchical head of the ministry and consequently has powers to issue circulars and directives laying down the ways in which the ministry, in all its various branches and services, is to operate. Ministerial oversight over these operations is exercised through the minister's *cabinet* and through the minister's ability to appoint his or her own nominees to senior posts. This ensures that the general orientation of the ministry's work is in line with the orientations defined by the government. However, long traditions of administrative autonomy and the absence of a strong political impetus for ministers to exert managerial control of their ministry mean that in practice the minister may intervene relatively rarely in the ongoing activities of many parts of the ministry. Here a major influence is the weight of the traditions and concepts specific to that particular ministry, and the concepts and approaches of the *corps* of officials of which it is made up.

Ministers are not forced by parliament to take a close interest in the individual decisions, and particular activities of the ministry. Equally members of parliament do not see the resolution of the personal grievances of their constituents as a very major part of their functions. Parliamentary questions (see Chapter 7) are limited in time and scope, and the executive actions of ministries virtually never scrutinized in detail unless some major public scandal prompts a parliamentary enquiry. The overall policy orientation of each ministry is scrutinized by

Parliament when the annual budget (appropriation) for that ministry is voted, but the subsequent execution of the policy is seldom followed up.

Parliamentary oversight over the work of the administration is relatively weak, but there are powerful internal administrative controls. A number of ministries have *corps* of inspectors attached to them; thus a *corps* of inspectors attached to the Ministry of the Interior oversees the activities of the national police force. Amongst other important inspectorates are the inspectors of social affairs, and the general inspectorate of the administration, which is in fact attached to the Ministry of the Interior, which oversees the activities not only of the central ministry but also of the prefectures. The most prestigious of all the inspectorates is the inspectorate of finance. These latter three inspectorates recruit the majority of their members directly from the graduating students of the ENA. Other inspectorates tend to recruit senior officials towards the end of their careers; indeed a post in such a *corps* may be a useful and honourable outlet for a senior official whose previous post is needed for a younger or more politically acceptable successor.

In practice, inspections are rare and episodic for any individual part of the administration. However, French financial procedures are generally tightly specified. Expenditure has to be authorized by someone other than the person actually responsible for disbursement, and the Ministry of Finance has one of its officials stationed in each ministry – the *contrôleur financier* – to undertake this. The courts of accounts, at central or regional level, undertake the subsequent audits, and report to the president of the Republic; the officials of the courts of accounts have the status of magistrates and the legal power to fine those found guilty of the improper use of state funds. Such auditing can occasionally reveal major scandals.

In general, internal oversight of the administration has been concerned with ensuring that it operates legally, in accordance with proper procedures. However, in 1988 as part of a wider programme of what he called public service renewal, Michel Rocard attempted to introduce provisions for far-reaching policy evaluation. In 1995 a circular from Prime Minister Juppé, taking forward a programme of administrative reform, identified evaluation as one of the core roles of the central administration and attempted to revivify it by linking it to devolved decision-making and ministerial modernization plans. However, the area is a potentially fraught one. Evaluation is liable to question the merits of the policy decisions that have been made, and while that may suit the technocrats it is likely to prove uncomfortable for politicians in a context of continuous political competition. It is scarcely surprising that ministers were not interested in encouraging studies. Indeed, evaluation has been described as 'a long series of failures' (Rouban, 1998a, p. 113). There is considerable resistance to notions of the monitoring of performance. In contrast to the position in the United Kingdom, the Budget Division of the French Finance Ministry 'remained strongly opposed to structural changes or even managerial principles because its predominant tools for public expenditure regulation remained public sector wages and cuts in intervention credits' (Bezes, 2001, p. 54). Indeed there is a surprising absence in France of internal financial management and information systems. As they expand their role into some elements of value-for-money audit – still a barely translatable concept – some of the regional Courts of Accounts are trying to develop such systems, but they will inevitably be difficult to graft onto already very cumbersome accounting procedures.

The French legal system includes a system of administrative courts. Ever since the Revolution it has been thought inappropriate for the ordinary civil courts to hear cases which involve complaints against the actions of the state; and it is, therefore, through a system of administrative courts that citizens must seek redress for grievances. Any action by the administration which contravenes general legal principles or which is specifically detrimental to a member of the public can be challenged before these courts, and the legal terms and conditions which govern employment within the public service are also enforceable within these courts. Access to them is relatively cheap and simple, but the courts are very busy, and cases may take a long time. Many citizens do pursue their grievances against the administration through these courts, which constitute an important source of protection for the public. Amongst the largest categories of cases which come before the administrative courts are those related to the individual employment conditions of officials, and also those concerned with taxation. Physical planning, and matters affecting the environment, have in recent years given rise to an increasing number of cases (Brown and Garner, 1983, pp. 189–90).

Appeals against the decisions of the administrative courts are heard by the Council of State (Conseil d'Etat) in Paris. The Council of State (see also Chapter 3) is a body which can trace its origins back to the royal councils of the pre-revolutionary monarchy. Nowadays it has two main functions: first it is the senior administrative court, acting especially as a court of appeal in administrative law cases. In fulfilling these functions the Council of State operates as a court of law. Secondly, the Council of State is the government's chief legal advisory body. The drafts of laws and of regulations are submitted to it before they are debated in Parliament or issued by the government and the government may also invite it more generally to give its views on legal questions. The government is not obliged to incorporate its amendments into the texts, or to have regard to its views, but they are usually taken seriously.

The independence of the Council's judgements and advice is enhanced by its status as one of the *grands corps*, with the consequent lifetime guarantees of employment and career and in addition the status and independence that comes from tradition, and membership of a small (around 300) and very highly regarded body, where promotion is automatic and dependent only upon seniority. There is a close sense of collegiality – literally an *esprit de corps*. A minority of its members are directly appointed later in their careers, often, but not always, from within other parts of the civil service.

There are, however, many situations where what is at stake is not so much the legality of the administration's activities as its fairness. In 1973 an 'ombudsman' was appointed following Scandinavian precedents. Called the *médiateur de la république*, the person concerned is appointed for a single term of six years (Clark, 1984). Complaints have to reach the *médiateur* through a member of the National Assembly or the Senate, although this rule has at times been quite flexibly interpreted – the *médiateur* sometimes begins to look into a complaint whilst advising the complainant to seek the help of a Member of Parliament. If the the complaint is judged well-founded, the action required to remedy the matter is recommended to the administrations concerned. Although there are no formal legal sanctions to back up the recommendations, they have largely been effective.

The *médiateur* makes an annual report to the President, which allows matters of general concern that have emerged from all the individual cases to be highlighted. Reports from the *médiateur* were important factors in the introduction, during the late 1970s, of further reforms which have enhanced the ability of members of the public to comprehend and scrutinize official decisions. In 1978 a law specified that individuals had the right to know what information was held about them on computerized records, including official records. Official records may not include information about an individual's social origins or political, philosophical or religious opinions. The application of the law is overseen by the *Commission Nationale de l'Informatique et des Libertés* (CNIL) – the national committee for computerization and liberties. A similar body, the *Commission d'Accès aux Documents Administratifs* – the committee for access to administrative documents – oversees the application of another law, also dating from 1978, which provides that citizens have a right to see all official documents except those specifically exempt.

Despite a legislative framework that provides a potentially impressive degree of open government, and continuous efforts over the past decade or so to render the administration less forbidding and to assist members of the public in their contacts with it – the provision of better information and reception services, for instance – in general, the image of the French administration remains one of remoteness, complexity and arcane procedures. The formal mechanisms for controlling the administration are substantial and extensive, but they are not reinforced by powerful political pressures. The opposition is more likely to attack the incumbent government over general policy than over the detailed execution of its programmes, and there is little crusading or investigative journalism. The climate, however, has been changing, even if slowly, partly as a result of decentralization (see Chapter 6) and partly as a result of the general growth of more 'liberal' ideas, readier to see the citizen not so much as the subject of the state but as the consumer of state services.

The Nature of Policy-Making: Image and Reality

The traditions and structures described above are important only in so far as they have real consequences for the shaping of public policy in France. The making and implementation of policies shapes the processes of public life in France and has a major influence on French social and political culture. The final section of this chapter looks at some of the consequences of the nature of the French administration and the debates that have surrounded the analysis of these consequences.

A technocratic republic?

The French administration began to recruit specialists to its service before the Revolution. By the middle of the nineteenth century it was already clear, from the discussions of what training should be given to civil servants, for example, that politicians and public expected the servants of the state to be expert and involved in a wide range of practical and technical matters. The *grandes écoles*, such as the *Ecole Polytechnique*, provided the confidence and expertise which reinforced their involvement. Despite a rhetoric of 'laissez faire' the state came increasingly, at the end of the nineteenth and into the twentieth centuries, to undertake activities in the sphere of economic development, especially the provision of economic infrastructure, and in the central provision of local services, whether education, policing, agricultural advice or public works. The experience of war merely reinforced this trend. The discrediting of some commercial and industrial leaders after the Second World War reinforced the view held by many senior civil servants at that period, especially the younger ones, that the renewal and reconstruction of the French state depended largely upon their efforts.

Public opinion has largely supported these claims. The fact that the civil service training schools form the apex of a very competitive education system means that those who succeed in gaining top level posts can easily be perceived as the most able members of society, and hence likely to produce the 'best' solutions. Moreover, problems of public policy and administration have not occupied a large space within French political debate and conflict. Many areas of public policy are thus 'depoliticized' so that civil servants have wide scope for autonomous action. Bruno Jobert has pointed out (Jobert and Muller, 1987; Jobert, 1989) that these themes come together in a 'scientists' consensus' linking the ruling elite, the professionals and public opinion. 'This sacred alliance of science and the state has been the ideological foundation of the concept of public service since the Third Republic. In that positivist age the best solution to the nation's problems seemed to be to let them be treated by scientifically trained professionals with the least possible interference from politicians' (Jobert, 1989). De Gaulle's reinforcement of the executive and tendency to call upon officials to full political posts reinforced this image.

Not the least of the paradoxes of the French system of policy-making has been the combination of sharp criticism of officialdom at all levels with considerable public support for the preservation of public services and a willingness to see officials protect their status and acquired rights. French governments have generally been attached to the notion that certain core public services must, in pursuit of the republican principles of equality, be provided by the state on an equal basis for all. The issue is further discussed in Chapter 10. However, the notion of a technocratic state which can be deduced from these characteristics has not gone unchallenged, and the following sections explore the debate.

French policy style

The debate about technocracy is linked to a debate about how policies are made and what the outcome of the policy-making process is. The particular features which combine in any one country to make these processes different there from elsewhere are sometimes described as the national 'policy style'. Observers of French public policy have noted the huge efforts of rebuilding and reconstruction undertaken after the war, the extent of social change in the post-war decades, and the rate of growth in the French economy up to the 1970s. The first two decades of the Fifth Republic saw a new impetus given to major projects and developments: the building of the new airport at Roissy, and of the new suburban rail network in Paris; the high speed train (*train à grande vitesse* – TGV) network; the vast improvement and modernization of France's previously very backward telephone system; the huge nuclear power programme which has resulted in the building of over 90 nuclear power stations; the programme of nationalization that accompanied the arrival in power of the Mitterrand government in 1981 and, in contrast, the privatizations between 1986 and 1988. All these seemed evidence that French policy 'style' was one that could be described as 'heroic'. The state, through the actions of its senior officials, could make large-scale decisions and sustain their implementation. The image is one of a strong and centralized state, capable of making and imposing far-reaching decisions (Elgie and Griggs, 2000, pp. 7–11).

The image is certainly not altogether false. These programmes have been successfully implemented. Civil servants were crucial to their launching, sustaining and achievement. Where a political decision has been taken to set a certain priority, and put large resources into it, the control of these resources gives the appropriate part of the administration considerable clout, and may result in a marked degree of success, as in the case of the modernization of telecommunications or the building of the TGV. But other efforts have failed or been watered down, and many other policy areas are handled in quite different ways. In such circumstances the evolution of policy can only be slow, incremental, indeed opportunist. In most circumstances and for most of the time the capacity and indeed the willingness of the French administration to formulate and implement a clear and distinctive policy may be limited (Cawson *et al.*, 1990).

Muller (1992) takes the argument further. He notes that many of the major policies of modernization and construction were based upon the particular vision of groups of civil servants for whom the constraints of the market were only a part of the constraints, including technological and industrial factors, which had to be overcome. The needs of the consumer were thought to be attained by the achievement of the technical objective of the policy. Consequently, the most successful projects – whether the construction of major new public works in Paris, or the TGV, or the Ariane rocket – were achieved where the demand was essentially political, not economic. The TGV is part of a very highly subsidized network which does not pay its way. Not only was this approach a very segmented one, it was, in the 1980s and 1990s, fundamentally challenged by two new features. They are, first, the increasing importance of European Union policies, which adopt a much more open, market-oriented approach (see Chapter 10) and, secondly, the impact of decentralization (see Chapter 6) which has increasingly meant the setting of policy agendas at local rather than central levels.

A shattered monolith

A major limitation upon the policy formulation and implementation capacity of the French administration is its fragmented nature. Over recent years this has increasingly been recognized, in contrast to earlier emphases, which tended to view the French administration as a vital constituent part of a powerful, monolithic, centralized and coherent state. Observations which focused upon the institutional structures and formal descriptions of the powers and responsibilities of the French administration reinforced this monolithic image. Little traits – the fact that only certain senior officials may be authorized to sign any letters emanating from a ministry, for example – emphasize a rigid hierarchy, as does a certain social and institutional deference shown to senior officials. It is not difficult to assume that the French administration must reflect a combination of the French taste for neat abstract rationality and Napoleonic organizational precision.

During the last 20 years this image has been repeatedly challenged. A number of factors have been identified which produce lack of cohesion, incoherence and conflicts within the administration. They include:

- policy and political disagreements between parts of the administration;
- 'territorial' conflicts within and between ministries;
- the relationship of parts of the administration with their external environment;
- the career patterns of certain administrators.

The policy and political disagreements that produce tensions between ministers (see above) are reproduced within the ministries. For example, conflicts between the Ministry of Finance and the spending ministries are endemic. Moreover, not only are all officials, even senior officials, not cast in the same mould, as a study of the ideological and career choices of the graduates of the ENA clearly shows, but they may also change their attitudes as they change posts and functions within the administrative framework to take on the approach dictated by the requirements, ethos and tradition of the job they happen to be doing (Suleiman, 1974, ch. IX).

A second powerful factor producing conflict is the definition of the scope of certain activities. In principle, the rational legal framework of administrative responsibilities precludes most such conflict. In practice, boundary disputes do arise. In 2002, disputes were reported between the Minsitry of Justice and the

Ministry of the Interior under a very activist minister who had already extended his empire by annexing the gendarmerie (*Le Point*, 26 July 2002). Conflict may result from a whole group of officials attempting to extend their field, as when the bridges and highway engineers moved into town planning, or the telecommunications engineers looked to the extension of information technology and electronic services to extend their range. It may also result from individual disputes between branches of ministries. Sometimes they are based on functions. For example, conflicts between technical administrative considerations and political or electoral considerations in policy formulation and implementation are almost institutionalized in the often fraught relationships between a ministry's divisions and the minister's *cabinet*. Both these factors are crucially influenced by administrative relationships with their external environment. In effect the fragmentation and divisions of civil society are echoed and reflected within the institutions of the state. For example, Pierre Grémion's highly influential study (1976) showed that prefects, ostensibly the channel through which the powerful central state secured the local implementation of policies (see Chapter 6) were constrained and deeply influenced by local pressures, and were to an equal degree the means through which local forces shaped and adapted policy to particular local circumstances. Similarly, Dupuy and Thoenig (1985) argue that policy may be differentially applied, as administrators seek to pass on its social, political and indeed financial costs. They cite the example of the local *gendarmerie* who will enforce regulations relating to long-distance lorry freight but only against vehicles originating outside their own *département* (French vehicle number plates make the identification of such lorries very easy).

Within the administration, moreover, different groups of officials or individuals have different personal and career interests. At the very top, the products of the different routes to the top – the graduates of the *Ecole Polytechnique* and the ENA, for instance – jealously guard the particular posts to which they feel they and those who shared their route to the top are entitled, and try to ward off encroachments by the rival establishment.

An interlocking elite

Such rivalries do not merely occur within strictly official posts. One of the marked characteristics of the social background to French government and politics is the closely interlocking nature of the elite which occupies the senior posts in every branch of activity – politics, the civil service, public enterprise, the big private companies, the media. In 1998 a study found that 66 per cent of the chairmen of the top 40 French companies had attended either the the the *Ecole Polytechnique* or the *Ecole National d'Administration* (Maclean *et al.*, 2001, p. 323). In 2002, the head of the employers' confederation (the MEDEF), Ernest-Antoine Sellière, was also an *énarque* as were seven out of 39 ministers in the Raffarin government, which also included one graduate of the *Ecole Polytechnique*. This closely linked elite is a relatively small grouping. One study has identified 2950 individuals holding directorships in the top 100 companies of industry in 1998 (Maclean *et al.*, 2001, p. 323). To this might be added the incumbents of senior civil service posts making a plausible total of perhaps 5000. It is based effectively on small-scale institutions, very much smaller than the 'old-boys networks' of 'Oxbridge' or the 'Ivy League' (Maclean *et al.*, 2001, p. 318; Ezra Suleiman in *Le Point*, 22 March 2002), which largely feed initially into government postings, and it is often underpinned by social contacts, family relationships and marital connections. It is reasonable to suggest that once the initial fierce academic hurdles of the entry competitions to the training institutions have been successfully surmounted, '[i]t is not primarily "what you know" but "who you know", not expert knowledge but clever networking, which still matters most in French business' (*The Economist*, 16 November 2002) and in the French public service today.

The Fifth Republic has seen a diminution in some aspects of *dirigisme* but an increase in the penetration of businesses by officials. Serving officials are quite often appointed to the boards of directors of public enterprises and companies in which the state has an interest (for the role of the state in relation to the boards of directors of the SNCF and of Airbus Industrie, see Suleiman and Courty, 1997, pp. 111–15). The competence of government officials in relation to economic and industrial matters is broadly accepted in France: because senior officials have reached their posts through jumping the highest hurdles in a stiffly competitive educational system; because the necessity for the state to be active in economic affairs has been largely unquestioned; and because experience in high-level policy areas is held to provide both a breadth of view and a network of contacts which careers within a firm or company cannot match, former officials, especially from the more relevant ministries, and with the *grands corps* fulfilling the roles that elsewhere headhunters play (Sadran, 1997, p. 132), are frequently appointed to senior posts in industrial and commercial concerns, whether public enterprises or private concerns.

Movement between public service and business, which is known as *pantouflage* – putting on one's slippers in the supposedly more comfortable ambience of the commercial or industrial world – is no novelty. It has been a feature of the careers, for example, of the Finance Inspectorate since the last century. However, it has become more widespread. In 1975, just over 10 per cent of the former students of the ENA were employed in the public or private enterprise. In 1997 the proportion had reached 20 per cent (Sadran, 1997, p. 131) and in 2002, 30 per cent of the top 400 French companies were headed by *inspecteurs de finance* (*Le Point*, 26 July 2002). Movement out of the public service seems to be occurring at an increasingly young age and more and more to be regarded as part of a standard career path. As the role of the state has changed, government intervention 'become more circumscribed' (Schmidt, 1997, p. 239) and ENA training somewhat more managerial, the attraction of movement has grown. 'French government elites', in Vivien Schmidt's words, have managed to preserve their position as France has moved from a state-lead to a market-lead economy. Moreover they 'could be confident that the increasingly independent and interdependent French businesses would be run as they would have run them themselves – or would run them themselves in the near future' (Schmidt, 1997, p. 236). The interlocking circles of cross-ownership and directorships which were a feature of privatization are further discussed in Chapter 10.

Industrial and commercial links run alongside the movement of officials directly from administrative life to political activity as parliamentary candidates, members of Parliament or ministers, discussed above. In these circumstances it is easy to be fearful that the interconnections were becoming damagingly close and the whole system unhealthy. In practice, whilst the social interconnections that result are undeniable, and the French political, administrative, financial, industrial and commercial elite is remarkably concentrated, it can also be argued that the damage is limited by two factors. The first is the fragmentation and divergent interests within both administration and the competitive world of industry and commerce. The second is the recognition of the dangers, attempts to regulate, such as the provisions since 1995 that officials must seek the authorization of an independent committee before taking up a post outside the civil service, and more intense scrutiny by judicial investigation.

Conclusion

The observation that France possesses a particularly small and rather strongly interconnected elite does not imply that this elite is not riven with conflicts that derive from position, background, values and ideologies and simple personal ambition. The structures of the machine express the desire of all governments to coordinate and make governing effective. The rhetoric of a strong and expert central authority persists, and the nature of the elite, and the expectations, rules and relationships of political – administrative relationships give the French central government machine a distinctive flavour. But as both Robert Elgie and Stephen Griggs (2000, Chapters 1 and 3) and Jack Hayward and Vincent Wright (2002, *passim*) have pointed out, a range of interpretations can be drawn from empirical observation and most reveal that the rhetoric is no more than words. The state can be strong in some areas and weak in others. The bureaucracy is no uniform and ideologically driven technocracy. Moreover the role of the central state is further complicated by its relations with local government, which are discussed in the next chapter.

6

Local Government

Chapter 1 examined the great geographical diversity of France, and drew attention to the way in which the territory of France was brought together over an extended period of time. The creation of a single nation state, with a fairly uniform pattern of administration was quite largely the product of deliberate policy and choice, and has occurred, in historical terms, relatively recently, in the period since the Revolution. The revolutionary ideals entailed an interpretation of liberty and equality which implied a uniform pattern of rights and obligations for all citizens, and hence an end to local diversity in legal and administrative customs. The exigencies of the revolutionary and Napoleonic wars resulted in the emergence of a system which would extract the necessary resources of money and manpower from a broad and diverse territory. What emerged appeared to be a highly centralized system under a controlling central administration. This chapter examines the administrative and political structures which underlie local – as opposed to central – government in France, at all sub-central levels. It will argue that the picture is far more complex than a simple centralized model suggests and that it is changing substantially and rapidly.

The Units of Local Government

Title Eleven of the constitution specifies *communes* (municipalities), *départements* (counties) including the overseas *départements*, and the overseas territories as the basic units of local government, but allows for the creation by law of other units. This occurred when the law of 2 March 1982 created regions. Article 72 provides that local government units must be administered by elected councils and the first direct elections to regional councils were held in March 1986.

France currently has four overseas *départements*, which are regarded as constituting part of metropolitan France and differ from the other *départements* only in that each also forms a region in its own right and therefore has two elected councils; one, the regional council, elected by proportional representation and the other, that of the *département*, elected by territorial divisions (*cantons*). Three of these *départements* are in the Caribbean – Guadeloupe, Martinique and French Guyana – and one – Réunion – is in the Indian ocean. The small archipelago of St Pierre et Miquelon off the Canadian coast, and the island of Mayotte in the

Comoros islands near Madagascar in the Indian ocean have a special regime. France currently retains three overseas territories, all in the Pacific – Wallis and Futuna, French Polynesia (including Tahiti and the Mururoa atoll used for nuclear testing) and New Caledonia.

The 'commune'

The basic unit of local organization in France is the *commune*. All *communes* have the same structures, and the same legal status and powers, although there is no uniformity in size between them, since they may consist of anything from a small hamlet or village to a very large town. At the 1999 census there were some 36 677 *communes*, 36 565 of them in metropolitan France. Some 21 000 of them have fewer than 500 inhabitants and a further 10 892 have between 500 and 2000 inhabitants, but only a quarter of the population lives in these small *communes*. Half the population of metropolitan France lives in the 2 per cent (874 out of 36 565) *communes* with over 10 000 inhabitants and 37 *communes* are cities of over 100 000 people. Paris, with over two million inhabitants, is simultaneously a *commune* and a *département* (Ministère de l' Intérieor, 2002, p. 14).

A plethora of attempts by central government to limit the problems caused by such fragmentation have had a limited but growing impact. Mergers are impeded by local loyalties and attachments to traditional boundaries (the *communes* are based upon pre-revolutionary parishes) have thwarted and daunted tidy-minded reformers. The financial and administrative resources of many *communes* are too small to allow them to operate effectively, while modern urban and suburban development has not respected centuries-old boundaries; consequently various devices have been used to overcome fragmentation (see Table 6.1 and 6.2). These include the creation of partnerships (*syndicats*) for pooling resources and rationalizing the provision of public services. They also include the legal authorization and organization, especially in large urban agglomerations, of consortia (*communautés*) of *communes* for one or more specific purposes with mandatory duties and their own revenue. A law of 1999 (the so-called Chevènement law) set out to reorganize and promote cooperation, in particular by abolishing some of the previous, weaker, frameworks and by offering subsidies. This approach seems to have been more successful than some of its predecessors (Levy, 2001, p. 112) since, by 2001, 90 new consortia had been created (see Table 6.1). *Communes* may, depending upon their size and resources, act in a wide number of areas. These can broadly be characterized as: the maintenance of public health and safety; the development of local infrastructure and public transport; the furtherance of local economic development; the provision and maintenance of buildings for nursery and primary schools; the provision of certain cultural facilities.

The *commune* is at one and the same time the territory for the lowest level of the state administration, and the basic unit of local government. Some communal responsibilities for matters such as public car parking, and refuse collection derive from an essentially administrative responsibility for good order, as does

TABLE 6.1

Extent of cooperation between *communes*

Type	Nature	Created	No.
Single purpose partnership (SIVU)	Pooled resources for service provision	1890	14 885*
Multi purpose partnership (SIVOM)	Pooled resources for provision of several services	1959	2 165*
Consortium of Communes (Communauté de Communes)	Planning and economic development, and some public services. Has tax raising powers	1992	1 717**
District	Provision of public services with stronger legal framework and some own revenue. Abolished as from 1 January 2002 by law of 12 July 1999	1959	171**
Consortium of Towns (Communautés de Villes)	Planning and economic development, and some public services. Abolished as from 1 January 2002 by law of 12 July 1999	1992	5*/0**
Urban Consortium (Communauté Urbaine)	Powers in 12 key areas and with own revenue. Since law of 12 July 1999 any new Urban Consortium must cover at least 500 000 inhabitants.	1966	12**
New Town partnerships	Planning, economic development and infrastructure in the nine new towns around Paris. To be transformed into Agglomeration Consortia	1983	8**
Agglomeration Consortia	Urban development and cohesion, infrastructure, services. Intended for areas of at least 50 000 inhabitants around a central commune of 15 000	1999	90**

Source: Calculated from Ministère de l'Intérieur, 2002, p. 16.
Notes:
* on 1 January 1999.
** on 1 January 2001.

the oversight or provision of the services of undertakers and of slaughterhouses. In the interests of the maintenance of good order some communes maintain a police force; such forces are usually small and their powers limited. In rural communes there may be a *garde champêtre* with a special concern for enforcing regulations relating to the countryside, for example concerning hunting.

Communes also have powers over town and country planning and some infrastructure development. All *communes* may draw up a communal plan designating the land use within their area (POS, *plan d'occupation des sols*). Since 1983, communes have had complete responsibility for the drawing up and approval of these documents; once the plan has been settled, the granting of planning permission for new or altered buildings within those communes which have

TABLE 6.2

Principal purposes of partnerships between *communes* (1 January 1999)

Purpose	Number of consortia engaging in activity				
	Single-purpose	Multi-purpose	District	Consortium of Communes	Urban Consortium
Waste disposal	713	743	195	606	11
Provision of Water	3 305	427			
Sewage	1 122	642	122	212	11
Provision of schools and related facilities	2 708	537	95	315	9
School transport	1 205	363			
Highways	351	906	86	587	5
Provision of energy	1 354	109			
Industrial estates	219	221	155	870	8
Protection of the environment	269	216	86	587	5
Support for industrial and commercial activities and employment	128	254	106	606	2

Source: compiled from Ministère de l'Intérieur, 2002, pp. 18–20.

a POS becomes a largely legal and formal matter for the mayor who must simply ascertain that the proposed construction accords with the plan. *Communes* also have some responsibility for infrastructure, especially for the construction and maintenance of local roads and paths, for drainage and water supply, and for street lighting. They may provide public transport. They may, with the assistance of state funds, and often in partnership with developers, become involved in the development or restoration of their areas. They do not directly build or administer low-cost housing, but they may set up or participate in the organizations that do (*habitations à loyer modéré*). They are not allowed to engage directly in industrial or commercial activities, but they may seek to attract investment and employment, for example through subsidies, the encouragement of tourism, and the creation of attractive conditions for life and work.

Communes have long had the responsibility for the buildings, upkeep and equipping of schools, and the 1982 laws reaffirmed this role in relation to primary schools. This responsibility is closely connected with the other cultural activities which *communes* may undertake – the provision of cultural centres, including facilities for young people or for the elderly, museums, theatres, and public libraries. Such activities are largely confined to medium-to large-size towns, and are much less common amongst small and rural *communes*; the central government, chiefly through the Ministry of Culture, is often heavily involved with subsidies and general oversight.

The powers and responsibilities of the *commune* may, in the case of large *communes*, provide scope for an important and effective municipal policy. Much depends, however, upon the relationships of the *commune* to other levels of government and to partners in the para-public and private sector. The *commune* is not simply an implementor of central policy nor, since 1982, is its activity strictly subject to prior approval by central authorities; but limitations of both finance and expertise constrain the autonomy of most *communes* except the largest and wealthiest.

The 'département'

In 1790 the revolutionary government divided France into *départements* (see map, p. 146). It wanted to replace the previous patchwork of customary and feudal rights and practices with a uniform system and law, before which all citizens (or rather, all male citizens) would be equal. The boundaries of the *départements* have remained relatively unchanged over the last 200 years. Their names were largely taken from geographical features, often the principal river of the territory; nowadays they also have a number, in roughly alphabetical order, familiar to many since it identifies the *département* of origin on the number plate of all French motor vehicles. There were originally 89, and later 90 *départements*: the growth of population around Paris resulted in the creation of five new *départements* in the Paris region in 1966 and in 1975 Corsica was divided into two, so there are now 96 *départements* in metropolitan France and four overseas. Each of the original *départements* was, it is said, so devised that no part of the *département* territory was further than a single day's ride away from the principal town, and certainly they are fairly uniform in geographical area, though, partly in consequence, not at all uniform in population. The Lozère has 74 000 inhabitants, the Nord 2.5 million.

Initially *départements* were administrative divisions devised from the centre for central purposes. Only in 1871 were *départements* recognized as units of local democracy, when an elected council replaced what had previously been an appointed advisory council. The decentralization laws of 1982 increased the autonomy of this council; but they also enhanced the status of the communal mayors, and introduced a new tier of local government, the region, with its own responsibilities and resources. The consequence is that the formal scope for action by the *département* remains quite limited. Nevertheless, since the early 1980s, *départements* have often been ready to take the initiative in formulating policies to tackle local problems. This is, however, still heavily dependent upon their relationships with other authorities. The *département* is also still an important territorial unit for the organization of central government activities.

The *département* is responsible for social work, including work with the disabled, the provision of children's homes and homes for the elderly. They also have a particular responsibility for dealing with poverty and social exclusion, and contribute towards the funds for basic income support (*revenue minimum*

France by *départements*

d'insertion), so that in 1999, welfare expenditure accounted for 60 per cent of their operational budgets (Delivet, 2001, p. 88). The *département* is also responsible for preventive medicine, such as screening for various types of disease and the provision of vaccination and child-health clinics. Since 1996 they have been responsible for fire and rescue services.

The construction and maintenance of most roads and bridges and of the smaller commercial and fishing ports forms part of the responsibilities of the *département* as, since 1982, does the building, maintenance and equipping of the *collèges*, which are the schools for the eleven to sixteen age group. The provision and payment of teachers is a matter for the central Ministry of Education. The running of school bus services, except within the limits of a single *commune's* transport area, is also now the task of the *département*. Following consultation with the *communes* they plan waymarked footpaths and protect and manage sensitive areas of natural beauty. They may also be involved in water supply and sewage and refuse disposal. *Départements* may also, like *communes*, provide for or subsidize museums, art galleries and other local cultural activities or associations.

The 'region'

During the 1950s it became clear that infrastructure development and economic restructuring might more effectively be planned at an intermediate level between the central government and the *département*. This was not a totally new idea; an initial attempt to create administrative structures at regional level had occurred under the Vichy government but, probably because of the Vichy associations, had been discontinued shortly after the end of the war. In the 1950s much of the impetus came from the economic Planning Commissariat who devised the grouping of *départements* which persists today, apart from the separation of Corsica from the Provence – Alpes – Côte d' Azur region, so that in 2002 there were 22 metropolitan regions, including Corsica with its special status, and 4 overseas. In 2002 the new government put forward a policy, accompanied by a constitutional amendment, for substantial further decentralization, especially to regional level, and this was accompanied by speculation about the merger of certain regions, so the number may reduce.

In 1964 regional advisory committees (*Commission du Développement Economique Régional* – CODER) were created in each region consisting of nominated members, to provide advice and guidance on economic development for the benefit of central government. In 1969 President de Gaulle proposed a reform which would have created elected regional councils, and put it as part of a package of reforms to the unsuccessful referendum in 1969 (see Chapter 4). A further, but more tentative, reform was introduced in 1972 for all the regions, except the Ile de France around Paris which was restructured by a 1976 law. Advisory regional councils were created, consisting of the members of the National Assembly and senators for the region together with members nominated from amongst their membership by the councils of the *départements* and some of the *communes*. It was only in 1982 with the Mitterrand government's decentralization laws that the region became a fully developed level of local government with directly elected regional councils. The first direct elections were held alongside the general election in March 1986.

The regions had, until 1982, no strictly executive functions at all. The 1982 laws specifically gave the regions executive powers, both by making the *président* (chairperson) of the council its chief executive, and by extending the scope of regional activities and allowing for the financing not only of investment but also of running costs. As a result of their background, the powers of the regions are largely related to economic development. They also look after all the non-staff costs of higher secondary schools (*lycées*). They have been notably active in this area, building 220 *lycées* between 1986 and 1992, compared with 60 built by the state in the preceding five years. They also have discretionary powers to fund buildings and other facilities for universities and to subsidize academic activities. They may subsidize cultural activities – orchestra, opera and theatre, for example. They must provide professional training, apprenticeships and employment support for young people and in 1997 this took up a third of their operational budgets (Berthon, 2001, p. 72). Regional resources are not large, although the size of their staff multiplied by six in the five years after 1981. Their budgets quadrupled between 1982 and 1988 and continued to grow, if at a lesser rate, thereafter. Since their operating costs are low, and they are not heavily committed to ongoing programme expenditure, they can spend substantial amounts in high-profile investment and subsidies, and, by concluding regional development planning contracts with the state, can match their own resources with state funds. They can also attract European Community funds, and they may borrow.

In 1982 it was envisaged that the regions would be increasingly responsible for economic planning. However, there was some ambiguity in the objectives, as between the regional realization of a national plan and local planning at a genuinely regional level, and critics grumble that the plans have largely served to compel regions to pay from their budgets what should have been provided by the centre, for example for the expansion of the universities. Nevertheless, planning contracts were agreed in 1984, and again in 1989 and 1994. Between 1994 and 1998 the centre contributed some 81 million francs to the planned investments, and the regions put in 84 million (Berthon, 2001, p. 74). Grandiose regional economic development initiatives have not been possible and the regions have concentrated upon underpinning areas of major importance to them, such as, for the Nord-Pas-de-Calais region, the Channel ferry ports.

The growing prominence of the regions in the political debate at the European Union level has also assisted the very rapid development of the political status and identity of the regions. They have taken their place in the European Union Committee of the Regions and sought to find partners and allies amongst regions in other member states, for example through groupings such as the 'Atlantic arc' group of regions. All the French regions (except the Auvergne) maintain offices in Brussels.

The Corsican conundrum

Geographical distance, linguistic differentiation, social structures and culture have always resulted in a sense of difference and distinction between Corsica and the mainland. Within Corsica, in a society which is almost impenetrable to outsiders, clan loyalties and codes of honour and revenge, organized crime, politics and the apparatus of the state are all deeply intertwined. The post-war period saw a growth both in political pressures for decentralization and the recognition and preservation of Corsican culture and of an autonomist movement, prepared to use violence to make its case (the *Front National pour la Libération de la Corse –* *FNLC*). One of the motives of the decentralization reforms of the early 1980s was to disarm this pressure. For this reason the 1982 law treated Corsica as a special case. So the 1982 law made the two *départements* of Corsica into a region and gave it some additional powers beyond those enjoyed by other regions. The separatist agitation and violence continued fairly unabated, and in 1991 a further reform classified Corsica as a unique form of local authority, with an elected assembly, a seven-person executive and particular responsibilities for cultural identity, although the Constitutional Council struck down a clause referring to Corsica as a historical and cultural community on the ground that it infringed the constitutional indivisibility of the Republic. But these measures have not solved the problem. This was brutally emphasized by the murder in 1998 of the prefect, M. Erignac. For many French people this was profoundly shocking: the prefect incarnates the state, and this assassination was a blow against the whole Republican system. The shock has been compounded by the continuing failure of the authorities to locate and arrest the presumed murderer.

The Jospin government in 2000 invited all the political groups represented in the Corsican Assembly to discussions on the legal status of the Corsica. An agreement – the 'Matignon agreement' – was reached, but resulted in the resignation of Jean-Pierre Chèvenement, the minister of the interior, who saw it as denial of republican principles. The proposal was to remove the distinctions between the two *départements* and the region, leaving a single assembly, to allow Corsican language teaching in schools, and to endow the Corsican Assembly with additional powers, including adapting national legislation to the island. Despite ongoing, rather technical discussions with members of the Corsican Assembly, little progress had been made before the general election.

The incoming Raffarin government in 2002 treated Corsica as an urgent priority with a rapid and high profile visit by Interior Minister Sarkozy. In March 2003 a constitutional amendment was adopted. One of its main objectives was to make possible the creation of local authorities with distinctive legal powers in the place of those which already exist. Such authorities would have defined powers to make by-laws. Unity, said the official communiqué when the amendment was first proposed, was not be confused with uniformity. The new provisions allow for pilot projects by which some regions may be given different powers from others. The Minister for Justice, presenting the proposals to parliament, said 'local authorities are in an especially good position to judge whether legislation achieves its aims, to identify weaknesses in it and to devise reforms to it'. While carefully phrased to apply potentially to any region, these provisions should avoid the situation in which any proposal to devolve powers to Corsica will be thrown out by the Constitutional Council in the name of the indivisibility of the Republic. Given the potential for other regions too to seize upon the opportunities offered they could eventually bring about a significant undermining of the Jacobin state.

The Electoral and Administrative Structures of Local Government

'Communes' and their mayors

Both the *département* and the region began as purely administrative territorial divisions, created to answer the needs of the central government. The *commune* has a longer history of existence as a unit of representative local government, but all three levels of government continue to be involved in a complex intertwining of local government and administration, and the local execution of central government functions. *Communes* are governed by an elected council (see Exhibit 6.1). The smallest councils, for *communes* with less than 100 inhabitants, have nine members, and the number of members rises in proportion to the population so that those *communes* with more than 300 000 inhabitants have 69 member

---

EXHIBIT 6.1

National and local electoral systems in France

Election	System	Electoral district
Presidential	Two-ballot 'first past the post'	Whole country
National Assembly	Two-ballot 'first past the post'	Single member constituencies
Senate	Indirect, by electoral college	*Département*
European Parliament*	Proportional by list	Eight large constituencies
Regional Councils*	Two-ballot list system: 25% to winner, 75% proportionately.	Region
Département Council (*Conseil Général*)	Two-ballot 'first past the post'	Subdivision of *département* (*canton*)
Commune Council (*Conseil Municipal*)	1. Fewer than 3500 inhabitants: two-ballot 'winner takes all' list system 2. Over 3500 inhabitants: two-ballot list system: 50% to winner, 50% proportionately	*Commune* (except for Paris, Lyons, Marseilles)

Note: * from 2004.

councils, apart from Lyons with 73, Marseilles with 101 and Paris which has 163 seats on its council. Elections are held every six years.

In small *communes* of under 3500 inhabitants, councillors are elected by a majority-vote system. The voter has as many votes as there are seats on the council. In *communes* of over 2500 inhabitants, candidates are obliged to group themselves into lists, each with as many candidates as there are vacancies, but voters may strike out a name on a list and replace it with a name from another list. In these *communes* there are two rounds of voting; candidates who obtain 50 per cent or more of the votes cast (and the votes of at least 25 per cent of the electorate) are elected at the first round. The remaining vacancies are filled by those candidates who achieve the highest scores in the second round. For *communes* with over 3500 inhabitants (except Paris, Lyons and Marseilles), a new electoral system was introduced in 1982. Candidates group themselves into lists of as many candidates as there are seats. Electors have one vote, which they cast for one of the lists. If any one of the lists obtains over 50 per cent of the vote in the first round, they are awarded half the seats and their share of the other half which are distributed in proportion to the votes cast amongst all those lists which have achieved at least 5 per cent of the votes. If no list has obtained over 50 per cent, then a second round is held between all the lists which have obtained at least 10 per cent of the votes. The list which obtains the highest number of votes at that stage takes half the seats, and the other half are divided proportionately between all those lists which have gained at least 5 per cent in the second round. The composition of the lists may be modified by the amalgamation of two lists, but no candidates may stand who were not already candidates in the first round on lists which gained at least 5 per cent of the vote. Nor may candidates who figured on the same list in the first round divide themselves amongst several lists in the second round. In these elections all residents who are European Union citizens may register as electors and vote.

One effect of this electoral system is to prevent the emergence of a 'hung council'; one single list is necessarily assured of a comfortable majority composed of its 50 per cent plus its proportionate share of the other half of the seats. A further effect of these provisions is the encouragement of alliances between parties, so that the first round can to a certain extent act as a 'primary' election, a subsequent merger of lists being shaped by the first round results.

Paris, Lyons and Marseilles are all subdivided into *arrondissements*, 20 in Paris, 16 in Marseilles and 9 in Lyons. Each *arrondissement* has its own council and mayor. One-third of the *arrondissement* council is made up of the members of the municipal council elected in the *arrondissement*. The two councils are elected simultaneously, and the lists of candidates contain as many names as there are seats on the *arrondissement* council. The electoral system is that applied to *communes* of over 3500 inhabitants. In Paris the council acts simultaneously as the *conseil municipal* and the *conseil général*.

The mayor is elected from amongst its members by the council of the *commune*. In *communes* of over 3500 inhabitants it is invariably the leader of

EXHIBIT 6.2

Mayors

Who is a Mayor?
Number of Mayors (2001): Total 36 674 Women 10.9 per cent (8.2 per cent in 1995)
Persons under age 40: 5.3 per cent Persons 60 and over: 28.5 per cent.

Occupation	men	women	total as percentage of all mayors
Farmers, agricultural professions	6 153	452	18.0*
Self-employed, business owners	2 447	91	6.9
Executives and senior professionals	7 853	720	22.7
Other professions	2 170	371	6.9
White-collar workers	2 094	574	7.3
Manual workers	537	24	1.5
Retired, or not economically active	11 727	1 714	36.7

Source: Compiled from Ministère de l'Intérieur, 2002, p. 107.
The representation of certain professions has changed markedly over the past three decades;
while fewer mayors are farmers the role has increasingly attracted the retired.

	1971	**1977**	**1983**	**1989**
Farmers, agricultural professions	45.3	39.5	36.5	28.5
Not economically active or retired	14.5	18.3	20.2	27.4

(Compiled from *Cahiers Français*, 239, pp. 61–2 and *Pouvoirs*, 60, p. 78)

How much time do they spend on their tasks as mayor (as a percentage of a sample
poll taken in 1987)?

Days a week	Mayors of communes with a population of		
	Fewer than 2000	**2000–5000**	**More than 5000**
Not more than one	11	3	0
Between one and three	61	29	15
Four or more	36	66	83
No reply	2	2	2
n = 500			

the majority list who becomes mayor, so that the voters can be said to have
some voice in the choice and electoral battles may be quite closely linked to the
personality of the potential mayors. Mayors are both the leaders and the chief
executives of their *communes*; they combine representational duties on behalf
of their *commune* with political and administrative activities on behalf of the
council, and with a number of functions on behalf of the state. As both an
elected representative and an official of the state, mayors are not accountable to
their councils; they cannot be dismissed by them. The powers combined by a
mayor are considerable: where national political groupings play a large part in
local political life the mayor is the main local political leader; the mayor is also

the chief executive of the council's decisions. The enlarged executive powers of the council since the 1982 reforms have reinforced the mayor's position in this role. In addition, the mayor exercises some of the prerogative powers of the state, especially in relation to the maintenance of law and order and the prevention of nuisances, so that by-laws on these matters may be made by mayoral decree. The mayor also acts for the state in the registration of births and deaths, and of marriages.

The position of the mayor has always been an interesting and complex one in relation to central politics and the central government. In many small *communes* the mayor will be a leading local figure, often with purely local connections, but sometimes a local person who has achieved a position in the central administration or national politics. A person who understands the operation of the machinery of national power may, it is often felt, be in an advantageous position to forward the interests of the local *commune*, even if many of the day-to-day duties of the position have to be carried out by a locally based deputy. It has been normal practice for many national political figures to be mayor of their local town, and for those who are mayors of large and important towns these positions can constitute a substantial power base. It was, for example, such a power base that facilitated an unsuccessful challenge to Chirac's leadership of the RPR by a number of Gaullist *notables* in 1990. A number of such mayors have held office for very long periods indeed, including the Gaullist Jacques Chaban-Delmas (prime minister during 1969–73) Mayor of Bordeaux from 1945 to 1995 when he was replaced as Mayor by the then serving prime minister, Alain Juppé, and Gaston Defferre, Socialist Minister from 1981 to 1986, Mayor of Marseilles from 1953 until his death in 1986. The mayor may thus be at the centre of an important network of political and municipal patronage and power. A desire to disperse power more widely, to remove some of the occasions for abuses, and to disarm criticisms that no one could carry two full-time jobs led both Jospin and Raffarin to require their ministers to abandon their mayoral offices (see Chapter 5).

In their capacity as officials of the state, mayors are subject to the oversight of the State's local representative, the prefect, and ultimately of the Ministry of the Interior, whose advice and directives are conveyed to the mayors through a multiplicity of circulars and instructions. Relationships with the local mayors continue to be a major preoccupation of the prefect in each *département*. Whatever the formal, institutional pattern of responsibility, the fact that a mayor is simultaneously representative and official blurs the picture; in *communes* of over 3500 inhabitants the mayor enjoys the legitimacy deriving from the voters' direct say in the election: the voters know, when they choose a list, who will be the mayor. In the smaller rural *communes*, the mayor enjoys local status and support in dealings with what may be seen as outside forces. Where the mayor is a major political figure, then relationships with central government bodies, and particularly the prefect, have always been very delicately balanced.

'Départements' and regions

Half the members of the *conseil général* of the *département* are elected every three years; each member thus serves a six-year term. In a bid to improve turnout, the elections are now arranged to coincide with those for the other levels – thus in 1998 the election took place alongside the regional elections, and in 2001 alongside the municipal elections. One member is elected for each *canton* (ward) of the *département*, by a two-round system similar to that used for parliamentary constituencies (see Exhibit 6.1). This electoral system has been in place since the 1870s. The *conseiller général* for any canton has very frequently been the mayor of one of the *communes*. Since the *département* was, until 1983, largely an administrative body rather than an entity of genuine local government, the *conseil général's* role was essentially that of providing a forum for the concerns of the *communes*.

It was not until 1986 that the regions became a full tier of local government. In that year the elections for the regional council, provided for in the 1982 decentralization laws, took place. Regional councils are elected for a fixed six-year term. The electoral system initially chosen (proportional representation by departmental list) failed, in a number of cases, to produce overall majorities. This made for particularly fraught situations when the National Front held a potential balance of power. In 1999 (following the 1998 elections) a new system was introduced which will operate for the first time in 2004. This will be a two-ballot single regional list system, but unlike arrangements for large municipalities the list with the overall majority (either 50 per cent at the first ballot or the majority at the second) will be attributed only 25 per cent of the seats, and the remaining 75 per cent will be divided amongst the second ballot lists with over three per cent of votes cast.

Given the functions of the region, described above, the administrative services attached to the region, including those transferred from the central government, are relatively small, though rapidly expanding. The chairperson (*président*) of the regional council is its chief executive; the post has been seen as a politically important and influential one, and leading politicians from the party or group holding the majority of the seats in the regional council have been elected. In certain regions in 1998, the election of the *président* proved to be of considerable political significance, as a test case on the willingness of the mainstream Right parties to ally with the National Front (see also Chapter 8). Several mainstream Right politicians gained presidencies with the support of the NF. Almost all promptly resigned, even at the cost in the Centre region, for example, of letting in a Socialist. The first Juppé government contained three regional *présidents* and the second one, four. Jospin equated the presidency of a regional council with a mayoralty, so ministers had to choose. Jean-Pierre Raffarin continued this approach, and set the example by resigning as *président* of the Poitou-Charentes regional council. Regional politics are steadily acquiring a higher profile.

The role of the prefect

The prefect who, until the 1983 reforms, played the key role in the administrative life of the *département* continues to occupy a prominent and central place. He (only six out of 116 prefects were female on 1 June 2000 (le Pors and Milonski, 2002, p. 60)) is the representative of the government in the *département*, and as such takes formal precedence. He plays a major representational role on official occasions, in uniform, and is provided with housing, expenses and an official car to enable him to do so. He is appointed by the president by a decision taken in the Council of Ministers. When Napoleon instituted the prefectoral system, the main task of the prefect in each *département* was to ensure law and order and loyalty to the government, to see that central government decisions were uniformly applied throughout the country, and to keep a steady flow of both taxation and conscripts to support the war effort. The prefect remains responsible for law and order, and for taking whatever measures are required to deal with emergencies and disasters. The prefect is also formally responsible for the oversight of all the services of the central government which operate within the *département*. The prefecture is located in the administrative centre of the *département*, usually the main town, though in some cases other towns have become larger and more important than the one designated nearly two centuries ago as the seat of the prefecture. The *département* is divided into *arrondissements*, each with a sub-prefect located in the principal town of the area. The structure was conceived of as a neat and rational one, which ensured that laws and instructions could rapidly be transmitted, via prefect and sub-prefect, to the mayors, and that they would be smoothly and uniformly executed (Machin, 1979) nor was the flow purely one way. The prefects were called upon to report regularly to Paris upon the conditions, events and state of opinion within their *département*.

In practice, matters were never quite so simple. First, although the prefect was the representative of the state within his *département*, he was also, very frequently, in effect the ambassador of his *département* to the central government. Prefects required the cooperation of mayors and other local leaders if the *département* was to run smoothly, and would endeavour to ensure consensus, and compromise solutions to avoid dispute and conflict.

Secondly, the prefect, as representative of the state, has also, almost from the beginning, been seen as the representative of the government, and hence directly implicated in the political stance of the government of the day. The duties of the prefects from the beginning included the requirement to try to keep local leaders and local society loyal to the regime, and in the circumstances of nineteenth and much of twentieth century France where regime and government were inseparable, this involved a highly political role. This undoubtedly at some periods meant that prefects could, and did, use their positions to try to influence elections in favour of the government in place. The development of organized, disciplined, mass-based political parties has diminished the possibility of such influence, but the prefect is still regarded as a highly political official (Schmidt, 1990, p. 385), and prefectoral posts are included amongst the *postes à discretion* (see Chapter 5) for which political views can be taken into account. A consequence of this very politicized image is that changes in political circumstances can be accompanied by a *valse préfectorale* – a prefectoral waltz – quite large numbers of prefects are moved from one *département* to another, or find posts elsewhere in the administration or indeed outside it.

Thirdly, the administrative role of the prefect was greatly complicated by the development of bureaucratic structures. From the beginning, the services of the Ministries of War, Justice, Finances and Education were placed outside prefectoral control, but other pre-existing bodies, such as the bridge and highway engineers, were brought under the prefect's control. Over the succeeding two centuries the central administration has become more complex, the number of individual ministries has grown, and the task of the prefect has in practice become much more one of coordination than of direction and control. As communications have improved, and especially since 1945, much more business has been carried out informally and directly between local services and their parent ministry, and the prefect may be involved, if at all, only in the formal processes. On several occasions since 1945 (in 1953, 1964 and 1970), attempts were made to reassert the primacy of the prefect, without marked success.

The decentralization reforms of 1982–3 had an impact upon the role and position of the prefect, but it might be argued that the changes in the prefect's role were largely illusory. The prefect's function in relation to the oversight of the local authorities did not change as might have been expected. Decentralization did bring structural changes. The councils of both *communes* and *départements* were given powers to determine their own budgets, rather than agree to a budget set by the prefect, and the chairperson (*président*) of the council was given a role as the council's chief executive. This meant the transfer of resources from central government ministries to the local authorities, and also the transfer of staff from the prefecture and other local offices of the central government to the service of the council. Large parts of the social work services (the *direction départementale des affaires sanitaires et sociales*) and some parts of the public works services (the *direction départementale de l'equipement*) as well as of the agricultural and forestry services have been transferred to the *conseil général*.

However, even before the decentralization legislation, the prefect's legal powers to draw up and then put into effect the local budget were inevitably matters for consultation and negotiation with the local council members, and the prefect's power to veto decisions on grounds either of illegality or inadvisability was seldom exercised. In many respects the decentralization legislation legalized what had long been informal practice, at least for the *départements* and the larger urban *communes*. The smaller rural *communes* still tend to look to the prefect for guidance and reassurance. Since the new legislation, neither budgetary nor policy decisions within the councils' areas of responsibility require prior approval by the prefect, but financial actions (except for those of *communes* of fewer than 2000 inhabitants, where the Ministry of Finance checks the accounts) are scrutinized by the local *Chambre Régionale des Comptes*, an independent audit body attached to the central audit institution, the *Cour des Comptes*. Prefects may draw the attention of the *Chambre Régionale des Comptes* to cases where local budgets are not being properly formulated or administered. This is no mere formality and has resulted in some important revelations of dubious practice and corruption (Mény, 1992, pp. 273–6). Equally, policy decisions may be referred by the prefect to the local *tribunal administratif* – administrative court – though only on grounds of illegality, not on the merits of a decision.

Paradoxically, moreover, the emphasis of several governments upon lessening the extent of governmental centralization has strengthened the position of the prefect in some respects. A law of 6 February 1992 laid down the general principle – linked to the Maastricht concept of subsidiarity – that decisions should always be taken as closely possible to the citizen, company or other body affected. This was followed up by a decree of July 1992 setting out what was called the Deconcentration Charter. The logical consequence – that the role of the central administration was not to make implementing decisions itself but to confer the power to do so on services at local level – was explicitly spelt out. Coordination and coherence were to be assured by the prefect. However, the local services were, and are, in fact rather autonomous and likely to be deeply involved with a local clientele and the preservation of local good relationships (Dupuy & Thoenig, 1985). The initial impact of the Deconcentration Charter was almost imperceptible. Juppé's modernization programme repeated the theme in a more robust way, and the Jospin government filled in the details in December 1997. The central administrations were to be confined to 'the tasks of forecasting, analysis, policy formulation, drafting legislation and evaluation. These regulatory functions must be clearly distinguished from the operational tasks of managing, applying regulations and providing benefits' (Rouban, 1996) and this reduction in tasks has been accompanied by some diminution in central staff numbers. Normally all decisions involving individual persons or firms are now taken locally, mostly by the prefect. The prefect continues to be clearly responsible for the local implementation of national and European Union policies. The dynamic of centralization has slowly produced changes, but not those which were anticipated. The number of actors within the system has multiplied and relations between the prefects and 'their' local leaders are no longer simple (Gleizal, 1995, p. 246). More and more the representatives of the central state find themselves in a position where they must negotiate, mediate, cajole, communicate and unite. 'As deconcentration blends into decentralization, it is often difficult to determine who is truly in charge: whether state agents are leading local authorities or the locals are leading the state' (Levy, 2001, p. 106). One very experienced prefect cites the example of local hospital administration. The hospital administration wants to balance its budget. The doctors want the most advanced equipment. The unions want good salaries and working conditions. The mayor, who chairs the hospital authority, wants to advance local concerns. The role of the prefect is to be responsible for the implementation of public health policy and remind all concerned that their actions must benefit patients (Bernard, 1992). 'It is...through the interactions of a multiplicity of actors that the definition and implementation of the general interest at local level is worked out'(Négrier, 2000, p. 127).

The Resources of Local Authorities

Until 1982, *communes*, especially the large ones, often had a good number of employees, but the non-executive roles of both the *département* and the region meant that they employed virtually no staff at all. The transfer of responsibilities, and the widening of the executive scope of all levels of local government meant that the number of local employees rose although those of the *communes* still constitute three-quarters of the total (see Table 6.3). The notion of the local public service as a career service is protected by the establishment of bodies at national level, for senior officials, and at the level of the *département* for others, which undertake recruitment, organize training, and will take responsibility for any official who has lost a post until a job can be found elsewhere.

Local authorities' sources of income 'constitute a veritable jungle of complexity' (Tulard, 2001, p. 155). About one-third of their operating expenditure is covered by central government grants, which have, since 1996, been held down by cash limits in the interest of holding public expenditure to levels conforming with the Maastricht criteria for monetary union. The other two-thirds of the current account resources come from the local authorities' own taxes, including taxes on land, property, housing and business. Until 2000 the *départements* were entitled to the vehicle licence tax for cars and small vans (the *vignette automobile*). This was abolished, more to appease disgruntled motorists protesting against the costs of motoring than to reduce local complexity, and replaced by increased central government grant.

TABLE 6.3

Local government staff on 1 January 2000

Type of authority	Number
Region	10 243
Département	164 526
Other*	61 385
Commune	933 608
Intercommunal Consortia	109 866
Private sector local bodies (cultural, leisure etc.)	97 469
Housing bodies, municipal banks etc.	61 874
Total	1 531 153
Employed by local authorities on youth and long-term unemployed employment schemes (*contrats emplois solidarité; emploi jeunes*)	156 598

Note: * Regional and Departmental bodies including Paris Prefecture of Police and *Département* fire services.
Source: Ministère de l'intérieur, 2002, p. 110.

EXHIBIT 6.3

Local government expenditure

Decentralization resulted in a transfer of resources to the various levels of local government:

Total resources of local authorities (in millions of Euro)

1982	1986	1996	1999
57	83	114	124

Resources and Expenditure by type of local authority in millions of Euro (1999)

	Communes	Départements	Regions
Resources	73.4	37.9	12.6
Expenditure	72.6	37.6	12.6

Taxation as a percentage of Gross National Product

Country	1985			1999		
	social security	local taxes	All taxes and contributions	social security	local taxes	all taxes and contributions
France	19.0	3.8	43.8	16.5	4.6	45.8
Spain	11.4	3.1	27.6	12.2	6.0	35.1
Sweden	11.9	14.7	48.3	13.2	15.8	52.2
United Kingdom	6.8	3.9	37.7	6.2	1.5	36.3

Source: Compiled from *Cahiers Français*, 1989, p. 239; Guy Gilbert, 'The Resources of the French Regions in Retrospect', in Loughlin and Mazey (1995); and www.dgcl.interieur.gouv. fr/donneeschiffrees/cadrage/ (consulted August 2002).

One reason for the relatively sheltered position which local government has enjoyed in France in the 1980s and the 1990s, even in face of the Maastricht pressures on public expenditure, was the fact that the Socialist governments of 1981 and 1988 did not wish to see the *grande affaire* of decentralization undermined by local dissatisfaction. An even more important reason is the strength of the defences which local affairs can mobilize against the centre.

Continuity and Change: Patterns of Local–Central Relationships

In the 200 years since the Revolution some of the patterns of relationships between central and local bodies became deeply embedded in the pattern of French administrative and political life. The decentralization reforms of the 1980s were a determined effort to shake up and change some of these entrenched habits. The changes may have been more modest than the rhetoric which surrounded them, but there have been important shifts in power. In analysing British local government, Rhodes (1992) concluded that central–local relationships depended upon an exchange of power resources, and a system of interdependence between sectoral and functional networks of actors. The development of French local government may have moved it closer to this model. The central command and control model was, as historical research has shown, never more than a myth. Scholars such as Gary Marks and Liesbet Hooghe, commenting upon the development of the European Union as a polity, have seen it as characterized by multilevel governance, moving away from a model of a controlling central government towards a complex pattern of decision-making, with partnerships developing between and across different levels. Local and regional voices have an influence in Brussels, and EU policy impacts directly in the local areas. This depiction is particularly applicable in the field of regional policy and the deployment of the European Union's regional and structural funds. Any evaluation of the evolution of local–central relationships in France needs to view them in this context and should not neglect a number of major factors:

- First, despite the origins of local government units as administrative rather than political bodies and, until recently, the very limited scope for genuine local government, the pattern was always complex. The neat organizational plan of the centralized state was balanced by the strength of local identity and local interests, with whom the agents of the central state were compelled to work. This may impact on the central government. The Ministry of Finance plan to rationalize tax assessment, whose failure cost Finance Minister Christian Sautter his job in 2000, could partly be ascribed to the ability of officials, unwilling to give up entrenched working practices, to rally local representatives to their cause on the basis that they risked losing 'their' tax office. A similar problem has until recently bedevilled attempts to improve the deployment of the police and the gendarmerie.
- Secondly, this balance was, and still is, assisted by the operation of the system of *cumul des mandats* – the holding of multiple electoral offices. Whilst multiple accumulation of offices is no longer possible, and ministers cannot now be mayors or *présidents* of major consortia or regional councils, the practice of being both a local councillor or mayor and a member of parliament is likely to continue. The consequence is that local politics tend to be very important to national politicians. They are often the means through which a local power base and local legitimacy is secured within a constituency or local area. Equally the local area has an effective advocate with central officials, ministers and their advisers.
- Thirdly, the complexity of the balance has not diminished. However apparently neat and rational the division of responsibilities between the four levels of government – *commune*, *département*, region, centre, – the boundaries are not straightforward. Local politicians seek to take the credit for tackling problems which are locally important. But they do not want to carry the can where the problems are intractable: 'responsibility for the care of the elderly stops

where medical policy begins, that for the prevention of delinquency where anti-drugs policy starts, responsibility for poor housing stops with the homeless. There would be a long list of areas which the state has been left with because they are difficult and there is little desire on the part of local elected councillors to be held responsible for the outcomes' (Grémion, 1992, p. 189). Equally, the prefects have reacted flexibly to the changes, laying an increased stress upon their role as coordinators and monitors of the implementation of policy, rather than executives. They have thereby retained a good deal of influence, now reinforced by the deconcentration measures.

- Fourthly, mounting social and economic problems – industrial adjustment, homelessness, unemployment, racial tensions, unrest in deprived areas – which have had political repercussions, have caused French governments of both Left and Right to introduce a number of new legal frameworks which cut across and complicate the structures introduced in 1983. These include the 1991 *loi d'orientation pour la ville* which provides for some sharing of resources between rich and poor *communes* (though it is expected to be 2010 before this is fully implemented) through devices such as *contrats de la ville* – city contracts – and *programmes locaux de l'habitat* – local improvement plans. The intention was that the state (often operating via the prefect) should encourage local authorities to review their policies – such as housing policy – to see whether they were in themselves producing problems such as homelessness and ghettoization and change them if required.

A second such law was the 1995 *loi d'orientation pour l'amenagement et le développement du territoire* recognizing the existence of *pays* – new territorial groupings following the patterns of life and work which do not necessarily respect administrative boundaries. Within these *pays*, plans for economic and infrastructural development may be drawn up. These may range from plans to provide basic services in neighbouring rural *communes* which happen to span regional boundaries to ambitious development plans for much larger areas, especially for mountainous and coastal areas. Some funds are provided, for example for the resiting of industry or development of former mining areas, but these are not extensive.

Finally, the 1996 *pacte de relance pour la ville* created a plethora of new *zones* which enjoy various advantages and fiscal exemptions in the interest of encouraging development and employment:

- 744 *zones urbaines sensibles* – some reduction in rents for public housing and some state-provided jobs in the 'public interest' sector;
- *zones de redynamisation urbaine* – new and existing businesses are exempt from the payroll tax;
- 44 *zones franches urbaines* – employers are exempt from taxes on their profits for five years and from employers' social security contributions provided that at least twenty per cent of their employees come from deprived areas.

There will be further attempts to improve public services, including public transport, and higher pay for officials such as teachers serving in these areas. The traditional model of local government as (republican) administration (Clark, 1998, p. 101) has become fragmented and politicized (Cole and John, 1995), and overlain by a complex network of new functional relationships organized more around specific problems than territorial uniformity.

- Fifthly, the nature of the French legal framework and of French administrative practice allows, within an apparently highly centralized system, for a considerable degree of local flexibility in the implementation of the law. Most French laws as passed by Parliament set out a broad framework for action. In ensuring the law is obeyed prefects and mayors may, and frequently do, take account of local conditions; if the enforcement of the law is challenged, the courts will be concerned to see that the intentions of the policy embodied in the legislation are being achieved. An example of the application of this discretion is in the general field of control of agricultural pollution; those concerned with implementation at local level will try to assist farmers to meet the national norms in ways that are appropriate to local conditions; but equally higher standards than the national level may be set locally, for example in North Brittany, where local shellfish production may be harmed by water pollution from intensive animal rearing.

- Sixthly, the effect of the decentralization has been to reinforce the powers of the local political elites. An important impetus in the movement for the decentralization reforms was the desire of local political leaders, especially mayors, to enlarge their scope for action without depending upon the cumbersome and often slow processes of obtaining authorization from central government bodies. Local leaders have undoubtedly been the main beneficiaries of the reforms. The reforms, especially the limitation of the *cumul des mandats*, have, however, opened up participation in local politics to a rather wider circle of active participants, tending to reinforce thereby the role of political party organization (Schmidt, 1990, pp. 267–77).

In France it can be argued that what is still formally a centralized system has in fact been made necessary by the considerable strength of local interests and influence. The prefectoral system ensures that the government hears the voice of local concerns, while the large size and geographical omnipresence of the *services déconcentrés* gives a substantial part of the central administration a stake in developments affecting those local bodies which are their neighbours and clients. Moreover, the very late development of national, organized, mass political parties in France has tended to emphasize the importance of local roots for politicians, often above political allegiance, and the *cumul des mandats*, even if now limited, has entrenched habits of political behaviour which ensure that local voices can be politically strong.

• Finally, the European Community has added a further element to the complex pattern. As European action and legislation extends, some of the paradoxes of the European dimension are becoming obvious. The European Community acts through the national governments of member states. It is the national governments who are signatories to the treaty, and who carry the responsibility of seeing that community policies are implemented and enforced. In so far as local authorities are in fact the bodies to whom the task of implementation actually falls, the central government is answerable for their actions to the European Court. Thus the European dimension may work to reinforce the oversight of the central authorities over the local authorities. Equally, however, the local authorities find in the policies or the subventions of the European Community a source of power and resources which reinforces their position. Pierre Moscovici, Jospin's Minister for European Affairs, argued in 1999 that 'close to 50 per cent of funds for territorial infrastructures and economic development come from Europe' (quoted in Gueldry, 2001, p. 183).

Conclusion

The decentralization reforms, including the creation of directly elected councils at regional level, have certainly altered the pattern of local government in France. Many of these alterations have been effectively the continuation or enhancement of previous trends. Problems remain. There are still very many – probably far too many – local government entities. There are now three sub-central tiers of government. Rivalries – sometimes seriously wasteful, for example in attracting investment – conflicts of responsibility, for example in training or in social services, and complexity are the consequence. The financing of local government activity is very complicated, and has for too long and in too many places been a hotbed of corruption (Wolfreys, 2001). Local political bosses, sometimes of astonishing political longevity, with a hold on party organization, and a foot in both national and local politics, can build formidable clientilist political machines. Amongst the beneficial effects of decentralization, however, have been an increase in local political pluralism, greater scope for managerial innovation and improved service delivery, and some increase in the sensitivity of local government to local needs (Schmidt, 1990, pp. 390–1; Levy, 2001, p. 96).

In arguing that local and central affairs in France remain very closely linked, through a complex administrative network, and through overlapping political elites at national and local level, this chapter has adopted what Elgie and Griggs (2000, p. 95) call the 'local governance' model of analysis of French local government and its relation with the central state. They rightly point out that the use of the term 'governance' in this context implies perhaps too fluid a set of relationships, and indeed that the model is no more than 'new variations on old themes' (p. 93) but these new variations have the merit of emphasizing the rivalries, cooperation and variations in competence, powers, policy-making and policy-implementing capacity between different local levels as well as between those levels and the central state. There are complex and interdependent relation-ships between the organizations and elites involved. The development of interconnections and integration in ways that do not take account of national boundaries, as well as increasing insistence by local populations on having a say in the development of the area in which they live, prompted, for example, by eco-logical and environmental concerns, are both likely to contribute to the shaping of the patterns of relationship. Some local authorities may well be growing in confidence and initiative, but the variety, and the fragmentation of the basic level of local government is also an important factor of weakness, and will long ensure a major role for the central government.

7

Parliament

Since the onset of the French Revolution, which was marked, in 1789, by the calling together of the Estates General, every government in France has recognized that it requires support from a representative body that embodies and visibly expresses the consent of a large proportion of the population. With the entrenchment of republicanism by the end of the nineteenth century, the principle, now embodied within the constitution, that national sovereignty belongs to the whole people, who exercise it through their elected representatives, was firmly established, although it was not until 1944, after a long history of struggle and debate, that women were recognized as fully forming part of the sovereign people and given the vote.

The Parliament of the Fifth Republic is deeply rooted in the principle of universal suffrage. The introduction in 1962 of direct election to the presidency (see Chapters 2 and 3), combined with the presence in the National Assembly of a presidential majority (see Chapter 8) had the effect for a while of concentrating political power and activity outside Parliament, if within an institution that could also claim to be supported by the sovereign people. During the 1980s, however, the strength of the rationalized and constrained parliamentary system with which the authors of the 1958 constitution had wished to replace the irresponsible and unstable patterns of the Fourth Republic became rather more evident. Both the Left and the Right have discovered the mechanisms which the constitution makes available to them. Parliament's chief function remains the legitimation, through the legislative process, of the programme of a government. In this role the Parliament of the Fifth Republic has been markedly more effective than its predecessor. Another main function of parliaments is 'to make the government behave' (Frears, 1990, p. 33). The French Parliament has in general performed this function less effectively. This chapter describes the structures and mechanisms of Parliament and considers its functions and the role it plays.

The Structure of Parliament

The National Assembly: voters and elections

The French Parliament consists of two houses, or chambers. The 'lower' house, the National Assembly, has 577 members, sometimes called 'deputies'. The French word is *député* which might better be translated as 'delegate'.

The right to vote for members of Parliament is enjoyed by men and women over the age of eighteen. The voting age was lowered from 21 to eighteen in 1974, by a law passed soon after Valéry Giscard d'Estaing won the presidency. Voters must be of French nationality and must not have been legally deprived of their right to vote. Such a deprivation, usually for a certain specified number of years, can form part of the penalty for certain criminal offences. Electors must also appear on the electoral register, which is revised each year.

Members of the National Assembly must be over the age of twenty-three and be French citizens. Most of them acquire their seats at general elections. A general election must be held at least once every five years: in 1967, 1973, 1978, 1986, 1993 and 2002, general elections occurred because the sitting Assembly had been in place for five years. General elections also happen after the dissolution of the National Assembly by the President. The general elections of 1962, 1968, 1981, 1988 and 1997 followed a presidential dissolution.

Some members of the National Assembly come into parliament at times other than a general election. Members (on average two a year) die or (as occurred in June 2000, but the event is rare) are removed following criminal conviction, or resign, perhaps because they wish to take up functions which are legally incompatible with a position as a member of Parliament. Posts as government ministers fall into this category, so, for example, in 2002, 22 people who had been elected to the National Assembly in the general election resigned before that Assembly even met to take up ministerial posts as the new government was formed. During the 1986–8 Parliament, which was elected by a list system of proportional representation, such vacancies were filled by the return to Parliament of the first unsuccessful candidate from the same party list as the outgoing member. For all the other parliaments since 1958, all candidates at an election have had to nominate, alongside themselves, a *suppléant* – a person to replace them should they be unable to continue as a member. By-elections occur only when the replacement as well as the original member dies or resigns, but usually happen about twice a year.

Election campaigns, which last officially for the three-week period between the nomination of the candidates and polling day, are subject to strict official controls. Some regulations cover the period before the opening of the official campaign, so that party political commercials on television are banned not only during the campaign but also in the six months before a parliamentary term is due to end, as are all forms of political advertising other than official posters of the regulation size and shape in the authorized sites during the campaign.

Candidates pay for the provision of voting slips in their names and their official posters and election addresses, but these costs, up to a limit of 50 per cent of permitted electoral expenditure, are refunded to all candidates who receive over 5 per cent of the votes. A candidate's total expenditure is limited to 38 000 Euro plus 1.5 Euro for every inhabitant of the constituency. Unofficial teams of nocturnal bill posters are equally a feature of French elections, and the art of finding the humorous or pointed riposte with which to embellish opponents' posters is highly developed. The exact time allowed for each candidate or party by the broadcast media is carefully measured; even studio debates may be timed by a stopwatch. In an attempt to prevent last-minute pressure and unfair influence, all such campaigning has to cease the day before polling day, and the publication of opinion polls is not permitted immediately before polling day. Between 1977 and 2001 the gap was seven days. Since the spring of 2002 it has been two.

The act of voting requires voters to place a slip of paper containing the name of the chosen candidate (and his or her replacement) in an envelope and post this into the ballot box. Empty envelopes, or those containing more than one slip, are counted as void or spoilt votes.

Most general elections since 1958 have been conducted under the constituency-based two-ballot system. One member is returned by each territorial constituency. To be elected at the first ballot a candidate requires over 50 per cent of all the valid votes cast (see Table 7.1). Otherwise all those candidates who have been voted for by more than 12.5 per cent of the registered electors and who do not stand down go on to a second ballot a week later. If no candidate – or only one – achieves 12.5 per cent the two with the most votes go forward. This system encourages *désistement* (agreements), at least at second ballot stage, between parties of similar political outlook, so that their best placed candidate goes forward. At the second ballot the candidate with most votes (a simple plurality of votes) wins.

In 1986 a proportional representation system was used, treating each *département* as a multi-member constituency. Its introduction was an astute, if cynical, manoeuvre. It was largely prompted by short-term party political considerations. The election for which it was used installed a right-wing government in power which restored the previous system, redrawing the constituency boundaries in a law drafted within the Ministry of the Interior in consultation with a committee of six 'wise men' and the Council of State and imposed on Parliament as an issue of confidence. Proportional representation for general elections is no longer on the political agenda.

The confirmation of the validity of elections, and hence the determination of the National Assembly's membership is not its own responsibility. A number of cases during the 1950s gave rise to decisions about membership of the Fourth Republic's National Assembly which were widely felt to have been based on highly political motives; this caused some scandal (Williams, 1972, p. 120), and the authors of the Fifth Republic's constitution removed such powers from the National Assembly and gave them to the Constitutional Council (see Table 2.2),

TABLE 7.1

Number of candidates elected at the first ballot

	1958	1962	1967	1968	1973	1978	1981	1986	1988	1993	1997	2002
Total seats	579	482	487	487	490	491	491	N/A	577	577	577	577
Elected at first ballot	35	103	81	166	60	68	157		120	80	12	58

Source: Compiled from Assemblée Nationale (www.assemblee-nat.fr/elections/historique-3.asp).

which adjudicates in cases where the election results are disputed, or electoral fraud or malpractice alleged.

The Senate

The Senate is the second chamber of the French Parliament. It represents the elected local authorities since each electoral constituency consists of one *département* in which the senators are elected by an electoral college comprising the members of parliament, the members of the *département's* council, and mayors and town councillors. The Senate consists of 321 members who must be over the age of 35, each of whom serves for a nine-year term. The Senate cannot be dissolved. One-third of the membership is replaced every three years. The members represent *départements* (including the overseas territories and *départements*) which are divided into three groups, all the members from one of the groups being replaced at each renewal. Twelve senators represent French citizens resident abroad. The method of election of senators gives a national political significance to the results of local elections, since the political complexion of local councils determines that of the Senate. This meant, for example, that the Senate of the first decade of the Fifth Republic reflected the results of local elections under the Fourth Republic, and with a high proportion of rather conservative independent members, was much less supportive of de Gaulle than the National Assembly. Socialist representation in the Senate increased in the early 1980s, following the left-wing gains in the local elections of 1977, and a similar effect occurred in 1995, when Senate elections in September followed municipal elections in June. In the late 1980s the representation of the Right increased following their gains in the local elections of the early 1980s. The process of political change in the Senate is slow, however, given the nine-year term of each senator and the Left have never commanded a majority there. Equally, although the National Front in 1995 gained the councils of three large towns (Toulon, Orange and Marignane) the party is not represented in the Senate.

Since laws must be passed in identical terms by both houses (see below) the Senate can and does influence legislation, often acting to amend and improve bills in technical ways. The Senate's relationship with de Gaulle was poor, largely because of the opposition of its members to the 1962 constitutional amendment. It survived the 1969 referendum which proposed its reform. The outcome of the 1981 election again resulted in a political division between the majorities in the two houses and the Senate constituted a source of difficulty for the Mitterrand government. Its opposition to the nationalization programme, the press reform bill and the laws reforming industrial relations slowed the legislative process. The Senate is also an element in the complex pattern of relationships which counterbalances the power of the central state by ensuring that local interests are well represented at the centre. The Raffarin government's constitutional amendment provides that laws relating to the powers of local authorities should always begin their passage in the Senate. The Senate has largely been unable to block governmental legislation although it can substantially amend it. In 2000, senators put down over 1 000 amendments to a bill on housing provision which would have a considerable impact on local authorities, and over 600 of them were passed (*L'Année Politique*, 2000, pp. 71–2). It also has the crucial ability to block the normal procedures for constitutional amendment, a power it has used.

The Members of Parliament: Characteristics and Conditions

The professional background of members of Parliament has varied according to the party balance within Parliament (Table 7.2 gives rather approximate indications). Thus the advent of a majority of the Left in 1981 resulted in an increase in the numbers of *députés* who had been teachers; out of 285 Socialist *députés*, 150 were former teachers. In the 1997 Parliament, there were some 130 teachers and university teachers. The Socialist Party has traditionally drawn a good deal of its activist membership from this group. The return of the Right reduced the figure for teachers to 73. The proportion of *députés* with backgrounds as junior employees or workers, small business or tradespeople and farmers has long been low.

The number of women members of Parliament in France has never been high. It was highest in 1945 just after women had gained the vote. The low proportion in the 1980s and 1990s, rising from between 5 and 6 per cent to 11 per cent in 1997 (and 12 per cent in 2002) directly prompted the parity laws (see Exhibit 2.7).

A feature of the French Parliament is the number of members who have formerly been civil servants – 40 per cent of members of the 1997–2002 National Assembly, although 62 per cent of these were in fact teachers and only 6.4 per cent of all members were former students of the ENA (Rouban, 1998b, p. 176). In 2002 the figure was 189, of whom 73 were teachers or university teachers. Officials may claim 'secondment' from the civil service during their period as *députés* and consequently have a particularly secure fall-back should electoral

TABLE 7.2

Representation of selected occupations in the National Assembly (rounded per cent)

Occupation	1978	1981	1986	1988	1993	2002
Education	20	33	25	28	13	12
Civil service	20	23	22	17	12	20
Farmers	3	2	2	2	4	2
Industrialists/ senior management	7.5	4	11	5	11	17
Employees and workers	4	6	2	3	3	2.5

Sources: 1978 to 1988 figures from Dreyfus and D'Arcy (1993, p. 85). 1993 figures from *Le Monde*, 1 April 1993 and *Pouvoirs*, 66 (1993). 2002 figures calculated from *Le Figaro*, 18 June 2002 and *Les Echos*, 19 June 2002. Categorization is not necessarily identical.

TABLE 7.3

Women in the National Assembly

Year	1981	1986	1988	1992	1997	2002
Total membership	491	577	577	577	577	577
Women	28	33	33	32	63	71
Percentage of women	4.7	5.7	5.7	5.5	10.9	12.3

defeat occur. For senior civil servants the contacts with politicians and political life that they have encountered during their official activities can assist the launch of a political career, although the number of members of the *grands corps* (see Chapter 5) who are members of the National Assembly has been falling – from a high point of 14 per cent in 1978 to 8.6 per cent in 1993 and 4 per cent in 1997 (Rouban, 1998b, p. 176).

French members of Parliament enjoy salaries calculated as the median of those paid to the highest grade of officials. The Communist Party always insisted that its members of Parliament should hand over this salary to the party. Its *députés* are then remunerated at the average rate for a skilled worker, and in the past when Communist representation in Parliament was substantial the surplus provided an important source of general party funds.

Another striking feature of the members of Parliament is the extent to which they may combine elective offices (*cumul des mandats*) (see Chapter 5). In 1981, 82 per cent of the *députés* held one or more elective offices at local level. Indeed 'mayors of major cities have a sort of natural call to be members of parliament' (Masclet, 1982, p. 110). Aproximately half of all members of every Parliament since 1958 have been mayors (Knapp, 1991, p. 19; Knapp and Wright, 2001, p. 147). During the 1970s and 1980s, concern about this practice of accumulation of offices grew. After the 1981 Socialist victory resulted in a broad programme for decentralization which involved increased areas of responsibility for elected councils at the level of the *département* and the introduction of a new tier of elected local government at regional level, this concern became increasingly pressing. Debate focused on the likelihood that where several offices were combined some of them, at least, would not be properly fulfilled. There was also some feeling that decentralization ought to mean a broadening of political participation and not simply the creation of further offices for those who already constituted a political elite. In addition, even though holders of multiple offices were only entitled to draw half pay for some of them, the propriety of allowing an individual to retain multiple salaries was questioned: in the mid-1980s Jean Lecanuet held five offices, at every level from the European Parliament to the *commune* of Rouen, and drew an income approximately twice that of the average basic salary for a member of parliament (Schmidt, 1990, p. 147). A law of 30 December 1985 permitted the holding in future of only two major elective offices at any one time. After the elections of 1988, the 577 members of the National Assembly between them held 812 local positions, and to comply with the law needed to 'lose' 141 of them. Faced with choices the *députés* almost all preferred to abandon posts at the level of region and *département*. None resigned as a mayor (Knapp, 1991, p. 35). In an interesting exception to this pattern in October 1989, former President Giscard d'Estaing preferred to retain his seat in the regional council of the Auvergne and the European Parliament, and give up his seat in the National Assembly, to which, however, he returned in 1993. He was re-elected *président* of the Regional Council in 1998. A further reform by a law of March 2000 restricted the combination of local elected offices, or the combination of any other post with membership of the European Parliament, even more tightly, but allowed national parliamentarians to continue as mayors.

Partly as a result of the close linkage between local and central political life symbolized by the practice of the *cumul des mandats* the task of a *député* is conceived as having particularly strong local connections. Members of Parliament are not a major means through which citizens plead their individual cases against the actions of the ministers and ministries – other channels are used for the redress of grievances of that sort. *Députés* are, however, perceived (somewhat erroneously) as able to procure individual favours for their constituents. They certainly are powerful pleaders for the broader interests of their constituency, and do develop strongly clientilistic relationships with the mayors and other leaders in their constituencies. In a centralized system, where much local development and activity is still subject to control and authorization by central government, and investment and economic development may be heavily influenced by central bodies, a *député* has an important role in trying to push forward his constituency's case within central government. It has moreover been powerfully argued (for example, by Ashford, 1982) that the absence (compared, for example, with the centralizing tendencies of the United Kingdom) of any assault on local government or, even in periods of economic recession, of attempts radically to restructure local government structures or expenditures, results from the strength of the links between local and central political levels, and the importance of central politicians' bases within their local areas.

The Organization of Parliamentary Work

As part of the reform embodied within the constitutional settlement of 1958 and intended to tip the balance of the institutions away from Parliament towards the executive, the constitution of the Fifth Republic contains detailed provisions for the organization of parliamentary work. These provisions contributed to the partial eclipse of Parliament during the first three decades of the regime. They were only one, and perhaps not the most important, amongst several factors which contributed at that period to Parliament's lack of prominence (see below). However, changes in the context in which Parliament operates, both political (the coming of *cohabitation*, for example) and institutional (the changing nature of the European Union and an increased role for the National Assembly in relation to European Union legislation) have led to changes in its habits and operation. Although its effect was principally to redistribute the calendar of sittings across the year rather than substantially to extend it, the extent of these changes was symbolized by the constitutional amendment of 1995, which altered the length of the parliamentary session.

In 1958 the constitution had limited the duration of parliamentary sessions in order, at least in part, to curb Parliament's appetite for business and limit its capacity to hinder and hamper the government. Moreover, the restriction of the matters about which it is permitted to legislate was expected to mean that it would need less time for its business. The Constitution therefore specified normal sessions of not more than 80 days following 2 October and for not more than 90 days following 2 April every year. In addition special sessions might be called at the request either of the government or of a majority of members of the National Assembly. Particular items of business which have to be specified in advance must constitute the agenda for such special sessions,which required presidential approval. Genuine emergency sessions occurred only very rarely. The half-day session in late August 1990 called to discuss the Iraqi invasion of Kuwait was the first session since 1959 to have been summoned in response to an international crisis (Maus, 1991, p. 68). However, from the mid-1970s onwards special sessions became the norm, while the brevity of parliamentary sessions produced unedifying spectacles such as the final passage, at the end of December 1987, of sixteen laws and seven ratifications of foreign agreements within 48 hours.

The constitutional amendment of 1995 changed these provisions. Parliament now meets on not more than 120 days (with the possibility of additional days on the decision of either the prime minister or a majority of members) in a single session lasting from the first working day in October to the final working day in June. The President has thereby lost powers to veto additional days. The provision for special sessions still exists, but they are rare: in the five-year legislature from 1997–2002 there were two, one in September 1997 (the new government had utilized the residue of the previous ordinary session in June, but recalled Parliament in September) and one in July 1998. In 2002 when the General Election took place in June a two-week special session was called in July. The new Parliament would otherwise not have met until over three months after the election. It approved revised financial appropriations and some initial tax cuts, to meet President Chirac's election commitments. This reform was also the logical next step in a process championed by Philippe Séguin, who presided over the National Assembly from 1993 to 1997. He had been particularly active in seeking to increase the profile of parliamentary activity, and had in the autumn of 1993 ensured the passage of a law which allowed for the reception in Parliament of distinguished foreign visitors, for the continuous televising of parliamentary sessions on a Paris cable television network, and for the regrouping of business on three days a week. It was hoped that the reform would allow members to organize their time more rationally between their parliamentary and local responsibilities and reduce absenteeism. The long single session would mean that Parliament would no longer be absent from public sight for extended periods.

Both Houses of Parliament are presided over by a *président* elected at the start of each new Parliament. The role of this *président*, especially in the National Assembly, has a clear political status, and election to it may be quite hotly contested. It usually goes to a senior political figure from amongst the governing coalition. For example, former Prime Minister Laurent Fabius took over as *président* in 1988, while in 1993 the election of Séguin, who had led the 'No' campaign in the Maastricht referendum, against his party's official line, 'was the pay-off for [general election] campaign loyalty; it was also a convenient way for Chirac to reward an important figure without the embarrassment of having to have him in the government' (Hanley, 1993, p. 425). In 2002 the *président* was Jean-Louis Debré who, it was said, had declined governmental office because he did not wish to abandon his office as mayor of Evreux.

The timetable of parliamentary business is effectively drawn up by the government, another measure introduced by the 1958 constitution to curb the excesses of the Fourth Republic. The government has the right to insist that discussion of its bills, and of any private member's bills which it accepts, takes priority except on one day a month when, under the 1995 constitutional amendment, the members of the house may decide the agenda. The drafters of the constitution were very wary of allowing any scope for members of Parliament to push through legislation on their own initiative, seeing this as one of the factors of incoherence that had undermined government in the Fourth Republic. Several decades of a tamed disciplined and generally majoritarian National Assembly had lessened such caution (see Table 7.6). The new provision provides more scope for backbenchers to insist on debating particular topics, and to advance private member's bill. In a majoritarian system these are likely to need at least tacit governmental support to succeed. Governments have occasionally found it useful to encourage private member's bills which advance highly controversial causes which they may support but with which they would prefer not to be strongly identified. One example was the 1999 law on civil solidarity pacts (PACS – see p. 26). However, in the absence of any concept of 'official' opposition to which time would be allocated, there is still almost no scope for the 'opposition' to initiate debates on particular issues other than by moving a motion of censure on the government, a very rare ocurrence.

The right to speak in the Senate and the National Assembly is not confined solely to their respective members, since ministers, who are not members of Parliament and consequently have no vote, may be present for debates and questions and speak.

Parliamentary questions are provided for. The practice of holding debates round questions (comparable to British adjournment debates), not uncommon in the first two decades of the Fifth Republic, has disappeared since 1975, largely because the parliamentary majority controlled the committee (the *conférence des présidents*) which decided which questions to accept and could prevent discussions that might incommode the government. Only two such debates took place in the 1997–2002 legislature, both in the 2000–2001 session, one concerned with food safety and one on institutional reform. Oral questions continue once a week. A weekly quota is allocated to each political group. Only the author of the question and the minister concerned may speak. After an initial attempt at a more vigorous question time in 1970, 'questions to the government', in addition to the oral question procedures, were launched in 1974. These questions are nowadays taken for an hour at the beginning of the Tuesday and Wednesday afternoon sittings. The time allowed is divided up very precisely between the political groups in the Parliament and during that time they may put to ministers questions of which only an hour's notice need have been given, although the name of the questioner and an indication of the minister concerned has to be provided longer in advance. These questions are concerned with immediate issues and problems and both questions and answers are limited to two and a half minutes. Despite both their being televised and the insistence of successive *présidents* that both questioners and ministers should not simply read from their notes, they do not normally provide a forum for highly charged political debate and conflict.

The laws which Parliament passes originate either as government bills (*projets de loi*) or as private member's bills (*propositions de loi*) (see Table 7.6). Bills are immediately sent for examination to a committee. The constitution (Article 43) limits the number of permanent committees to six in each house (see Exhibit 7.1). This limitation was to ensure that they would be large and general, and to remove the possibility that specialized committees might act virtually as alternative ministers, subject to lobbying by interested parties and able to produce laws which differed fundamentally from those initially submitted to them. It is within these committees that the bulk of the detailed examination of the bills and proposed amendments (see Table 7.6) occurs. The committee hears the minister concerned, if the bill is a

---

EXHIBIT 7.1

The committees of Parliament

The National Assembly committees	The Senate committees
Cultural, family and social affairs	Cultural affairs
Foreign affairs	Foreign affairs, defence and the armed forces
National defence and the armed forces	Economic affairs and the plan
Finances, the economy and the plan	Social affairs
Constitutional laws, legislation and general administration	Finances
Production and trade	Constitutional laws, legislation, voting rights, regulation and general administration

TABLE 7.4

National Assembly and Senate: the passage of Acts of Parliament*

	1994	1995	1996	1997	1998	1999	2000
Without a joint committee	37	13	39	16	28	32	21
With agreement in a joint committee	25	12	29	4	5	8	10
Without agreement in a joint committee	1	0	1	7	13	11	19

Note
* excluding those ratifying treaties and conventions.
Source: Compiled from *L'Année Politique 2000*, p. 175.

governmental one, but may also undertake other enquiries and investigations. A report is produced which is presented to the plenary sessions of the National Assembly, indicating the text and the amendments which the committee supports. Following the completion of the committee's report, the bill, when it appears on the agenda, comes before a plenary session of the National Assembly, where it will normally be discussed article by article and may be amended. A final vote confirms the adoption or rejection of the final version of the whole law. The law is then passed to the other house, where a similar procedure ensues.

The result of the discussions in the other house may be some divergence from the text originally approved where it was first discussed. In this case the text returns to the original house for a vote on the amended version. If an agreement is still not reached a procedure known as the 'shuttle' (*navette*) occurs. The text may be passed back and forth until agreement is reached. However, the government may interrupt this process and set up a joint committee of members of the two houses to attempt to arrive at an agreed text. Where this proves impossible, or where the two houses still refuse to approve an agreed text, the constitution provides that the National Assembly shall have the last word.

When the National Assembly majority is a Socialist one, agreement between the two houses has tended to be more difficult. Under the Socialist governments of 1988 to 1993, nearly half of all disputed texts (79 out of 163) were finally adopted without the Senate's consent. With a majority from the mainstream right, there was very seldom a failure to reach agreement, but after 1997 the proportion of laws adopted without consent rose again sharply (see Table 7.4).

The Functions of Parliament: Opportunities and Constraints

Parliaments in liberal democracies usually fulfil a number of functions: they enact legislation; they may act as an arena for political debate; they may provide the government with the formal expressions of support it needs to maintain its legitimacy; they may constitute a forum for the exchange of information, serving both to educate their members, and through them the voters in the policies, needs and constraints of government, and to act as channels for the expression of the grievances of the citizen; they may control and supervise the work of the administration; they may be the place where political apprenticeships are served, providing a reservoir of potential ministerial office holders.

Legislation

The French Parliament enacts legislation. However, unlike some parliaments, its ability to do so is not absolute. Parliamentary sovereignty is limited by the constitution. First, the 1958 constitution specifies the areas in which Parliament may make law (see Exhibit 7.2). These areas cover the fundamental aspects of the organization of society, so that, for example, nothing can be made a criminal offence except by a parliamentary law. Parliamentary powers were extended by constitutional amendment in 1996 to encompass the enaction of the social security budget, an important element of taxation which had previously been dealt with solely by governmental regulation, as many aspects of the detailed application of these fundamental principles still are. They are thus not directly subject to parliamentary control. Secondly, the laws which Parliament passes have to conform to the principles set out in the constitution. It is the Constitutional Council (see Chapter 2) which has the responsibility both for determining whether Parliament is acting outside its sphere of competence, and for ensuring that constitutional principles are respected. The president, the prime minister, the presidents of the Senate and the National Assembly, or at least 60 members of the Senate or at least 60 members of the National Assembly may ask the Constitutional Council to examine the constitutionality of a proposed law after it has been voted but before it is officially promulgated.

Governmental resources, procedural and political
The legislative action of Parliament is not only constrained by constitutional provisions, it is also largely determined by the government. Indeed, governments tend to judge whether Parliament is 'working well' by the efficiency with which the government's policy objectives are translated into legislative measures. In this, they are assisted by two types of resources, procedural and political (Maus, 1989). In 1958 the authors of the constitution were particularly concerned that governments must be enabled to get their laws through. They envisaged the possible prolongation of the shifting and unstable coalitions of the Fourth Republic, and wanted to give governments better possibilities of insisting, procedurally, upon the passage of their legislation. This explains the (now slightly mitigated) governmental control of the parliamentary agenda discussed above, as well as the restriction on the number of committees. More important is the provision of Article 44 paragraph 3 of the constitution which enables the government to insist that a draft law, or any part of it, should be taken as a whole along with such amendments as

---

EXHIBIT 7.2

The powers of Parliament

Article 34 of the Constitution.
Laws shall be voted by Parliament.
Laws determine the rules concerning:

- civil rights and the fundamental guarantees granted to the citizens for the exercise of their public liberties; the obligations imposed by national defence upon the persons and property of citizens;
- the nationality, status and legal capacity of persons, marriage contracts, inheritance and gifts;
- the determination of crimes and misdemeanours as well as the penalties imposed therefor; criminal procedure, amnesty, the creation of new juridical systems and the status of the judiciary;
- the basis, the rate and the methods of collecting taxes of all types; the issue of currency.

Laws shall likewise determine the regulations concerning:

- the electoral system of the parliamentary Assemblies and local assemblies;
- the establishment of categories of public institutions;
- the fundamental guarantees granted to civil and military personnel employed by the state;
- the nationalization of enterprises and the transfer of the property of enterprises from the public to the private sectors.

Laws shall determine the fundamental principles of:

- the general organization of national defence;
- the free administration of local communities, their powers and their resources;
- education;
- property rights and civil and commercial obligations; a legislation pertaining to employment, unions and social security.

  The financial laws shall determine the financial resources and obligations of the state, under the conditions and with the reservations to be provided for in an organic law. Laws pertaining to national planning shall determine the objectives of the economic and social action of the state. The provisions of the present article may be detailed and supplemented by an organic law.

---

the government chooses to accept. This procedure, known as the 'block vote' (*vote bloqué*) acts as a 'guillotine' to cut short plenary discussion, and may also serve to prevent dissent within the majority coalition from being expressed – the text has to be accepted or rejected in its entirety. This procedure was used quite frequently, in the first decade of the Fifth Republic, but since 1970 the number of such votes has gone into double figures in only four years, and it was not used at all by the Jospin government between 1997 and 2002.

A second important procedural device is the provision of paragraph 3 of Article 49 of the constitution whereby a government may declare a particular text an issue of confidence. The text will automatically be regarded as being approved unless a motion of censure is tabled and voted. Governments have used it to ease or speed up the passage of legislation. The Socialists who had been highly critical of the procedure had recourse to it eleven times between 1981 and 1986, despite their absolute majority, and Chirac used it seven times in 1986 in the context of a *cohabitation* government whose limited life span – change of some sort at the election of 1988 was seen as inevitable – meant speed was important.

Between 1988 and 1993 the Socialist governments of Prime Ministers Rocard, Cresson and Bérégovoy, facing a hung parliament and thus rather closer to the situation which the authors of the constitution had originally envisaged, used the provision a total of 39 times, in order to gain approval of nineteen different laws. The presence of secure and relatively disciplined majorities since 1993 has (see Table 7.5) removed the need for frequent recourse to a procedure which is not without its risks. In November 1990 the Rocard government survived a censure motion tabled against a law increasing social security contributions by a margin of only five votes. It was however again resorted to in 2003 for a highly contentious bill altering the local electoral system.

A third constitutional provision allows the government to attempt to avoid altogether detailed discussion of potentially contentious matters that have to be regulated by law. This is the possibility of obtaining from Parliament delegated authority to legislate by regulation for a certain period in a certain field. Called a *loi d'habilitation*, the device has been used to avoid the emergence in public debate of divisions of opinion amongst the majority. It may also be used to speed

TABLE 7.5

Use of Article 49, paragraph 3 (Bill declared by government to be an issue of confidence 1 January 1959 to 1 April 2003)

Governments	Total	Censure motion tabled	No censure tabled
Debré 1959–62	4	4	0
Pompidou 1962	3	1	2
Pompidou 1962–67	0	0	0
Pompidou 1967–8	3	3	0
Couve de Murville/ Chaban-Delmas/ Messmer/Chirac 1968–76	0	0	0
Barre 1976–81	8	7	1
Mauroy/Fabius 1981–6	11	7	4
Chirac 1986–8	8	7	1
Rocard/Cresson/ Bérégovoy 1986–93	39	8	31
Balladur/Juppé 1993–5	3	3	0
Jospin 1997–2002	0	0	0
Raffarin 2002–	1	1	0

Source: complied from www.assemblée-nat.fr/connaissance/consulted 15 August 2002.

TABLE 7.6

Legislative activity 1997–2001

Session	Government bills passed	Private members' bills passed	Laws to ratify treaties and conventions	Amendments tabled	Amendments passed
1997–8	30	23	50	10 709	2 722
1998–9	34	19	40	13 835	3 472
1999–2000	37	43	61	12 326	4 182
2000–1	25	16	23	8 479	3 754
2001–2*	17	17	31	4 885	2 237

* October to February.
Source: compiled from www.assemblee-nationale.fr (consulted 16 August 2002 and 10 January 2003).

up legislation. The use of the procedure became more controversial during the period of *cohabitation*. President Mitterrand twice refused to sign the regulations which the government had drawn up under such a law. On the first occasion it was to mark his disagreement with the privatization programme. On the second occasion the *loi d'habilitation* concerned the new constituencies proposed under the return to the two-ballot system. Parliament ought, the President said, to have its say on its own membership. In both cases the government very hastily put the proposed legislation directly to Parliament as a normal law, and in the circumstances was able to carry its majority with it. The laws were duly promulgated. Since 1985 the provision has been used only thirteen times. Nine of these laws related to overseas territories (five of them to the tiny territory of Mayotte) and one dealt with the very special circumstance of the need to change sums specified in francs in legal texts to euros ahead of the changeover (http://www.assemblee-nat. fr/connaissance/collection/2.asp).

Secondly, the government does, of course, have political resources to assist it with the passage of its business through Parliament. Until 1986 all presidents were supported by a presidential majority within Parliament. Even during periods when party discipline was not well established, as was the case between 1958 and 1962, or when the presidential majority was constituted by a coalition whose coherence was fragile, for example during the presidency of Giscard d'Estaing, governments have largely proved able to mobilize political appeals to ensure the passage of their legislation. Between 1978 and 1981, for example, the Gaullist party within the National Assembly caused a number of problems for President Giscard d'Estaing and Prime Minister Barre, but never went so far as to risk a possible dissolution and general election. The governments of the second Mitterrand presidency, under Michel Rocard and Edith Cresson, also managed to put together majorities for the legislation they wished to carry. One factor was a marked decrease in the amount of legislation introduced. In the first 30 years of the Fifth Republic an average of 74 government bills a year were introduced, but between 1989 and 1993 the average fell to 56 a year. (Elgie, 1991, p. 12; Maus, 1995, p. 180). More recent periods have seen substantial legislation to ratify treaties and conventions, as Table 7.6 shows, and the passage of considerable numbers of private member's bills, but rather restrained governmental activity. This may be accounted for in part by the government's ability to act via regulation.

From the government's point of view the legislative function of the Parliament of the Fifth Republic has worked well. Very few governmental policies have been stymied by activity within Parliament. Where the government has ceded and withdrawn a bill it has usually been in response to intense pressure of public opinion, manifest for example in demonstrations like those concerning university reform in 1986. Nevertheless, private members can play an important role in the legislative process.

The role of members

The legislative role of the member of Parliament may seem reduced, by a combination of constitutional mechanisms and political pressures, to a purely formal one. Methods do exist, however, for members to influence legislation. One of the dilemmas within Parliament is the balance that has to be struck between the largely political function of supporting – or opposing – governmental policy on a broad base, and the more technical function of going through proposed legislation with an eye to improving it technically, to some extent regardless of the policy that it embodies. There is some scope for members to fulfil this latter function, for example in acting as *rapporteurs* for a bill as it moves through a committee, where there may be considerable scope for influence. In the last decade or so, however, the sharpness of much political debate has penetrated even to the committees, to the detriment, in the eyes of some commentators, of their function as places where the privacy of the proceedings allowed at least some partisan cleavages to be set aside.

Backbenchers can also propose amendments, and do so, sometimes in substantial numbers, as Table 7.6 suggests. A very high proportion of amendments adopted in fact derive from the government, or from the committees in which they have a majority, but backbenchers can by their amendments cause considerable difficulties for the government.

Private members may introduce bills, though only if they will have no effect upon public resources or taxation. Until 1995 the time available for the discussion of private member's bills was so limited, that many such bills were never discussed at all unless the government supported the proposal or incorporated it into a bill of its own. This happened in six cases during the spring session of 1990. Since 1995 markedly more private member's bills have been successful (see Table 7.6), albeit sometimes with governmental support as in the case of the PACS law. The impact of the allocation of monthly days for the discussion of private member's bills can be gauged, for example, by the fact that 10 of the 16 private member's bills passed in 2000–1 were discussed on those days, and five of them originated outside the Socialist Party.

Nevertheless, members' perception of their role in the legislative process is emphasized by the fact that often very few actually turn up to take their part in the debates or even to vote in person. On one notorious occasion in the autumn of 1987, when the National Front members of Parliament created a considerable disturbance in the chamber partly in protest at such absenteeism, there were, for an afternoon and evening debate on a law about drug abuse, only 25 members out of 577 present. It is equally the case that duties elsewhere – as mayors, or as councillors, or, until the reform of 2000, as members of the European Parliament – are likely to keep members away.

Votes are taken in the National Assembly by electronic means. All the members have their own places in the semicircular chamber, and each place is equipped with an electronic gadget which registers a vote when a key is turned in it. Until 1993 it was possible for a party representative to turn the keys of a large number of absent colleagues when a vote was taken. The Constitutional Council on 23 January 1987 decided that even when the constitutional provision that a member's vote is 'personal' and Parliament's own standing order limiting proxy voting had manifestly been flouted during the vote on a bill, the law so passed was valid. Dissatisfaction with the abuses to which the system could give rise led to a reform of the procedure in 1993 which has not, however, resulted in marked improvements in attendance.

The focus of political conflict

Every vote in favour of a measure proposed or supported by the government is implicitly a confirmation of that government's position and right to govern. The constitution provides, in Articles 49 and 50, for that legitimacy to be formally and explicitly confirmed or disavowed. The prime minister may present his programme to Parliament, or make a general policy statement. If he makes that programme or statement an issue of confidence and is defeated in the National Assembly the government must resign. But governments rarely do this: not all have even presented their programmes to the Assembly on appointment, although Jean-Pierre Raffarin did do so during the special session which followed the 2002 election. Motions of censure may also be proposed, and if they are successful, the government's resignation must follow. But the conditions for the tabling and voting of a motion of censure are tight. Such a motion must be proposed by one-tenth of the members of the Assembly, and members whose motion has been unsuccessful may not propose another during that parliamentary session (except in cases where a motion of censure is required to oppose a bill on which the government has invoked Article 49 paragraph 3, see above). A majority of all members must actually vote in favour of the motion for it to pass. Abstentions consequently count as votes against the motion. The votes have sometimes been close. In May 1992 Prime Minister Bérégovoy survived a vote of censure over the reform of the common agricultural policy of the European Community by only 3 votes out of 577. But during the Fifth Republic only one motion of censure has succeeded, in October 1962. Prime Minister

Pompidou resigned, de Gaulle dissolved the Assembly, Pompidou stayed in office until the elections, and was immediately reappointed as prime minister after the Gaullist electoral success.

Parliament under the Fifth Republic has not been the place where sharp political debate has been focused. There are a number of reasons for this: the reduced powers of Parliament; the rate of absenteeism; the limitations on questions; the existence of coalition governments; the fact that ministers are not actually members of the house; all these factors undoubtedly contribute to the absence of intense and adversarial conflict. Probably even more important has been the extent of presidential government for much, though not all, of the Fifth Republic. The general orientation of government policy could be attacked only through proxies in the Assembly, and presidents have responded to the political climate through press releases, interviews or press conferences, speeches, visits and television appearances. Governments have often not thought it necessary to make statements to the National Assembly about issues of political concern. There was, for example, no statement about the sinking of the Greenpeace boat *Rainbow Warrior* in Auckland harbour by agents of the French security services in 1985, despite massive press speculation and the eventual resignation of the Minister of Defence. The prolonged period of *cohabitation* did produce rather more government statements – an average of about four a year – sometimes on domestic issues of concern, such as, in early 2000, the coastal oil-spill of late 1999, or decentralization policy, in 2001, but more often on international problems – Kosovo in 1999, the Seattle riots of 1999, the events of 11 September 2001 and Afghanistan. It is at least possible that the habit will persist. Nevertheless, that media attention to the proceedings of Parliament is limited is both cause and effect of a perception that important politics happens elsewhere.

During and after the first period of *cohabitation* the National Assembly gained a slightly higher profile, and not just because of the rowdy tactics adopted by the end of 1987 by the National Front *députés*. Since governmental policy at that period was largely determined by the prime minister, who does appear in the Assembly, and in a situation where the government could not necessarily be sure of a majority, parliamentary debates might be seen as having some point. While the French parliament may not be a forum for the sharpest and most adversarial political debates (the press and, increasingly, television fulfil that role) it is not an arena that leading politicians feel they can afford to ignore. Former prime ministers (for example, Rocard, Balladur, Fabius, Juppé and Barre) and – even more notably, after a brief absence when he preferred the European Parliament – a former president, Giscard d'Estaing, continue to seek re-election and to serve as members.

Political education and the expression of grievances

Members of the French Parliament have access to a very large amount of information. Moreover, almost all *députés* hold periodic surgeries in their constituencies, and may also hold working meetings with the mayors and local councils of each *commune* in the constituency. In addition, computerized databases are now available to all members. Compared with their counterparts in the United Kingdom or Germany, however, they have limited access to specific research assistance, such as that provided by the House of Commons Library, or by the research staff of the political parties. French members of Parliament are assisted in dealing with this flood of information by the secretary and the personal assistant, paid for from Parliament's funds, to whom they have been entitled since the early 1970s.

Parliament itself has made some effort to remedy some of the gaps in its research and information base. In 1983, what amounts to a standing committee on science and technology was created – the Office for the Evaluation of Science and Technology Policy. This consists of eight *députés* and eight senators, with an advisory council of 15 scientists, charged with the task of explaining to Parliament the choices that have been made within science and technology policy. The result has been a number of solid reports on major technological and environmental issues, such as the semiconductor industry and the management of domestic and industrial waste. The impact of the Office has not been politically substantial, but it has contributed to increasing the technical competence with which some issues are discussed. It was followed in 1996 by an Office for the Evaluation of Legislation, constituted of equal numbers of senators and *députés*. Its role is, at the request of either house, to undertake studies into the effectiveness of legislation and make recommendations for simplification, but by 2002 it had produced only two reports, and had negligible impact. There are in addition one specialized joint 'delegation' and three separate but parallel ones with the task of providing information for the two houses: the joint delegation is concerned with demography and was set up in 1979 amidst concern for a possible fall in the birthrate after the legalization of abortion and contraception; parallel but separate groups in the two houses look at the national plan, at land-use planning and sustainable development, and at women's rights and equal opportunities for men and women.

The efficacy of Parliament as a place of political education and information depends chiefly, however, not on the quantity and quality of information available, but mainly on the nature and level of debate and the extent to which Parliament is perceived, by government, members and media, as a major forum for such activities. The TV cameras are now present within the National Assembly. Perhaps more importantly, since 1989 some of the meetings of the parliamentary committees have been open to the press. On the whole the committees have chosen to open up those of their meetings which are concerned with the gathering of information rather than those in which draft legislation is discussed. This development nevertheless suggests that members of Parliament are becoming increasingly aware of a potentially wider role for parliamentary activity.

Members of Parliament may also be a channel through which citizens can express their grievances, although this function is less developed in France than in the United Kingdom. A study of written questions to ministers showed that over half of them sought a decision in a matter affecting an individual or a particular group. Nearly a quarter of the questions requested further explanations of legal or taxation provisions or administrative decisions. The members can pass complaints of maladministration to the *médiateur de la république* (see Chapter 5).

Supervision and control

The annual debates on the budget, when each ministry's spending plans for the coming year are discussed within Parliament, provide an opportunity for members to scrutinize policy intentions. Debate is limited by the brief time available – usually one day's debate is devoted to each part of the budget – and the issues concern future expectations more than past performance. Members may, however, put direct questions to the minister during the debate.

Parliament's functions of supervision and control are carried out essentially through the procedures of questions and committee enquiries. Questions to the government, though more developed than in the past, with two televised sessions a week, are, inevitably, more ritual than probing. More seriously, there is little evidence that questions are taken very seriously by the government and its officials. Many of the written questions put by members to ministers remain unanswered. When the National Assembly was dissolved in 2002, some 22 per cent of the written questions that were put that session remained unanswered. Over the four previous 'normal' years the proportion of unanswered written questions had equalled around 15 per cent, a proportion very similar to that experienced in the mid-1980s. A senior British official was once staggered to hear his French opposite number say of a certain topic 'My Minister has been asked a question about that. We don't propose to answer it.' Even when questions are answered, replies may be delayed long after the official time limit.

Committees of enquiry may also be set up. Since 1977 such committees of enquiry have held legal powers to call for witnesses and documents, and to undertake visits of enquiry. Proposals to set them up have often seemed like an opposition device to exploit government embarrassment and been opposed by the majority, so no committee of enquiry was set up at all before 1970 (Dreyfus and D'Arcy, 1997, p. 120). Their impact was until the late 1980s limited by the fact that all evidence was taken in secret, and no very embarrassing conclusions were likely to be forthcoming when, as was the case, governmental supporters formed the majority in any committee. Committees of enquiry were set up in both Senate and National Assembly in late 1986 to enquire into the causes and consequences of the student demonstrations that year but were hampered by the ability of the police to refuse to provide information on national security grounds. In the National Assembly this committee was the only one to be set up during the first period of *cohabitation*. The Senate proved initially to be the less inhibited of the two houses in the matter, producing, for example, a notable report on the consequences of the oil spillage following the wreck of the *Amoco Cadiz* in 1978. The

National Assembly began to develop its activities in this area later, and in the context of the greater freedom of manoeuvre provided by a minority government. In May 1990 for the first time the Assembly put into effect a new agreement that each parliamentary political group may once a year call for a debate on the merits of setting up a committee of enquiry into some topical issue. Clearly such a proposal is more likely to be defeated than not, but in 1990 the outcome was the creation of two such committees, one on water pollution and water resources, and one on the operation of the public agency that has the task of assisting immigrant workers. Indeed, since 1990, from two to four such committees have been set up each year. They have increasingly focused on salient topics, including the activities of the security forces in Corsica (1999) and food safety and animal feedstuffs in the wake of the BSE problems (2000 and 2001). In consequence, their impact, which was for a long period very muted (Frears, 1990, p. 37), has begun to grow.

The European dimension

The relationship of France to the European Community has for a very long time been perceived principally as a matter of foreign relations (see Chapter 10). These are explicitly a matter for governmental and indeed presidential action and – in contrast, for example, to their Danish, British and Irish counterparts – French governments have resisted any suggestion that they should be bound by parliamentary opinion in their negotiations within the Council of Ministers (Lequesne, 1993, ch. 6). Parliament has necessarily been associated with the implementation of EC measures, especially in the relatively rare cases where the application of a directive has involved the passage of a law. There is a complex procedure, involving the advice of the Council of State, to determine whether the provisions of a directive fall into the legislative or regulatory sphere (Sauron, 2000). In general, however, very little attention was paid to European Community matters until the 1990s. In 1976, as it became more apparent that the parliaments of the newer member states were finding means of ensuring for themselves a role in these matters, attention was focused on the relations between the parliaments of the member states and the European Parliament by the need to legislate to fix the arrangements for the first direct elections to the European Parliament in 1979. At this point the Constitutional Council held that, in order not to infringe the principle of national sovereignty laid down in the constitution, the law must provide for election to a body which neither had nor would acquire real legislative powers. In this context, and as fears grew of increasing erosion of the role of the French Parliament, a successful private member's bill established small groups (*délégations pour les Communautés européennes*) of members in each House, with the task of reporting on proposals for EC legislation. They were limited in their effectiveness by the difficulties they experienced in obtaining adequate information from the French government, and by the jealousy with which the standing committees of both houses guarded their own rights. The *délégations* were little more than diffusers of information and occasional intermediaries between the political process and the various interests or groups who were liable to be affected by proposed EC legislation and sought to draw attention to its potential impact.

The creation of the single European market and the prospect of further institutional reform reopened the debate about the appropriate role for a national parliament. In May 1990, after a prolonged negotiation between Senate and National Assembly, a new law, again based on a private member's bill, reinforced the *délégations*. They were doubled in size, from 18 to 36 members; members of National Assembly who were also members of the European Parliament were permitted to be appointed to them; they were given more formal powers to hear ministers and representatives of the EC institutions; the government was obliged to transmit European Commission proposals to them at the point when they are passed to the Council of Ministers, and the Committees of the two houses may consult them on any law which touches on areas subject to EU policy. In 1990 the practice of occasional debates on European community affairs was also instituted and this has, as noted above, been extended to a monthly session in the National Assembly since 1994. The debates around the ratification of the Maastricht Treaty raised the stakes. The amendment to the constitution which was made to provide for the implementation of the Maastricht Treaty contained a provision which incorporated into the constitution the government's obligation (which already existed under the 1990 law) to communicate European Community legislative proposals to the National Assembly and allowed the houses, either in a plenary debate or through the *délégations*, to give their opinions. This constitutional amendment, proposed by a Socialist member of Parliament, raised the status of European Community business. The perceived need for constant parliamentary vigilance over European affairs was one of the justifications for the introduction of the single session in 1995.

A nursery of political talent

The role of the French parliament as a nursery and reservoir for the political leadership of the country is much more limited than that, for example, of the British parliament. It remains a feature of the political system of the Fifth French Republic that it is possible to make a political career very largely outside parliament. A number of ministers (see Chapter 4) have never been members of parliament. Of the prime ministers of the Fifth Republic only Chaban-Delmas, Mauroy, Rocard and Jospin have spent much time as members of the National Assembly. Election as a *député* may, nevertheless, for leading politicians, be a necessary confirmation of democratic legitimacy, and if they have never been elected they may, as Pompidou and Barre did, seek a safe seat after arriving in a prominent position. Neither Pompidou nor Barre immediately served as members, since their ministerial post was incompatible with doing so. Both did eventually enter the Assembly, following dismissal or defeat – Pompidou in 1968, and Barre after the Socialist victory in 1981.

The fact that governmental teams may be drawn from a far wider arena than just parliament may in part be both cause and effect of the fact that the French parliament is not the pre-eminent location for political conflict and debate. Reputations as politicians are not to any great extent made or lost within parliament. Elisabeth Guigou's memoirs strongly suggest that she found attendance in the National Assembly a chore rather than an opportunity: understandable, perhaps, given the disgraceful tendency of the members to engage in derogatory and insulting sexist banter, especially at the expense of female ministers (Guigou, 2000). Moreover, apart from 1986 to 1988 the National Front has been almost completely absent from parliament, yet it is undoubtedly a major political force in France, and its leader reached the second round of the presidential election in 2002.

Conclusion

Un Député, pour quoi faire? – what use is a member of parliament? – was the title of a book published in 1982 (Masclet, 1982). In the light of the constraints illustrated above it seems a pertinent question. Yet parliament is essential in all the main roles discussed above. Governments simply cannot get legislation passed if they cannot carry parliament with them, as President Giscard d'Estaing discovered when he was forced to rely on the votes of the opposition in order to get his abortion law reform through. President Mitterrand had a similar experience when his government accepted amendments to his education reform bill in 1984 in order to get it through only to find that these changes made it much more broadly unacceptable. In 1998 the Jospin government's broadcasting bill had to be withdrawn and reintroduced.

Before 1986 it was sometimes argued that the apparent powerlessness of parliament concealed a latent power which might be revealed if and when the political balance changed and the president no longer commanded an acquiescent majority within the National Assembly. *Cohabitation* revealed the scope for action by prime minister and government rather than president, but the relationship between government and parliament was little affected. It proved, in the event, that the political and procedural devices which had before 1986 largely assisted the president to ensure the implementation of his programme could also be used by a prime minister with an adequate backing. The president could, and did, force the prime minister back onto the mercy of parliament, but the government found there the support which it required. Although the person chiefly responsible for the governmental programme could now be present at debates and in theory be called to account, which had not been the case when that person was the president, in neither 1986, 1993 nor 1997 did the accountability of the government notably increase.

The period between 1988 and 1993 was exceptional in that the government was not based upon a party or a reasonably coherent coalition holding a parliamentary majority. The scope for parliament to play an active role visibly increased. The Rocard government was obliged to change, amend or even drop bills – for example in June 1990 the proposed reform of the French legal profession – in order to ensure the passage of their legislative programme. Finding a coalition within parliament to support each individual measure became a major task for the prime minister, though one in which he was aided by continuing habits of rather weak party discipline and the presence in the National Assembly of nearly a score of members who were not formally attached to any of the parliamentary political groups. Although this position has not been repeated, its impact, and the vigorous leadership of Philippe Séguin between 1993 and 1997, has aided the emergence of a somewhat more assertive and vigorous parliament.

Private members, even the *rapporteurs* on specific items in parliamentary committees, may not have enormous influence, but they do have some, and while the proportion of private member's bills and amendments passed is not large, neither is it insignificant. The scope for action produced by the absence of a substantial and fairly disciplined majority such as characterized the first 30 years of the regime has resulted in a number of developments (for example, the growing role for committees) and the changed pattern of activity since the 1990s, especially the enhanced European dimension, is likely to endure.

Parliament in France has been, to an extent that may seem to observers from certain other traditions deplorable, apathetic about insisting upon its rights. It has not managed to harass the government over answering questions. The Senate, where the sense of independence is greater, if only because senators serve guaranteed nine-year terms, was initially willing to use committees of enquiry to a larger extent than the National Assembly, which has now followed suit, but neither house has established any kind of mechanism for regular examination of ongoing public policy issues. Parliament has been content to see the implementation of laws it has passed greatly delayed when the administration has proved unable or unwilling to issue the necessary implementing regulations, and even to see its wishes anticipated or frustrated, as when in 1981 the Minister of Justice issued instructions to magistrates to take into account the anticipated reform of the very controversial law and order (*sécurité et liberté*) bill before Parliament had discussed its repeal or replacement. Perhaps more importantly, it has in almost all cases (except the contaminated blood affair) left to judges and the media the role of discovering the facts and calling to account those involved in the web of corruption and scandals that has entangled so many leading politicians. Indeed it has rather compliantly and complacently passed laws amnestying those who have (for their party's, not their own, benefit) breached the law on political finance. This has not assisted its public standing or reputation.

Ironically, it was the advent in 1988 of a government which shared the president's political orientation but did not enjoy a majority which most encouraged the assumption of a rather more assertive role by Parliament. This followed the experience, during the 1980s, of genuine changes in the political orientation of the government, and hence also of the opposition. There is now a sense that the opposition of today, which has its place within parliament, may indeed constitute the government of tomorrow. This perception, and the scope and importance of the issues with which legislation has recently dealt – decentralization, privatization, nationality and citizenship amongst many other things – may gradually be producing a somewhat more lively and active institution than that of the 1960s and 1970s. A sense of the need to ensure a prominent role for the national parliament in the face of the growing ambitions of the European Union and the European Parliament has also contributed to a higher profile for Parliament. At the same time, however, it has become apparent that, even within a more parliamentary interpretation, the constitution can and does provide a framework which permits a government, if with effort, bargaining and occasional concessions, to carry out its programme in a way that the governments of the Fourth Republic could not.

8

Party Politics in France

This chapter is concerned with the aspects of French politics that are most immediately and obviously visible to the observer, whether that observer is French, or an outsider. It is in the act of voting that citizens in democratic countries are most conscious of their role as individuals in political life. France's 'rapid fire electoral cycle' (Szarka, 2000, p. 23) has the consequence that French political life can seem to exist in a state of permanent campaigning, and indeed there are few years when an election is neither forthcoming, and the subject of debate and campaigning, nor just completed and hence the subject of analysis and associated triumph and recrimination.

It is nowadays rare, at levels above the *commune*, for an individual to stand for, let alone win, an election on the strength on his or her own personality and ideas alone. Electoral success tends to depend upon a party organization. Shared convictions, ideas and approaches about the shape which society should take and the policy approaches required to bring into reality a common vision of a better future normally hold together the adherents of any particular party. Theorists regard them as a means by which the desires, preferences and aspirations of citizens can be aggregated into a form which will enable them to be transformed into action. In France, however, there are important qualifications to be made to the general theories. Individuals may have important parts in political life because of who they are, not what they believe or which organization they belong to. Political parties may arise or be maintained out of shared support for a particular leader, or even out of naked opportunism rather than out of strongly held and coherently formulated beliefs. Loyalties to particular party groupings may not be seen as very compelling or constraining. Splits occur, as do fusions, which, however, may leave behind a rump of intractable adherents of the previous formation. Thus most of the little left-wing *Parti Socialist Unifié* (PSU) fused with the Socialist Party in 1974, but a rump remained for a while, from which a candidate, Huguette Bouchardeau, stood in the 1981 presidential election. Similarly in 1998 a number of the participants in the *Union pour la Démocratie Française* (UDF) confederation fused into a party, but *Démocratie Libérale* stayed out. In 2002, however, DL joined the *Union pour la Majorité Présidentielle* (UMP), which duly became a single party the *Union pour un Mouvement Populaire*, as did many, but not all of the UDF members, a rump of whom maintained a separate party, stood separately in the legislative elections and formed a distinct parliamentary group. Political debate revolves around discussion of moral principles and broad ideas, and also around very specific personalities. Party programmes and manifestos are often, though not always, slight and vague. The effect is kaleidoscopic, and to the external observer confusing.

The parties' fortunes have fluctuated, and their approach, strategy and tactics have varied. The first decade of the Fifth Republic was dominated by the emergence of the Gaullist Party, and the development of a governing coalition. The 1970s were the period in which the Socialist party was building up the position and support that led to its victory in 1981. During the 1980s and 1990s the political pattern shifted again, as the four major parties ceased to dominate voters' choices, the Communist party declined, the extreme right National Front became prominent on the political scene and the Ecologists also started to attract votes. Table 8.1 lists the state of play in 2002.

This chapter analyses the party system and the fortunes of the parties, especially since 1981. As Colette Ysmal (1990) argues, the old social and ideological cleavages still shape parts of the political structure, but they no longer suffice fully to explain shifts in voting preferences and the emergence of new political forces.

TABLE 8.1
Selected political parties in France, 2002

Party	Created	Background	Seats 1997	Seats 2002	Presidential candidate 2002	Percentage of votes cast first ballot 2002
Lutte Ouvrière (LO)		Trotskyist.	0	0	Arlette Laguiller	5.71
Parti Communiste Français (PCF)	1920	Marxist–Leninist. Split from SFIO.	38	21	Robert Hue	3.37
Parti Socialiste (PS)	1969	Refoundation of Marxist SFIO (founded 1905). Merged with smaller groups including CIR (1971) and PSU (1974).	240	140	Lionel Jospin	16.17
Parti Radical de Gauche	1996	Split from Radical Party as MRG in 1973. Changed name 1996.	12	7	Christiane Taubira	2.31

TABLE 8.1 (continued)

Party	Created	Background	Seats 1997	Seats 2002	Presidential candidate 2002	Percentage of votes cast first ballot 2002
Pôle Républicain (PREP)	1992	Socialist/Republican. Split from PS as *Mouvement des Citoyens* following Chevènement's resignation from government. Renamed 2002.	7	0	Jean-Pierre Chevènement	5.32
Les Verts (V)	1984	Ecologist/Green. Created from merger of several Green movements.	7	3	Noël Mamère	5.24
Force Démocrate	1995–1998	Christian Democrat. Originated with MRP (1944). Part of UDF confederation from 1978. Merged into UDF 1998.				
Démocratie Libérale	1997	Liberal, 'Orleanist' non-Gaullist right. Derived from Giscardian RI (from 1977 PR) founded 1962. Part of UDF confederation 1978–98.		2	Alain Madelin	3.9
Union pour la Démocratie Française	1998	Non Gaullist Centre-Right. Began as umbrella for pro-Giscard confederation 1978, founded as free-standing party 1998.	108	23	François Bayrou	6.83
Rassemblement pour la République (RPR)	1976	Gaullist. First Gaullist party founded 1948, refounded 1958. Amalgamated into the UMP 2002.	135			

TABLE 8.1 (continued)

Party	Created	Background	Seats 1997	Seats 2002	Presidential candidate 2002	Percentage of votes cast first ballot 2002
Union pour un Mouvement Populaire (UMP)	2002	Formed as federation of RPR, DL, and many UDF members for 2002 legislative elections as the *Union pour une majorité présidentielle.* Constituted into a party with new name October 2002.		355	Jacques Chirac	19.88
Rassemblement pour la France (RPF)	1999	Eurosceptic national populist group, constituted by Pasqua, formerly RPR, with MPF. De Villiers broke away again in 2000.	2	0		
Mouvement pour la France (MPF)	1994	Eurosceptic conservative group led by de Villiers, formerly PR. Constituted RPF with Pasqua 1999, but re-emerged when de Villiers broke away 2000.	1	0		
Front National (FN)	1972	Extreme Right. Formed from merger of several Extreme Right groups.	1#	0	Jean-Marie Le Pen	16.85
Mouvement National Républicain (MNR)	1998	Break away from FN			Bruno Mégret	2.34
Chasse, Pêche, Nature, Tradition (CPNT)	1989	Pro hunting and countryside			Jean Saint Josse	4.22
Others			29*	17**	4***	

Notes:
Removed for electoral malpractice and replaced at by-election by a socialist.
* Other Right: 14, Other: 1, Other left: 14.
** Other Right: 6, Regional Parties: 1, Other: 1, Other Left: 8.
*** Olivier Besancenot (LCR-Trotskyite).   Daniel Gluckstein (LT).   Corinne Lepage.   Christine Boutin (dissident RPR pro-family).

A whole range of other considerations come into play, including the credibility of the different parties, their strategies, the impact of their leaders, especially the presidential candidates, and the force of the issues before the voters at the moment of the election. The consequence over the period has been an unprecedented mobility in electoral choices and party political fortunes.

The Shadow of the Past: Cleavages and Party Organization

During the first half of the twentieth century the overall structure and nature of the French party system was distinctive. Not only was the party system a multi-party system, as opposed to the broadly two-party systems of Britain and the United States (Duverger, 1964, Book 2, ch. 1) but also there was a great variety of internal organization and structures within the parties themselves. This history continues to shape some of the aspects of the French parties into the twenty-first century.

Hague and Harrop (2001, ch. 11) argue that there are five normal functions for parties in liberal democratic states:

- to provide links between the rulers and the ruled, especially to facilitate the flow of political communication;
- to aggregate interests, by transforming 'a multitude of specific demands into more manageable packages of proposals';
- especially when in government, to set and implement collective goals for society;
- to provide the mechanism through which the political elite, especially the top political leadership, emerges;
- to be 'objects of powerful emotional attachment (or antagonism), exerting a powerful influence upon the opinions and behaviour of their supporters'. This process is known as 'partisan identification'.

The failure of the plethora of French political parties in the multi-party system of the Third and Fourth Republics to fulfil these functions was widely recognized. Indeed the constitution of the Fifth Republic was, as we have seen, partly shaped to provide institutional mechanisms that would compensate for the absence of parties that could do these things.

The origins of this plethora lay in the various divisions of opinion within France identified in Chapter 1, and the fact that the lines of division within society did not coincide (Criddle, 1987, pp. 137–8). These cleavages included those originating from the Revolution, such as those between republicans and anti-republicans, and between clerical and anti-clerical opinion. There were also the cleavages originating from the industrial revolution, such as those between working classes and bourgeoisie, and those between groups that favoured an interventionist state acting to promote social welfare, and those that wanted a minimal liberal state. In a situation where no compromise is possible between opposing points of view, and where there is no agreement on which cleavage is the most crucial one, the result will be a range of different parties or groups (see Table 8.1). These parties were almost all too small to bring together and articulate within a single programme the demands and desires of large numbers of the voters. They tended therefore to concentrate upon the issues that were most important to their own particular voters, and could not provide support and endorsement for a broad programme of government. Republicanism as such is little contested at the beginning of the twenty-first century, even if some of its implications may be challenged by the extreme right, and the divisions between clerical and anti-clerical have largely been swamped by secularism. However, other lines of division remain powerful, including that which separates the upholders of a structured, autonomous 'indivisible' state (for example Charles Pasqua on the right or Jean-Pierre Chevènement on the left) from the 'modernizers' with a more flexible, Europeanizing, decentralized vision (Elgie, 2000, p. 8).

French parties have also frequently been weak in their internal structures. In terms of Duverger's classic categorization of political party structures (1964, pp. 17–22) many of the parties were 'caucus parties' – loose networks of local leaders, which came together to form electoral committees when there were elections, but made no attempt to organize mass support or produce national programmes. Many members of Parliament under the Fourth Republic, including two future presidents, Giscard d'Estaing and Mitterrand, were elected on the basis of their personality or local roots, without national support or genuine party affiliation, though they might come together with other members of Parliament to form loose and undisciplined parliamentary groups. Only the Communist and the Socialist Parties differed significantly from this model. There was consequently no real concept of party discipline. This trait too persists. The UDF has been described as 'little more than an electoral cartel' (Cole, 1998, p. 141), and as the 'home of traditional *notable* conservatism', based around local leadership and even, as in the case of President Giscard d'Estaing and a number of other Centrist politicians, inheritance from father or grandfather (Bell, 2000a, p. 82).

Personalities, Power Bases, Fission, Fusion

The absence of the notion of a disciplined party organized around a coherent and credible programme helps to explain the third cause suggested by Criddle for the inability of the parties under the Third and Fourth Republics to achieve the normal functions of parties. The parties were unable to provide adequate support for any governmental programme especially since the electoral systems made it difficult for any one party to dominate. No party was strong enough to govern alone, and those parties that were able to make working coalitions – after 1947 for over 20 years the Communist Party ceased to be an acceptable coalition partner – could not ensure that their supporters would uphold the coalitions for any length of time. In these very fragmented conditions politics could become strongly personalized, with debate and loyalties focusing around the personality and approach of particular leaders.

These characteristics, in various forms, have also persisted into the beginning of the twenty-first century. A strongly articulated and detailed manifesto is not necessarily a precondition for election. The UMP, formed in haste after the presidential election in 2002, even if not altogether unforeseen, had little time to do anything more than assert that its main *raison d'être* was support for President Chirac and his prime minister, and insist that those candidates it supported must, if successful, join its parliamentary group rather than reverting to groups reflecting their previous allegiances. In its principal purpose it was sharply reminiscent both of the precursor of the RPR at the beginning of the Fifth Republic, and of the UDF in 1978–81. Some parties seem at times to be little more than convenient vehicles for personal political ambitions. Thus Szarka (2000, p. 26) notes that the *Parti Radical de Gauche* (PRG), while containing some members with a commitment to a Radical heritage, has equally served from time to time as a repository for those who either did not wish to be too closely associated with the Socialist Party or were not acceptable in it, such as the flamboyant, populist businessman, Bernard Tapie, who led its list in the 1994 European elections. That list also included ecologist Noel Mamère, who was subsequently, in 2002, rapidly drafted in as the presidential candidate for *Les Verts* when their initial choice, economist Alain Lipietz, proved ill-adapted to the political task.

Where the culture of party loyalty is weak, and, as we shall see, the imperatives of alliances necessitate overtures to other groups, switches of loyalty can occur. The political careers of President Mitterrand, and of Prime Ministers Rocard and Jospin took them through membership of several political groups. It has been by no means unheard of for persons who have served as ministers under governments of the mainstream Right to do so later under governments of the Left – Michel Jobert, and Jean-Pierre Soisson are examples. Equally, when disagreements arise, splits occur (see Table 8.1). Jean-Pierre Chevènement formed the *Mouvement des Citoyens* (MDC – now *Pôle Républicain*) after his resignation from the government in 1992. Charles Pasqua picked the provocative title *Rassemblement pour la France* (RPF – echoing de Gaulle's 1948 *Rassemblement du Peuple Français*, also RPF) for his Euro-sceptic breakaway group, set up initially to contest the 1999 European election. The *Front National* split in 1998, with both parts claiming the name and the assets, a dispute resolved in favour of Jean-Marie Le Pen's faction in the law courts. Conversely, mergers and fusions have strengthened some of the leading parties. However, as noted above, the result may not be the total disappearance of a previous party.

Electoral Systems and the Survival of Multipartyism

For so-called 'first order' elections – the presidential and parliamentary elections which can potentially bring about substantial change in the nature of central government – the introduction of the two-ballot system in 1958 had a clear impact. Under the two-ballot system any candidate who has gained above a certain minimum proportion of the vote may stand in the second ballot, but there are clear advantages in avoiding too much fragmentation of the vote. Whilst at the first ballot, voters can and do express their personal convictions, at the second ballot they can frequently be persuaded to vote for the candidate most likely to win amongst those whom they find not unacceptable. In the presidential election such a situation is forced upon the voters by the provision that only two candidates may stand at the second ballot. The outcome has been what was frequently, in the late 1960s and 1970s, described as the 'bipolarization' of French politics. Talk of 'bipolarization' however, can with hindsight be seen as misleading in so far as it suggests that France was moving towards a two-party system. It is much less misleading if it serves to indicate that what had emerged was a much more clear-cut notion than existed before 1962 of the existence of a government and an opposition (see Figure 8.1).

The development of notion of 'the opposition' in France depended, first, upon the existence of a relatively clear-cut choice, such as was presented especially by the presidential elections. Despite much speculation in 1995 about the possibility of the two second-round candidates emerging from the same (RPR) party, only in 1969 and 2002 have the presidential elections not resulted in a clear-cut choice between Left and Right, and in 2002 the legislative elections which followed produced a National Assembly in which two parties – the governing UMP and the opposition PS – between them occupied nearly 90 per cent of the seats. A second factor was the acceptance by all the parties of the nature of the Fifth Republic's institutions, and the withering away of serious proposals to overthrow the whole constitutional settlement. Instead it has been possible for *alternance* – the complete replacement of one governing coalition with another – and *cohabitation* to emerge, both of which are predicated on electoral choices between a government and an opposition.

The emergence of potentially alternating governing and opposition coalitions has not, however, led to the development of a two-party system. Within the coalitions the individual parties persist, and struggle for dominance, place and influence. There are a number of explanations for the survival of multi-partyism.

FIGURE 8.1

Percentage share of valid first-ballot votes cast
(rounded to nearest whole number)

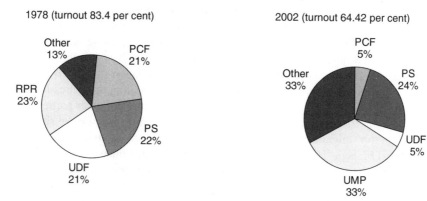

1978 (turnout 83.4 per cent)

2002 (turnout 64.42 per cent)

- First, the varied and conflictual ideological heritage of some of the parties makes some combinations unthinkable, even if in fact many ideological differences have lessened almost to disappearing point (Mény, 1995, p. 191). Indeed, disputes over the acceptability or not of cooperation with potential allies have been a key factor in conflict and splits, especially on the Right.
- Secondly, existence as a separate entity may mean that a party can even in first-order elections exact at least a share of the spoils. Standing as a presidential candidate provides any individual, and the party backing them if there is one, with a considerable measure of publicity and some political capital. Rivalry within recognized parties is counterproductive: it took Balladur's supporters (Nicolas Sarkozy, for example) a number of years (and the RPR defeat in 1997) to begin to regain their posts and influence in the RPR after 1995. But standing on the basis of a distinctive political formation may be helpful. The 1997 Jospin government contained two ministers who had been his rivals in the 1995 election.

  The two-ballot system has encouraged the formation of alliances before the election. In 1997 the PS stood down in favour of the Greens in 30 seats, and ran joint candidates with the MDC in 48. The result was parliamentary seats for both which they would almost certainly not have gained otherwise. However, in 2002 there were only minimal agreements on the Left. The two-ballot system also allows for a system of 'primary' elections (*désistement*), so that the partners within the coalition can put up individual candidates in the first round and agree that the best placed candidate from the coalition should go forward to the second round. In 2002 as in 1993 and 1997 this occurred with a reasonably good grace in many of the seats where both Communist and Socialist candidates were still confronting each other after the first round.
- Thirdly, electoral systems for second-order elections, as Exhibit 6.1 shows, include a substantial component of proportional representation, even if that for *communes* of over 3500 inhabitants, for example, has been carefully devised so as to ensure that a 'hung council' cannot occur. Small parties can and do profit from these arrangements. Where local implantation is strong, a small party may retain its identity and gain council seats, control of *communes* and Members of the European Parliament. This local power base may, as for the PRG, for example, provide the necessary standing to permit fruitful negotiations with their bigger ally. The group that might otherwise have been no more than a rural lobby group, *Chasse, Peche, Nature, Tradition* has made no alliances, but was enabled by proportional representation to gain five MEPs in 1999, in addition to the regional and local councillors they already held. They have sufficiently succeeded in worrying politicians of other parties as to render the transposition into French law of the EU directives on the shooting season for migratory birds almost impossible (even though PS secretary general François Hollande threatened his members that the party would refuse to support them at the next election if they voted against the bill (*L'Année Politique*, 2000, p. 86)) and its non-implementation a breach of EU law.

Electoral systems can, however, be manipulated. The furore which resulted when, in the early months of 2003, changes were proposed in the electoral system for Regional Councils arose from fears that a two-ballot system with a high second-ballot threshold would effectively eliminate small parties for whom seats on regional councils are an important resource.

- Fourthly, new parties have emerged outside the major alliances. Two such parties emerged in the 1980s, first the National Front and subsequently the Greens, both discussed below. The National Front was much assisted by the adoption, for the 1986 general election, of a proportional representation electoral system. The return to the two-ballot system in 1988 did not, however, result in its diminution as a national political force, even without seats in the National Assembly. It lost all but one of its parliamentary seats in 1988, failed to gain any in 1993 and, when the one it did win in 1997 was removed for elect-oral malpractice, did not win it back at the by-election. Even after its success in the 2002 presidential elections, it took no seats in the subsequent legislative election.

The party system of the Fifth Republic is a weak and fragmented system, made all the more confusing by the plethora of tiny groups which emerge at election time and whose sole *raison d'être* seems to be to harvest resources (see Exhibit 8.1). The 2002 legislative elections resulted in the declaration to the

---

EXHIBIT 8.1

Party proliferation and finance

In an attempt to tackle some of the causes of corrupt fund-raising by political parties a 1988 law provides that any party that registered itself with the Committee that supervises electoral expenditure and put up at least 50 candidates in metropolitan France (or one in the overseas *départements*) would be entitled to a subsidy, amount-ing in 2002 to 1.66 Euro per vote cast. In consequence some five million Euro a year was disbursed between 1997 and 2002 on about 20 little groups. The money has to be accounted for, but not to be spent on any particular purpose. Brice Lalonde, a former presidential candidate and minister, leader of the small Ecology party *Génération Ecologie* uses it to pay his salary as the party leader, for example.

In 1993 a small Ecology group, *Nature et Animaux* gained 640 000 votes and hence revenue of 275 000 Euro over the subsequent five years. However, in 1997, renamed *Nouveaux Ecologists du Rassemblement Nature et Animaux* it managed only 100 000 votes and 153 000 Euro a year.

Parties or leaders may use an election as a way of gathering initial resources. In 2002 a taxpayers' party, the *Rassemblement des Contribuables Français* put up 150 candidates hoping to gain both funds and respectability, while *Energies Démocrates*, launched three weeks before the start of the campaign by the former Chair and Managing Director of Air France, Christian Blanc, was also hoping that 57 candidates would allow the party to garner resources for the coming years (*Le Point*, 24 May 2002, p. 40).

Committee which oversees political financing of no fewer than 210 parties, about thirty of which had been created within the three months preceding the election. In total 8446 candidates stood for the 577 seats, a rise of over 30 per cent compared to 1997, with, for example, 26 candidates (13 on the left or extreme left, 11 on the right or extreme right and two unclassifiable) standing in one constituency (Levallois-Perret) (*Le Monde*, 8 and 19 June 2002, *Le Figaro*, 19 July 2002). There were understandable calls for reform of the financing system.

The bigger parties, however, lack adequate organizational and financial resources, partly because their membership, about which they are consistently secretive, is small. Subscriptions certainly provide no adequate base for party activity. This poverty and the importance of local roots rather than party identification for political success reduce the incentives for party loyalty (Mény, 1995, p. 182–7). In addition, the lure of the presidency encourages jockeying for position and personal rivalries and may split and weaken parties. This was true of the UDF in the run-up to the 1988 elections and of the Socialist Party in the early 1990s. It was starkly illustrated by the emergence of two RPR candidates in 1995. It fosters the obsession of the French media with the personal relationships between politicians not their policies (Laughland, 1994, p. 94). Since presidential candidates feel that they must transcend party it encourages the erosion of ideological difference which Mény argues has already reached the point where 'party labels constitute convenient indications of the orientation of the [politician] on the political landscape, but tell little about real allegiances, programmatic orientations or indeed ideological choices'(1995, p. 184). It is argued (Bilger-Street and Milner, 2001, p. 509) that 'available data suggest that...Left–Right values (rather than party allegiance as such) strongly influence opinions', and that 'there remains a basic division between the two camps and they continue to make enemies of each other' (Elgie, 2000, p. 16).

Hague and Harrop suggest that it is important that parties should act as objects of attachment and focuses for political activity. Democracy in liberal representative democracies depends upon citizens being able to look to parties as a channel to prioritize decisions and resolve conflicts. Over the first two decades of the Fifth Republic the four major groups did this with considerable success. Parties with distinctive orientations which could be seen as serious contenders for governmental office and thus as offering a real possibility of implementing programmes took 87 per cent of the votes cast in 1978, with a low rate of abstention.

All four major groups were (or would be, following *alternance* in 1981) in government. But a range of factors have led to a rather different position at the beginning of the twenty-first century. In the 2002 presidential election the second ballot run-off involved one candidate (Jean-Marie Le Pen) whose party (the Front National) not only had no likelihood of being a participant in government, but failed to win a single seat at the subsequent legislative elections. Those parties which had been in the governing coalition prior to the elections or were to be so after them took only just over 64 per cent of the votes cast, which meant that under half of the electorate (approximately 48 per cent) voted for them (see Figures 8.1, 8.2 and 8.3). It is in this context that the activities of pressure groups and the functions of direct protest which are discussed in the next chapter have to be considered. But some of the explanation lies in the evolution of the big parties, and this is discussed below.

Party Development and Change

The parties of the left: the demise of French communism

The first general election of the Fifth Republic sent the Communist vote plunging to just under 19 per cent – a figure that was for a long time thought to represent the bedrock of *Parti Communiste Français* (PCF) support. The party relied upon a number of traditional sources of support: the traditional industrial working class, located, for example, in the Communist districts around Paris; an equally traditional protest vote, found in the areas and amongst those groups that had long taken an 'anti-establishment' stance, which gave the PCF, for example, a rather surprising vote amongst the small peasant farmers of the South West; the young, especially the educated young, for whom a Communist vote was part of an assertion of rebellious identity; and those intellectuals for whom the PCF was the concrete expression of their Marxist belief system. After the Second World War the party's support was strengthened by the undeniably heroic and leading role it had played in the Resistance.

The party was closely controlled by its leader and its central politburo, secretive and disciplined, faithfully following the twists and turns of Soviet policy. As the Cold War intensified through the 1950s the PCF, following its expulsion from government in 1947, held itself grimly apart from the governmental process, denouncing the Fourth Republic, and equally vehemently refusing de Gaulle, his constitution of 1958 and his amendment of 1962. Some of the Fifth Republic's institutional arrangements, for example the two-ballot electoral system, were quite clearly designed to disadvantage the PCF.

The PCF, however, were in an ambiguous position in relation to the governmental system. They had formed part of the government until 1947, continued to campaign in parliamentary elections to seek to win seats in the National Assembly, and to support, or even put up, candidates for the presidential election. They also played an important role in local government. So the party has consistently been part of the political system which it has consistently denounced.

The process of decline for the PCF has been inexorable and now seems irredeemable. In 1978 it held onto the votes of just over one in five of the voters, despite vacillation in its alliance with the PS, concluded in 1972 and denounced in 1977, the PCF having realized that it was not the dominant partner. Its sharp decline began from 1981, and by 2002 it contrived to hang on to only 21 seats in the National Assembly. A number of causes can be suggested:

- First, the Leninist appeal to the example of the Soviet Union as the harbinger of a Communist better world for the workers was steadily eroded as information became more readily available and the plight of the dissidents of the

1960s and 1970s could not be entirely ignored. As David Bell points out (2000a, p. 149), there was always a paradox 'between what the party was (a wing of the international Communist movement) and why people voted for it (for many reasons, including idealism and patriotism, but not because of its subordination to the Soviets)'. But both sides of the paradox were undermined by the collapse of East European Communism in 1989.

- Secondly, the party failed, in the 1980s and 1990s, to maintain its centralized, Stalinist internal discipline. Various groups of dissidents and modernizers emerged so that, for example, Pierre Juquin stood against the official PCF candidate in the 1988 presidential election. Robert Hue's more open style after he took over as First Secretary in 1994 reduced the conflicts. He retained the tight local organization of 'cells' and federations, but attempted to update the PCF's vocabulary and approach (Szarka, 2000, p. 28). The party's desire to modernize was underlined by the installation of a woman First Secretary, Marie-George Buffet, in 2001, but it had already been substantially weakened.
- Thirdly, the discrediting of Marxism as an intellectual framework following the collapse of its practical manifestations in Eastern Europe reduced the PCF's appeal in particular to intellectuals and students, who had constituted a key part of its backing.
- Fourthly, the massive changes in employment and lifestyle amongst those involved in heavy manufacture, or living in strongly working-class areas, undermined the PCF's strongholds. Employment in heavy industry dwindled, and people in previously solidly Communist areas have become more mobile and, with the spread of television, popular music and other elements of mass culture, less dependent upon the party and the local community for their leisure and lifestyle.
- Fifthly, the PCF's implantation in local government, where PCF mayors and councils have a well-deserved reputation for effectiveness, has given it a bedrock which distinguishes it from other parties, but this is being eroded. It has throughout the Fifth Republic been one of the leading parties in local government, although it lost its last town of over 100 000 inhabitants, Le Havre, in 1995, and even in the municipal elections of 2001 controlled 90 councils in *communes* of over 9000 inhabitants (Bilger-Street and Milner, 2001, p. 513). It has held on in the 'red belt' around Paris, but partly through the personality and record of its local leaders. Local management has become more diverse, less distinctive, while it has also failed to convince voters that it has discarded its 'industrial "workerist" ideology to find new, service-sector-based urban regeneration strategies' (Bilger-Street and Milner, 2001, p. 514).
- Sixthly, the PCF is being challenged in its traditional role as spokesman for the poor and exploited. The veteran Trotskyite Arlette Laguiller's record of fighting five presidential elections seems to have enhanced her appeal, and the rise of anti-globalist, anti-big capital protest sentiment may also be reflected in the extreme left vote in the 2002 presidentials, where not only Laguiller but also the *Ligue Communiste Révolutionnaire*'s Olivier Besancenot scored more highly than Hue. The protest vote is also catered for by the *Front National*.

- Finally, the need for political alliances has posed a particularly acute dilemma for the PCF. The Common Programme of the Left in the 1970s was accepted as the only tactic that would allow the party to return to the place in government which it had enjoyed between 1944 and 1947. 'L'union est un combat' said its central committee (Portelli, 1987, p. 166). The PCF's abandonment of it in 1978 was resented even within the party as having prevented the victory of the Left in 1978, and when in 1981 Mitterrand won, four Communist ministers entered the government, all of them senior figures within the party, although the most prominent members of the leadership were not offered ministerial posts. However, both the 1983 local elections, and the European elections of 1984 showed continued decline, and at the government reshuffle that followed those elections, in which the general unpopularity of the Mitterrand government had been demonstrated, the Communists left the government and the party returned to outspoken criticism of the Socialists. But it did not abandon the tactic of electoral agreement with the Socialists, which enabled it to benefit from the swing to the left in the 1997 parliamentary election. Jospin rewarded its support with three ministerial posts. The PCF has been effectively compelled to hitch its fortunes as a junior partner to those of the Socialists, doing well, as a consequence, in the regional elections of 1998, and very poorly when it tried the gimmick of an independent 'double parity' – men/women, Communists/non Communists – list in the European elections of 1999 (*Regards sur l'actualité*, June 2000, p. 39). There has been no plausible response – could there be one? – to David Bell's pertinent question: 'If a "revolutionary" party turns reformist why vote for the copy, why not vote for the real thing?' (2000a, p. 165).

The parties of the left: the rollercoaster ride of the socialists

The 1960s were a dispiriting decade for the Socialist Party. The SFIO was largely discredited by its association with the Fourth Republic and, although it endorsed the new constitution, by 1962 it was clearly opposing de Gaulle and the way in which he was shaping the Fifth Republic. Parts of the party favoured alliance with the Communists, and others retained the party's earlier profound anti-Communism. The party's tactics did not prove conspicuously successful; the performance of the Left was creditable in 1967, but the aftermath of the May 1968 events brought a surge of Gaullism. The Socialist candidate, Gaston Defferre could only attract a humiliating 5 per cent of the votes in the 1969 presidential election.

In 1969 a reconstructed party, the *Parti Socialiste*, replaced the SFIO. The movement towards the PCF which was to lead to the 1972 common programme made a tentative beginning, and the new party began to install younger and more diverse local party officials within its organization, and to recruit new members. But the new First Secretary, Alain Savary, was not an electorally appealing figure, nor a charismatic leader, and the absence from the party of François Mitterrand who clearly did possess the necessary qualities seemed increasingly senseless (Bell and Criddle, 1988, p. 60). In July 1971 Mitterrand joined the new party, and three days later became its First Secretary.

Between 1971 and the end of the 1980s the story of the Socialist Party was one of a steady gain in credibility and electoral solidity, confirmed by its winning of an absolute majority in the National Assembly elected in 1981 (see Figure 8.2). The 1986 election reduced its share of the vote, and put it into opposition. Mitterrand's victory in 1988 was, unlike 1981, not followed by concomitant success for the party in the subsequent legislative elections, but the result was good enough to sustain a minority socialist government for the full parliamentary term. Within most European contexts a score of between 30 and over 37 per cent, which the Socialist Party achieved in three general elections between 1981 and the end of the decade, seemed respectable, especially since party support was increasingly spread across the whole of France (Hanley, 1989, p. 19).

During the 1980s the PS seems to have been 'in tune with the times' (Frears, 1991, p. 81; Bell and Criddle, 1988, p. 208). It built upon changes in the social, professional and employment structures of France in the last two decades. It benefited both from changes in the Roman Catholic Church and from the increasing secularization of society. It attracted women in a period when they had become increasingly conscious of their position within society and politics. It also, during the 1980s, proved able 'through social and political 'networking', to adapt to changing ideological and social conditions within the electorate and to adopt new social movements' (Machin, 1994, p. 41). Howard Machin suggests that the PS was, more than any other party, able to establish sympathetic links with the anti-racism movement, and particularly with the young generation of French-born

FIGURE 8.2

Votes and seats for the Socialist Party at National Assembly elections

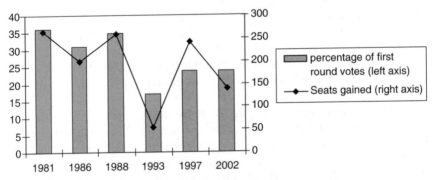

Source: Ministry of the Interior and www.parties-and-elections.de/fr.

children of parents of North African origin. Similar links were also established with the student movement. It was, Machin argues, the ability of the PS to be attractive to these new movements that throughout the 1980s prevented it from being outflanked by other groups.

A third factor that has affected the PS's place within the political system has been its role as a party of government. The Socialists had long-standing and deep roots at local and municipal level. These local bases provide opportunities for patronage, and hence encourage clientilism, but also corruption especially where the party is in control of the local administration. However, following Mitterrand's election in 1981 which was not widely or confidently forecast, and the sweeping success of the Socialist Party which achieved an overall majority in the National Assembly, the party had to find its place, in government at national level, in a presidential system which suited Mitterrand well enough – not, he said, made to measure for him, but fitting him nonetheless – but whose rhetoric allowed for no special place for the President's party.

The consequences were, as John Gaffney points out, that the party had to shift from a perception of itself as concerned chiefly with largely rhetorical and ideological left-wing support for a charismatic leader whose success would almost automatically herald major social change and progress to realizing that it must be 'a party representative of a huge grouping of French citizens and providing rational, competent and incrementalist government. The realities of government were to be the motor of this change' (Gaffney, 1990, p. 66). The constraints of the domestic and international economic situation meant that the priorities and the language of the Socialist government had, from 1983, to shift, under the influence of ministers such as Delors and Bérégovoy, to an emphasis on rigour, on the value of the *entreprise*, on the need for nationalization to provide not a motor for the transformation of industry but rather an opportunity for firms to restructure and return to profit. The president and the government carried the party with them, and it went into opposition in 1986 having established its credentials as a moderate and legitimate party of government, with a number of real achievements to its credit, including an economic record that was at least as good as that of most of the other members of the European Community, and major change, stemming from the decentralization programme, in local government. By the early 1990s the PS had moved a long way since 1981. It had clearly become a progressive but moderate social-democratic party.

Three interlinked factors – the effect of Mitterrand, the adaptation of the party to the changing social and political context, and its reshaping of itself as a pragmatic, centre-left, social-democratic party of government – helped the PS to create and sustain for itself, for a decade after 1980, a place as the major single party within the French party system. However, the PS's position proved far from secure and 1993 constituted a brutal reversal. Although the party has since improved its share of the vote it has not returned to the levels of the 1980s. Several reasons have been advanced for the 1993 results. First the 'anti-incumbency' tendency which has seen defeat for the sitting government in all the legislative elections since 1981 undoubtedly played a part. The government gained little credit for achieving growth in GDP per capita, for holding down inflation, and for much industrial adjustment. Unemployment in the late 1980s and early 1990s remained intractably above the OECD average and rising. At the same time, the adjustment and deregulation that had begun under the Chirac government, the Single Market and the reforms of the Common Agricultural Policy were adversely affecting several hitherto rather sheltered groups within the economy. Two years later Chirac was to identify need to tackle 'social fracture' as one of the key features of his successful presidential campaign although his very rapid abandonment of the measures he proposed to heal it contributed to his meteoric fall from popularity in his first few months. In 1993 the elements of that fracture – unemployment, feelings of insecurity, perceptions of growing inequalities, and increased levels of social exclusion – were visible and rebounded on the Socialists. The issue is one on which social democratic governments are particularly vulnerable, since the improvement of the material well-being of all of society is one of their most specific missions.

Secondly, President Mitterrand, ailing and aging, was no longer an asset but rather an increasingly controversial and scandal-beset figurehead. The party did not gain from its identification with him. Moreover, allegations of corruption, including financial malpractice in party financing and scandalous misjudgement in the contaminated blood affair, damaged the party's image. Such problems were by no means confined to the Socialists, but they bore particularly hard upon an incumbent government.

Thirdly, the party, always an uneasy federation of different *courants* – factions associated with a particular personality or ideological tendency – had been riven by infighting amongst those who hoped to be its candidate in the 1995 presidential elections. The party was 'demoralised and divided' (Bell, 2000a, p. 182). Finally, the Maastricht referendum campaign of 1992, which Mitterrand had expected would be a firm endorsement of his position, proved to be no such thing, but a difficult and narrowly-won campaign which 'split the PS from its own "Eurosceptic" voters in the urban working class' (Bell, 2000a, p. 182). Mitterrand in the 1970s and 1980s had succeeded in bringing together the traditional left-wing vote with a more middle-class, educated, professional, modernizing electorate. But that synthesis was finally blown away by the Maastricht referendum. The opposition at that point between those social groups who viewed the future with optimism, and those who felt that their interests and security were threatened, 'was a catastrophe for the Socialist Party, costing it more than any other party' since a 'no' vote in the referendum by a voter who had previously voted Socialist was in nearly half the cases translated into a vote for a different party in 1993 (Grunberg, 1993, p. 214).

Although 1997 did not bring the party up to its 1980s share of the vote, it brought it back to power. Again, the 'anti-incumbency' factor played a part. The popularity of the government had plummeted, and the president's with it. Jospin's somewhat austere, didactic, moralistic image proved attractive to voters. Moreover, he had done well enough in the presidential campaign to consolidate his hold over the party, so that infighting was controlled.

Another reason for the 1997 success was the ability of the party, between 1996 and 1997, to sustain a coherent strategy of alliances with other political groups to complement or replace the alliance with the Communists, whose results from the early 1980s were so poor that they could no longer provide sufficient support to enable the Socialists to sustain a majority of the Left. In the early 1990s Michel Rocard's 'big bang' approach – a proposal for some sort of merger between ecologists, dissident Communists and Socialists, which he had talked of during the 1993 election campaign – failed to prosper. At the 1994 European elections the Socialists found themselves in competition not only with ecologists and a 'Sarajevo' list put together to protest against inaction over the war in Bosnia, but also with a list headed by a former Socialist minister, Jean-Pierre Chevènement, and, much more seriously, a list put up by their erstwhile allies in the *Mouvement des radicaux de gauche*. This list attracted 12 per cent of the vote, compared with the Socialists' 15 per cent. Some have seen in the apparent encouragement offered by Mitterrand to Bernard Tapie, the media hero, business tycoon, football club owner and ultimately discredited leader of the MRG list, a deliberate (and successful) ploy to ruin Rocard's chances and ensure thereby that an old adversary would never occupy the Elysée. Jospin from 1995 moved quickly to negotiate the basis of the 'plural left' coalition, first with *Les Verts* and then with the PCF, the left-wing Radicals and Chevènement, that produced electoral agreements, avoided splitting the left-wing vote and enabled all the partners to benefit from the swing against Juppé's discredited government. While the impact should not be exaggerated, the presence of FN candidates in 132 constituencies for the second round, 76 of them (of which the left won 46) involving three-cornered fights between the FN, the mainstream right and the plural left, and hence the splitting of the non-left vote, also assisted (Ysmal, 1998 SL, pp. 297–9; *Le Figaro* 8 June 2002).

The 2002 defeat resulted in the loss of over 40 per cent of the PS seats in the National Assembly. For the plural left coalition the sanction seemed severe: of the 1977 leaders, Jospin for the PS, Hue for the PCF, Voynet for *Les Verts*, Baylet for the PRG and Chevenèment, only Baylet remained in parliament, and he is a senator and not involved in the contest. Jospin had withdrawn from politics after his first round defeat in the presidential election, and the other three had been beaten in their constituencies. There were other notable casualties, most spectacularly perhaps the architect of the 35-hour week, former minister of Social Affairs and mayor of Lille, Martine Aubry. However, of 22 ministers in the previous government who represented themselves, 15 succeeded and in fact 2002 saw very little change in the first round score of the PS. If it had not returned to the levels of the 1980s, it had equally not fallen back to those of 1993.

The PS government benefited from a mood of national optimism when, in 1998, economic growth and a fall in unemployment coincided with the victory of France's multi-ethnic football team in the World Cup played in France. But by

2002 it was suffering from the disillusion of voters who saw frustratingly little progress in improving comfort, security and stability in employment, or law and order and prevention of violence. Moreover, the plural left was without a single, high profile leader after the rapid departure of Jospin following his defeat. While anti-incumbency reactions help to explain the left's defeat, the success of the mainstream right in holding together its new coalition, avoiding any split in the mainstream right vote, and, in the backlash after the presidential election, in holding off the FN, explains much of its victory.

Allies of the plural left: the Greens

The ecology movement, which grew out of the general concerns for conservation and ecological problems that emerged particularly after 1968, initially consisted largely of fragmented and often locally based groups. These were largely peopled by grass-roots activists with very little central or political organization. Indeed, the movement was, as it generally continues to be, characterized by a distrust of leadership. A presidential candidate in 1974 attracted only a minuscule vote, although a Paris-based group achieved 11 per cent of the vote in the Paris municipal elections in 1977. There was an ecologist list in the European elections of 1979, which gained 4.39 per cent of the vote, and an ecology candidate (Brice Lalonde) in 1981, though neither had an organized political base. In general their electoral performance was very modest throughout the 1970s and 1980s, in contrast to the Greens of West Germany, for example, who were aided by the German electoral system.

At the time of the European election in 1984, and in reaction to Lalonde's decision to cooperate with more established political forces, a confederation of ecology movements was created as a unifying political force. It came to be known as *Les Verts* (the Greens) a shortened version of the full title, *Les Verts confédération écologiste – parti-écologiste*. In 1988 the Green presidential candidate, Antoine Waechter achieved just under 4 per cent.

A high point for *Les Verts* came in 1989, assisted by electoral systems where proportional representation operated. In the municipal election it averaged over 9 per cent of the vote in the 94 towns of over 20 000 inhabitants in which its candidates stood (Cole, 1989, p. 27). At the 1989 European elections later that summer the party achieved over 10.5 per cent of the votes and nine seats. The party's performance in 1989 was a considerable surprise, although well in line with general political trends throughout Europe.

The high hopes engendered by these results, and by favourable opinion polls, were soon disappointed. One reason was the apparently ineluctable tendency of the Ecologists to fragment, engendered in part by the 'somewhat anarchic individualism' (Frears, 1991, p. 108) of their activists and also by disagreements over strategy. Whilst *Les Verts* under Waechter refused all alliances, Brice Lalonde in 1992 set up a rival party, *Génération ecologie* (GE), intended largely to capture the ecological protest vote in the forthcoming regional and general elections and deliver it to the Socialists at the second ballot. The consequence was that a high score in the regional elections for the Ecologists taken together (nearly 14 per cent) was split almost equally between the two contenders. However, this was sufficient to win a number of seats at regional level, and hold the balance of power in the Nord-Pas-de-Calais region, where a coalition between Ecologists and Socialists resulted in a female councillor from *Les Verts* becoming president of the Regional Council.

The two ecology parties managed to patch up an agreement for the 1993 general election, but the result was profoundly disappointing. With under 8 per cent of the vote between the two parties on the first ballot, only two candidates even went through to the second ballot and both were defeated. Further splits and dissension followed. *Les Verts* evicted Waechter from the leadership in favour of Dominique Voynet, who had emerged as a media personality during the campaign. Under her the party moved more clearly in favour of a strategy of alliance with the alternative Left, such as dissident Communists and left-wing former Socialists, while also being wooed by Rocard as part of his 'big bang' approach. Fragmentation was all too visible at the European elections of 1994, when *Les Verts* presented one list, *Génération écologie* another, and Noël Mamère, a former GE leader, figured prominently on Tapie's list. Neither ecology list achieved more than 3 per cent of the votes. In 1995 Voynet was the sole ecologist candidate but her results, at 3.32 per cent, were back to the levels of a decade previously. However, the campaign had established the Greens as the only plausible ecology party, and it marked the beginning of 'the conversion to political realism of the party leadership' (Szarka, 2000, p. 30). The agreements which constituted the plural left brought 7 Green *députés* into the National Assembly in 1997 and Voynet into government, although in 1998 the party lost the regional presidency it had held. The proportional representation national list system enabled a Green list headed by 1968 figurehead Daniel Cohn-Bendit to do relatively well (9.72 per cent) at the 1999 European Elections, despite the presence of a rival list led by Waechter. But such scores are not reflected in other elections and in 2002 the Greens improved on their 1995 presidential score by only two percentage points, with Noël Mamère, as their candidate. The landslide defeat of the left reduced them to only three seats in the National Assembly.

Fragmentation, strategic incoherence and infighting have all wreaked havoc on the Ecologists' electoral fortunes. Their ideology and political approach have not proved sufficiently robust to capture and hold a large and stable group of followers, especially in a climate of economic difficulty and unemployment. They can be seen as too identified with a single issue, which in 1998 was a priority for only 21 per cent of the electorate, compared with 61 per cent who saw unemployment as a crucial issue (Santeny, 2001, p. 215) Those who perhaps share some of their ideals do not necessarily vote for them (Machin and Guyomarch, 1994, p. 304). For some they provide an opportunity for a protest vote – 38 per cent of Voynet's voters in 1995 voted for her because they did not like any of the others – but such support is always liable to be fickle (Santeny, 2001, p. 215) and 'the Greens remain uncomfortably perched at the margin of the system' (Hayward, 2001, p. 275).

Parties of the mainstream right: the Gaullist party

Gaullism is one of the few political creeds to be identified by the name of a single individual. De Gaulle, despite the strength of vision that constituted so powerful a part of his charismatic personality, never produced a specific or coherent political statement. His most important published works are his memoirs. The 'certain idea' or, in another translation, the 'precise image', (Charlot, 1970, p. 67) of France which de Gaulle evoked at the start of his memoirs meant a commitment to the international status and independence of France. His complex and ambiguous personality provided scope for a range of interpretations of what loyalty to his vision might actually mean. In supporting him his followers were generally expressing rather unfocused aspirations for the unity and standing of France. 'To French voters the Gaullist party offered a charismatic leader; the heroic aura of the resistance; loyalty to institutions that offered a stable government for the first time in the twentieth century; *gloire*; a sure barrier against communism, and economic prosperity' (Knapp, 1990, p. 140).

The adjective 'Gaullist' – perhaps it should be neo-Gaullist – has remained attached to the *Rassemblement pour la république* founded, in 1976 by Jacques Chirac, and superceded, in the autumn of 2002, by the *Union pour la Majorité Presidentielle*, which has since 1981 constituted a key element in the 'government/opposition' political system (see above and figure 8.3). The emergence of the Gaullist Party was of crucial importance to the political development of the Fifth Republic for two major reasons:

- First, it provided for the first decades of the regime a solid parliamentary basis for the entrenchment of the Fifth Republic's institutions. The framers of the

FIGURE 8.3

Votes and seats for the mainstream right* at National Assembly elections

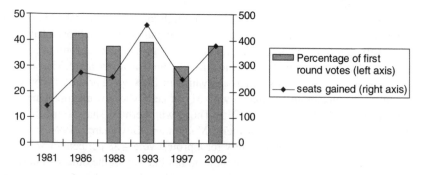

* RPR and UDF (2002 UMP and UDF).
Source: compiled from www.parties-and-elections.de/fr.

Constitution had not expected the power of the President and government to be based upon the existence of a largely disciplined governing majority. But such a majority existed, and the Gaullist Party was the dominant element in it. Political practice and expectations shifted to accommodate this fact.

- Secondly, the Gaullist Party was the first mass-based disciplined party of the French right. It did not – at least initially, but see Mény (1995) and Knapp (1994) for the argument that it is now no different from the other parties – look just to the local standing of its candidates as a basis for electoral support nor, unlike the earlier RPF, and much to the surprise of some commentators, did it depend solely upon the charisma of de Gaulle himself, for it survived his resignation and his death. Modern techniques of central organization, of the selection and briefing of candidates, of attracting voters and marketing the party's appeal were developed. The effect of this, in the 1960s and 1970s, was to provide a haven for a large right-wing electorate, putting great pressure upon fragmented parties of the centre, and encouraging the formation of alliances and larger groupings both on the Right and between the parties of the Left who needed to ensure their own defence, indeed survival.

The survival of the Gaullist party resulted from the strengths of its party organization, from the development of a system of local leaders (*notables*) who can rely on their local power and their local record, and, crucially from Jacques Chirac's leadership (formally until 1994) and the organizational and financial resources that could be channelled into the party, especially, from 1977 to 2001 if with contested legality, through the RPR stronghold in the Paris City Hall, when first Chirac (to 1995) and then Jean Tibéri was mayor (Knapp, 1999, p. 113).

In the 1960s the defence of the institutions which de Gaulle had imposed was the central Gaullist concern. As these institutions became embedded and uncontested this essential element of Gaullist identity became irrelevant. Gaullism, Andrew Knapp asserts (1994, p. 185) has no core ideology, although it is always right-wing, nationalist and relatively authoritarian. David Bell (2000a pp. 66–7) discerns an ongoing tension between a market and free-enterprise oriented strand and a more populist, more socially oriented strand reflected, for example, in Chirac's 1995 election promises.

The RPR of the 1990s and the start of the twenty-first century has faced a number of challenges and difficulties. First, there have been problems of internal dissent and rivalry. These became visible after the defeat of 1988, and particularly acute in 1992. Although the party leadership stuck to support for the ratification of the Maastricht Treaty in 1992, prominent members of the party, notably Philippe Séguin and Charles Pasqua, campaigned for a 'no' vote. RPR members of Parliament (72 out of 127), senators (70 out of 90) and members of the European Parliament (3 out of 13) supported a 'no' vote despite the leadership's position (Buffotot, 1993, p. 280). The landslide victory in the 1993 general election and the appointment of an RPR prime minister encouraged, rather than prevented, the emergence of two plausible Gaullist candidates, Balladur as well as Chirac, in the 1995 presidential election. Each candidate needed to find a distinctive appeal. Chirac's was, much more than before, based on notions of a mitigated and social market. He was unable, once in office, to keep the contradictory promises of his campaign. The result was a vertiginous drop in public approval.

Rivalries continue to be a problem within the party. With the trauma of defeat eventually leading to some healing of the rift between those who had supported Balladur and the followers of Chirac, the party was faced in 1999 with the abrupt resignation of Séguin as party president, and as head of the joint list for the European elections between the RPR and DL. At those elections the party was also faced with a Euro-sceptic list headed by former party grandee Charles Pasqua. The first woman to head a major French party, Michèle Alliot-Marie, took over as party president. In 2001 Séguin was the party's official candidate for the mayoralty of Paris. Sitting mayor Jean Tibéri (supported by Pasqua) put up a dissident list, and the right lost out to Socialist Bernard Delanoë.

The second challenge to the RPR has been its alliances and relationships with other parties. The success of Valéry Giscard d'Estaing rather than the Gaullist Chaban Delmas in 1974 was a severe blow, but since Giscard's defeat in 1981 the RPR has pursued a strategy of electoral alliance with the non-Gaullist mainstream right for elections at all levels. In the 1999 European elections, however, the RPR shared its list with only one of the non-Gaullist parties, DL, and was faced with a competing UDF list. In the run-up to the 2002 elections the RPR, and especially Alain Juppé, worked hard to enlist the support of all the non-Gaullist mainstream right. This did not succeed in preventing a separate UDF candidate, François Bayrou, who went on to put up some 200 UDF candidates in the legislative elections. The strategy did lead on to the constitution of a new political grouping, the *Union pour la Majorité Presidentielle*, involving the RPR, DL and much of the UDF. No candidates were put up with an RPR label and the party accepted the conditions: first, that candidates should accept the decision of the central organizers as to who should stand in each constituency. A second aspect was that the UMP was declared as a political party, even though it was not to be formally constituted until the following October. Hence the subsidy payable for each vote would go to the UMP, not to the RPR or other contributing groups. In effect this meant the end of the RPR in its previous form, and its president, Michèle Alliot-Marie, finding that 95 per cent of her executive committee (*bureau politique*) were in favour, agreed to an extraordinary general meeting of the party in autumn 2002 where it dissolved itself. Chirac thus unhesitatingly killed off the party he had himself created (*Le Point*, 7 May 2002, p. 42). Finally, candidates were required to undertake that once in the National Assembly they would remain within a single UMP parliamentary group. This would contrast with previous experiences, for example in 1988, where candidates returned on the basis of electoral alliances and single designations within constituencies broke apart to form separate parliamentary groups. It remains to be seen whether this extended successor to the RPR and some of the non-Gaullist parties (see below) will be able to discipline, marshal and control the even more disparate strands and tendencies within it. Even before its formal creation there was vigorous debate going on as to the wisdom of allowing, within its constitutional arrangements, for the formal representation of different *courants*. As one commentator pointed out, these *familles de pensée* already included, at least, republican Gaullists, liberals, both 'social' and 'societal' strands of non-left wing ideas, and centrist decentralizing pro-Europeans (*Le Point*, 19 July 2002, p. 34).

Another acute problem of alliances arises in relation to the FN, especially at local level. Their growing electoral presence has resulted in some attempts to steal their clothes. The law and order and anti-immigration policies of Charles Pasqua, minister of the interior in both 1986–8 and 1993–5, were aimed at accommodating this section of the electorate. However, as Andrew Knapp points out, this, combined with the need also to accommodate alliances with the non-Gaullist mainstream right, has had the paradoxical effect of increasing the salience and legitimacy of the issues on which the FN campaigns while seeming not wholeheartedly to embrace the consequences (Knapp, 1999, p. 118). The FN has profited thereby. The mainstream right has moreover in some cases had second-round votes from the FN to thank for its successes. But alliances and agreements have been few and far between – and all at local levels, as in two regions in the south between 1986 and 1992 (Bell, 2000a, p. 135). The RPR's leaders generally have held firm in their refusal of any agreement or alliance, even when, for example, relationships with the FN caused real difficulties at regional level after the 1998 regional elections. A former secretary-general of the RPR, Jean-François Mancel, was promptly expelled from the party when he said he saw no reason not to work with FN councillors (*L'Année Politique*, 1998, p. 45). An RPR councillor elected to the presidency of the regional council in Haute Normandie with FN votes immediately resigned the post, leaving the way open for the PS. Chirac announced before the vote for the 2002 election that any UMP candidate who came to any agreement with the FN would be automatically ejected not only from the UMP but from any presidential majority.

Gaullism, or rather neo-Gaullism, may be dissolving into a large catch-all federation of the mainstream right in the shape of the UMP. It seems probable however, that sharp distinctions between mainstream left and mainstream right will, in France as in the rest of Europe, be increasingly difficult to sustain, and it is notable that some of the most controversial of the policies of the Jospin government are not such as to be instantly overthrown. The incoming Raffarin government in 2002 observed that the 35-hour week, bitterly opposed by the right when it was introduced, was now an established part of the social expectations of the French people, and could not be undone. Performance in government may increasingly become the touchstone, especially with the *quinquennat* for both president and national assembly. It remains to be seen whether the generally centrifugal forces of French politics can be countered by the tactical need to hang together.

Parties of the mainstream right: the non-Gaullist right

Three main strands have fed into the non-Gaullist mainstream right; right-wing independence, radicalism and Christian democracy. Of these, Christian democracy has the clearest ideological contours. Like Christian democracy in other European countries such as Germany, in France it grew out of the social doctrine of the Roman Catholic church in the late nineteenth and early twentieth centuries, with an orientation that was 'cross-class and anti-liberal' (Bell, 2000a, p. 105), arguing for a middle way between liberal capitalism and Marxism (Irving, 1973, p. 55). One outcome was the formation, in 1919, of a Roman Catholic trade union, but it was not until 1944 that a political party developed (the *Mouvement républicain populaire* – MRP). The MRP was a party of the centre during the Fourth Republic, principally divided from the Socialists, with whom they worked closely, by the Socialists' anti-clericalism and the MRP's suspicion of the atheist Marxist foundations of the Socialist approach. Politically, however, the centre is an uneasy and uncomfortable place, and the centre parties, which flourished briefly in the political space left by the discrediting of the Right in the post-war years, have dwindled. The MRP supported De Gaulle's return to power and formed part of his first government, but suspicion of unchecked central power caused the party to oppose the proposals for the direct election to the presidency when they were introduced in 1962, and it was affronted by De Gaulle's policies on European integration, to which, like Christian democratic parties elsewhere, it was deeply committed. However, in the electoral structure of the Fifth Republic it needed allies. The Socialists' growing rapprochement with the PCF was anathema to Christian democrats and during the 1970s they allied themselves definitively with the non-Gaullist right, becoming in 1978, part of the Giscardian UDF federation. Then known as the *Centre des Démocrates Sociaux*, it was one of the two largest component parts of the federation. In 1995 it was refounded as *Force Démocrate* (FD), seeking to extend its appeal beyond its Christian roots.

The second element of the non-Gaullist right has its origins in the Radical party, founded in 1901, which, like the Christian Democratic MRP had been a medium-sized party with 10 to 15 per cent of the vote each before the demise of the Fourth Republic. It was anti-Communist, anti-clerical and liberal. Forced to choose by the emergence of the rift between government and opposition and the possibility of *alternance*, the *Parti Radical* split, one part constituting what is now the *Parti des Radicaux de Gauche*, and the other eventually coming under the umbrella of the UDF federation, and diminishing to insignificant proportions by the end of the century. With the reconstitution of the UDF in 1998, it retained its separate identity as a component of the party 'largely so as to be able to celebrate its centenary in 2001' (Knapp, 1999, p. 129). At its 103rd Congress in October 2002 it voted to become an associated body of the UMP in which it is now likely to disappear.

The third element of the non-Gaullist mainstream right derived from the conservative independents elected to the parliaments of the Fourth and the early Fifth Republics under the 'independents and peasants' label. In the 1962–7 National

Assembly, where the Gaullist Party did not enjoy an absolute majority, they formed part of the presidential majority and looked to the young Valéry Giscard d'Estaing as their leader. He had taken over a parliamentary seat from his grandfather in 1956, and had thus depended for his first steps in politics on his personal, local and family connections, rather than on ideology or party organization. He began to set about fashioning a political power base for himself. Initially this took the form of a parliamentary 'study group' of the Independents and Peasants' members who had followed him, plus a number of young politicians, some of whom had come like him through the elite civil service recruitment and training process and shared his rather technocratic style. This group he called the Independent Republicans (*Républicains indépendents* – RI).

Giscard d'Estaing's victory in the 1974 presidential election campaign was due to a well conducted campaign, to his success in presenting himself as a competent, modern, progressive, forward-looking candidate, who was nevertheless firmly within the safe framework of the coalition that had governed France since 1958, and also to the disunity of the Gaullists and the defection of a good number of them to his cause. His party base was still relatively weak. With the approach of the 1978 general election and following the local elections in Paris, where Chirac had defeated Giscard d'Estaing's candidate, Giscard d'Estaing needed a political backing upon which he could depend and which could counterbalance the Gaullists. This he succeeded in creating, first by the relaunch of the Independent Republicans as the Republican Party (*Parti Républicain* – PR) in 1977, and then by the creation of a federation of the PR with other non-Gaullist elements of the majority.

The *Parti Républicain* increasingly embodied the neo-liberal, free-market elements of the mainstream right. Always prone to infighting between its leaders, and not immune from secession – in 1994 Philippe de Villiers broke away to set up an anti-European party – in 1997 it was refounded as *Démocratie Libérale* under the free-enterprise oriented Alain Madelin, briefly finance minister under Juppé in 1995 until his rigorous, public-expenditure-cutting reformist policies proved unpalatable to president and prime minister.

These were the various strands that Giscard d'Estaing, looking to enlarge his support not only within the conservative right, but also within the centre, brought together into a federation, created shortly before the 1978 election, whose title, the Union for French Democracy (*Union pour la Démocratie Française* – UDF) echoed that of the book he published during his presidency – *Démocratie Française* (1976).

The UDF was a weakly organized group, an uneasy confederation (though it did have a small number of 'direct' members) that remained close to the classic formula of a cadre party. It has consequently been susceptible to rivalry amongst its leading personalities and to dissidence amongst its constituent groups. During the 1980s it just succeeded in surviving the disruptive effects of the ambitions of some of its leaders, such as François Léotard, and of intense rivalry between ex-President Giscard d'Estaing and ex-Prime Minister Barre in the run-up to the

1988 presidential election. However, the alliance continued to experience divisions, and the three diverse, 'cadre-party' components were never really federated (Knapp, 1999, p. 124). In 1988, for example, the RPR and the UDF put up only one candidate in each constituency for the first round, under a joint label. However, once the successful candidates reached Parliament, division occurred, not only between RPR and UDF, but within the UDF, for the CDS members and other 'Barrists' split from the rest of the 'Giscardian' UDF to form a separate Parliamentary group and put up a separate list for the 1989 European Parliament against a joint list backed by the RPR and the remains of the UDF and headed by Giscard d'Estaing. Moreover, the minority Rocard government was courting the centre – his government actually included four UDF ministers. By the end of 1991, however, most of the dissident CDS had been driven back to the UDF, and a degree of unity within the federation and the alliance with the RPR were both patched up for 1993, but the 1992 Maastricht referendum provoked the secession of de Villiers. For the general elections in 1988, 1993 and 1997, and European Parliament elections in 1989 and 1994 , it continued to be linked to the RPR in a difficult marriage of convenience from which it drew the benefit of a higher level of parliamentary representation than it could expect if it were confronted by direct electoral competition with the RPR. In 1995, in the absence of a candidate of its own, its leaders divided their support between Balladur and Chirac, with the bulk of the support going to Balladur who was 'transformed by default into a UDF candidate' (Cole, 1995, p. 330).

However, 'UDF history could be written as a competition between the Christian Democrats and Parti Républicain' (Bell, 2000a, p. 92), and the fragility of the federation became clearly evident when the outcome of the regional elections forced the UDF to decide whether to expel those five DL or UDF members who owed their presidencies of regional assemblies to FN support. In the aftermath, and as the RPR manoeuvred to reinforce its dominant position over the whole of the mainstream right, the UDF split. A new UDF was created as a single formation, not a federation, dominated by FD, while Madelin took DL out to stand on its own, but to join up with the RPR in a joint list for the European Elections of 1999. He himself stood as first-round presidential candidate in 2002. Such a campaign provides a platform for ideas but rather little leverage. However, desiring to federate the whole of the right, Chirac drew his new prime minister, Jean-Pierre Raffarin, and five ministers from DL, which merged into the UMP.

The new UDF put up its own list for the European elections in 1999, and its leader, François Bayrou, as a presidential candidate in 2002. Bayrou resisted the blandishments of the UMP for the subsequent legislatives, although nine of Raffarin's ministers and 25 per cent of the UMP candidates were drawn from his organization (*Le Figaro*, 8 June 2002). He refused the UMP's conditions which would channel all the official state funding to the new formation and called for a continuing 'plural' majority. In the event, the UDF managed to field 200 candidates, many of them standing against UMP competitors, of whom 29 were successful, and hence retained its own parliamentary group.

Some 25 years of attempts to federate the non-Gaullist mainstream right had never produced a convincing or durable outcome. The rump of the UDF has been marginalized and the foundations laid for a large party regrouping most of the mainstream right. However, many of the divisive dilemmas – free market or social solidarity, greater or less European integration, possible cooperation with at least part of the extreme right, or total rejection of any relationship – will persist in the new formations, as will personal ambitions. It seems improbable that the kaleidoscope has ceased to turn.

The extreme right: the National Front

The rise of the National Front through the 1980s was the most striking development within French political life in that decade (see Figure 8.4). The extreme Right was not a new phenomenon within the French political spectrum. By the early 1970s Jean-Marie Le Pen (see Exhibit 8.2) brought together into a single political organization – the *Front National* (FN) – a wide variety of strands of extreme Right opinion. A good deal of support for the FN, at least initially, came from those who were still bitterly resentful of the French abandonment of Algeria. This resentment had probably helped to achieve a 5 per cent first-ballot score for the extreme Right candidate in the presidential election of 1965. Support also came from some remnants of the xenophobic, anti-modernization, anti-state movement amongst small shopkeepers, farmers and small businessmen, known, after the name of its leader Pierre Poujade, as Poujadism. This had flared briefly in the 1950s, and Le Pen had been one of the Poujadist deputies in the National Assembly. As the credibility of the FN grew during the 1980s, support came also

FIGURE 8.4

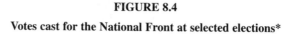

Votes cast for the National Front at selected elections*

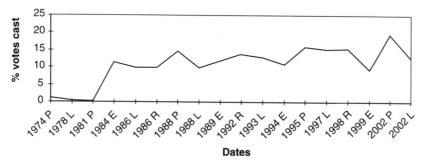

Dates

- * Percentage of valid votes cast.
- P = Presidential, L = Legislative, R = Regional, E = European.

EXHIBIT 8.2

Jean-Marie Le Pen

Jean-Marie Le Pen was born in Brittany in 1928. His experience in the Resistance as an adolescent fuelled a virulent anti-Communism, and he became involved in right-wing student groups while registered as a law student in Paris. He then joined the army, and was sent to Indo-China as a parachutist. He subsequently returned to his law studies, but quickly became involved in Pierre Poujade's movement and in 1956 was elected to Parliament by a Paris constituency as a Poujadist, becoming its youngest member.

He almost immediately left his parliamentary duties to rejoin his regiment, and whilst serving in Algeria was suspected of being involved in torturing an Algerian prisoner. He has never been convicted for this, though the accusation continues to haunt him. At this period he lost one eye in a brawl at an electoral meeting, and for a while his public image involved the sporting of a somewhat sinister eyepatch. He left the Poujadists and was re-elected to Parliament in 1958 as an independent, losing his seat in 1962.

He continued to be active in politics, supporting the 1965 presidential campaign of the extreme Right candidate, Tixier Vignancourt. In 1972 he founded the National Front. Towards the end of the 1970s he inherited a fortune bequeathed to him by one of the earliest members of the FN.

He stood as a candidate in the presidential election of 1974 gaining less than 1 per cent of the vote, and took only just over 3 per cent of the vote in his Paris constituency in 1978. In 1981 he could not assemble the necessary signatures for a nomination as a presidential candidate.

From the 1980s, Le Pen, having been a very marginal and little known political figure, acquired a degree of media notoriety, which he exploited fully. A scandalous divorce in 1987 – his ex-wife sought to embarrass him by being photographed wearing nothing but an apron – had no noticeable impact upon his political prospects. His crude outspokenness has resulted in much litigation. He has managed to rebut charges of anti-Semitism, but his 1987 reference to the Holocaust as 'detail' of history was damaging, whilst in 1988 an extremely offensive pun again alluding to the Holocaust provoked the departure from the party of the only FN member elected to Parliament in the 1988 election.

In between the two rounds of the 1997 legislative election, Le Pen physically assaulted a socialist candidate, an offence for which he was banned from holding public office, initially for two years, subsequently reduced to one, from April 1998. He was able to head the FN list for the 1999 European elections. His performance in the 2002 presidential elections (Figure 8.4) was an extraordinary testimony to personality and charisma.

---

from some intellectuals critical of marxist influence and what they saw as western decadence. Some monarchists were attracted to the FN, as were some Catholics who disliked the liberal changes that had occurred in the Roman Catholic church since the 1960s. Thuggish and violent elements also found an outlet in the FN. It is a populist but parliamentary movement, so 'the issues that it raises and the themes that it champions are chosen to make an electoral appeal' (Bell, 2000a, p. 127)

The initial impact of the National Front was minimal. (see Figure 8.4). The first sign of a change in the fortunes of the FN came when Le Pen himself took over 11 per cent of the vote in a Paris *arrondissement* in the municipal elections of spring 1983, though nationally the FN secured only 0.3 per cent of first-ballot votes. In November and December that year the FN list spectacularly scored over 16 per cent in a municipal by-election in Dreux – a town with a large immigrant population – and made a pact with the local Gaullists which resulted in the election of an FN member on the second ballot. Scores in another town by-election and in a parliamentary by-election in which Le Pen himself stood that autumn confirmed a dramatic rise in votes. In the 1984 elections to the European Parliament the FN took 11 per cent of the national vote, and gained 10 seats.

The 1986 general election in France was also conducted under a proportional representation system, so a vote for the FN of just under 10 per cent brought the party 35 parliamentary seats. However, with the return to the previous ballot system in 1988, an only slightly diminished proportion of the votes produced only one *député*, who later left the party. A parliamentary by-election in December 1989 returned the FN candidate, so the party continued to be represented in the National Assembly until 1993, when a higher proportion of the vote failed to yield any seats. The sole candidate returned in 1997 was ousted for electoral malpractice and replaced by a socialist at the consequent by-election.

During the 1990s the FN was able to gain control of a number of *communes*. It gained Toulon, Orange and Marignane in 1995, and Vitrolles, where second in command Bruno Mégret's wife (he had been disqualified) was returned as mayor in a notorious municipal by-election in 1997. In all these towns it sought to practise its principles of national preference for French citizens and of support for what it saw as specifically 'French' culture.

The isolation of the FN was brought into focus by its continuing failure to convert votes into seats and by the 1998 regional elections and the election of the regional assembly presidents that followed. Some in the FN, and especially the technocratic Bruno Mégret, were looking closely at the role of the very right-wing MSI in Berlusconi's Italy and advocating rapprochement with the mainstream right. Moreover, the question of the succession to Le Pen was opening up. Such tensions came to a head in 1999, partly as a consequence of Le Pen's proposal that, in the expectation that he would still be banned from standing, his second wife should head the European Parliament list (Rillardon, 2000, p. 100). Mégret summoned a special party congress and persuaded it to vote him in as leader. At the European elections there were two lists: one, headed by Le Pen, for the FN, he having resorted to the courts to ensure that he retained both the name and the capital assets. The other was headed by Mégret whose party had taken the name *Mouvement National Républicain*. Mégret's list, with only 3.28 per cent of the votes, failed to take any seats, while Le Pen's list fell back to 5.69 per cent and 5 seats. At the municipal elections of 2001 Toulon was lost, Mégret held on to Vitrolles, where his wife was mayor, and Marignane, and the FN held Orange, but no further gains were made, and, although the extreme right took 10.3 per cent of the total vote in those *communes* where there were far right candidates, it 'shrunk back to its heartlands: [with councillors in] 297 towns compared to 456 in 1995' (Bilger Street and Milner, 2001, p. 514).

Against this background Le Pen's winning through to the second ballot of the 2002 presidential election was as unexpected as it was shocking. No opinion poll predicted it. Indeed a string of polls between 10 and 18 April 2002 showed the estimated vote for him at between 11 and 14 per cent, well behind Jospin's scores of 16 to 19 per cent (http://elections.lemonde.fr/presidentielle). It has been argued that had any poll in fact suggested such a possibility the impetus to stop him would have succeeded in doing so (*Le Monde*, 21 June 2002). The result was a strong display of anti-Le Pen feeling. On the May Day holiday some 400 demonstrations took place across France, involving, it was reckoned, a total of a million and a half people. In Paris the march of about 400 000 demonstrators was one of the largest for over fifty years. Turnout at the second ballot rose from just under 72 to nearly 80 per cent. Le Pen took 13.41 per cent of the votes of all registered electors (17.78 per cent of votes cast), just over 50 000 more than his and Mégret's combined scores on the first ballot. Since these results could not be converted into success in the National Assembly elections, and given the strength of feeling demonstrated and the well-attested resolution of most of the main-stream right in refusing cooperation, it is clear that the FN will remain an outsider in national-level political life. Nor is it apparent what its fate will be when Le Pen, aged 74 at the time of his appearance on the second ballot, can no longer act as the charismatic figurehead. But the resonance of the FN themes, and its marked capacity to involve its sympathizers, for example in its own May Day (Joan of Arc) processions, and to mobilize its activists, mean that it cannot be ignored nor too lightly dismissed.

The reasons for the emergence and current position of the FN are undoubtedly complex, but a number may be suggested. They are closely interlinked and interdependent, and explanations have to be sought in the conjunction of a number of factors rather than in any single or dominant cause. For the purposes of analysis the factors can be divided into three groups: those related to the issues around which Le Pen focuses his programmes; those related to the structure of the electorate and the electoral system; and those related to legitimacy, credibility, respectability and publicity.

Amongst the factors that relate to issues are, first, that the FN has latched on to certain issues which have found a considerable echo in parts of the electorate, and has found a style of expression, based on alleged plain speaking and the supposed common sense of the ordinary person, in posters, party political broadcasts and other campaigns, that has proved attractive. Among the main issues on which the FN has successfully campaigned have been those which appeal to feelings of insecurity amongst the electorate in times of economic and social change, recession, restructuring and Europeanization; 'because it knows that is is not likely to be in office, it can afford to pay less attention to nuances' (Hanley, 2001, p. 309). The theme of the need for security, in the sense of the repression of crime and the enforcement of law and order, has been closely linked to the much stronger and simpler theme of hostility to immigrants and immigration. The FN attacks the European Union's provision for freedom of movement and the abolition of frontier controls. It opposed the extension of voting rights at local and European elections to citizens of the Union who are not French nationals, seen as the thin end of a wedge which would lead to voting rights for all immigrants. There is also a general theme of protest against the evils of modern society, with denunciations of drug addiction and the spread of AIDS.

The initial impact of the FN came soon after France had experienced the major political upheaval of *alternance*, and the advent of a left-wing government. France had been experiencing a recession and a rising rate of unemployment throughout the 1970s. The centre-right governments of the 1970s had attempted to combat this through austerity measures and restructuring. They had also responded with law and order legislation to concerns about crime and hooliganism. Equally, there was nothing new about an undercurrent of hostility to immigrants, which had produced tougher immigration controls and repatriation schemes during the 1970s. For some, the change of government in 1981 did not produce the radical social transformation for which they had hoped. For them a vote for the FN was a protest vote against the failure of past hopes. For others the new government, allied with the Communists, looked like the first step on a dangerous road towards Communist totalitarianism, which the traditional right had not been strong enough to resist. The failure of the mainstream right to present a strong, unified and credible opposition or to provide solutions in government channelled such protest to the FN. The perceived inability of the Left to effect radical change was mirrored by disillusion with the Right in the mid-1980s, and again when Balladur's government in 1993 and Chirac's promises in 1995 did little to ease unemployment, cut taxes or lift the burdens which economic adjustment placed on the unskilled and disadvantaged. 'It was the failure of the Centre-Right rather than of the Left that provided Le Pen with his opportunity for a political break-through' (Hayward, 2001, p. 281)

The National Front, although largely devoid of any explicit economic ideology, has consistently rejected the competition-oriented, globalist logic which the parties that are, or have been, in government see as inescapable in a world of increasing economic interdependence. It is now able to latch on to the anti-globalization themes that are becoming stronger in protest politics. 'Globalization' is used as a catch-all slogan for the ills of the French economy just as 'immigration' can be used for the ailments of French society (see Chapter 10). The EU, presented as a technocratic would-be superstate with ambitions to level down the distinctiveness of France and especially its welfare safety nets, is just a first step on the road to this globalization. In 2001, 70 per cent of FN sympathizers thought that the EU failed to protect France from the effects of globalization, compared to a national total of 54 per cent (SOFRES, 2002, p. 126). The FN advocates withdrawal from, and renegotiation of, the European Treaties and the Schengen convention. It is explicitly protectionist, not a free-market party, having inherited from earlier extreme-right movements an anti-capitalist, anti-technocratic approach, and appealing to sectors that feel threatened by economic modernization – 'all those who feel they may have something to lose' (Hanley, 2001, p. 310).

As politicians of all the mainstream parties became increasingly mired with the stains of corruption and illegality, the result was increasing disaffection of the voters and refusal to support the mainstream parties, a refusal from which the National Front benefited. In 2001, 57 per cent of FN sympathizers thought the political parties had too much influence, compared to a national total of 43 per cent (SOFRES, 2002, p. 122). The FN insists that it is the only clean party.

The factors that relate to the structure of the electorate and of the voting system include the following:

- It is possible to discern, as was first clearly emphasized by the Maastricht referendum in 1992, a cleavage in France between relatively affluent, optimistic, educated voters and more disadvantaged, less educated, more peripheral voters who constitute a strong populist strand in French politics. Alain Duhamel (*Le Point*, 3 May 2002, p. 54) defines them as those who have confidence in the society that is being constructed, and those who are frightened or horrified by it. The National Front articulates the fears and desires of an important section of these latter voters.

- Geographically, the FN's heartlands are in Alsace and Lorraine, in the South East, and around Paris. In some of the areas where it is important, such as the Provence–Alpes–Côte d'Azur area, the FN could from the beginning exploit certain traditional extreme Right sympathies. Moreover, the South and South East in 2001 had, alongside Paris, the highest rates for crimes against persons and property (*The Economist*, 23 February 2002), which also fuels the FN vote.

- Proportional representation, both for the European elections and for the 1986 general election, gave the FN its crucial point of entry into the political institutions. The return to a constituency based system has since resulted in minimal representation for the FN in the National Assembly, although it retains MEPs. Nevertheless, from the mid-1980s, once represented in the European Parliament and the National Assembly, the party acquired, in public and media perception, the status of a legitimate part of the political scene that had to be treated seriously.

It is notable that the peaks of the FN's electoral appeal have occurred in the first ballot for the presidential elections (see Figure 8.4). The personal appeal of Le Pen, especially in circumstances where there is truly no likelihood of the FN actually taking power, is undoubtedly a crucial factor. And as Catherine Fieschi has pointed out, what presidential elections do is open up particular opportunities for 'rally' politics. This aspect of politics, which De Gaulle himself espoused, and which the Fifth Republic, through its second-ballot presidential duel 'institutionalised and...domesticated' (Fieschi, 2000, p. 81), allows space for a candidate who appeals to notions of unity, to fears of 'the break-up of the nation...in favour of, not only a corrupt or...inept political class, but also of "special interests", fragments of the nation' (p. 82). The leader is not perceived as indulging in 'real' politics because they divide, but rather, through charisma, and through the 'folklore' and showbusiness aspects of his party activities and campaigns, he creates a sense of unity and of belonging that transcends divisions. This is Le Pen's strength, and undoubtedly weighed heavily in the 2002 presidential election results. What Mégret knew, and what the party has never successfully been able to operationalize, is that at the level of every other election except that for European Parliament (where the existence of a single national list also allows a special place to appeals to national unity) classic party organization and politics are indispensable.

Le Pen's ability to exploit this aspect of Fifth Republic politics was crucial to the growth of the legitimacy and credibility of the FN. Le Pen proved to have a personality and demeanour that parts of the electorate found reassuring and not threatening. Despite occasional horrific and revealing lapses – for example, his reference to the holocaust as 'a mere detail of history' – he distanced himself from the wilder and more overtly anti-Semitic and racist statements of some of his followers. He has contrived to draw together, partly within his own life history (see Exhibit 8.2), many of the traditional themes of the far Right – the nationalism of the 1930s, the anti-Gaullism of Vichy, Poujadism, *Algérie française*, and traditionalist Roman Catholicism (Charlot, 1994, p. 120). The FN has contrived to make many of the themes of these ideologies admissible within general political discourse (Birenbaum, 1992, p. 310). The presence of FN members in the National Assembly from 1986–8 and in the European Parliament and their largely respectable behaviour (with only occasional outbreaks such as the occasion in October 1987 when they created a virtual riot in the chamber of the National Assembly in protest against the absenteeism of members of the established parties) gave the party the public status of a legitimate participant in the political system, with the accompanying press and television exposure.

The FN has been described as the party of discontent and fear (Mayer and Perrineau, 1989). In the 1990s and at the start of the new century, many long established certainties are threatened. Farmers find themselves exposed to change through the reform of the European Community Common Agricultural Policy and the WTO agreement. BSE and genetically modified crops loom over the safety of daily food. Shopkeepers suffer from increases in competition. Unemployment, albeit diminished, looms for both the underqualified workers whose jobs are disappearing and for the middle manager and white collar worker whose qualifications are no longer an automatic passport to stable and respectable existence. A SOFRES poll in June 2001 found 83 per cent of FN sympathizers thinking that globalization was a threat to employment and businesses, compared to a total percentage of 55 (SOFRES, 2002, p. 117). To all these groups, the FN offers a utopian vision of the retrieval of a (mythical) national past and national identity (Perrineau, 1993, p. 152; Yves Mény in *Le Point*, 3 May 2002). Only the educated upper professional classes seem to be largely immune to these blandishments.

The FN is not merely a party of protest, but also the outcome of the emergence of an important new cleavage that runs not so much between Left and Right as between the 'establishment' and those who are profiting, or at least not suffering, from change, and the 'anti-establishment' disadvantaged groups.

The FN is not a Fascist party. It does not reject the regime. It is not particularly bellicose. It tries hard, if not totally successfully, to maintain its credibility and respectability and has established itself firmly within the political spectrum. It can pose dilemmas for both mainstream left and mainstream right. For both, it points up the necessity to avoid the fragmentation which can allow the FN to creep ahead. It was probably the lingering effects of the 1999 schism as well as backlash against the presidential results which kept the FN below the 12.5 per cent needed for a place in the second ballot in an increased number of constituencies in 2002 compared with 1997. The installation of the *quinquennat*, meaning that presidential elections which favour 'rally' politics and parliamentary elections which require 'party' politics will probably coincide, is likely to hinder it. Mégret seems a negligible threat. His performance in the presidentials gives him little leverage and his party lacks resources: after 1999 he sought to take up his rights to return to his employment as an *ingénieur des ponts et chausées*, while continuing to run his party (Rillardon, 2000, p. 102). The loss of his organizational abilities and networks may be more harmful. At local levels, at least in its heartland, the FN may continue to pose dilemmas for the parties of the moderate Right. For the moment the new UMP is firmly opposed to compromise. But this is an issue with potential to split apart the new party and expose again the fragility of the mainstream right.

Conclusion

The party political landscape of France has changed markedly over the period of the Fifth Republic. The first two decades of the Fifth Republic saw the emergence of larger parties, more firmly organized, even if their financing remained a matter for mystery and scandal. They act within Parliament, in general, in a disciplined way, partly through the operation of the mechanisms invented to ensure precisely that (see Chapter 7). But since the early 1980s the scene has changed again. Power is still largely shared between the successors of the big four of the early 1980s. But around them, like comets and asteroids amongst the planets, is a penumbra of smaller parties, some relatively ephemeral, some more durable. The *Gauche Plurielle* coalition of the Jospin Government encompassed five parties. The nature of election campaigns, with a concentration of media attention upon the leaders, and especially the demands of the presidential campaigns, has increased the focus of politics upon personalities. The system, with its provision for proportional representation in some elections, can accommodate new entrants. Nor is it always unforgiving to mavericks. If Jean-Pierre Chevènement and all his MDC lost their seats in 2002, Philippe de Villiers was returned at the first ballot.

FIGURE 8.5

Voter protest 1981–2002

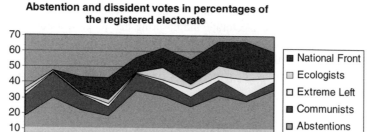

The 1970s and 1980s were marked by the massive decline of the Communist Party. Despite the rise of the FN at the end of the 1980s it could be argued that 'the political extremes which under the Fourth Republic represented nearly half the electorate, account[ed], even [then] for no more than one-fifth' (Charlot, 1989, p. 34). In the 1990s the parties of the centre ground of political life continued to dominate. The crucial electoral choice still seemed to be perceived as being between moderate Right and moderate Left, as Lionel Jospin's unexpectedly good performance in 1995 demonstrated. All the mainstream parties have adapted to the institutions and practices of the Fifth Republic and to the *alternance* they have made possible.

However, the 1990s began to provide evidence of a new phenomenon – a considerable disaffection towards the processes of political representation. The turnout at elections has dropped steadily (see Figure 8.5). There has been a growth in the levels of spoiled or blank votes. It is always possible for a voter to turn out in order to put nothing into the envelope which should contain the voting slip, as a gesture of protest. Jean-Marie Le Pen ostentatiously did this at the second ballot of the presidential elections in 1995, indeed the level tends to be highest at this stage when choice is limited (4.85 in 1995, 4.29 in 2002).

Moreover, the levels of what is quite clearly a protest vote have risen. In the earlier decades of the post-war period the PCF could sweep up a good proportion of the votes of those who objected to their own position, to the elites and the establishment, to capitalism, competition and Europe, and who dreamt of a revolutionary and rosy future. In the 1980s, and especially from 1989, this dream became unsustainable. But economic and social change was urgent and ineluctable. So the 1990s also saw a marked rise in the number of votes for the smaller groups, the extremes and the anti-establishment parties, which together now amount to over one-third of all votes cast. Governments with a solid majority of seats are not supported by a majority of the electorate. The UMP took only

33 per cent of the vote at the first ballot of the parliamentary election in 2002, and 47 per cent at the second ballot even though Chirac had achieved a massive majority of the votes cast (82 per cent) and even of the total electorate (62 per cent) against Le Pen in the second round of the presidential election only a month before. Re-engaging this electorate and ensuring that its protest does not take on 'wildcat', unregulated, possibly violent and highly disruptive forms (see Chapter 9) is undoubtedly now the biggest challenge for the mainstream 'parties of government' if they are to fulfil adequately their functions as parties within a representative liberal democracy.

9

The State and Civil Society: Pressure and Interest Groups

The French constitution proclaims the sovereignty of the people. It is from this sovereignty that the legitimacy and authority of the government derives. The tradition of direct suffrage, dating back to the French Revolution firmly locates the exercise of this sovereignty in the casting of a vote. Political parties have developed as the means by which voting choice can be organized, channelled and expressed. Political parties, however, are by no means the only channels through which citizens may choose to voice their opinions or seek to express their interests, needs and demands. A very large number of groups, societies and associations exist within France and they too have important roles to play in shaping both policy-making and policy implementation. Many clubs and societies exist for purely social, sporting, recreational or cultural reasons, but even they may occasionally be stirred to more political action, as when representatives of the local anglers' societies began, in Brittany during the 1980s, to take legal action against farmers whose agricultural activities polluted the water. Moreover, there is a long and strong tradition of street protest and direct action, which also influences governmental activity and politicians' priorities.

It has sometimes been argued that the French are not 'joiners'; that the strength of family ties, and of individualism within French society has meant that there has not been a strong social tradition of membership of associations or clubs of any sort. However, even in 1951, 41 per cent of the respondents to a poll were members of a voluntary association (Wilson, 1987, p. 14). The Ministry of the Interior records the number of new groups registered at the prefectures. Over 60 000 were founded in 1997, and in 2001, at the centenary of the law which authorizes and regulates them, some three-quarters of a million were registered (Keeler and Hall, 2001, p. 51).

Nevertheless, there has long been a strand in French political life and thought which has deplored the existence of such groups, or at least any propensity they may have for involvement in public activity. There have been those, like General de Gaulle, for instance, who have felt that the expression of popular sovereignty ought not to involve any intermediate groupings between the citizen and the result of the vote (Wilson, 1987, p. 13). This tradition is rooted in the views of the

227

eighteenth century philosopher, Jean-Jacques Rousseau, who saw the state, in its role as the organizer and guarantor of society, as embodying a general will which ought directly to express the interests of all. 'It is therefore essential,' he wrote, 'if the general will is to be able make itself known, that there should be no partial society within the State and that each citizen should express only his own opinion' (Rousseau, 1762). This view is no longer widespread. In 2001, 69 per cent of respondents to a poll felt that consumers' and citizens' movements had inadequate influence (SOFRES, 2002, p. 123).

In 1791 a law was passed, in the interests of an unconstrained expression of the general will and of revolutionary equality, which dissolved the old guilds and other associations and prevented the formation of any group which would represent a special or particular interest or need. This *Loi le Chapelier* was repealed in 1884, and in 1901 a further law recognized citizens' rights to freedom of association and provided a legal basis upon which an association or society could exist.

In much French thinking, the state, as the overall custodian and guarantor of the organization of society, has a clear role in relation to any formal grouping of citizens. While it is not illegal to form a purely private club, any group which wants protection or legal status, for example to protect its funds against embezzlement, must register its existence and its aims and objectives with the local prefecture (see Exhibit 9.1). The role of the state in relationship to clubs and associations in general frequently extends beyond mere legal recognition. Almost all clubs will expect to get some financial assistance or subsidy, even if only of a very modest amount. This largesse derives from the *commune* although the other levels of local government and even central ministries may also produce funds. Whilst mayors may recognize that handing out a few hundred francs annually to the local anglers may not greatly enhance their electoral fortunes, on the whole they prefer not to put this to the test by refusing, and the associations expect it.

In many cases a voluntary group, often a small one, demonstrates a social need, and the state will then take over the action necessary to meet the need, sometimes continuing to use the association as its agent, but effectively providing a very large part of the necessary resources. A notable exception to this process was the family planning movement. The *Mouvement Français pour le Planning Familial* was founded in 1956. Since the promotion of contraception was strictly speaking illegal until 1967, the state could not become involved, and so in its early years the movement was, in John Ardagh's words 'a remarkable and rare example in France of effective unofficial civic action on a national scale' (Ardagh, 1988, p. 344).

The relationship between the state and the various groups, at all levels, is thus very complex. The state has always maintained ambiguous relations with interest groups. On the one hand, it rejects them in the name of its own theoretical sovereignty; on the other, it establishes such close relations with them that it is sometimes difficult to distinguish between public and private interests or institutions

---

EXHIBIT 9.1

La vie associative

Many French thinkers, politicians, lawyers and officials hold a concept of the state as the body through which power is legitimated and organized; as such the state exercises public power with the task of ensuring the peacefulness, security and good order of society. The state therefore maintains a general oversight over all activities within society, providing the necessary legal and administrative frameworks. The 1901 law on associations was intended to do this chiefly for cultural and religious associations, clubs and societies. It also had the effect of legalizing the existence of political parties (Hanley, 2002, p. 22). It continues to provide the means through which any association, club or society can have an existence before the law, giving it, for example, the right to own money or property. In 2001 there were estimated to be over 750 000 associations in France

Any group of people has the right to found an association. However, if the association wishes, for example, to open a bank account or obtain premises, then it must set out its aims and objectives, provide itself with a constitution on an approved model, and declare these at the office of the local prefect. Its existence will be announced in the daily government publication, the *Journal Officiel*. If the association wishes to extend its legal capacity – for example, to receive legacies, it must obtain from the Minister of the Interior a declaration that it is 'of public utility'. It then becomes subject to 'supervision' (*tutelle*) of its finances by the authorities. The government may abolish any association whose aims are held to be a threat to public order.

This official oversight of associations, clubs and societies means that it is possible to have a fairly clear view of the number and type of associations that exist. It engenders a feeling that associations are in some ways a part of public rather than private life, and that the activities of associations (*la vie associative*) constitute a special sector of the life of society as a whole. This has a double effect. First, many associations look to the authorities to provide them with subventions and financial support. Secondly, since their status is similar to registered charities in the United Kingdom, for example, public bodies and authorities often look to associations, or indeed create them, as the channel through which desirable activities can be undertaken, for example, the care of the handicapped or the promotion of cultural activities.

(Mény, 1989, p. 391). Alongside the many interest groups characterized by these features, the main categories of which are described below, there are broader, less organized movements. Some persist, others wax and wane over time, and their role is frequently reactive protest. It is not easy to distinguish boundaries between the various types of groups, but they do differ in their role and their impact upon the making and implementation of policy. First it may be appropriate to categorize them in terms of their own internal structure, objectives and functions. Secondly, they may be considered in the light of their relationship to the state, and, the types of impact that they have upon public policy and functions. Clearly these two types of description overlap, but for the sake of clarity this chapter now takes them in turn.

The Nature of the Interest Groups

This section considers the functions of the groups under four headings:

- parastatal groups,
- social partners,
- pressure and lobbying movements and groups,
- clubs and societies.

Parastatal groups

There are, in France, a number of groups of which membership is compulsory for certain individuals or enterprises, and which are entitled to levy dues. They are controlled by elected representatives, not government officials, and they have the functions of organizing certain aspects of economic life, often undertaking essentially public functions as agents of the state. They may also serve, however, to represent the functional interests of their membership to the state, and may be consulted and conferred with. The main organizations of this type are the various 'chambers': chambers of commerce (*chambres de commerce*), chambers of agriculture (*chambres d'agriculture*) and chambers of trades (*chambres de métiers*). These bodies may have important roles in the implementation of government policy. For example, the chambers of agriculture act as government agents in the management of various types of agricultural grant and subsidy such as the funds available to assist in the restructuring of agricultural holdings. Chambers of commerce may have a very wide range of activities, financed through government subsidy, levies on their members, and income generated. They often run local facilities, such as airports and tourist information. They may contribute subsidies to the local business schools, which they have often helped to create and on whose governing bodies they are almost always well represented (Chafer, 1988, p. 18). The larger chambers of commerce run extensive export advisory services for local business, dispensing state funds for export support.

The essence of these groups is that although they are organized as private groups membership is in fact compulsory, and they are legally assimilated to the public sector:

> These chambers...are real corporate organisations in the traditional sense of the term. They enjoy fiscal advantages and disciplinary or regulatory powers and play a semi-public role in matters such as public investment and the organisation of the profession. Integration and the overlap of public and private roles have been pushed furthest in these institutions. (Mény, 1989, p. 394)

Social partners

These groups do not have the characteristic of compulsory membership. They, too, however, have recognized roles in certain public functions, although they also have a clearer role in the representation and defence of the economic interests of their members, not only in relation to the state, but also in dealings with other groups. They were largely born out of the political and ideological background of the class struggle.

The most important of these groups are the trade unions and the employers' organizations. Given their conflictual relationships, both with the state and with each other, it may seem perverse to describe them as social partners, although that is the terminology increasingly used, perhaps more in hope than belief, within the European Union, and it does reflect the recognized roles that such groups may play, for example, in social security organizations.

The level of trade union membership is low. Recent estimates of a figure that is extremely difficult to ascertain with any accuracy suggest: that around eight per cent of the workforce is unionized (down from about 25 per cent at the beginning of the Fifth Republic); that this is amongst the lowest proportions of the workforce in the major industrialized countries, and that the union membership is increasingly an ageing one (*L'Etat de la France*, 2002, p. 484). The French trade union movement has always been characterized by fragmentation. As Jack Hayward has pointed out, notions of democracy and socialism had developed in France before the emergence of an industrial workforce on a large scale. The consequence was that workers' groups did not develop as part of a labour movement concerned broadly with the amelioration of the conditions of workers within the current political system, largely through collective bargaining. Rather they emerged as 'weak and fragmented...unions whose prime function was that of ideological mobilisation outside and against the liberal democratic system' (Hayward, 1986, p. 57).

The oldest (1895) and largest of the French union confederations is the *Confédération générale du travail* (CGT). It developed with an explicitly Marxist analysis of industrial relations, and a general ideological commitment to the bringing about of a socialist society. It was traditionally strong in the steel, construction and chemical industries, in the ports, the mines and the railways, and it retains its bastions in the public sector gas, electricity and railway undertakings (Milner, 2000, p. 42). In 1947, in the atmosphere of the developing cold war, the union came under Communist control. Thereafter the relationship between the leadership of the CGT and that of the French Communist Party (PCF) was very close, though not formal. The CGT was long regarded as the instrument of the PCF's industrial relations policy. Not all members of the CGT are members of the PCF, or even particularly committed to the Communist line, and since the mid-1990s it has tried to assert its autonomy, but in 2000 the majority of its executive belonged to the PCF (*L'Etat de la France*, 2002, p. 489) The union, like all other unions in France, experienced, during the late 1970s and the 1980s, a very sharp decline in membership, which may now have levelled out. Its candidates can still command about one-third of employees' votes for industrial tribunal (*conseils de prud'hommes*) membership.

After the assertion of Communist control over the CGT in 1947, a non-Communist element broke away and in 1948 set up a rival confederation, the

Force ouvrière. Noted for its virulent anti-Communism, and attracting a relatively high proportion of white-collar workers, from banking, insurance, the health services and the middle to lower ranks of the civil service, it has attempted to maintain its distance from all the political parties and from any specifically political objectives. Its stance in relation to issues such as worker participation has been fairly radical, and it has included a Trotskyite wing, whose influence grew in the 1990s. Its membership held up well until 1985 (Headlam, 1989, p. 32) but has declined sharply since. It has now adopted a generally conflictual stance, chosing at its 2000 congress to be 'alone against the world', hostile to globalization and Europe (*L'Etat de la France*, 2002, p. 490).

The CFDT, on the other hand, has, under the first woman to lead a major union confederation, Nicole Notat, its secretary-general from 1992 to May 2002, been moving away from conflictual and left-wing politics. This union emerged in 1964 out of the Roman Catholic *Confédération Française des Travailleurs Chrétiens* (CFTC). The CFTC owed its origins to late nineteenth century Catholic social movements, developed by the Roman Catholic Church to attempt to combat the influence of Marxist socialism amongst the workers. In 1964 a large proportion of the union elected to break its formal links with the church, and this group renamed and reformed itself, becoming the CFDT and developing a more political analysis of society while moving quite rapidly towards the left. Many of its leaders continued to be left-wing Catholics, and in the period after the end of the 1960s when the Socialist Party was reforming itself, and attracting increasing support from left-wing Catholics, amongst other groups, the CFDT also moved quite close to the Socialist Party. It did not, however, benefit markedly from the accession of a Socialist government to power in 1981. The CFDT attempted to maintain a generally supportive but nonetheless clearly distinct relationship with successive Socialist governments, but this did not succeed in preventing a decline in membership numbers, although it now claims to have been growing steadily throughout Nicole Notat's period in office.

These union confederations consist of individual unions representing workers and employees across the whole spectrum of occupations. They are not, however, the only unions or union confederations. There are major groups representing particular occupational sectors, in particular the middle-class white-collar union representing middle management and executives, the *Confédération Générale des Cadres*. This is a rather small confederation, which has been losing support, but, along with the four confederations already described (CGT, FO, CFDT, CFTC) it is specifically named in the Code of Labour Law as automatically to be deemed a representative organization for the purpose of collective agreements. This automatic recognition for purposes of collective bargaining has been important in the context of negotiations for the implementation of the 1997 law on the 35-hour week. The status is resented by the non-associated unions which represent other groups, particularly the teachers, traditionally a sector in which levels of unionization could reach two-thirds, and by other autonomous unions. Most teaching unions were for most of the post-war period federated in the very large and influential *Fédération de l'Education Nationale* (FEN). With a total of perhaps half a million members, its strength could give it an important voice in some professional matters. The move by the Socialist government in 1984 to change the status of church schools was partly a result of FEN pressure. The defeat of the changes was a blow to the FEN which found itself unable thereafter to oppose further reforms. An attempt to reform the union structure in 1992 by making it a much more federal body resulted in the expulsion of some of its component groups and a schism. In 1993 a new education union, the *Fédération syndicale unitaire* was founded, which claims 180 000 members and whose overall influence, measured by the success of its candidates in elections to the various professional bodies, is greater than that of the FEN (Mouriaux, 1994, p. 114; *L'Etat de la France*, 2002, p. 493). The residual FEN (now *UNSA-education)* then linked up with a number of other moderate unions, particularly a public service union with a strong membership in the police, to form the *Union Nationale des Syndicats Autonomes* (UNSA), which has also been a haven for unionists leaving the public service components of the increasingly radical FO. In the education sector, as elsewhere, fragmentation and division is a major characteristic of the unions, whose influence is certainly weakened thereby.

Farmers also have separate unions, of which the largest and by far the most influential is the *Fédération Nationale des Syndicats d'Exploitants Agricoles* (FNSEA) although there are other smaller rival groups.

In addition there are a wide range of small independent professional associations and unions concerned to defend the professional interests of their members. These may be the independent unions, often of workers within a particular enterprise, which are often accused of being the creatures and tools of management, although they have become important in the car industry, for example. They may also be the associations of those with a particular background or job, for example those which unite the former students of an elite educational institution, or doctors, or lawyers. These do act in the defence of their members' material interests even though they might not recognize themselves as a union, nor do they necessarily have a recognized status as a representative body, but they may moreover themselves be highly fragmented. A left-wing lawyer is likely to belong to the *Syndicat Nationale de la Magistrature*, a moderate right one to the *Union Syndicale des Magistrats*.

Employers, too, have their own organizations. The representation of business is less fragmented than is that of labour. The principal organization is the *Mouvement des Entreprises de France* (MEDEF). This is the renamed (from 1998) continuation of the *Confédération Nationale du Patronat Français* (CNPF), which was founded in the post-war period as a response both to a militant workforce, and to the *dirigiste* tendencies of the state in the face of industrialists and employers who had been discredited by the failure of many of them to rally to de Gaulle and the Resistance during the war. De Gaulle famously remarked to a gathering of industrialists soon after the Liberation that he had not seen many of them in London. The MEDEF is itself a federal body. It combines within itself both commerce and industry. Its representative role has always been particularly important in general matters such as social security and taxation. Its active leader, Ernest-Antoine Seillière, elected in 1997, achieved the change in name, but largely failed in the attempt to oppose the introduction of the 35-hour working week. The MEDEF was, however, successful in preventing the use of the unemployment benefit funds, jointly managed by employers and unions through the UNEDIC *(Union pour l'emploi dans l'industrie et le commerce)*, to finance the costs of the shorter working week. Seillière then embarked upon an ambitious attempt to promulgate a *refondation sociale*, pushing back the tide of state regulation of social and working conditions in favour of collective agreements with the unions in a number of areas. On the employers' side he managed to associate the owners of small businesses, grouped within the *Confédération générale des petites et moyennes entreprises* (CGPME), and the *Union professionelle des artisans* with the agreements. His allies on the union side were the more reformist of the unions, especially Nicole Notat's CFDT. The CGT and FO both refused to sign. Nor is it clear that national agreements result in local effects. However, the high profile of the activities, the alliance with the CFDT and the reinforcement of the MEDEF position by two rulings of the *Conseil Constitutionnel* (in December 2001 and February 2002) which annulled parts of the proposed legislation implementing the 35-hour week, resulted in a growth in the political influence of the MEDEF, and, Susan Milner argues, 'to a large extent set the domestic agenda for the 2002 elections' (Milner, 2002, p. 341). This influence may have been greater at political rather than grass roots level. In 2001 only 9 per cent of respondents to an opinon poll had confidence in Seillière's role in reforming social and industrial relations in France, as compared with 28 per cent for Nicole Notat (SOFRES, 2002, p. 302).

Pressure and lobbying movements and groups

Trade unions and employers' associations are, of course, very largely concerned with pressure and with lobbying to further the interest of their members. However, they are regarded as having a broader general interest in the organiza-tion of relationships within society, reflected, for instance, in the specific right of union membership granted by the constitution. Nevertheless, the boundary between them and pressure groups is hard to establish. Indeed, in the sense that any particular group may at some time seek to influence the decision-making process, the definition of a pressure group becomes very wide indeed.

'Non-occupational' groups (Wilson, 1987, pp. 48ff) do exist in France, even if there are few of the large, national voluntary 'public interest' associations with interests in particular policy areas that characterize some aspects of interest-group politics in some other countries; there is no French equivalent of the United States's National Rifle Association that campaigns for the right to carry arms or the British Royal Society for the Protection of Birds; whilst French consumers' organizations developed much later than, and were partly modelled upon, the British Consumers' Association. Wilson categorizes such groups as either 'advocacy groups', concerned with advancing the cause of those who seek services from the state, or as 'public interest' groups. Amongst the advocacy groups he includes the organizations representing former servicemen which were very influential during the Fourth Republic, and have continued to ensure that there is a government minister with special responsibility for them, the student groups, the family associations, the parent-teacher associations, and the women's movement.

Clubs and societies

'*La vie associative*' is the collective French term used to describe the activities of all sorts of associations and clubs (see Exhibit 9.1). Despite the traditional stereotype, supported by anecdotal evidence (Ardagh, 1988, pp. 290–305), which portrays the French as generally highly attached to life within the rather narrow confines of family and perhaps business contacts, and wary and suspicious of involvement in voluntary, cultural or recreational activity within the community, change occurred from the 1970s. Associations flourish, and are used as a framework not only for social, cultural or sporting activities, but for many voluntary and charitable purposes, and for the channelling of public funds. So associations may range from a handful of academics seeking to attract and administer research grants with minimal bureaucracy to families of persons with a mental illness seeking to provide support and practical help. A great many associations, not only the volunteering and charitable ones, require and expect a measure of public subsidy, which may come from the local *commune*, the *département*, the region or central government. There is no vigorous culture of fund-raising to support such local activities; it is hard to identify the French equivalent of the jumble sale or coffee morning. Many cultural, recreational and charitable associations are largely run by salaried employees, working as *animateurs* of the various activities. It has sometimes been said that the expansion of such activities during the 1970s produced, in those working in this sphere, a noticeable new group of potentially influential voters for the Socialist Party, attracted, partly as a result of the type of work they did, with its emphasis on the collective good and public provision, to a party of the moderate left. Certainly all governments over the past 30 years have sought explicitly to encourage *la vie associative*, undeterred by the paradox of state action in pursuit of what must be essentially voluntary and personal activities.

Most clubs and associations are small and local. They always have the potential to become involved in lobbying and pressure activities to protect the interests of their members, or promote a cause. As Dieter Rucht points out:

> Though not all these groups are concerned with politics, and some only occasionally so, we can conclude that there exists an extremely rich and multifaceted associational spectrum which creates both needs and opportunities for political participation. For the most part, participation in this context does not mean directly engaging in professional politics, but rather taking part in societal activities which, however, may have an indirect impact on policy-making. For example, the many voluntary associations active in matters of social welfare and health reduce the load and cost of state activities in these areas. (Rucht, 2000, p. 95)

Their activities can perhaps be distinguished from those of the much larger and looser groupings usually known as 'social movements'. These are symbolized by mass demonstrations which bring 'together scores of associations, voluntary groups and individual citizens in a spontaneous movement of public defiance' (Waters, 1998a, p. 170). Their goals are usually large scale policy change, even if their bedrock may be local groupings and community structures, which mobilize people, outside the classic political organizations, around local issues – for example, nature protection, living conditions, local provision for immigrants (Waters, 1998b, p. 496). However, 'social movements tend to form loose networks without a clear-cut membership, a definite programme and statutes, and elected bodies. Social movements may incorporate organisations...but as a whole they do not form an organisation' (Rucht, 2000, p. 97).

France has a particularly strong tradition of social protest, and provides clear examples of social movements of different types, trajectories and fates. Four such movements are discussed briefly below. Other examples – for example the movements for regional autonomy in Britanny, largely defused by the development of decentralization, and Corsica, still violently active, or the movement for the rights of homosexuals – could have been chosen but those outlined below illustrate the similarities and differences in the movements. They are the student movement, the ecology movement, the women's movement, and the anti-racist and solidarity movement.

Students

Students are by definition a changing and transient population. Student generations are short and may not share the goals, aims, or degree of commitment to activism of their predecessors. Nevertheless, they do constitute a definable group of which large sections have at various times during the Fifth Republic been mobilized in ways which have had important effects. Students very often have dual concerns, both for those issues which most directly affect the nature and quality of their education, and for much broader and more general political issues. In 1968 these two concerns fused, under the leadership, not of the more established student or political organizations, but of various ad hoc groups, some more or less inspired by Trotskyite or Maoist views, and of a few charismatic individuals, to bring about what is variously known as the student revolt, or the student uprising, or simply the events of May 1968 (see Exhibit 9.2).

The strength of the student protests, directed initially at the shortcomings of the French educational system, but rapidly widened into criticisms of almost every aspect of French social, political and cultural life, and revulsion at the brutal police repression acted as the catalyst for a general strike, fuelled by discontent at working conditions and wage levels. Secondary school children, broadcasting journalists, civil servants and many others became involved in impassioned discussions of what working conditions, social relations, and the shape of society and politics should be. The art of the poster and the slogan blossomed. The effects of the general strike were far-reaching and uncomfortable; no one was unaffected.

EXHIBIT 9.2

May 1968

Main events: chronology

March–April	Student agitation at the Nanterre campus calling for improved conditions
2 May	Nanterre campus closed by university authorities
3 May	Students occupy courtyard of Sorbonne. Police called to clear courtyard. Violent clashes and numerous arrests
6 May	Riots in Latin quarter (university area) of Paris, 422 students arrested, about 600 injured. Extent of police violence causes much adverse comment
11–13 May	Two major unions, CGT and CFDT, call for a general strike on 13 May, which is widely observed
16–17 May	Renault workers take over factories at Boulogne-Billancourt (Paris) and elsewhere demanding better wages and conditions. Workers' strikes spread
26–27 May	Number of strikers has risen to over 9 million. Negotiations between unions and government
27 May	Grenelle agreement between unions and government results in offer of 7 per cent general pay rise
29 May	De Gaulle makes secret visit to General Massu at French base in Baden, Germany
30 May	Second broadcast by de Gaulle. General election called. Demonstration in Paris in support of the government
14–16 June	Students abandon occupation of the Sorbonne and the Odeon theatre
17–24 June	Car workers are amongst last to return to work
23 and 30 June	Two rounds of the general election. Gaullists win overall majority in the National Assembly

Causes

A wide range of causes have been suggested for these events. Bénéton and Touchard (1970) enumerate eight major explanations that were offered at the time, ranging from psychological disturbance to deliberate subversion. Some are patently far-fetched. Those who took part had varied motives. The events acted as a catalyst for the expression of a huge range of grievances and discontents that had found no other outlet. The marginalization of the trade unions and the weakness and fragmentation of political opposition in the first decade of the Fifth Republic all contributed. The violence of the police and the vacillations of the government were also key factors in turning student protest into a major 'event', indeed an uprising.

Effects

The immediate outcome of the events was the Gaullist victory in the June general election, and a general wage rise that fuelled inflation and contributed to the 1969 devaluation of the franc. Over a longer term, the idealism of May 1968 fed into the revival of the Socialist Party during the 1970s. Mendras and Cole (1991, p. 229) see May 1968 as an important turning point in the development of French society, symbolizing the rejection of austerity and narrowly constraining moral codes. However, they also say that the areas in which nothing changed are probably more important than those where substantial change occurred. The events of May 1968 were vivid and dramatic; their legacy is obscure and ambiguous.

The government seemed briefly to waver, and for a little while it was possible to believe that the times were truly revolutionary. And then the government reached an agreement with the main unions – the Grenelle agreement – and wage levels were raised. The calling of a general election, which eventually produced a strong right-wing backlash, defused the political situation. The students went on holiday.

The crisis was diagnosed by some as the outcome of a blocked and stagnant society, where genuine opposition was difficult, and channels for the effective expression of grievances inadequate or non-existent, where management was distant, personal and patriarchal, and relationships within families and within the educational system rigid, formal and old-fashioned. In such a society, it could be argued, pressure builds up until a gasket blows; a violent upheaval releases the pressures, and the system settles back, relatively unaltered.

After 1968, student activism was virtually non-existent for some 15 years. However, activism revived in the 1980s, if focused more specifically on the concerns of young people. Between 1986 and 1995, students and young people succeeded in bringing about the withdrawal of three measures affecting them – the Devaquet bill reforming higher education in 1986, the 1994 proposal to reduce the minimum wage for young people, and in 1995 further proposals to reform aspects of higher education. Students have also been conspicous participants in other protests and demonstrations, such as those organized by anti-racist and solidarity movements, and in the 2002 demonstrations against the National Front following Le Pen's success in the first round of the presidential election.

Women

The women's movement – perhaps more accurately 'movements' for there were a range of sometimes cooperating and sometimes competing groups – in France is often traced back to the events of May 1968 (see Duchen, 1986). The movement can be categorized as a 'new social movement' since it 'express[ed] new issues…absent from…the mainstream political agenda' (Waters, 1998a, p. 171). Its tactics were not the mass demonstration but rather consciousness raising, argument, lobbying, petitions and targeted gestures. The women's movement in France has been notable for its intellectual, literary and cultural character, and the influence of psychoanalytical theory. The French term for women's liberation, *Mouvement de liberation des femmes*, was, in the 1970s, adopted and registered as a trade mark by one particular group, of a distinctive intellectual, psychoanalytical and separatist persuasion, thus preventing its formal use by others. This not unnaturally caused consternation and resentment amongst other women's groups. However, there were also campaigns around specific areas of special concern, such as the liberalization of laws on contraception and abortion. The movement seemed to have dissipated in the 1980s and 1990s, because, it could be argued (Waters, 1998a, p. 172), its objectives had largely been achieved. However, it continued to exist in the small local groups, not all of whom would necessarily recognize themselves as belonging to the women's movement as such, who concern themselves with issues such as the welfare of immigrant women or of battered wives (Reynolds, 1988a and 1988b; Appleton, 2000, p. 72; Allwood and Wadia, 2000). And at the end of the century the movement for parity revived women's campaigning and resulted in constitutional amendment (Exhibit 2.7).

Environmentalists

The environmental or ecology movement is also often traced back to the events of 1968. In fact, groups and associations concerned with the conservation of nature had existed since the nineteenth century, but they were small, fragmented, and largely ineffectual. During the 1970s a number of campaigns began which attracted national attention. For example, the long-running dispute over the attempt by the army to extend its firing ranges in the remote Larzac plateau, where José Bové (see Exhibit 9.3) became active as a protestor and a farmer, began in 1971, and continued until one of the first acts of the Mitterrand government in 1981 was to cancel the proposals. The dispute was eventually settled in 1985. Similarly, following examples in West Germany and the United Kingdom, in the mid-1970s, objections to the civil nuclear programme, previously unheard of, began to be voiced. It is worth noting that, unlike the case of the United Kingdom, there has never been, in France, any significant movement against nuclear weapons, so there was no linkage

---

EXHIBIT 9.3

José Bové

Born in 1953, José Bové spent some of his childhood in Berkeley, California, where his parents were working. Back in France he was, as a schoolboy, involved in the 1968 events (see Exhibit 9.2). He dropped out of university in the early 1970s, joining the environmental and anti-militarist protests and action against the army's appropriation of land on the Larzac plateau for training, for which he was jailed for three weeks in 1976. He occupied a farm in the military-owned land, farmed sheep and produced Roquefort cheese. The dispute about the land was settled in 1985, but Bové's activism continued. In 1987 he helped to found the *Confédération Paysanne*, to support small producers. He also joined the Greenpeace protests against the revival of nuclear testing in 1995.

In the late 1990s his protests took on a strongly anti-globalization and anti-American emphasis, prompted by opposition to genetically modified crops, and by fury at the 100 per cent duty imposed by the USA on Roquefort cheese in riposte to the EU banning of the import of American hormone-treated beef. Part of this protest took the form, in 1999, of the sacking of a branch of McDonald's in Millau in south-west France. For this he was condemned to a further short term of imprisonment. When it was eventually enforced he entered prison defiantly, as a martyr in the anti-globalization cause and, aided by his moustachioed Asterix-like appearance, as an emblem of what was presented as the resistance of the 'ordinary' French person to change and Americanization. He particularly condemned what he called *malbouffe* (bad eating) – uniform, processed, fast food prepared and consumed without the wholesome ingredients, care and time traditionally devoted to good French cooking. Bové's international profile grew with the rise of the world-wide anti-globalization movement.

between the issues of civil and of military nuclear use. Although President Mitterrand, immediately he came to power in 1981, cancelled the construction of a nuclear power station on the Breton coast against which a prominent campaign had run, the rest of the extensive nuclear programme went ahead under the Socialists. As a movement the environmentalists have been weak and fragmented. A plethora of small local naturalists' and conservation groups continue to exist, now federated in the *Fédération Française des Societés de la Protection de la Nature*. During the 1970s some of the ecologist groups, like their counterparts elsewhere in Europe, began to develop political strategies (see Chapter 8) and by the 1990s the environmental movement constituted an example of a social movement which had transformed into a political party.

Anti-racism and solidarity

By the end of the 1980s the women's, student and ecological movements had all ceased to be recognizably social movements as defined above (p. 236) (Bell, 2001, p. 188). However, social mobilization and protest has not disappeared. New movements emerged characterized instead by an affirmation of social and political rights, and of the democratic values of equality and solidarity (Waters, 1998a, 1998b; Bell, 2001; Appleton, 2000). The anti-racist movement, which grew as a direct response to the rise of the National Front (see Chapter 8), is one example. While there are a number of more or less structured organizations, such as SOS-racisme, initially sponsored by the Socialists, and the *Mouvement Contre le Racisme et Pour l'Amitié Entre les Peuples* (MRAP – linked to the PCF), anti-FN rallies – as at the time of the 2002 elections – tend to bring together a vast range of individuals and groups without strong connections. Ironically, since the FN claims to be an anti-system party, the anti-racist movement also canalizes a strong strand of anti-system feeling.

The anti-racist movement is – as, for example, the title of the MRAP suggests – closely interlinked with what has been described as the solidarity movement. This is concerned with civic and humanitarian issues, such as third-world development, and the rights of asylum seekers and refugees or the homeless. This movement can be seen as embracing very long-standing groups, such as the *Ligue des Droits de l'Homme*, founded at the time of the Dreyfus affair, or Amnesty International, alongside well-known humanitarian organizations, such as *Médecins sans Frontières*, but also more spontaneous groups and activities in support of – or even by – disadvantaged groups. One example would be the 1997 mobilization against the proposals of the Juppé government to tighten the law on illegal immigrants (Waters, 1998a, p. 170). Another would be the occupations of churches in Paris, and, following the closure of the Sangatte asylum seekers' camp, in Calais, by asylum seekers. These movements, like the environmental movement, also, if almost paradoxically, overlap with the now world-wide anti-globalization movement, through organizations like *Attac*, a group campaigning initially for the installation of the so-called 'Tobin tax' to assist economic development but bringing together a wide range of anti-globalization issues.

The Role of the Groups: Context, Tactics and Responses

Many of the groups described above explicitly do, and all potentially may, play a political role, in the sense that they will seek to influence decisions, finding solutions to problems that will be to the liking and benefit of their members, or more generally seeking to contribute to the shaping of society in ways they find congenial. In determining the scope of the groups' influence, their relationship with the political authorities becomes crucial. Various attempts have been made to apply to the relationships between the French groups and the state the theoretical models which are in general use to describe patterns of state-group relations in other Western liberal democracies. Those who have done so have tended to find the exercise rather unsatisfactory. Knapp and Wright (2001, pp. 299–337) contrast four theoretical ways of describing relationships between the state and the groups with what Wright called 'the untidy reality' (Wright, 1989, pp. 254–93). Frank Wilson discusses various theoretical formulations and whilst he finds some features from each of them present in French interest group politics, he also concludes that 'none of the four models...is sufficient to describe the reality of group/government relationships in France' (Wilson, 1987, p. 241). Wilson insists upon the importance of idiosyncratic factors such as the nature of the personalities involved on both sides, and the salience of any particular issue within public opinion at any time. He notes that whilst there is a temptation for analysts of politics to regard the groups' relationship with the authorities as their most important priority at any one time, they do in fact all have a multiplicity of other tasks which will affect their overall behaviour. Jack Hayward remarks (Hayward, 1986, p. 46) that in considering the relationship between the state and the groups, the state is often regarded as monolithic; in fact, much recent research has shown the administrative authorities to be highly fragmented, so that different parts of the administration are likely to maintain very different styles of relationships with the groups.

The groups in context: the role of the state

There are, however, a number of specific statements that can be made about the role of interest and pressure groups in France. First, the role of the administrative authorities in shaping the ways that groups can operate and the success that they may have in advancing their cause is a very powerful one. There are a number of reasons for this. A constant theme throughout the foregoing description of the nature of the groups has been the dependence of many of the groups upon state determined legal frameworks, upon state subsidies, and sometimes upon publicly financed personnel. Secondly, the structure of the Fifth Republic's institutions has resulted in a strong political – administrative executive. There is a very large scope for administrative discretion and the work of parliament is largely dominated by governmental priorities (see Chapters 3, 4, 5 and 7). Groups which are seeking to achieve specific goals are likely to do so through contacts within the central administration or the local authorities. Hence parliament, unlike, for example, the United States' Congress, is not a place where competition occurs between lobbies and groups with conflicting interests. In this respect the Fifth Republic differs from the Fourth Republic, which was sometimes described as a *régime des intérêts* (Wilson, 1987, p. 216).

Thirdly, the notion of the state as being above conflicting, partial interests and their special pleading persists in the rhetoric of ministers and of administrators. The 'pluralist' notion that democracy involves unfettered competition between the various interests, within a relatively free-market and deregulated framework has little place within the institutional ideology of the Fifth Republic, where the notion of the general interest is important as is the sense that 'there is "one best way" of attaining public purposes' which can be discerned and imposed by the state (Hayward and Wright, 2002, p. 10). In France the mainstream ideas that have determined the attitudes of many political actors have regarded the notion of the individual or group as capable of acting outside the state as definitely radical. At least since 1945, the state has been expected to play a major strategic role within society. To stress that the rhetoric and ideology of the state implies a kind of moral aloofness and authoritarianism is not to suggest that the state actually succeeds in being very powerful or effective. No perception of the public interest really provides much guidance as to where, or indeed whether, to run a motorway or high speed rail line or site a nuclear power station. But the rhetoric does provide the state with a weapon against the groups if it chooses to use it.

Whilst the groups operate within a context that gives the state a pre-eminent role, it is also true that the state, in its various manifestations, also needs the groups. Some groups are needed, first, to assist in the process of the implement-ation of policy. Indeed, the parastatal groups described above may carry out the disbursement of state funds and subsidies, and the state also relies upon some trade associations for the disbursement of state funds and the collection of statistics. The trade unions have a much larger role in society than their size and fragmentation might warrant because of the part they play in running the social security system, including the health insurance schemes, sickness benefit and retirement pensions. The trade unions organize candidates for election as work-ers' representatives to all the industrial tribunals. The implementation of the 35-hour week was also heavily dependent on negotiation with the unions.

Secondly, some parts of the state need the groups as their allies in the process of competition and conflict within the administration. The relationship may in effect be a patronage relationship but the size and importance of any patron's client groups will enhance the patron's standing and influence within the admin-istration. For example, in the early 1970s the French government appointed a Minister for the Environment, in response to a number of pressures that had come from the environmental movement, but equally from the developing international concern with environmental issues, and in 1973 a free-standing ministry was created, though for most of the period since then it has been attached as a junior ministry to other departments. One of the ministry's greatest weaknesses was its lack of adequate links into a powerful and cohesive pressure group. As noted above, the environmental movement is very fragmented, and lacks a coherent peak organization. Until the political development of the movement meant that environmentalists came to form part of the governing coalition in the early and late 1990s, the ministry could not link into ideas that had been given prominence and priority at either national or local levels, or utilize public opinion sensitized by powerful non-governmental sources.

In contrast, the Ministry of Agriculture, whose priorities are frequently sharply different from and opposed to those of the Ministry of the Environment, is strongly linked into such a network of contacts with the farmers' unions, especially the FNSEA and its 'sister organization' (Roederer-Rynning, 2002, p. 112) the *Centre National des Jeunes Agriculteurs* (CNJA). Close linkages may act a brake as well as a support. Edith Cresson, first Minister of Agriculture of the Socialist government in 1981, fearing this and distrusting a body that had cooperated very closely with the policies of previous governments, made attempts to promote rival organizations to the FNSEA, for the government. What resulted was virulent confrontation with the FNSEA which the rival groups, not being sufficiently powerful or at home with the new status accorded to them, could not counteract. Within a few years Cresson had been replaced and the government had moved back into a closer relationship with the FNSEA. The continuing unwillingness of the French government to contemplate rapid or radical reform to the EU Common Agricultural Policy, for example at the European Council in Berlin in April 1999 (*European Voice*, 1–7 April 1999), is a testimony to the ongoing influence of the FNSEA.

Similar relationships have developed in other sectors. In formulating a policy for any particular sector of social or industrial activity, a good deal of specialized information and advice is required. Research into the relationships between the administration and industry has revealed the extent to which the bodies actually involved in the industry concerned enjoy what has been described as a 'monopoly of legitimate expertise' (Bauer and Cohen, 1981). In many cases those bodies are the individual firms, which effectively act as pressure groups in the pursuit of their own interests. 'The information available to governments concerning costs, technology and future prospects tends to come from the industry itself. In an uncertain world it is difficult to test wisdom by first principles, and the critical element of strategic judgement is based on information which cannot easily be queried by civil servants' (Cawson *et al.*, 1990, p. 361). This was as true for the implementation of privatization as it was for the 'contractualised dirigisme' which preceded it (Hayward and Wright, 2002, pp. 190 and 195).

The state needs some groups, but it is important to be clear about the limitations of this assertion. First, whilst the French administration may develop detailed policies in collusion with certain groups and on the basis of information and expertise supplied by them, the relationship does not amount to that kind of partnership between the state and the main interest organizations for the determination of major political goals for which the term 'corporatism' is sometimes used. 'Corporatism...involves a process of bargaining between actors representing monopolistic organizations and (because we are speaking here of "public" policy) actors representing the state' (Cawson *et al.*, 1990, p. 6). This simply does not occur in France as a way of determining the very broad strategies of public policy – the choice between privatization and nationalization, for example, the approach to be taken in relation to closer European integration, or, as in 1995, major reform to the social security system. Where such bargaining does occur is in relation to very specific policies and goals. What emerges may be called a 'policy community'. Within that community, individuals, both politicians and administrators and those representing functional interests, and groups of various kinds will cooperate, bargain, negotiate, and conflict:

> The policy-making process is conceived as operating within semi-pluralistic, elitist decision-making communities, which in the case [for instance] of economic and industrial policy give pride of place to the discretion of actors in the major business firms, to the public and private bankers and to the politico-administrative leaders, exercised within a framework of domestic and international constraints. (Hayward, 1986, p. 38)

A second qualification to the statement that the state needs some groups is that the state does not need any and every group, and may exercise a great deal of choice as to those groups with whom any part of it may choose to interact. A common distinction made by those who analyse the groups is that between 'insider' groups and 'outsider' groups. 'Insider' groups are those deemed to be useful and supportive, given particular official recognition, consulted, included in the membership of the vast range of consultative and joint committees which various parts of the administration sponsor or run. These groups are regarded as *interlocuteurs valables*, respected and responsible. A group's status is not necessarily fixed and invariable but may relate to the issue at hand, and may change over time. It has been observed, for example, that one of the features of the French industrial policy community in the 1970s and 1980s was its ability to exclude the trade unions from influence in that area (Hayward, 1986, p. 66). Nor, even under a Socialist government, did the unions play a determinant role in formulating the laws reforming the shape of industrial relations passed in the early 1980s (the *lois Auroux*), or, twenty years later, in the introduction (as opposed to the implementation) of the 35-hour week. On the other hand in 1991, all the confederations except the CGT signed the collective agreement with the employers' federation on vocational training that was forthwith translated almost verbatim into law, and the unions succeeded in blocking plans to reform public sector pensions in 2000, and in frustrating Christian Sautter's proposed reform of the tax assessment and collection services. Moreover, they have a formal place in the determination of conditions of service, disciplinary matters and promotion procedures within the civil service and belong to the tripartite bodies which run the social security system. *Coordination Rurale*, created in June 1991 by right-wing cereal growers, in protest against the price cuts introduced in the 1991 MacSharry reforms of the EU Common Agricultural Policy, began with a campaign of violent and conflict-ual demonstrations, but by 2000 had done sufficiently well in elections to the *Chambres d'Agriculture* (see above) to be granted status as a recognized repre-sentative organization for the sector.

Yves Mény has noted that policy communities may be fragile, and alter as external constraints change, the most striking source of change being the European Community. The EC provides opportunities for 'outsider' groups to go over the head of the French government, as happened when a supermarket chain took action in the European court to force the abandonment of a fixed retail price for petrol. Moreover, the EC's rules on competition and the single market lessen the ability of some groups to use a position buttressed by state regulations to protect themselves against competition, as has occurred with the auctioneers (Mény, 1989, pp. 395–6) and the legal profession. *Electricité de France*, as a nationalized industry, has been in a strong position to pursue its own interests and impose them and has done so effectively. Nevertheless the French energy policy network has also had to change, as the opening up of the European energy market has left the big monopoly suppliers (*Electricité de France, Gaz de France*) lobbying the European Commission and other EU member states along-side the French government in defence of a French conception of public services (see Chapter 10).

However close and collusive the relationship between the state and any group, it should, thirdly, be noted that the power and legitimacy of the state is such that no group in France can unequivocally 'capture' parts of the state and impose its own priorities unconditionally. There is no doubt that groups with interests of their own seek to deploy their relationships with the state as a resource in their activities. Even the civil servants, who on the one hand seek to enforce the polit-ical and administrative priorities of the political executive, on the other have pro-fessional interests of their own which they defend, sometimes ferociously, as a group. Public sector workers, who constitute a quarter of the workforce, are much more strongly unionized than other groups – 26 per cent compared with eight per cent overall – and they have been virulently active in protecting their job security, working conditions, retirement ages and pension rights. However, the farmers, for example, organized in the FNSEA, and always very close to the Ministry of Agriculture, have not been able to capture total control over agricultural policy, or even to dictate the French stance in Common Agricultural Policy discussions in Brussels. Some areas have enjoyed considerable freedom of manoeuvre as a result of their particular position within the state. But the state has not been a totally acquiescent or compliant partner and cannot necessarily protect groups or industries against the pressure of external forces, for example, EC policies, as the hunters of southern France found to their cost. *Chasse, Peche, Nature, Tradition* has turned to political representation and gained seats in local councils and in the European Parliament. Other groups have turned to lobbying directly in Brussels, an activity initially much discouraged by the French government which felt that ministers and officials were the only legitimate representatives of the one and indivisible state within international fora.

The groups and politics

Pre-emption and incorporation

One of the ways in which pressure groups contribute to the political life of France is by the contribution of ideas and concerns to the general flow of political debate and competition, and by alerting public opinion to specific issues. The contribution of the groups to the political development of the country in this way may seem indirect, but it can nevertheless be substantial. This is particularly true of the broader groupings of interests that are described above as 'movements'. What occurs is a process familiar in relatively pluralist democracies: as an issue grows in salience and attracts public attention it may, though not necessarily without conflict, attract the attention of one or more of the organized political groups. The role of the group or movement is often to mobilize initial support and public interest. In some cases the issues will be sufficiently broad and radical to ensure that the movement continues, even after the issue has been incorporated within the political and administrative structures. In other cases the group or movement may dwindle as the issue moves into the mainstream political agenda. The ecology movement is an example of a movement that has faced the dilemmas of this process in a particularly visible and acute form throughout Europe. It is the case that for many of the movements their relative distance from the more structured and perhaps rigid institutions may result in greater scope for the expression of radical and creative ideas (Hayward, 1978).

The regional groups such as the Breton and Corsican movements were, for example, one of the forces that influenced the decentralization reforms of the early 1980s. The Breton movement has faded in importance as the place of the Breton language and culture has been increasingly recognized and the region has developed economically. Corsican nationalism, however, has increasingly manifested itself in feuding and violence on the island, including, most shockingly to the majority of French people, the murder of the prefect, Claude Erignac. The Corsican question was one of the first to be tackled by the Raffarin government, when the high profile Interior Minister, Nicholas Sarkozy, paid an early visit to the island. The constitutional amendment on decentralization proposed in October 2002 will apply to all regions, but has been crafted to allow for the possibility of extensive devolved powers for Corsica in ways that will get around the Constitutional Council's insistence that there can be no special status for any one part of the indivisible republic.

The women's movement was not the only influence upon the social reforms of President Giscard d'Estaing's presidency, but those reforms included a number of measures taken in response to the post-1968 women's movement and a new sensitivity in government circles to 'women's issues'. The divorce laws were liberalized and abortion legalized. In 1981 under Mitterrand a ministry for the rights of women was created, under an energetic woman, Yvette Roudy. The cabinet status of the ministry did not survive the advent of the right-wing Chirac government and it has not since regained the high profile which it had under Roudy. A highly cynical view would see the whole tale of government attention to women's issues as symbolic or opportunistic, an attempt to woo an increasingly politically aware group in society. Siân Reynolds (1988b, p. 159) points out that it would be naive to suppose that women's rights had ever been a major priority with the Socialist Party and that overtly feminist groups, by 1986, 'felt that "going official" had rather demobilized independent feminism'. Less cynical would be the observation that the high profile and energetic efforts of Yvette Roudy did result in women's issues coming more firmly on to the Socialists' agenda, and that recognition of the genuine, if unspectacular, achievements of 'institutional feminism', including, for example, the 1992 law against sexual harassment at work, may have assisted in 'the rallying of the feminists to the Socialist banner' of which 'the PS and Mitterrand reaped the electoral fruits' (Machin, 1994, pp. 49–50).

Similar patterns of attempts at incorporation and pre-emption can be seen in attempts in the 1980s by the Socialists to harness to themselves the anti-racist movement, through their sponsorship of SOS-Racisme. The challenge to established parties by the Ecologists resulted in the adoption of a more ecological rhetoric, especially by the Socialist Party, and eventually the conclusion of political alliances.

Contestation and direct action
Collusion with the political authorities, or co-option into the traditional political structures are not the only ways in which groups may seek to have political effects. There is a long tradition in France of direct action and confrontation with the authorities. In 2001 there were 800 officially authorized political demonstrations in Paris and 1461 demonstrations for better pay, conditions or job security (*The Economist*, 16 November 2002). Such action may be organized by relatively established groups, as for example, at Air France in 1993 when union-sponsored strikes caused the withdrawal of drastic restructuring plans and precipitated the resignation of the chairman of the company. In October 1995 a massive one-day strike by public sector workers against a public sector pay freeze brought France to a virtual standstill, and this was followed in November and December by much more extensive strikes in the public sector (see Exhibit 9.4). In 2002 a series of strikes by doctors, begun under the Jospin government, resulted in the Raffarin government increasing payments to general practitioners. But protests and strikes may also be the result of small autonomous committees or local groups. This was the case with the railway strike of the winter of 1986–7, with the almost countrywide traffic jam along the main *autoroutes* resulting from lorry drivers' protests in 1983 and 2000, and with sit-ins in employment offices by the unemployed in 1998.

EXHIBIT 9.4

1995 – discontent and protest

The late autumn of 1995 witnessed an outbreak of social and political discontent and unrest that proved longer lasting and more disruptive than any since 1968. A number of political and public policy issues came together in strikes, demonstrations and protest. The context was:

- The aftermath of the presidential election of May 1995. Jacques Chirac's programme had appeared to promise a combination of tax cuts – 'It is possible to cut taxes... Compulsory contributions must be reduced' (Chirac, 1995, p. 19) – and reduced unemployment – 'I cannot accept so many young people, so many executives, unemployed. I am not resigned to the inevitability of long-term unemployment... We must act differently' (Chirac, 1995, p. 11). But between spring and autumn, unemployment began to increase, industrial production and sales dropped, the economy scarcely grew.
- The economy. Although the minimum wage was increased by four per cent, the Juppé government, in its September budget, raised taxes in an attempt to keep France on course to meet one of the Maastricht Treaty conditions for participation in a European single currency from 1999 (a budget deficit of no more than 3 per cent). A freeze on civil service pay was announced, affecting some five million employees. The money markets lost confidence in the franc after the September budget, and raised interest rates followed.
- Deficits in the social security system. The complex system is composed of a combination of insurance based funds, managed by joint bodies including representatives of employers and unions, and government contributions. It provides generously for pensions and health care and for unemployment benefit.
- Privatization proposals which included the state-owned telecommunications enterprise, France Telecom. This, combined with requirements imposed by the competition policy of the European Community for greater competitivity, threatened the jobs and working conditions of the employees.
- Conditions in French universities which were were crowded, underequipped, poorly housed and indebted.
- A re-emergent terrorist threat, linked to the highly unstable political situation in Algeria. A police clampdown followed.

In October and November 1995 a wave of demonstrations and protest occurred. Students, especially at some of the new smaller universities, demonstrated for better conditions. Simultaneously, heavy-handed police methods against those who might be Islamic fundamentalist terrorists or sympathizers were producing hostility and violence in the housing estates and suburbs where many of those of North African origin live. Civil servants and public sector workers mounted very large marches and demonstrations against their pay freeze. Proposals to reform the social security budget, including an attempt to reduce patients' open access to specialists within the health service, and to extend the qualifying period for receipt of a full pension, met with fierce protests. Public sector employees, including those from France Telecom, and from the railways, where spending cuts threatened reduced state subsidy, and hence service and job cuts, were at the forefront of the protests. A transport strike stopped rail services, buses and the Metro. Power station workers reduced energy output. By early December nationwide strikes or days of protest were being called by teachers, lorry drivers, postal workers, airline staff, tax officials and even doctors.

$\longrightarrow$

> ⟶
>
> The events provided a graphic insight into many of the issues, difficulties and paradoxes of French politics. The government appeared tightly constrained between their European policy, which involved the meeting of the Maastricht single currency convergence criteria and the maintenance of the linkage of the franc to the Deutschmark, and its domestic consequences. The opening up, as a consequence of European liberalization and globalization, and liberalization of sectors, from telecommunications to banking, that had previously been much protected by the state, caused painful adaptations without a powerful ideological rhetoric to legitimize them. Rising social expectations, and increased costs in medical services and pensions, are difficult to accommodate in a period of recession and global competition. The issues surrounding the repercussions in France of difficulties and conflicts in Algeria were again thrown into sharp focus.
>
> These events cast a long shadow. Widely regarded as being a major cause of the heavy defeat of the Juppé government in 1997, they had a strongly inhibiting effect on government willingness, under both Jospin and Raffarin, to tackle the problems of the public sector or the social security and pensions systems (see Chapter 10).

Direct action is noisy, causes inconvenience and may catch the headlines. It is very infrequently (with 1995 as an exception, though even then the effects were long-term and indirect, see Exhibit 9.4) clearly politically effective. However, there have been notorious occasions when action has followed such tactics, which tends to encourage those who resort to them. In 2000, lorry drivers blocked roads in both Britain and France in protest at rising petrol prices. Indeed it was said that the British action was inspired by the success of the French, and certainly the French drivers achieved negotiations with the government and agreement to a subsidy for the small operators. But such success can no longer be taken for granted. Repetition of such action in the autumn of 2002 was rapidly foiled when the police showed an unwonted willingness to move in and the drivers were threatened with loss of their driving licences. But the effects of direct action are frequently less apparent. The largest strike and demonstration movement of the Fifth Republic, the events of May 1968, whilst it may have had far-reaching effects upon social and cultural expectations, and provided an impetus for later social movements, had very limited long-term political effects. Where the French government is strongly constrained by other political factors, especially those which arise from the interdependence of modern nation states, results may be particularly limited; the violence of the steelworkers in 1978–9 may have improved the redundancy terms they were offered, but did not avert restructuring and eventual privatization any more than did the action at Air France, of which, by 2002, the state owned only 54 per cent.

Nor should the phenomenon be exaggerated. The numbers of working days lost through strikes declined through the 1980s. Violent direct action, although always newsworthy, is sporadic and isolated.

Conclusion

Despite the constitutional rhetoric of indivisibility, France is a highly fragmented and pluralistic society, with a wide range of organizations that bring together people with a shared interest, and that may seek, persistently or from time to time, to influence the political and administrative decision-making processes. Very many such groups are fragmented, divided along ideological or territorial boundaries, often very small, and frequently in conflict with other groups. There are very few large national level organizations or lobbies.

Nevertheless, one of the main roles of such groups is to place issues of concern to important groups of the population firmly upon the political and administrative agenda. Paradoxically, the fulfilment of such a role may often weaken the groups. Mendras and Cole (1991, *passim*, but especially p. 228) argue that the large social movements of the 1970s which took their impetus from May 1968 are almost extinct. Their causes have been absorbed either by governmental action – decentralization, the creation of the Ministry of Women's Rights – or by co-option into the programmes of the political parties. Howard Machin (1994, pp. 49–50) points out the role of the Socialist party in incorporating the priorities and in some cases the leaders of the movements into its structures.

Similarly the position of the trade unions remains ambiguous. In an industrial environment where many French firms are still strongly dominated by a relatively authoritarian boss, and 'French workers correctly perceived the process of decision-making within the firm as essentially unilateral' (Gallie, 1983, p. 98), many of the improvements in working conditions that in other countries are likely to be the results of collective bargaining have traditionally been the result of political agitation and action by the state. For this reason, both the conditions under which redundancies may be declared, which are always monitored by the state officials of the *Inspection du Travail*, and the introduction of flexible working hours were matters for political controversy and legislative action through the 1980s and 1990s, including not only the 35-hour week legislation, but also the 'social modernization' law (*loi sur la modernisation sociale*) which sought to protect jobs. Whilst contestation on behalf of the workers is fundamental to the reason for their existence, the unions also need their status as representative organizations and social partners if they are to influence developments, as Nicole Notat's CFDT clearly recognized. The early 1980s' reform of industrial relations law had mixed results for the unions. It gave extensive rights of consultation to workers over matters such as health and safety. However, although the unions may, and do, field lists of candidates for the workplace committees, they have lost any monopoly of representation, and may be seriously stretched by the need to find enough militants to fulfil these functions. In 1996 the Juppé government gave Parliament rather than the joint body of unions and employers the task of setting health and social security spending. On the other hand, union strikes and demonstrations frequently enjoy the support of public opinion, and there is public outrage at incidents such as the decision in the late 1990s of the leading British retailer Marks and Spencer to close its Paris store and sack the staff. The resulting litigation slowed down the process.

Despite apparent fragmentation and weakness, the interest groups and lobbies thus continue to play a crucial and lively role in the formulation and implementation of political programmes and the administration of policies. In this area, as in others, the role of the state as a key actor, both in constituting the framework within which these activities occur, and in the activities of its own different parts within the complex pattern, is a distinctive feature of the French system.

10

Policy Making and Politics: Issues and Approaches

The political dimensions of everyday life for the citizen of, or resident in, France are complex and cross-cutting. Media reports tend to highlight political rivalry between competing ideologies or (increasingly) personalities. Protests, processions and soundbites make news reports and briefly highlight specific issues which may or may not be distinctively French. The problem of rising insurance premiums against medical complications which caused a strike of obstetricians at the new year in 2003 was common to most developed countries; the sharply rising birth rate in 2000 and 2001 (ascribed by some, in part, to the impact of the 35-hour week) which made the problems acute was particular to France (*Le Monde*, 4 December 2002) as was the administrative response, which required the regional prefect to inventory resources and requisition both hospital beds and specialists if necessary (*The Guardian*, 2 January 2003). But beyond the frequently ephemeral news items the resident also engages with politics and policies in innumerable almost automatic actions of daily life – for example, carrying an identity card, paying VAT on purchases, working for certain hours, or consulting a doctor. And certain political issues have, over the last two or three decades, proved to have a particular resonance. Moreover, this chapter argues, it is increasingly impossible to take France as an example of autarchic policy-making. However powerful the rhetoric of national politicians seeking to assert that the decisions they make are crucial and determinant, and it is both powerful and frequently justified, all member states of the EU now operate in an interdependent and pooled policy-making arena. This chapter therefore starts by examining France's relationship with EU policy-making, and goes on to look at economic policy, at policy on the *services publics* and at immigration and nationality policy. These three selected areas provide the context in which the governmental and political processes described in the preceding chapters actually operate, and which are in turn affected by the outcomes of those processes.

France and the European Union

The development of the EU

Much of the original impetus for the creation of an international body with supra-national powers came from Jean Monnet and the Commission of the French Plan for Reconstruction and Modernization which he headed. The founding of the earliest Community authority, the European Coal and Steel Community (ECSC), arose from a French initiative devised by him and propounded in 1950 by the then Foreign Minister, Robert Schuman. The immediate objective was to solve polit-ical and economic problems relating to the rehabilitation of Germany and the organization of the coal and steel industry that were of great concern to France. A further French initiative for the creation of a European Defence Community involved too great a surrender of control over national defence forces for many French politicians to accept, and was defeated in the French Parliament in 1954 by an unlikely alliance involving both Communists and Gaullists.

The structures of the ECSC, and those which followed in 1958 for the European Economic Community and Euratom, were strongly influenced by French models and patterns of administration, and tended initially to provide a milieu into which French administrative assumptions meshed rather easily. As the European Community institutions have gradually developed a life of their own, so French administrators, politicians and voters have been obliged, sometimes painfully, to come to terms with new methods and approaches.

When the European Economic Community was set up, an important part of its political base was in effect a bargain between Germany and France, that involved the opening of the very large West German market to French agricultural produce in return for freer access for the products of German manufacturing industry to what had been a very protected French market. Some of the officials and pol-iticians involved also hoped that the EEC would accelerate the operation of the market forces that were forcing the French economy into becoming more com-petitive and acquiring modernized capitalist structures, a transformation which the 1945 nationalization of about half the French banking system and the creation of the Planning Commission (which was able, in its early years, to deploy large Marshall Aid funds) had only begun.

De Gaulle came into power just as the EEC and Euratom were being set up. He had been opposed to French participation in them, but he did not repudiate them. Instead he attempted to shape the Communities and French participation within them to accord more closely with his view of French national interest. His attempt to promote a looser political structure allowing the Community to develop into a more intergovernmental forum for cooperation in fields such as foreign and cultural policy – both areas in which, at that time, French pre-eminence amongst the six founder members was likely to be uncontested – foundered on the resistance of the other member states. He was, however, successful in preventing British membership of the Community during his life-time. He wished to prevent the challenge to French leadership that he thought

British membership would bring and any opening up of the Community to greater American influence.

Following a major confrontation between France and the other member states of the Community in 1965, during which the French representatives withdrew from the main decision-making bodies of the Community – though not from some of the day-to-day management bodies – de Gaulle succeeded in establishing the so-called Luxembourg Compromise of 1966. This was the principle, which endured until the late 1980s, that a member state had the right to veto proposals that it regarded as contrary to its vital national interests. France was also able to cut back some of the ambitions of the Commission of the European Community for faster movement towards a more federalist approach, and to ensure a shift in the balance of power within the Community institutions towards the Council of Ministers where national interests were most fully represented.

However, the period of confrontation during 1965 also made it clear that the pressures upon the French government were not solely political. Economic interests were clearly involved. French farmers were benefiting in important ways from the Common Agricultural Policy (CAP); this helps to explain why the CAP, which scarcely figures in the Treaty of Rome, took so high a priority in the early years.

The complexity of the French approach to the European Community has stemmed from the fact that it has always included elements both of Jean Monnet's vision of the inevitable logic of greater European cooperation, and of Gaullist rhetoric. Each successive President since 1958 has encouraged and developed progress in certain areas. For de Gaulle, the Common Agricultural Policy and the customs union were key economic factors that were of crucial importance to France. President Pompidou encouraged the admission of the United Kingdom, the Republic of Ireland and Denmark to the Community. He was seen to be a leading influence over the summit at the Hague in 1969 which set a renewed agenda for the Community, involving enlargement, and also proposing (as it turned out rather prematurely) progress towards economic and monetary union.

Over the next decade France retained a leading role in the development of the Community. The partnership between President Giscard d'Estaing and Chancellor Helmut Schmidt of West Germany built upon the privileged relationship between their two countries which had begun with the relationship between German Chancellor Adenauer and de Gaulle in the early 1960s. Franco-German initiatives were responsible for a number of the advances made by the Community during the second half of the 1970s, especially the development of the European Monetary System (EMS) and of the political cooperation machinery, which again echoed the Gaullist emphasis on intergovernmental machinery, and on the primacy of political – that is, foreign policy – considerations. In institutionalizing the summit meetings of the heads of government of the Community into a regular European Council, Giscard d'Estaing also emphasized the importance France placed upon political impulsion for the Community deriving from the member states rather than primarily from the Commission.

During the 1980s the French supported the development of a single European market, and the signing of the Single European Act which provided the institutional basis for the single market and for further movement towards integration. At the start of the 1990s, however, the balance within the founding bargain upon which the European Community had been based was unsettled by the unification of Germany, creating a very large state with a population which considerably exceeded that of France. President Mitterrand was far from enthusiastic initially about the speed and nature of the unification process. France subsequently accepted it with a good grace and continued to insist that the Franco-German axis must remain the pivot about which the Community – or rather, after 1993, the European Union – would continue to turn.

Underlying the French approach consistently was the 'Gaullist paradigm' (Cole, 2001, p. 58). De Gaulle's rhetoric was the rhetoric of national independence and the importance of the nation state – in contrast to the earlier vision of Monnet and Schuman whose major concern was with the practical politics of economic interdependence within Europe. None of de Gaulle's successors has felt able to jettison the Gaullist language about the status and role of France, a language linked to a view about the need for a European identity and role to counterbalance what would otherwise be the absolute domination of the superpowers. If some of France's fellow member states suspected that talk of the interest of Europe essentially covered a concern for French national interests simply and solely, such language nevertheless allowed successive French governments to claim the status of 'good Europeans'. The features of this paradigm are:

- a cultural attachment to European values and civilisation, notably as embodied by France;
- a Europe prepared to protect its industry and agriculture;
- the promotion of common European policies where these do not endanger French interests;
- a marked anti-Americanism and advocacy of an independent security and defence identity;
- a tight community based on a Franco-German directorate.... ;
- a preference for intergovernmental over supranational institutions. (Cole, 2001, pp. 58–9)

Developments in the 1990s put this approach under increasing strain. The protection of industry, of cultural values (for example, against the import of American films and TV programmes) and indeed of agriculture along the traditional French lines all proved increasingly problematic. The Franco-German relationship in the 1990s became more complex and less reliable. 'France's leadership role in the EU for the past 40 years had been predicated on its confidence that French leaders could persuade their German counterparts – without going to the actual effort of persuasion itself – to reach joint solutions to shared problems' but since the conclusion of the Maastricht treaty in 1992, this confidence has proved increasingly difficult to sustain (Drake, 2001, p. 457).The French had accepted the move towards Economic and Monetary Union, and in the event reluctantly acquiesced in a system of governing EMU, based, like the German *Bundesbank* model, on central bank independence. But they tried, with minimal success, to achieve political control that would temper any concentration upon price stability as the sole objective of the European Central Bank (ECB); they ensured that the word growth was added to the agreement, on which the German government insisted, to enforce this (the stability and growth pact) and they agreed to the appointment of a Dutchman, Wim Duisenberg, as the first governor of the ECB only on the understanding that he would be replaced before the end of his full term by the French candidate Jean-Claude Trichet. Only in June 2003, when Trichet was finally acquitted of all charges related to a cover-up of huge losses by the *Crédit Lyonnais* bank in 1992 when it was still nationalized, was the way opened for the implementation of this agreement.

Moreover, the end of the cold war produced a queue of Central and East European countries applying to join the European Union, of which eight, alongside Cyprus and Malta, will accede in 2004. The French had been far from enthusiastic about previous enlargements, which were seen as damaging to the vision outlined above, of a small, tight, and French-led European Community. However, increasingly, enlargement to Central and Eastern Europe has been accepted as inevitable (Howarth, 2002, p. 355). It may be that former President Giscard d'Estaing's outspoken attack in December 2002 on Turkey's candidacy for the EU (which was relatively well-received in French press comment) represented an attempt to draw a line in the sand in defence of the 'Gaullist paradigm' for it expressed anxieties both about values and civilization and about dilution of the 'European project' into no more than a free-trade area. The challenges which the new enlargement poses to the 'traditional French preference for a strong Europe with weak institutions' are substantial (Cole, 2001, p. 59; Drake, 2001, p. 456), for both the content of policies and the methods of policy-making are having to be changed to accommodate it. This has resulted in conflict with the Germans over future expenditure, the reform of the CAP, and, at the negotiations leading to the Nice Treaty at the end of 1999, over the weighting of votes in the Council of Ministers, to reflect Germany's greater size. It is clear that 'the profound differences in French and German visions of the EU's future remain' (Howarth, 2002, p. 364). Both President Chirac (since 2002 with Prime Minister Raffarin) and Prime Minister Jospin and his government accept that change, especially in the institutional structure, is inevitable, and indeed promoted and brokered a number of changes in the much-criticised negotiations for the Nice Treaty. The French government has supported the debate on the future of Europe launched in the aftermath of Nice, and the setting up of the Convention on the future of Europe chaired by former President Giscard d'Estaing, and the drafting of a European constitution. However, the 'Gaullist paradigm' still shapes many political and public attitudes to the EU, and governmental vision of exactly what form the structures should eventually take is not clearly defined. The issue did not form part of the electoral programmes of either Chirac or Jospin in 2002, even if both clearly reject strongly federalist ideas, refusing, for example, notions of a European president for both Commission and Council of ministers – a European president should be chosen from, and preside over the Council – and speaking, in a phrase coined by former French Minister and Commission President Jacques Delors, of 'a European federation of nation states'.

The evolution of attitudes

The debate round the ratification of the Maastricht Treaty in 1992 proved a crucial moment in awakening much French public opinion to the potential impact of the European Union. Although the political and economic elite were (with a few notable exceptions, such as Philippe Séguin, Philippe de Villiers and Charles Pasqua) in favour of ratification, the referendum outcome was very close and the proportion of the French respondents who reply positively to the Eurobarometer question whether EU membership is 'a good thing' has dropped from a high point of over 70 per cent in 1987 to just under 50 per cent in 2002 (Usherwood, 2002; Flood, 2002). The implications of membership of the EU were only slowly recognized amongst many politicians and officials, who had regarded it largely as a matter for foreign policy and remote from domestic concerns. This is partly explained by the ease with which French political and administrative working practices fitted in with a Community system, by the skill of French negotiators and by the relatively unchallenged leading role France was able to play in the EC for its first three decades. Moreover, until the appointment of Jacques Delors, French commissioners of the European Communities had gained little prominence, even if one of them (Raymond Barre) went on to become prime minister. The ministries in Paris had not been much concerned to acquaint themselves with the procedures and law of the Communities. Surprisingly, perhaps, relatively few French high-fliers had occupied senior posts in the Brussels administrations. It had been notoriously difficult to ensure the implementation of rulings by the European Court of Justice in France. Only in the 1990s did the French Parliament take steps to develop a system of parliamentary scrutiny of European legislation (see Chapter 7).

Until the Maastricht referendum the political elite, with the tacit consent of a large proportion of the population, supported the process of European integration as it was perceived from France. Since the early 1990s there has been a growth in criticism of the EU and a marked increase in the ability of critical groups to make their voices heard, via the media and in the competition for votes (Usherwood, 2002). For example, in the 1994 EP elections, de Villiers' revisionist group (see Table 8.1) sent 13 members to the EP, and, jointly with Pasqua, achieved the same result in 1999, although they have been markedly less successful in parliamentary and presidential elections. Neither of them stood in 2002, while Jean-Pierre Chevènement, standing on a 'left-Gaullist' national republican platform amidst a bandwagon of publicity and alleged support (Cole, 2002, p. 321), eventually picked up only 5.3 per cent of the first ballot.

The stances of the various parties and groups vary widely. Of the many political groups, only the National Front (and possibly the Trotskyite LCR and LO) currently call for withdrawal from the EU, although others, such as Pasqua and de Villiers, call for a return to an earlier – pre-Maastricht – condition or, like the PCF and the Greens, advocate substantial reform of policies and institutions (Flood, 2002). The bases of the criticisms offered also vary markedly. Most emphasize technocracy and lack of democratic accountability as features of the EU, and, unlike elsewhere, even the right-wing 'Euro-sceptics' are concerned about the equation of the EU with neo-liberal globalization, to which they are opposed, and with atlanticist USA and NATO-led security and defence policy. But while the more left wing groups are looking for a redistributive social Europe and a more open policy towards immigration and asylum-seeking, those on the right emphasize national sovereignty, and the need to protect national values (Hanley, 2001, *passim*; Flood, 2002).

Analysis of exit polls suggests that 'Europe' has loomed largest as an issue in EP elections, but even then was a dominant concern only for a minority (perhaps 37 per cent), while at other elections the salience of the issue has been very low (for the absence of any debate on Europe in the 2002 campaigns see Cole, 2002, p. 324) . However, it can be argued that in public opinion as a whole, there are 'quite high levels of dissatisfaction with aspects of the EU's governance and the direction of integration' (Flood, 2002). The constraints, as well as the opportunities of EU membership are now more than ever a matter for discussion, especially since policy-making and the conduct of economic and societal activity in a great many areas can no longer occur in isolation from the processes and outcomes of EU policy-making.

The organization of French input into EU policy-making

Some discussion of the EU – for example the criticisms of *Chasse, Pêche, Nature, Tradition* – treats the EU as an external force intervening in a hostile and unaccountable way. Given the complexities of the EU decision-making system, such treatment is unsurprising. However, no area of policy-making is now unaffected by 'Europeanization' – reorientation such that 'E[U] political and economic dynamics become part of the organisational logic of national politics and policy-making' (Ladrech, 1994, p. 70). Two aspects of this process hence become crucial: one is the influence which French policy actors have upon the formulation of EU policy, and the other is the ways in which implementation and repercussions of the resultant decisions impact upon what happens in France.

French ministers and officials have had to accommodate to a style of policy-making which is less 'top-down' than has been frequently the case in France. Those who formulate policy in Brussels are relatively open and may be receptive to lobbying. Political considerations play an important part in policy formulation. With the extension of EP powers embodied in the Maastricht and Amsterdam treaties, attention has to be paid to the views of MEPs. Political considerations are crucial at the stage of negotiation within the Council of Ministers with which the legislative procedure culminates. It is expected that measures will be drawn up after a broadly consultative and consensual approach, whilst in France (see Chapter 4) policy formulation requires skills in the confrontation of divergent points of view and the imposition of the *arbitrage* that results (Hayward and Wright, 2002, p. 135). It is also expected that the outcome will then be applied uniformly, whereas in France it frequently arises that measures are adapted to fit needs on the ground only after promulgation through a mechanism of dispensations. The administration of the European Commission and the secretariat of the Council of Ministers are fairly hierarchical organizations, with an immense range of nationalities, and an organizational maze of committees in which networks of personal relationships like those upon which the French elite rely in Paris may be difficult to form, although Jacques Delors himself drove many of his policies forward in this way. It may not always be possible, as it more frequently was within a much smaller Community, and still is in Paris, to fix a matter by a well-placed telephone call. The French have only slowly discovered the necessity of lobbying, and experience it as constraint upon their policy-making.

The president and his staff, the prime minister, other ministers, the officials of the ministries, the French representative at the European Community in Brussels, Parliament, the political parties and the pressure groups all play a greater or lesser role in the production and coordination of French input in the EU policy process.

The president and his staff at the Elysée have a major role in formulating the French approach. De Gaulle set the tone and the agenda of the French approach to the European Community during his presidency. All subsequent presidents have been influenced by his style. Even under *cohabitation*, 'high politics', such as the French input into the negotiations leading to enlargement or treaty changes, have always been handled in the Elysée. It is the president who attends meetings of the European Council, and consequently it is upon his staff that the main burden of the task of preparing for them falls. This occurred, for example, in 2000, when France's incumbency of the Presidency of the European Council coincided with the final negotiations for the Nice treaty. *Cohabitation*, however, which from 1997 until 2000 had worked rather smoothly on EU issues, did impede the smooth running of these much criticized negotiations, since inconsistencies between the approach of president and prime minister caused tactical difficulties and were seized upon by a hostile press. But under all political configurations, the president has consistently dominated the policy-making process in relation to key aspects of European integration. He 'regards all EU matters as ultimately and often actually his preserve at the decisive phase' (Hayward and Wright, 2002, p. 162).

The prime minister also plays a part in the formulation of policy relating to the European Community, especially at the more day-to-day level. As EC policy comes increasingly to involve a range of different aspects of policy, the coordinating role of the prime minister and his office described in Chapter 4 has become important in this sphere also. The government department responsible for coordinating policy towards the Community, the *Secretariat General de la Comité Intérministerielle pour les questions de coopération économique européenne* (SGCI) is usually attached to the prime minister's office.

The prime minister is most likely to be deeply involved in the making of policy towards the European Union when there are financial implications, for example in the setting of the multi-annual budgetary plan for the EU, or difficult choices concerned with the internal political impact of the policies, for example in the handling of the Bovine Spongiform Encephalopathy (BSE) crisis. Edith Cresson during her short tenure of office tried to mobilize industrialists and bankers in support of a more active industrial policy for the European Community, an attempt which did not survive her period in office. French policy in relation to the longer-term plans for financing the EC: (the so-called 'Delors packages') required prime ministerial intervention. Moreover, the prime minister has to undertake the task of justifying the outcome of EC decisions to Parliament, so that Pierre Bérégovoy was faced by a vote of censure over the reform of the CAP in 1992, and Edouard Balladur also faced difficulties at the time of the conclusion of the GATT negotiations at the end of 1993.

The SGCI serves as the main centre for the coordination of policy and for liaison with the French representation in Brussels. The SGCI was set up initially in 1948 to handle relationships with the newly emerging European bodies – such as the Organisation for European Economic Co-operation (OEEC), which is now the Organisation for Economic Co-operation and Development (OECD). This was set up as a body that would transcend and overcome the fierce interministerial rivalries, which have by no means disappeared, between the Finance Ministry, the Foreign Ministry and then, but far less so now, the Planning Commission, and handle all relationships with Brussels.

This system has essentially survived. The SGCI, with some 160 staff, transmits the EC proposals as they arrive from Brussels to the appropriate 'lead' ministry. The line to be adopted is then settled at a meeting – there are about 1100 a year – called by the SGCI. If agreement cannot be reached, the matter may be passed on to the prime minister's personal staff for the prime minister's decision. But such prime-ministerial intervention occurs only in about 10 per cent of cases. Quite often the political clout of the secretary-general of the SGCI – who is an official – is sufficient to allow decisions to be taken within the SGCI that all will accept. The SGCI also takes steps to see that French MEPs are kept well informed of the line on any issue that the French government supports.

Much of the detailed negotiation in Brussels is undertaken by the staff of the permanent representation there. Observers who are familiar with the Brussels machinery note that the French officials who negotiate are normally well briefed and well prepared on the principles underlying any proposed course of action. Their tendency is to formulate a logical and thoroughly well-thought-through case often derived from the principles at stake and then to press it on the basis of rational and tenacious argument. Although they will act on the basis of instructions from the SGCI, these instructions are not always written and formal. On technical details French negotiators are perceived as often less well-supported by back-up staff than other delegations.

A former French permanent representative in Brussels commented upon the scope which he enjoyed to act autonomously and to exercise his own judgement. He would not necessarily expect to consult Paris for instructions at every point as the negotiations developed. This was a consequence of the autonomy of judgement and decision that senior French officials expect to enjoy (see Chapter 5) and of the continuity of French approach and policy towards the Community. It is also a consequence of the priority which the French place on a leadership role which will involve initiating, rather than reacting to proposals wherever possible and ensuring that they are well furnished with allies in the Council of Ministers (Hayward and Wright, 2002, p. 145). Contrasting his experience with that of the British, who have a notably more regular and formal requirement to report upon the progress of negotiations and seek written instructions, the former representative observed that whilst the French system enabled him to respond with greater rapidity and flexibility, it also meant that the maintenance of continuity and consistency was more heavily dependent upon a limited number of people.

The French Parliament is slowly developing a role in relation to EU matters. The fact that under the French constitution many EC directives can be implemented in France through governmental regulation, when they do not concern those areas where law must be made by Parliament, has resulted in an elaborate procedure for determining the status of any piece of legislation (Sauron, 2000) but also limited the amount of public discussion. The Single Market proposals and the 1992 rhetoric were important factors in changing the situation (Maus, 1991, p. 77). The French parliament (see Chapter 7) is now attempting to ensure some national democratic scrutiny of EC legislation similar to that undertaken by the British, Irish and Danish parliaments. The impact is likely to be limited, but is symptomatic of a growing public concern, noted above, with the implications of the development of European integration. French proposals for the constitution for the EU included suggestions of a new chamber for the EP to allow national parliaments to play a greater role in the formulation and endorsement of European policy.

French arrangements for input into EU policy-making illustrate the combination of ideological rhetoric and pragmatic, almost opportunistic, management that tends to constitute the formulation of policy. It is a combination which operates within a fragmented political and administrative system, which is legally and formally rational and highly structured, but which works partly because complex and interlocking informal relationships constitute not only checks and balances, but also flexibility and opportunities. The closely interlinked Parisian elites facilitate communication. Most of the secretaries-general of the SGCI have been members of one of the *grands corps*, and although Elisabeth Guigou was not, she had served as an official in the very high status Treasury Directorate of the Ministry of Finance.

Economic Policy

The health of the national economy is a major priority of every government, and has a powerful effect upon the citizen's everyday experience. A key moment in the shaping of economic policy in the last two decades of the twentieth century was the so-called U-turn of 1983. The strategy of the Mitterrand government from 1981 had been a state-directed programme of modernization and development, with a particular ambition to increase employment. Its components included the nationalization of the leading industrial and banking companies, with state aid intended to produce modernizing investment, more jobs and better working conditions. Where nationalization did not occur, sectoral programmes protected areas where France was expected to have an advantage, such as the furniture industry. Public sector jobs were created and the minimum wage and social benefits were increased, in line with a rhetoric of solidarity, but in the expectation that demand would grow. The strategy could not endure. It resulted in higher social charges upon employers, – and Mitterrand's argument for a 'European social space' which would ensure that France's European competitors carried comparable charges proved unavailing – in large budget deficits, and in a rapidly worsening balance of trade as higher consumption sucked in imports. Either France would have to abandon the pegged exchange rates of the European monetary system, pull back from a European system of free movement of goods and protect her own system, or to devalue and change strategy. In March 1983 Mitterrand chose the latter course. That 'regime defining' choice resulted from, and in, a recognition of the limits on national freedom of action imposed by the international economic context (Clift, 2002, p. 326; Hall, 2001, p. 176). The main lines of economic policy that emerged after 1983 have remained very constant, under successive governments of both Right and Left.

Economic and Monetary Union and the Euro

At the heart of the direction chosen in 1983 was a commitment to economic integration within the EU. Rather than withdraw from the European Monetary System, the continued linking of the Franc to the German Deutschmark was affirmed. This resulted in a strong and relatively stable franc – the *franc fort* – but it also meant that in order to remain competitive with a relatively high exchange rate, costs had to be cut. Market mechanisms became the key levers to produce restructuring and adjustment. Following the adoption by the EU of the Single European Market programme, championed by Jacques Delors, the French social democrat who had been Minister of Finance in 1983 and in 1984 became President of the European Commission, the French government between 1985 and 1989 removed price and exchange controls and deregulated the financial markets.

Acceptance of the proposals initially embodied in the Maastricht Treaty for the development of the European Monetary System which led in 1999 to the creation of the Euro, followed on 1 January 2002 by the introduction of notes and coins, entailed the loss of autonomy for the Bank of France and the disappearance of the Franc. But if the alternative were the de facto domination of the European economy by the Deutschmark and the German central bank (the Bundesbank), then, in the French government's view, it might be preferable to have a European central bank where a French representative would have an equal voice. Economic and monetary union would ensure that Germany would be locked into a European process and not simply achieve domination by default, as a result of her economic and industrial strength.

The budgetary and public spending discipline that had been imposed by the *franc fort* policy was formalized by the obligation to meet the Maastricht criteria for membership of the Euro which limited both the annual budget deficit and the overall level of public borrowing. These obligations were continued after the creation of the Euro through the Stability and Growth Pact. Doing so has resulted in a number of tensions and dilemmas for the government, epitomized by the attempts of Jacques Chirac in his electoral campaign in 1995 to suggest that it would be possible to meet these obligations, to reduce unemployment, and to ensure social solidarity and an end to exclusion. The massive public protests of 1995 (see Exhibit 9.4) underlined how difficult it would be to carry through the policies required; the sudden and early general election of 1997, linked to the need to reinforce the position of the government as the necessary cuts began to bite, produced a coalition government of the left that was faced with the same problems. Prime Minister Jospin, and Dominique Strauss-Kahn (Minister of Finance until he was forced to resign by the repercussions of allegations that he had, while not in office, received unjustified payments for fictitious consultancy), helped by a relatively booming economy until 2001, were able initially to increase taxation on individuals (to increase social security funding), and to reduce the general government deficit from 3.0% of GDP in 1997 to 1.4% in 2001 (though it was to rise anew to 3.1% in 2002); inflation stayed low and the ratio of public debt to GDP declined in each of the three years from 1999 to 2001. Global economic growth, and the relatively successful adjustment and productivity growth in French companies permitted tax cuts. Some were to the advantage of low earners and small and medium sized enterprises in 2000–1. The value added tax was cut by one percentage point in 2000 and, in the same year, Laurent Fabius (Minister of Finance) announced a three-year programme of tax cuts for 2001–3. The introduction of the Euro notes and coins ran very smoothly, and produced less of an outcry about the alleged rounding up of prices than it did in Germany. But the economy turned down in 2001–2, and widely recognised economic competence did not win Jospin or the Socialist Party the 2002 elections. The Raffarin government was faced with the requirement placed on them by President Chirac's election pledge to reduce income tax by 30 per cent over his five-year term. Given the slowdown in the global economy, and the difficulty of making effective cuts in a number of key areas such as the public service wage bill, the process of producing new budgetary plans proved difficult and protracted. Finance Minister Francis Mer, insisting in October 2002 that the Stability and Growth Pact was not 'set in stone', persuaded the EU to allow France until 2006 rather than 2004 to arrive at a general government financing requirement close to balance, but later, and in the face of EU Commission criticism, insisted that France's budgetary policy and political priorities were a matter for national decision, even if that meant a continued deficit (*The Economist*, 16 November 2002).

French governments have thus since 1983 broadly accepted the disciplines and obligations of the neo-liberal macro-economic policies involved in the Economic and Monetary Union (EMU). However, they have equally consistently fought to ensure that as much space as possible is left for the furthering of French interests. This (see above) partly motivated support for the EMU, but also the attempt, at the Amsterdam Treaty negotiations and thereafter, especially during France's tenure of the EU presidency in 2000, to develop 'economic government' for the EU, at least through the creation of a strong group of the finance ministers of the Eurozone countries with the task of counterbalancing the ECB's concentration on low inflation. In these aims, France has faced resistance both from Germany, determined to maintain ECB independence, and from Britain which wishes to ensure that important decisions are not taken in a forum from which the British are absent. Mer's insistence on the priority of national decisions continues France's ambiguous relationship with her European context.

Employment

The 1983 U-turn was in part a decision to ensure that a sound currency, market-led adjustments and low inflation were given priority over social goals. This strategy, known as 'competitive disinflation' effectively shifts the burdens on to wages, whose share in the corporate sector's value added went down over the 1980s and 1990s, and on to employment. This was particularly acute in the early 1990s, when the Franc shadowed the Deutschmark and thus had to emulate the high interest rates that were part of the price the Germans were paying for reunification. Indeed, because of Exchange Rate Mechanism (ERM) constraints, French rates had to be even higher than German ones. Unemployment rose from 8.3 per cent in 1983 to over 12 per cent in 1997. Since concern about unemployment was the major consideration for French electors in all the elections of that period, governments have needed to find whatever means they could to counter the social exclusion that unemployment produces. These include reduction of the social security and tax burden on firms that take on additional workers or employ low-paid workers. There was also a massive expansion of school education, with the aim that 80 per cent of pupils should achieve the *baccalauréat* qualification at 18, of vocational education, and of higher education, the intention being to produce a more highly skilled workforce. In addition the introduction of the 35-hour week was intended directly to increase employment, and may have done so, though it is hard to tell to what extent the reduction of unemployment to 9 per cent by 2002 has also been due to a general economic upturn. And despite job-creation schemes for young people, such as the *emplois jeunes* scheme launched in 1997 which is said to have created 100 000 jobs by 1999 (Milner, 2001, p. 333), youth (under 25) unemployment remains stubbornly high, peaking at around one in four in the early 1990s and still around one in five. Some politicians and commentators see the unemployment rate as a consequence of a rigid and regulated labour market – 'second out of 17 OECD countries in 1997 for strictness of regulation' (Milner, 2001, p. 331) – with high social security and taxation charges, and exacerbated by the Jospin government's legislation on 'social modernization'. But there is a great deal of public support for employment protection, including the powerful guarantees enjoyed by public service workers, and even a government of the right is subject to the general expectation that the state will underpin social protection. In general 'the simultaneous desire to protect and liberalise has led to greater state intervention, partly in response to public unease about unemployment' (Milner, 2001, p. 331).

Privatization

A further element of the economic policy that followed from the 1983 U-turn was the move away from nationalization towards partial or full privatization of public sector companies. There are a number of key aspects to the French privatization programme.

First, although the motivations for the programme have varied and the rhetoric has depended upon the nature of the government in power there has been an almost continuous programme of privatization since 1983. It began, almost clandestinely, with the need to find investment capital for state-owned companies under conditions of budgetary rigour after 1983. Finance Minister Delors began to permit the state-owned companies to issue non-voting shares and to sell off subsidiaries. The ideological impulsion of the 1986 government of the Right was clear and its programme extensive and rapid. Its stated intention was to privatize 12 major groups, comprising some 65 companies. Before the 1987 stock market crash put an end to this, 30 companies had been privatized. Mitterrand in 1988 declared that he favoured neither nationalization nor privatization, but the government found that partial privatization to allow the sale and acquisition of cross-shareholdings with other European companies was a requirement for the formation of Europe-wide alliances in the face of the single market. The return of the Right in 1993 produced a further major wave of privatizations, though this slowed as conditions became more difficult after 1995. Ironically, the largest programme of, frequently partial, privatizations in terms of its value was undertaken by Dominique Strauss-Kahn in the first two years of the Jospin government between 1997 and 1999. It was referred to as 'opening up of capital', and can seen as 'pragmatic and tactical...aimed at facilitating international links and cross shareholdings inside and outside France' (Hayward and Wright, 2002, p. 213; Cole, 2001, p. 178).

Second the uses to which the proceeds of privatization have been put have varied. In 1986–8 they were virtuously used to reduce the national debt. From 1993 to 1995 they were used largely for budgetary purposes before another change of tack in the policy over the use of such proceeds. They thus helped finance programmes aimed at reducing unemployment. They also provided much needed finance to Air France and the big bank *Crédit Lyonnais*, both of which were by 1993 suffering huge losses. Successive governments eventually spent more rescuing *Crédit Lyonnais* than they had on their share of the construction of the Channel Tunnel (Hall, 2001, p. 178). In these cases the French government has had to negotiate carefully with the European Commission to ensure that its help did not fall foul of EU rules outlawing state aid to competitive industries. In the case of *Crédit Lyonnais* as in that of the ailing insurance company GAN, the rescue package was agreed to by the EU competition authorities only on condition of full privatization. In 1997–9 the proceeds again repaid subsidies that had covered companies' losses, and helped to reduce the government borrowing figures as the date for the EMU approached.

Thirdly, the privatization programme over quite a long period exhibited an 'obsessive concern to avoid foreign control' (Hall, 2001, p. 178). For this reason the privatizations of 1986–8 and 1993–5 involved the creation of interlinked cross shareholdings between specially picked firms, political allies of the government and intended to provide stable core shareholdings that would be proof against bids for foreign control or political upheaval on a change of government. From 1995 onwards, however, these stable core shareholdings began to break up: foreign shareholders had been admitted as part of the price of international alliances, and they tended to support the operation of a market-driven logic. Takeovers have occurred, such as that of the insurance company UAP by AXA in 1996, and of the oil company Elf-Aquitaine by Total-Fina in 1999. French privatization has differed from similar programmes elsewhere in the caution shown about admitting the full rigour of market forces. It has also differed in its hesitation in relation to major public utilities. A further difference has been a greater willingness to accept a mixture of public and private stakes in a number of companies, for example the defence and electronics company Thalès. This is intimately linked to the issue of public services, to which this chapter now turns.

Services Publics

The Treaty of Amsterdam contains, at French insistence, a clause recognizing a special role for 'general interest' or 'public' services. The strikes and demonstrations of autumn 1995 (Exhibit 9.4), and again (albeit on a smaller scale) autumn 2002, provide evidence for the attachment of much of the French population to the notion of *services publics*. The Amsterdam Treaty clause was part of an attempt by the French government to protect what can be seen as a traditional French conception of service provided in the general interest against the liberalizing and deregulating implications of the single market and EU competition policy. Part of the intense French debate on globalization, of which the EU may be seen by its critics as a vector, is a fear that it will undermine what the Socialist Party in 2000, in terms that would be broadly acceptable across the political mainstream in France, defined as the role of the state 'the guaranteeing of equality of opportunity and social cohesion, the reduction of risk, and the affirmation of a new security and new rights' (cited in Hanley, 2001, p. 305). To this mission the public services are held to be crucial. They have become a 'mobilizing myth', a key part of the discourse of modern political culture. The notion is underpinned by certain legal rules: a public service must be provided continuously, must be equally accessible by all, must meet public needs. It does not automatically follow that public services must be provided by publicly owned concerns, although in so far as tasks identified as being in the general interest are contracted out, their provision is subject to special legal rules.

The extent to which the provision of any type of service or good is to be considered a matter of public service is far from clear, and the boundaries can vary: classic French analysis suggested that there were three grounds on which they might be so categorized (Chevallier, 2002, pp. 183–4). The first is that a natural monopoly exists, and the state must ensure that it is not used to extract unfair profits. On the other hand, a public service may need to enjoy a monopoly in order to ensure that it can recoup the costs of its obligations to provide a continuous, universal and equal service (Bodiguel *et al.*, 2000, p. 24). Under French law, public services may levy charges but must not be created for financial gain. The provision of energy and transport are held to fall into this category. The second ground is the existence of an indivisible collective good, such as defence or education, and the third is the need to rectify the failings of the market. However, in the last analysis the categorization of any activity as a public service is a value-driven, political decision, which in France is held to relate to citizenship and the values by which the republic choses to define itself (Bodiguel *et al.*, 2000, p. 25).

Closely linked to the notion of public services as providing indispensable public goods which could and should not be left to the whims of rapacious market organizations is the notion of the protected status of public service employment. *Fonctionnaires* (see Chapter 5) enjoy almost total job security, guaranteed advancement to certain levels, and pensions based on fewer years of contributions than in the general pensions regime. Some public utilities – especially posts and telecommunications – were until the 1980s integral parts of the civil service. When in the 1980s they were gradually detached, transformed from a single ministry into separate more or less commercial enterprises, and France Télécom eventually, in 1997, partially privatized (while retaining its public service mission and consequently the constraints of continuity of service and universal provision), careful provision had to be made to ensure that all the existing staff retained all the benefits of their *fonctionnaire* status: only newly engaged staff are employed on private law contracts. Although they are not *fonctionnaires* the employees of *Electricité de France – Gaz de France* and the *Societé Nationale des Chemins de Fer Français* (SNCF – the railway) enjoy similar conditions.

In this context the French government has consistently mounted a determined defence of their public services and monopoly utilities against pressures stemming from EU policies or political fashion to liberalize or privatize.

Liberalization of air transport within the EU was achieved in the late 1980s, following an abrupt and still largely inexplicable about-turn by the then minister of transport in the Council of Ministers in 1986, but massive help continued to be given to Air France, and its restructuring in the face of competition was painful and slow. However, determined rearguard actions were fought against the opening up to competition, especially foreign competition, of the markets for postal and telecommunications services, and for energy. The French government eventually proved unable to stand out against the single-market pressures of the other EU member states, some of them far from happy at seeing French companies, including EDF, take a substantial share of their liberalized utilities markets – electricity, water and rail services in the UK for example – whilst their government defended national monopolies on its home turf. The French have had to accept the directives supported by a majority of EC members. That on telecommunications resulted in the opening of its markets in January 1998; on postal services the (Right-wing majority) National Assembly in 1996 adopted a resolution opposing the liberalizing directive, and the EU directive will, at French insistence, not be applicable until 2003 (Cole, 2001, p. 173). Resistance to opening up of the energy market has been equally strong. The EU directive on the electricity market dates from 1996. It was not transposed into French law until 1999. The French government under Jospin conceded some liberalization for large consumers but repeatedly attempted to block EU attempts to ensure the opening up of the domestic consumer market, but under the Raffarin government agreement was reached that by 2007 all commercial users and households in France will be allowed a free choice of their provider of both gas and electricity. At least partial privatization of EDF and GDF is likely to follow.

Moreover, on the one hand France is a party to international agreements, such as the World Trade Organisation agreements, aimed at opening up markets and encouraging global competition. There are strong pressures on a government committed by membership of the Euro to budgetary discipline to encourage commercial effectiveness and self-sufficiency in the utilities, and to open up the French utilities market to external competitors. On the other hand, there are substantial obstacles:

- The government, and the technical *grands corps*, whose fiefdoms the public utilities have been, are wary about relinquishing too much control.
- The utilities have very substantial unfunded pension obligations which, as the demographic pressure worsens, will make them unattractive to private buyers. The government had to agree to taking on half of France Télécom's liabilities to achieve its partial privatization.
- Public employment and the guarantees it offers has long been seen as social safety valve (Rouban, 1996). It provides an antidote to social frustration by offering the prospect of guaranteed secure employment and advancement. Liberalization is equated with globalization, job losses and insecurity. The rhetoric of the general interest and republican values provides an almost

universally accepted justification for interests that affect a very wide swathe of the population. One estimate has suggested that 57 per cent of French adults are either civil servants, or the children, parents or spouses of civil servants.

The public services will continue to be a sensitive issue in French political life. Even if they vary – more in degree than in fundamental approach – in their responses to the challenges they pose, none of the mainstream parties fundamentally contests the doctrinal importance attached to them.

Immigration and Race Relations

The unexpected emergence of Jean-Marie Le Pen as a second-round contender in the French presidential election in 2002 highlights the salience of issues of immigration and race relations in France. Le Pen's party, the FN, emerged in the 1980s with a clearly anti-immigrant and xenophobic agenda, and has not lost that aspect of its ideology. Amongst the reasons why voters chose Le Pen are real anxieties around the politics of immigration and of what in other countries, but, revealingly, not in France, are known as race relations. Associated with these, rightly or wrongly, are other issues such as violence, especially but not only in schools in deprived areas, drug dealing and crime. While some of the xenophobia is directed against foreign institutions such as the EU, much is focused upon immigrants from Africa, especially the Maghreb, and their descendants. There is certainly some popular feeling that crime – from which one opinion poll in September 2002 found that half the respondents felt they were often at risk (*The Economist*, 16 November 2002) – is disproportionately the work of members of ethnic minorities. Whether or not this view is correct is impossible to say, since in the interests of republican equality, no distinctions are made in official statistics. It is at least arguable that crime is primarily a consequence of unemployment, poverty, social exclusion and poor education, which bear particularly hard upon the ethnic minority population (for the size of such groups see Chapter 1).

The framework of policy on the rights of non-EU citizens to move into France as workers is relatively simple. The end of the post-war boom saw, in 1974, a law suspending legal immigration by non-EU citizens as workers into France, at first temporarily, and, by the early 1980s until 1998, permanently. This, however, left a number of problems for immigration policy. First, whilst legal immigration was tightly controlled and effectively limited to family reunification, clandestine and illegal immigration continued. In 1981 Mitterrand attempted to deal with this by regularizing the position of those already established, while promising firmer measures to restrict it. There is some evidence, including the fact that less than half the estimated number of illegal immigrants actually applied for regularization in 1991 (132 000 out of an estimated 300 000) that the numbers were, as Patrick Weil argues, always overestimated and that public perceptions and hostility were based not on reality but on 'the visibly increased concentration of immigrants in certain areas' (Weil, 2001, p. 217). The result, however, was increased mistrust of official policy, which certainly contributed to the level of support for the FN.

It was in response to that mistrust, and to pre-empt some of the appeal of the extreme left that in 1993 Minister of the Interior Charles Pasqua introduced a tough set of laws aimed at further controlling inward movement. The laws were the subject of notable tussles with the Constitutional Council, but even when amended still produced a much more repressive regime. The result was a marked decrease in legal immigration flows over the next few years (Weil, 2001). But the 'zero immigration' which Pasqua purported to promise was never a realistic option – even at the lowest point in 1995 there were still nearly 14 000 authorized non-EU migrants – and some areas of public opinion continued to be hostile. In 1996 Minister of the Interior Jean-Louis Debré (son of the Fifth Republic's first prime minister) sought further repression of clandestine immigration, for example by dislodging illegal immigrants on hunger strike from a church in 1996, and through the 1996 Debré laws which aimed, amongst other provisions, to make it a criminal act to lodge an illegal immigrant. This was met by large demonstrations and a mobilization of anti-racist groups, the extreme left, intellectuals and students in support of the so-called '*sans-papiers*'. Jospin on his appointment in 1997 appeased Socialist Party pressure for a rapid repeal of the Pasqua and Debré laws by asking an expert, Patrick Weil, for a report, and in 1998 a moderately liberalizing package, improving conditions for family reunification and allowing the immigration of persons with certain skilled qualifications, was enacted (Weil, 2001, pp. 219–20).

Secondly, in the face of proliferating ethnic and political conflict throughout the world and since legal immigration for economic reasons was no longer possible, asylum requests escalated sharply, peaking in 1989. Changes in procedures followed, speeding up the processing of requests, but also, from 1991, preventing asylum seekers from working legally while their requests were processed. Policy and public attitudes also changed, and asylum seekers were increasingly perceived as would-be economic migrants. In 1985 France adhered to the Schengen convention, aimed at removing frontier controls and harmonizing visa and asylum policy between its signatories: this became operative in 1995, and following the Treaty of Amsterdam was brought into the EU machinery, although some EU member states were, and remained, outside the arrangements. Part of this harmonization involved the creation of facilities at ports and airports to detain those whose applications were being processed, and a general agreement that asylum requests should be dealt with in the country where the asylum seeker first arrived. That this is not necessarily a realistic solution was underlined by the tension surrounding an asylum seekers' refuge, opened by the Red Cross, at Sangatte near Calais. The British accused the French of not doing enough to deal with the asylum seekers or to protect the traffic across the Channel by tunnel and ferry from clandestine travellers. The asylum seekers, mostly Kurdish and Afghani, sought to reach the UK whose language they spoke, where there were communities of their origin which they could join, and where identity cards were not essential. The energetic interior minister of the Raffarin government, Nicholas Sarkozy, brokered a deal with the British in the autumn of 2002 to resolve the immediate problem, but the root causes have not gone away. French policy continues to be that asylum should be a matter for national not EU decision, and, in line with EU policy, that there should be a clear distinction between flight from political persecution and economic migration.

The third problem for immigration policy is the nature of the treatment to be accorded to migrants and asylum seekers who are legally settled in France and their descendants. Two issues arise: one is the question of citizenship and voting rights. In 1993, as part of the generally tougher package, a nationality law removed from French-born children of immigrant parents the automatic right to French nationality. Now such nationality had to be explicitly sought, a change intended to ensure that such citizens had made a deliberate choice in favour of the values of French civic culture. In 1998 the Jospin government reverted to automatic accession to French citizenship at age 18. A further ramification – that of whether non-EU non-French nationals residing in France should be allowed to vote at local elections, given that they are subject to taxation and are users and clients of local services – remains on the table. It will require a constitutional amendment, as did the extension of such rights to EU citizens as required by the Maastricht Treaty, and is not likely to be taken forward by a government of the Right. The other issue is the question of the relationship between differing ethnic and religious cultures within French society. The sense that republican values are universal and imply monoculturalism at least at civic level is very strong. The right of the individual to hold his or her private beliefs is acknowledged and these beliefs may, following the 1989 ruling of the *Conseil d'Etat* that made the wearing of the Muslim headscarf or other religious insignia in state schools a matter for local decision, be manifested. But *communautarisme* – the existence of culturally distinct communities – is regarded as dangerous. French political elites, and public opinion are 'torn between France's multicultural reality and their monocultural aspirations' (Hayward and Wright, 2002, p. 23). 'Integration' is the official term for the desired outcome; the government's advisory body in this area is called the High Council for Integration (*Haut Conseil à l'Intégration*). But in the absence of an active anti-discrimination policy – as opposed to purely formal non-discrimination – discrimination and exclusion persist. For example, according to Patrick Weil, 26 per cent of young people of Algerian origin have a *baccalauréat* but the unemployment rate amongst them is 41 per cent, as compared with 16 per cent of comparably qualified native French (Weil, 2001, p. 225). Alongside support for the openly xenophobic NF there has been a decline in willingness openly to express racist attitudes to opinion pollsters, but even so 38 per cent of respondents admitted to being racist in 1998, while the previous year well over 50 per cent expressed the view that there are 'too many Arabs in France' (Hayward and Wright, 2002, p. 236). Despite the optimism induced by the very multiracial team which won the Football World Cup in 1998 (though it markedly failed to do so in 2002) it is perhaps unsurprising that French young people of North African origin whistled at the Marseillaise at football matches in 2001 and 2002.

Conclusion

The policy areas discussed above all exemplify on-going continuities in French policy-making. None of them could have been discussed outside the framework of EU as well as specifically French decision-making. Other areas – for example defence and security policy, or health and welfare state policy – could have been chosen, and are well discussed elsewhere (for example in Guyomarch *et al.*, 2001, or in Elgie, 2000). But all illustrate the tensions and dilemmas of a political and governmental elite faced with internationalization, Europeanization, ideological conflict, and challenges to legitimacy and policy decisions from both more or less vocal groups, and more or less fragmented public opinion.

11

Conclusion

France's experiences and traditions of politics and government have given her a quite specific place in the political history of Western Europe. France stands firmly within the tradition of liberal democratic capitalist states. Indeed, as we saw in Chapter 1, the principles of the French Revolution, deeply anchored within French political culture, played a major part in defining, for the whole of Europe, what notions of democracy and a liberal view of human rights might mean. French state structures, developed as the nation state consolidated, incorporated within the revolutionary principles as the expression of the will not of the monarch but of the sovereign people, and refined by Napoleon, persisted alongside the revolutionary principles. The consequence was a basis for government and politics which, at least from the early modern period of history, differed quite markedly from that found in English-speaking countries.

The deep divisions within the French polity resulted, from the Nineteenth Century onwards, in a highly fragmented political party system. Under the Fifth Republic the system has become capable of encompassing a broad notion of potentially alternating government and opposition coalitions. Throughout the period the principal political contests have consistently been between Left and Right, but the picture has never been entirely clear cut. While some of the old cleavages (for example that between clerical and anti-clerical camps) have weakened, new divisions of opinion and interest, for example between Europhiles and Eurosceptics, the town and the country, those who are pessimistic or optimistic about the impact of globalization, have begun to appear and were reflected in the results of the 2002 elections. The logic of party financing, organization, leadership and electoral appeal, and changes in the social basis of politics (see Chapter 1) propelled the emergence of one dominant party on the Left in the 1990s and seem to be having the same effect on the mainstream Right in the new century. But there are still substantial numbers of votes for the extremes on the Left, and, more markedly, on the Right. As in other West European countries the political contest has focussed around economic organization and competence, especially in the tackling of unemployment, while issues of law and order have also become highly salient. On some issues there is marked consensus: the level of support for President Chirac's anti-war stance at the time of the 2003 war in Iraq was very high. There is also an almost universal commitment to the desirability of protecting the

273

rather secure social safety net enjoyed by all except the socially excluded. French party politics thus retains a degree of distinctiveness, despite having become in some ways less different from its neighbours over the course of the Fifth Republic. The shadow of de Gaulle has greatly diminished.

Not only did administrative and political development differ in France, so did the shaping of the country's economic framework. French capitalism emerged in a country where the dominant, though not always the unchallenged, view was that the interest and prosperity of the country were best served by the subordination to state authority of the forces of private greed and profit-seeking that are the motor of capitalism (Hayward, 1986, p. xiii). For complex social and economic reasons full-blooded capitalism developed relatively late in France, so that, again, assumptions, habits and practices differed from those of the English-speaking countries, even though the values and practices of capitalism are shared.

Although France is often described as having a strong and centralised state the strength of the countervailing forces means that the state is far from being overbearing or dictatorial. In the first place, as we saw in Chapters 3, 4 and 5, to talk of 'the state' as if it were a single unified entity, with a clear and consistent purpose, is misleading. It is not only the case that political priorities and the sense of direction from the top can vary as governments change, but also that differences and conflicts exist throughout all levels of the state institutions. Moreover, there is considerable scope, as the discussion of local government structures in Chapter 6 showed, for varying interpretation and implementation of policies at local level.

Equally France is not a highly pluralistic political society. Although, as Chapter 9 demonstrated, differing groups and economic interests make demands, and compete for the resources with which to satisfy them, even in recent years it has never been accepted in France that the task of the state should merely be to preside in a fairly neutral fashion over the interaction of competing demands. Presidential candidates offer, and voters expect, a vision of the future of society and, as Chapter 10 suggested, the tradition of legitimate and competent intervention by the state has enabled governments to act decisively. Finally, France is not a corporatist political system. The state is not merely an equal partner with the groups that perform the main social and economic functions in society. However, its ability to act heroically has weakened. A somewhat despairing perception of the disappearance of old forms of social and economic protection and of the unwillingness or inability of the EU simply to provide the old comforts to a larger territory may lie behind the anti-EU sentiment discussed in Chapter 10. The 2002 vote for Le Pen can be seen as 'a cry for help' (Yves Mény in *Le Point*, 3 May 2002, p. 38). As Vivien Schmidt pertinently observes 'while the state has given up tremendous power through its de-regulating, decentralizing, liberalizing and Europeanizing reforms, and thus has less capacity for action, it still perceives itself, and is perceived by society, as wholly responsible for what occurs within France' (Schmidt, 2000, p. 162).

France, is thus neither a centrally-planned, nor a pluralistic, nor a corporatist political system. Rather it is a mixed system in which market forces interact with civil society and with the preferences of the government of the day. These preferences are determined sometimes by partisan allegiance and ideology, frequently by European, international or constitutional constraints, sometimes – and perhaps to a greater extent in France than, for example in the United Kingdom – by views about administrative rationality or desirability.

In France governmental preferences have a particular force. This force derives from the tradition of state authority based upon the structures and presuppositions of Roman law, upon the emergence of the absolutist monarchy as the focus of the nation state's life, and upon the notion of political economy, which gave public power a predominant role in the control of economic activity. As Jack Hayward points out:

> The normative weight of national tradition was tilted in favour of state force rather than market forces and it was taken for granted that governments could decide what they wanted to happen and were able to make it happen provided they had the will.
>
> However a governmental predilection to act as though it is sovereign is separated from its capacity to do so by the countervailing constraints that social and economic forces exert upon it. (Hayward, 1986, p. xiii)

The liberal capitalist economy has its own autonomy and its own constraints. The French government develops ideas about the shape and balance of the national economy that it wishes to see, but is obliged in the end to leave not only the detail but also much of the broad strategy of economic activity to those whose livelihoods, whether as companies or as individuals, stand or fall by the economic decisions and choices that they make. Moreover, economic activity is less and less conscious of national boundaries. Integrated economic and monetary policy within the European Union, a currency shared with eleven other states, the condition of the international economy, the competitiveness of imports and exports and many other factors combine to affect the decisions of companies and investors in ways which governments seek to influence but cannot control.

One of the themes of this book has been the extent to which France's membership of the European Union has induced reform and change in structures, from the Constitution downwards, in relationships and in political choices. It is true that EU membership has often been the wind tunnel down which the winds – often experienced as very chilly winds – of global competition, business internationalization and economic rigour have been funnelled. But it would be a mistake to conceptualize France as simply a victim of these forces. The leadership of France has been active in shaping many of the decisions, in offering French models – of agricultural development, of social solidarity, of a vision of European security and defence – as exemplars for Europe. Whilst none of these models has been wholly successful, they have been influential and the debates continue. One of the ongoing debates is whether the end of the Twentieth Century has witnessed the end of *l'exception francaise* – French exceptionalism. The debates, shifting though they have been, turn out crucially to focus not so much on France as an exception but on France as a distinctive example and model. Old habits have changed and for France, as for other Western countries, the context of government and politics has broadened. So France's experiences of change in the final decades of the century can be portrayed as 'a variant on more widely-shared experiences of the reshaping of distinctively-structured national polities and national economies' (Lovecy, 2000, p. 221).

Amongst much change and evolution France is perhaps no longer exceptional or exemplary, but she is still different. The context has broadened, and within this '[s]overeignty... is likely to be increasingly split between the different levels of government abroad as well as at home; it is shared between the French state (itself increasingly decentralised) the E[U] and the market itself. And what this complex structure guarantees is concern about and debates on French identity, on the ability of the French *nation* to define and defend its originality even when the *state* that used to be its straitjacket loses or gives up many of the powers it used to have' (Hoffman, 1995). The governmental apparatus and political system of France will shape the responses to these new challenges. The values, priorities, concerns and traditions that have characterized French identity are carried within them as much as within the social life and civil society which they both shape and reflect.

Guide to Further Reading and Resources

Good general introductions to the government and politics of France are, paradoxically, much more available in English than in French. Bell (2002) is an excellent recent example. Cole (1997) and Howarth and Varouxakis (2003) both range more widely over social and cultural issues while Elgie (2003) concentrates on the institutions. For those with the necessary background Knapp and Wright (2001) is extraordinarily comprehensive, lively to the point of being provocative, and very clear. Mény (1998) is an excellent short discussion, now available in English. Hewlett (1998 and 2003) has a distinctive and thought-provoking stance. In French the broadest general discussion of the institutions is in Dreyfus and D'Arcy (1997). Chevallier *et al* (2001) is a very comprehensive chronological survey, much enlivened by periodic sharpness of tongue. Elgie and Griggs (2000) survey the different analytical and theoretical approaches taken by academic analysts to key themes in the study of French politics.

McMillan (1992) and Larkin (1997) are invaluable for the historical background of the twentieth century, and Gildea (2002a) is an excellent history of the post-war period. For more detailed history, the *Nouvelle Histoire de la France Contemporaine*, published by Seuil and largely available in English translation as the Cambridge History of Modern France is an indispensable starting-point. On the Vichy period Paxton (1972) is the classic work with Jackson (2001) and Gildea (2002b) providing major detailed studies. No book on the Fourth Republic has surpassed, or even equalled Williams (1972). Hazareesingh (1994) provides a detailed analysis of the intellectual and political traditions of modern France.

Eck (1998) is clear study of the French economy. The impact of economic developments on society is one, but only one, of the themes of the immensely readable Ardagh (2000). Perry (1997) and Flower (1997) provide background studies of numerous aspects of French society and culture, while Girling (1998) offers a critical outsider's perspective. A treasure trove of statistical information on French society is attractively presented in Mermet, editions of which appear every two years. The regularly updated editions of *L'Etat de la France* (Paris: La Découverte) provide a well documented overview of many political, policy, social and economic issues, while the regular volumes issued by SOFRES survey public opinion.

This book has attempted to set the framework for an understanding of the handling of political issues, conflict and decision-making in contemporary France. The issues themselves are discussed in detail in Guyomarch *et al* ((2001) and Elgie (2000) and see also Maclean (1998), Keeler and Schain (1996) and Flynn (1995). The journals *West European Politics, Modern and Contemporary France* and *French Politics* are key sources of academic analysis and discussion. In French the most important journal is the *Revue Française de Science Politique*. Each issue of *Pouvoirs* is devoted to a different theme, but also includes a chronology of recent institutional and political developments. *Regards sur l'Actualité, Problèmes Economiques et Sociaux* and *Cahiers Français*, all produced by the official publications office, the *Documentation Française* are also very useful.

The internet has now become a crucial resource for those studying French politics. All French ministries maintain informative websites.

Those of presidency – http://www.elysee.fr –
the prime minister – http://premier-ministre.gouv.fr –
the Constitutional Council – http://www.conseil-constitutionnel.fr –
and the two houses of Parliament – http://www.assemblee-nationale.fr and http://www.senat.fr – are particularly useful, and regularly updated.

The *service public* website at http://www.service-public.fr is the main portal for access by French citizens to governmental services and provides links to the sites of ministries and local authorities.

Official reports, studies and other documents can be found at http://www.ladocfrancaise.gouv.fr, and statistics and related studies at http://www.insee.fr.

All the political parties maintain websites, for example http://www.u-m-p.org/. Links to their sites, those of the Trade Unions and many other organisations can be found at http://www.adminet.com/poli/.

News as it breaks can be followed at http://fr.news.yahoo.com/politique/.

The French Embassy in London maintains an English language website of information about France at http://www.francealacarte.org.uk/ressources/index.html.

The French versions of the standard search engines such as http://fr.yahoo.com/ or http://www.google.fr are helpful, and some universities maintain pages of useful links – see for example http://www.les.aston.ac.uk/freweb.html or http://www.utm.edu/departments/french/french.html.

More specialised studies of the themes covered in this book include Hayward and Wright (2002) on central government, Hayward (1993) and Bell (2000b) on the presidency and Elgie (1993) on the prime minister. Hanley (2002) and Bell (2000a) study the party system and the parties. On Parliament there is Huber (1996) and on local government Cole and John (2001) and Institut International d'Administration Publique (2001). Allwood and Wadia is a comprehensive study of the role of women in French politics. On economic policy and local development Levy (1999) is detailed and stimulating. On social movements Duyvendak (1995) and Tarrow (1998) are recent studies. Guyomarch *et al* (1998) and Gueldry (2001) deal with French relationships with the EU. Dyson and Featherstone (1999) and Howarth (2000) are authoritative accounts of the process of monetary union.

Bibliography

Allwood, Gill and Khursheed Wadia (2000) *Women and Politics in France* (London and New York: Routledge).

Anderson, R. D. (1977) *France 1870–1914* (London: Routledge & Kegan Paul); (1984 New York: Routledge, Chapman & Hall).

Appleton, Andrew (2000) 'The New Social Movement Phenomenon: Placing France in comparative perspective' in Elgie, Robert (ed.) *The Changing French Political System* (London: Frank Cass) pp. 56–75.

Ardagh, John (2000) *France in the New Century: portrait of a changing society* (London: Penguin Books).

Ashford, Douglas (1982) *French Pragmatism and British Dogmatism* (London: Allen & Unwin; New York: HarperCollins).

Avril, Pierre and Jean Gicquel (1993) *Le Conseil Constitutionel*, 2nd edn (Paris: Montchrestien).

Bauer, Michel and Elie Cohen (1981) *Qui Governe le Groupes Industriels?* (Paris: Seuil).

Bell, David S. (2000a) *Parties and Democracy in France: Parties under Presidentialism* (London: Dartmouth).

Bell, David S. (2000b) *Presidential Power in the Fifth French Republic* (Oxford and New York: Berg).

Bell, David S. (2002) *French Politics Today* new edition (Manchester: Manchester University Press).

Bell, David S. and Byron Criddle (1988) *The French Socialist Party: The Emergence of a Party of Government* 2nd edn (Oxford and New York: Clarendon Press).

Bell, David S. and Byron Criddle (1994) *The French Communist Party in the Fifth Republic* (Oxford: Clarendon Press).

Bell, Laurence, (2001) 'Interpreting Collective action: methodology and ideology in the analysis of social movements' *Modern and Contemporary France* 9(2), pp. 183–96.

Bernard, Paul (1992) *Le Préfet de la République: le chêne et l'olivier* (Paris: Economica).

Berthon, Christine (2001) 'The Role of the Region' in Institut International d'Administration Publique *Local Government in France* (Paris: La Documentation Française, series 'Getting to Know French Administration) pp. 69–83.

Bessy-Pietri, Pascale, Mohamed Hilal and Bertrand Schmitt (2000) 'Recensement de la population 1999: Évolutions contrastées du rural' *INSEE Première*, no. 726, juillet at http://www.insee.fr/fr/ffc/docs_ffc/IP726.pdf consulted 7 January 2003.

Bezès, Philippe (2001) 'Bureaucrats and politicians in the politics of administrative reforms in France (1988–1997)' in B. Guy Peters and Jon Pierre (eds) *Politicians, Bureaucrats and Administrative Reform* (London: Routledge/ECPR Studies in European Political Science) pp. 47–60.

Bigaut, Christian (1997) *Les Cabinets Ministériels* (Paris: LGDJ).

Bilger-Street, Hélène and Susan Milner (2001) 'The municipal elections of 2001' *Modern and Contemporary France* 9 (4) November 2001, pp. 507–22.

Birenbaum, Guy (1992) *Le Front National en Politique* (Paris: Balland).

Bodiguel, Jean-Luc, Christian Albert Gorban and Alain Supiot (2000) *Servir l'intérêt générale* (Paris: Presses Universitaires de France).

Boëldieu, Julien and Catherine Borrel (2000) 'Recensement de la population 1999: La proportion d'immigrés est stable depuis 25 ans' *INSEE première*, no. 748 Novembre at http://www.insee.fr/fr/ffc/docs_ffc/IP748.pdf (consulted 7 January 2003).

Bornstein, Stephen E. (1994) 'The Politics of Scandal' in Peter Hall, Jack Hayward and Howard Machin (eds) *Developments in French Politics* revised edn (London: Macmillan and New York: St Martin's Press).

Brown, L. and J. F. Garner (1983) *French Administrative Law* 3rd edn (London: Butterworth).

Buffotot, Patrice (1993) 'Le Référendum sur l'Union Européenne' *Modern and Contemporary France* NS1 (3).

Buffotot, Patrick and David Hanley (1996) 'Chronique d'une victoire annoncée: les elections présidentielles de 1995' *Modern and Contemporary France* NS4 (1).

Carcassonne, Guy (1997) 'Les rapports du president français et du premier minister' *Revue française d'administration publique* No. 83, juillet–septembre, pp. 397–409.

Carcassonne, Guy (ed.) (2000) *La Constitution, introduite et commentée* 4th edn (Paris: Seuil).

Carcassone, Guy and Olivier Duhamel (2001) *La Ve République 1958–2001: histoire des institutions et des régimes politiques de la France* (Paris: Armand Colin).

Cawson, Alan, Peter Holmes, Kevin Morgan, Anne Stevens and Douglas Webber (1990) *Hostile Brothers: Competition and Closure in the European Electronics Industry* (Oxford and New York: Oxford University Press).

Chafer, Tony (1988) 'Business Education in France: An Expanding Sector' *Modern and Contemporary France* 34 (July).

Chapsal, Jacques and Alain Lancelot (1979) *La Vie Politique en France depuis 1940*, 5th edn. (Paris: Presses Universitaires de France).

Charlot, Jean (1970) *The Gaullist Phenomenon* (London: Allen & Unwin).

Charlot, Jean (1989) 'Les Mutations du Système des Partis Français', *Pouvoirs*, 49.

Charlot, Jean (1994) *La politique en France* (Paris: Le Livre de Poche).

Chevallier, Jacques (2002) *Science Administrative* 3rd edn (Paris: Presses Universtaires de France).

Chevallier, Jean-Jacques, Guy Carcassonne and Olivier Duhamel (2001) *La Ve République 1958–2000: histoires des institutions et régimes politiques de la France* (Paris: Armand Colin).

Chirac, Jacques (1995) *La France pour tous* (Paris: election brochure).

Claisse, Alain (1972) *Le Premier Ministre de la Ve République* (Paris: LGDJ).

Clark, David (1984) 'The Ombudsman in Britain and France: a comparative evaluation' *West European Politics* 7(3) (October).

Clark, David (1998) 'The Modernization of the French Civil Service: Crisis, Continuity and Change' *Public Administration* 76 (1), pp. 97–115.

Clift, Ben, (2002) 'The Political Economy of the Jospin Government' *Modern and Contemporary France* 10 (3), pp. 325–7.

Cole, Alistair (1989) 'The French Municipal Elections on 12 and 17 March 1989' *Modern and Contemporary France* 39 (October) pp. 23–34.

Cole, Alistair (1995) 'La France pour tous? – The French Presidential Elections of 23 April and 7 May 1995', *Government and Opposition* 30 (3), pp. 326–46.

Cole, Alistair (ed.) (1990) *French Political Parties in Transition* (Aldershot and Brookfield, VT: Dartmouth).

Cole, Alistair, (1998) *French Politics and Society* (New York and London: Prentice Hall).

Cole, Alistair (2001) 'The *Service Public* under stress' in Robert Elgie (ed.) *The Changing French Political System* (London: Frank Cass) pp. 166–84.

Cole, Alistair (2002) 'A Strange Affair: the 2002 French elections' *Government and Opposition* 37 (3), pp. 317–42.

Cole, Alistair and Peter John (1995) 'Local Policy Networks in France and Britain: Policy Coordination in Fragmented Political Subsystems' *West European Politics* 18 (4), pp. 89–109.

Cole, Alistair and Peter John (2001) *Local Governance in England and France* (London: Routledge).

Collard, Sue (1992) 'Mission impossible: Les Chantiers du Président' *French Cultural Studies*, ii, pp. 97–132.

Crozier, Michel (1963) *Le Phénomène Bureaucratique* (Paris: Seuil).

Dauphin, Sandrine (2002) 'La parité à l'epreuve des elections' *Modern and Contemporary France* 10 (1) (February), pp. 59–73.

Dauphin, Sandrine and Jocelyne Praud (2002) 'Debating and implementing Gender Parity in French Politics' *Modern and Contemporary France* 10 (1) (February), pp. 5–11.

De Gaulle, Charles (1959) *Mémoires de Guerre: le salut* (Paris: Plon).

Debbasch, Charles *et al.* (1985) *La Ve République* 2nd edn (Paris: Economica).

Debré, Michel (1958) 'Discours devant le Conseil d'Etat 27 août 1958' in Quermonne, Jean-Louis (1980) *Le Gouvernment de la France sous la Ve République* (Paris: Dalloz) pp. 621–31.

Delivet, Philippe (2001) 'The role of the *département*' in Institut International d'Administration Publique *Local Government in France* (Paris: La Documentation Française, series 'Getting to know French administration) pp. 85–98.

Drake, Helen (2001) 'France on Trial? The Challenge of Change and the French Presidency of the European Union, July–December 2000' *Modern and Contemporary France* 9 (4) November, pp. 453–66.

Dreyfus, Françoise and François D'Arcy (1997) *Les Institutions Politiques et Administratives de la France* 5th edn (Paris: Economica).

Duchen, Claire (1986) *Feminism in France from May '68 to Mitterrand* (London: Routledge & Kegan Paul).

Duclaud-Williams, Roger (1997) 'Education' in John Flower (ed.) *France Today* 8th edn (London: Hodder and Stoughton).

Duhamel, Olivier (2000) *Le Quinquennat* (Paris: Presses de Sciences Po).

Dupuy, François and Jean-Claude Thoenig (1985) *L'Administration en Miettes* (Paris: Fayard).

Duverger, Maurice (1964) *Political Parties* (London: Methuen; New York: Routledge, Chapman & Hall).

Duyvendak, Jan Willem (1995) *The Power of Politics: new social movements in France* (Boulder, Colorado and Oxford: Westview Press).

Dyson, Kenneth (1994) *Elusive Union: The Process of Economic and Monetary Union in Europe* (London and New York: Longman).

Dyson, Kenneth and Kevin Featherstone (1999) *The Road to Maastricht: Negotiating Economic and Monetary Union* (Oxford: Oxford University Press).

Eck, Jean François (1998) *La France dans la nouvelle économie mondiale* 3rd edn (Paris: Presses Universitaires de France).

Elgie, Robert (1991) 'La Méthode Rocard Existe-t-elle?' *Modern and Contemporary France* 44 (January).

Elgie, Robert (1993) *The Role of the Prime Minister in France 1981–1991* (London: Macmillan; New York: St Martin's Press).

Elgie, Robert (2000) 'The Changing French Political System' in Robert Elgie (ed.) *The Changing French Political System* (London: Frank Cass) pp. 1–19.

Elgie, Robert (2003) *Political Institutions in Contemporary France* (Oxford: Oxford University Press)

Elgie, Robert and Stephen Griggs (2000) *French Politics: Debates and controversies* (London: Routledge).

Elgie, Robert and Howard Machin (1991) 'France: The Limits to Prime Ministerial Government in a Semi-Presidential System' *West European Politics* 14 (2) (April).

Eling, Kim (1999) *The Politics of Cultural Policy in France* (London: Macmillan).

Emeri, Claude (1985) 'Les déconvenues de la doctrine' in Olivier Duhamel and Jean-Luc Parodi (eds) *La constitution de la Cinquième République* (Paris: Presses de la Fondation Nationale des Sciences Politiques).

Favoreu, Louis (1998) 'La Place du Conseil Constitutionnel dans la Constitution de 1958' in *La Constitution de 1958 à quarante ans* http://www.conseil-constitutionnel.fr/dossier/quarante/q 18.htm (consulted 22 July 2002, p. 4).

Ferrandon, Benoît (2002) 'Entreprises: La nouvelle donne' *Cahiers Français* 311 pp. 39–44.

Fieschi, Catherine (2000) 'Rally Politics and Political Organisation: an institutionalist perpective on the French Far Right' *Modern and Contemporary France* 8 (1) pp. 71–89.

Flood, Christopher (2002) 'Euroscepticism: A Problematic Concept (illustrated with particular reference to France)' paper presented at the University Association for Contemporary European Studies Conference, Belfast, September.

Flynn, Gregory (ed.) (1995) *Remaking the Hexagon: The New France in the New Europe* (Boulder, CO; Oxford: Westview Press).

Fourastié, Jean (1979) *Les Trentes Glorieuses* (Paris: Fayard).

Fournier, Jacques (1987) *Le Travail Governmentale* (Paris: Presses de la Fondation Nationale des Sciences Politiques).

Frears, John (1990) 'The French Parliament: Loyal Workhorse, Poor Watchdog', *West European Politics* 13 (2) (July).

Frears, John (1991) *Parties and Voters in France* (London: Hurst; New York: St Martin's Press).

Gadrey, Jean (2002) 'Une économie des services' *Cahiers Français* 311, pp. 20–5.

Gaffney, John (1990) 'The Emergence of a Presidential Party: The Socialist Party', in Alistair Cole (ed.) *French Political Parties in Transition* (Aldershot and Brookfield, Vermont: Dartmouth), pp. 61–90.

Gallie, Duncan (1983) *Social Inequality and Class Radicalism in France and Britain* (Cambridge and New York: Cambridge University Press).

Gaxie, Daniel (1986) 'Le Ministre', *Pouvoirs*, 36, pp. 61–78.

Gildea, Robert (2002a) *Marianne in Chains: In Search of the German Occupation 1940–1945* (London: Macmillan).

Gildea, Robert (2002b) *France Since 1945* paperback edn (Oxford: Oxford University Press).

Girling, John (1998) *France: political and social change* (London: Routledge).

Giroud, Françoise (1977) *La Comédie du Pouvoir* (Paris: Fayard).

Giscard d'Estaing, Valéry (1976) *Démocratie Française* (Paris: Fayard).

Gleizal, Jean-Jacques (1995) 'En guise de conclusion: la recomposition du système politico-administratif' in Jean-Jacques Gleizal (ed.) *Le retour des préfets* (Grenoble: Presses Universitaires de Grenoble) pp. 245–9.

Grémion, Cathérine (1992) 'Que reste-t-il des administrations déconcentrées?' in Muller, Pierre (ed) *L'Administration Française Est-Elle en Crise*? (Paris: L'Harmattan).

Grémion, Pierre (1976) *Le Pouvoir Périphérique* (Paris: Seuil).

Grunberg, Gérard (1993) 'Que reste-t-il du parti d'Epinay?' in Phillippe Habert, Pascal Perrineau and Colette Ysmal (eds) *Le Vote Sanction* (Paris: Départment des Etudes du Figaro et Presses de la Fondation Nationale des Sciences Politiques) pp. 185–215.

Gueldry, Michel (2001) *France and European Integration: Toward a transnational polity?* (Westport CI and London: Praeger).

Guigou, Elisabeth (2000) *Une femme au coeur de L'Etat* (Paris: Fayard).

Guy, Gilbert (1995) 'The Resources of the French Regions in Retrospect' in John Loughlin and Sonia Mazey (eds) *The End of the French Unitary State: Ten Years of Regionalization in France 1982–1992* (London: Frank Cass).

Guyomarch, Alain, Howard Machin, Peter Hall and Jack Hayward (eds) (2001) *Developments in French Politics 2* (London: Palgrave).

Guyomarch, Alain, Howard Machin and Ella Ritchie (1998) *France in the European Union* (London: Macmillan).

Habert, Philippe, Pascal Perrineau and Colette Ysmal (1993) *Le Vote Sanction: les élections législatives des 21 et 28 mars 1993* (Paris: Département des études politiques du Figaro & Presses de la Fondation Nationale des Sciences Politiques).

Hague, Rod and Martin Harrop (2001) *Comparative Government and Politics: An Introduction*, 5th edn (London: Palgrave).

Hall, Peter A, (2001) 'The Evolution of Economic Policy' in Alain Guyomarch, Howard Machin, Peter Hall and Jack Hayward (eds) *Developments in French Politics 2* (London: Palgrave) pp. 172–90.

Hamon, Léo (1985) 'Du référendum à la démocratie continue' in Duhamel, Olivier and Jean-Luc Parodi (eds) *La Constitution de la Cinquième République* (Paris: Presses de la Fondation Nationale des Sciences Politiques) pp. 504–21.

Hanley, D. (1989) 'Waiting for the President: The Political Year in Retrospect, September 1987 to August 1988' *Contemporary France* vol. 3 (London: Printer).

Hanley, David (1993) 'Socialism Routed? The French Legislative Elections of 1993' *Modern and Contemporary France* NS1 (4).

Hanley, David (2001) 'French Political Parties, Globalisation and Europe' *Modern and Contemporary France* 9 (3) August 2001, pp. 301–12.

Hanley, David (2002) *Party, Society and Government: Republican Democracy in France* (New York and Oxford: Berghahn Books).

Harrison, Martin (1993) 'The President, cultural politics and media policy' in Jack Hayward (ed.) *De Gaulle to Mitterrand: Presidential Power in France* (Brighton: Harvester Wheatsheaf; New York: New York University Press).

Hayward, J. (1978) 'Dissentient France: The Counter Political Culture' *West European Politics* 1 (3) (October).

Hayward, J. (1986) *The State and the Market Economy* (Brighton: Harvester Wheatsheaf; New York: New York University Press).

Hayward, Jack (ed.) (1993) *De Gaulle to Mitterrand: Presidential Power in France* (London: Hurst).

Hayward, Jack (2001) 'In Search of an Evanescent European Identity: the demise of French distinctiveness' in Alain Guyomarch, Howard Machin, Peter Hall and Jack Hayward (eds) *Developments in French Politics 2* (London: Palgrave) pp. 257–85.

Hayward, Jack and Vincent Wright (2002) *Governing from the Centre: Core executive coordination in France* (Oxford: Oxford University Press).

Hazareesingh, Sudhir (1994) *Political Traditions in Modern France* (Oxford and New York: Oxford University Press).

Headlam, Allan (1989) 'Le Paysage Industriel Français: Les syndicates et l'emploi', *Modern and Contemporary France* 37 (April).

Hewlett, Nick (1998) *Modern French Politics: Analysing Conflict and Consensus since 1945* (Cambridge: Polity).

Hewlett, Nick (2003) *Democracy in Modern France* (London: Continuum).

Horne, Alistair (1979) *A Savage War of Peace: Algeria 1945–1962* (Harmondsworth: Penguin and New York: Penguin USA).

House, J. W. (1978) *France: An Applied Geography* (London: Methuen; New York: Routledge, Chapman & Hall (1979)).

Howarth, David (2000) *The French Road to European Monetary Union* (London: Palgrave).

Howarth, David (2002) 'The European Policy of the Jospin Government: a new twist to old French games' *Modern and Contemporary France* 10 (3), pp. 353–70.

Howarth, David and Georgios Varouxakis (2003) *Contemporary France: An introduction to French Politics and Society* (London: Edward Arnold).

Howorth, Jolyon (1991) 'France and the Gulf War: From Pre-war Crisis to Post-war Crisis' *Modern and Contemporary France* 46 (July).

Howorth, Jolyon (1993) 'The President's Special Role in Foreign and Defence Policy' in Jack Hayward (ed) *De Gaulle to Mitterrand* (London: Hurst) pp. 150–89.

Huber, John (1996) *Rationalizing Parliament: Legislative Institutions and Party Politics in France* (Cambridge: Cambridge University Press).

Institut International d'Administration Publique (2000) *Local Government in France* (Paris: La Documentation Française, series 'Getting to Know French Administration).

Irving, R. E. M. (1973) *Christian Democracy in France* (London: Allen & Unwin).

Jackson, Julian (2001) *France: The Dark Years 1940–1944* (Oxford: Oxford University Press).

Jenkins, Brian and Peter Morris (1993) 'Political Scandal in France' *Modern and Contemporary France* NS1 (2).

Jobert, Bruno (1989) 'The Normative Frameworks of Public Policy' *Political Studies* 37 (3) (September).

Jobert, Bruno and Pierre Muller (1987) *L'Etat en Action* (Paris: Presses Universitaires de France).

Jones, H. S. (1993) *The French State in Question* (Cambridge: Cambridge University Press).

Keeler, John and Martin Schain (eds) *Chirac's Challenge* (New York: St Martin's Press).

Keeler, John and Peter Hall (2001) 'Interest Representation and the Politics of Protest' in Alain Guyomarch, Howard Machin, Peter Hall and Jack Hayward (eds) *Developments in French Politics 2* (London: Palgrave) pp. 50–67.

Keeler, John T. S. (1985) 'Confrontations Juridico-politiques: Le Conseil Constitutionnel face au Gouvernement Socialiste comparé à la Cour Suprême face au New Deal', *Pouvoirs*, 35, 133–48.

Knapp, Andrew (1990) 'Un parti comme les autres: Jacques Chirac and the Rally for the Republic' in Cole, Alistair (ed.) *French Political Parties in Transition* (Aldershot and Brookfield, VT: Dartmouth) pp. 140–84.

Knapp, Andrew (1991) 'The *cumul des mandats*, Local Power and Political Parties in France', *West European Politics* 14 (1) (January).

Knapp, Andrew (1994) *Gaullism Since De Gaulle* (Aldershot: Dartmouth).

Knapp, Andrew (1999) 'What's Left of the French Right? From Conquest to Humiliation, 1993 to 1998' *West European Politics* 22 (3), pp. 109–38.

Knapp, Andrew and Vincent Wright (2001) *The Government and Politics of France* (London: Routledge).

L'Année Politique, (2000) (Paris: Éditions Événements et Tendences).

Ladrech, Robert (1994) 'The Europeanization of domestic politics and institutions: the case of France' *Journal of Common Market Studies* 32 (1), pp. 69–88.

Larkin, Maurice (1997) *France Since the Popular Front: Government and People 1936–1986* 2nd edn. (Oxford and New York: Clarendon Press).

Laughland, John (1994) *The Death of Politics: France under Mitterrand* (London: Michael Joseph).

Le Pors, Anicet and Françoise Milowski (2002) *Piloter l'accès des femmes aux emplois supérieurs: premier rapport du Comité de pilotage pour l'égal accès des femmes et des hommes aux emplois supérieurs des fonctions publiques* (Paris: La Documentation française).

Lequesne, Christian (1993) *Paris-Bruxelles: comment se fait la politique européenne de la France* (Paris: Presses de la Fondation Nationale des Sciences Politiques).

L'état de la France, un panorama unique et complet de la France (2002) (Paris: La Découverte).

Levy, Jonah D. (1999) *Tocqueville's Revenge* (Cambridge, Mass., Harvard University Press).

Levy, Jonah D. (2001) 'Territorial politics after decentralisation' in Alain Guyomarch, Howard Machin, Peter A Hall and Jack Hayward (eds) *Developments in French Politics 2* (London: Palgrave) pp. 92–115.

Leyrit, Claude (1995) *Les Partis Politiques et l'Argent* (Paris: Le Monde editions).

Lochak, Danielle and Jacques Chevallier (1986) *La Haute Administration et la Politique* (Paris: Presses Universitaires de France).

Loiseau, Hervé (2002) 'Le rétrécissement du secteur public depuis 1985' *Cahiers Français* 311, pp. 36–8.

Lovecy, Jill (2000) 'The End of French exceptionalism?' in Robert Elgie (ed.) *The Changing French Political System* (London: Frank Cass) pp. 204–24.

Luchaire, François, Gérard Conac and Gilbert Mangin (1989) *Le Droit Constitutionel de la Cohabitation* (Paris: Economica).

Machin, Howard (1977) *The Prefect in French Public Administration* (London: Croom Helm; New York: St Martin's Press).

Machin, Howard (1979) 'The Traditional Structures of Local Government in France' in Jacques Lagroye and Vincent Wright (eds) *Local Government in Britain and France* (London: Allen and Unwin).

Machin, Howard (1989) 'The Evolution of the French Parties and the Party System' *West European Politics* 12 (3) (October).

Machin, Howard (1994) 'Changing Patterns of Party Competition' in Peter Hall, Jack Hayward and Howard Machin (1994) *Developments in French Politics* revised edn (London: Macmillan; New York: St Martin's Press) pp. 85–101.

Machin, Howard, (2001) 'Political Leadership' in Alain Guyomarch, Howard Machin, Peter A. Hall and Jack Hayward (eds) *Developments in French Politics 2* (London: Palgrave) pp. 68–91.

Machin, Howard and V. Wright (eds) (1985) *Economic Policy and Policy Making under the Mitterrand Presidency* (London: Pinter; New York: St Martin's Press).

Machin, Howard, and Alain Guyomarch (1994) '1990–1994' in Peter Hall, Howard Machin and Jack Hayward (eds) *Developments in French Politics* 2nd edn (London: Macmillan) pp. 298–322.

Maclean, Mairi, Charles Harvey and Jon Press (2001) 'Elites, Ownership and the internationalisation of French Business' *Modern and Contemporary France* 9 (3) August, pp. 313–25.

Maclean, Mairi (ed.) (1998) *The Mitterrand Years* (London: Macmillan).

Masclet, J.-C. (1982) *Un Député, pour quoi faire?* (Paris: Presses Universitaires de France).

Massot, Jean (1979) *Le Chef du Gouvernement en France* (Paris: Documentation Française).

Massot, Jean (1987) *L'Arbitre et le Capitaine* (Paris: Flammarion).

Massot, Jean (1991) 'Le Président de la République et le Premier Ministre' in Chagnollaud, Dominique (ed.) *Bilan Politique de la France 1991* (Paris: Hachette).

Massot, Jean (2002) 'La machine élyséenne' *Après-demain* 440/441 janvier–mars, pp. 29–32.

Maus, Didier (1989) 'Parliament in the Fifth Republic' in Paul Godt (ed.) *Policy-Making in France* (London: Pinter; New York, Colombia University Press).

Maus, Didier (1991) *La Pratique Constitutionelle Française 1 octobre 1989–30 septembre 1990* (Paris: Presses Universitaires de France).

Maus, Didier (1995) *Les Grands Textes de la Pratique Institutionnelle de La Ve République* (Paris: Documentation Française).

Mayer, Nona and Pascal Perrineau (eds) (1989) *Le Front National à Découvert* (Paris: Presses de la Fondation Nationale des Sciences Politiques).

McMillan, James (1992) *Twentieth Century France: Politics and Society 1898–1991*, 2nd edn (London: Edward Arnold).

Meininger, Marie-Christine (2000) 'The Development and Current Features of the French Civil Service System' in Hans A. G. M. Bekke and Frits M. van der Meer (eds) *Civil Service Systems in Western Europe* (Cheltenham: Edward Elgar) pp. 188–211.

Mendras, Henri with Alistair Cole (1991) *Social Change in Modern France: Towards a cultural anthropology of the Fifth Republic* (Cambridge: Cambridge University Press).

Mény Yves (1989) 'The National and International Context of French Policy Communities' *Political Studies*, 37 (3) (September).

Mény, Yves (1992) *La Corruption de la République* (Paris: Fayard).

Mény, Yves (1993) *Le système politique français* (Paris: Montchrestien).

Mény, Yves (1995) 'The Reconstruction and Deconstruction of the French Party System' in Flynn, Gregory (ed.) *Remarking the Hexagon: The New France in the New Europe* (Boulder: Colorado; Oxford: Westview Press).

Mény, Yves (1998) *The French Political System* (Paris: La Documentation Française).

Mermet, Gérard (2000) *Francoscopie 2001: Comment vivent les français?* Paris, Larousse

Milner, Susan (2000) 'Trades Unions, a new civil agenda' in Gino Raymond (ed.) *Structures of Power in Modern France* (London and New York, Macmillan).

Milner, Susan (2001) 'Globalisation and Employment in France: between flexibility and protection?' *Modern and Contemporary France* 9 (3), pp. 327–37.

Milner, Susan (2002) 'The Jospin Government and the 35 hour week' *Modern and Contemporary France* 10 (3), pp. 339–51.

Ministère de la Fonction Publique (1999) *La Fonction Publique de l'Etat 1998–9* (Paris: La Documentation Française).

Ministère de l'Intérieur (2002) *Les Collectivités Locales en Chiffres* at http://www.dgcl. interieur.gouv.fr/publications/CL_en_chiffres/accueil_CL_en_chiffres_2001.htm. (downloaded 13 August 2002).

Ministère de la Culture et de la Communication (1980) *Des Chiffres pour la Culture* (Paris: Documentation Française).

Mollet, Guy (1973) *Quinze Ans Après* (Paris: Albin Michel).

Monnet, J. (1978) *Memoirs* (London: Collins; New York: Bantam Books).

Mouriaux, Réné (1994) *Le Syndicalisme en France depuis 1945* (Paris: La Découverte).

Mouriaux, René and Geneviève Bibès (1990) *Les Syndicats Européens à l'Epreuve* (Paris: Presses de la Fondation Nationale des Sciences Politiques).

Muller, Pierre (ed.) (1992) *L'Administration Française est-elle en crise?* (Paris: L'Harmattan).

Muxel, Anne (ed.) (2001) 'Les Français et la Politique' *Problèmes Politiques et Sociaux* No. 865 (Paris: La Documentation Française).

Négrier, Emmanuel (2000) 'The Changing Role of French Local Government' in Robert Elgie (ed.) *The Changing French Political System* (London: Frank Cass) pp. 120–40.

Oberdorff Henri (1997) 'L'administration des sommets de l'Etat en France' *Revue française d'administration publique* No. 83, juillet-septembre, pp. 411–21.

Parodi, Maurice (1981) *L'Economie et la Société Française depuis 1945* (Paris: Colin).

Paxton, Robert (1972) *Vichy France: Old Guard and New Order* (New York: Columbia University Press).

Perrineau, Pascal (1993) 'Le Front National: La force solitaire' in Phillippe Habert, Pascal Perrineau and Colette Ysmal (eds) *Le Vote Sanction* (Paris: Départment des Etudes du Figaro et Presses de la Fondation Nationale des Sciences Politiques) pp. 137–59.

Perry, Sheila (ed.) (1997) *Aspects of Contemporary France* (London: Routledge).

Peters, B. Guy, Rod Rhodes and Vincent Wright (1997) 'Introduction: Tendances convergentes et spécificités nationales' in *Revue française d'administration publique*, no 83, juillet–septembre, pp. 381–95.

Pinchemel, Phillippe (1987) *France: A Geographical, Social and Economic Survey* (Cambridge and New York: Cambridge University Press).

Portelli, Hugues (1987) *La Politique en France sous la Ve République* (Paris: Grasset).

Portelli, Hugues (1990) *La Politique en France sous la Ve République* 2nd edn (Paris: Grasset).

Quermonne, Jean-Louis (1980) *Le Gouvernment de la France sons le Ve République* (Paris: Dalloz).

Quermonne, Jean-Louis (1991), *L'Appareil Administratif de l'Etat* (Paris: Seuil).

Quermonne, Jean-Louis and D. Chagnollaud (1996) *Le Gouvernement de la France sous la Ve République* 5th edn (Paris: Dalloz).

Rémond, Burno and Jacques Blanc (1989) *Les Collectivités Locales* (Paris: Presses de La Fondation Nationale des Sciences Politiques/Dalloz).

Rémond, Réné (1982) *Les Droites en France* (Paris: Aubier).

Reynolds, Siân (1988a) 'Whatever Happened to the French Ministry of Women's Rights?' *Modern and Contemporary France* 33 (April).

Reynolds, Siân (1988b) 'The French Ministry of Women's Rights 1981–1986: Modernisation or Marginalisation' in John Gaffney (ed.) *France and Modernisation* (Aldershot: Avebury; Brookfield, VT: Ashgate) pp. 149–69.

Reynolds, Siân (ed.) (1986) *Women, State and Revolution* (Brighton: Wheatsheaf; Amherst: University of Massachusetts Press).

Rhodes, R. A. W. (1992) *Beyond Westminster and Whitehall: the sub-central governments of Britain* 2nd ed (London: Routledge).

Rhodes R. A. W. and Patrick Weller (eds) (2001) *The Changing World of Top Officials: Mandarins or Valets* (London: Open University Press).

Richardson, Jeremy (1982) *Policy Styles in Western Europe* (London: Allen & Unwin).

Rillardon, Vincent (2000) 'Front contre Front' *Modern and Contemporary France* 8 (1) pp. 99–102.

Rioux, Jean-Pierre (1980) *La France et la Quatrième République, Tome 1. L'Ardeur et la Nécessité* (Paris: Seuil).

Roederer-Rynning, Christilla (2002) 'Farm conflict in France and Europeanisation of Agricultural Policy' *West European Politics* 25 (3), pp 105–24.

Rondin, Jacques (1985) *Le Sacre des Notables* (Paris: Fayard).

Rouban, Luc (1998a) *La Fin des Technocrates* Paris (Presses de Sciences Po).

Rouban, Luc (1998b) 'La Politisation des fonctionnaires en France: Obstacle ou nécessité?' *Revue française d'administration publique* No 86, avril–juin, pp. 167–82.

Rouban, Luc. 1996. *La Fonction Publique* (Paris: La Découverte).

Rousseau, J.-J. (1762) *The Social Contract*, Book 2, Ch. 3 (trans. G. D. H. Cole, revised edn.) (London: Dent, 1973).

Rucht, Dieter (2000) 'Political participation in Europe' in Richard Sakwa and Anne Stevens (eds) *Contemporary Europe* (London: Palgrave) pp. 85–108.

Rudelle, Odile (1985) 'Le Général de Gaulle et l'élection directe du Président de la République' in Duhamel, Olivier and Jean-Luc Parodi (eds) *La constitution de la Cinquième République* (Paris: Presses de la Fondation Nationale des Sciences Politiques) pp. 101–27.

Sadran, Pierre (1997) *Le système administratif français* (Paris: Montchrestien).

Safran, William (1995) *The French Polity* 4th edn (London and New York: Longman).

Sainteny, Guillaume (1991) *Les Verts* (Paris: Presses Universitaires de France: Que Sais-je? no. 2554).

Sainteny, Guillaume (1994) 'Le Parti Socialiste face à l'écologisme' *Revue Française de Science Politique* 44 (3) June.

Sainteny, Guillaume (2001) 'L' ecologisme français entre prêsent évanescent et avenir incertain' *Modern and Contemporary France* 9 (2) May, pp. 209–20.

Sauron, Jean-Luc (2000) *The French Administration and the European Union* (Paris: La Documentation Française).

Schifres, Michel and Michel Sarazin (1985) *L'Elysée de Mitterrand* (Paris: Alain Moreau).

Schmidt, Vivien (1990) *Democratising France* (Cambridge and New York: Cambridge University Press).

Schmidt, Vivien (1997) 'Running on empty: the end of *dirigisme* in French economic leadership' *Modern and Contemporary France* 5 (2), pp. 229–41.

Schrameck, Olivier (2001) *Matignon-Rive Gauche* (Paris: Editions du Seuil).

SOFRES (2002) *L'état de l'opinion 2002, présenté par Olivier Duhamel, Philippe Méchet* (Paris: Seuil).

Stewart, J. H. (1951) *A Documentary Survey of the French Revolution* (New York: Macmillan).

Stone, Alec (1992) *The Birth of Judicial Politics in France: The Constitutional Council in Comparative Perspective* (Oxford and New York: Oxford University Press).

Suleiman, Ezra (1974) *Politics, Power and Bureaucracy in France* (Princeton, NJ: Princeton University Press).

Suleiman, Ezra (1978) *Elites in French Society: The Politics of Survival* (Princeton, NJ: Princeton University Press).

Suleiman, Ezra and Guillaume Courty (1997) *L'age d'or de l'etat, une métamorphose annoncée* (Paris: Seuil).

Sutton, Michael (forthcoming) *France's Stamp on European Union*.

Szarka, Joseph (2000) 'The Parties of the French 'Plural Left': An uneasy complementarity' in Robert Elgie (ed.) *The Changing French Political System* (London: Frank Cass) pp. 20–37.

Tarrow, Sidney (1998) *Power in movement, social movements and contentious politics* 2nd edn (Cambridge: Cambridge University Press).

Thomson, David (1969) *Democracy in France Since 1870* 5th edn (Oxford: Oxford University Press).

Thuillier, Guy (1982) *Les cabinets ministériels* (Paris: Presses Universitaires de France: Que Sais-je no. 1985).

Thuillier, Guy and Jean Tulard (1984) *Histoire de l'administration Française* (Paris: Presses Universitaires de France: Que Sais-je no. 2137).

Tournier, Fréderique (1995) 'François Mitterrand et l'affaire Bousquet' *Modern and Contemporary France* NS3 (3).

Tremblay, Manon (2002) 'Les élites parlementaires Françaises et la parité: sur l'évolution d'une idée' *Modern and Contemporary France* 10 (1) (February) pp. 41–57.

Tulard, Marie-José (2001) 'The Financial Resources of Local Authorities' in Institut Internationale d'Administration Publique *Local Government in France* (Paris: Documentation Française) pp. 151–72.

Tuppen, John (1983) *The Economic Geography of France* (London: Croom Helm and New York: Barnes & Noble).

Usherwood, Simon (2002) 'Opposition to the EU in France: a Challenge to French Leadership' paper presented at the University Association for Contemporary European Studies conference, Belfast, September.

Wahl, N. (1959) 'The French Constitution of 1958: The Initial Draft and its Origins' *American Political Science Review*, 53 (June).

Waters, Sarah (1998a) 'New Social Movement Politics in France: the rise of civic forms of mobilisation' *West European Politics* 21 (3), pp. 170–186.

Waters, Sarah (1998b) 'New Social Movements in France: une nouvelle vague citoyenne?' *Modern and Contemporary France* 6 (4), pp. 493–504.

Weber, Eugen (1979) *Peasants into Frenchman: the modernisation of rural France* (London: Chatto & Windus; Stanford, CA: Stanford University Press).

Weil, Patrick (2001) 'The Politics of Immigration' in Alain Guyomarch, Howard Machin, Peter A. Hall and Jack Hayward (eds) *Developments in French Politics 2* (London: Palgrave) pp. 211–26.

Wilcox, Lynne (1994) 'Coup de Langue: The amendment to Article 2 of the Constitution' *Modern and Contemporary France* NS2 (3).

Williams, Philip (1970) *Wars, Plots and Scandals in Post War France* (Oxford: Oxford University Press).

Williams, Philip (1972) *Crisis and Compromise: Politics in the Fourth Republic*, paperback edn (London: Longman).

Wilson, Frank L. (1987) *Interest Group Politics in France* (New York: Cambridge University Press).

Wolfreys, Jim (2001) 'Shoes, Lies and Videotape: corruption and the French state' *Modern and Contemporary France* 9 (4), pp. 437–51.

Wright, Vincent (1989) *The Government and Politics of France* 3rd edn (London: Unwin Hyman).

Wright, Vincent (1993) 'The President and the Prime Minister' in Jack Hayward (ed.) *De Gaulle to Mitterrand* (London: Hurst) pp. 101–19.

Wright, Vincent, (1994) 'The Administrative Machine: old problems and new dilemmas' in Peter A. Hall, Jack Hayward and Howard Machin *Developments in French Politics*, revised edn (London: Macmillan) pp. 114–32.

Wright, Vincent (1997) 'Démocratiser l'Élite Française: Regard d'un Britannique' *Pouvoirs* 80 (l'ENA): 101–120.

Wright, Vincent (2000) 'The Fifth Republic: from the *Droit de l'Etat* to the *Etat de droit*? in Robert Elgie (ed.) *The Changing French Political System* (London: Frank Cass) pp. 94–119.

Ysmal, Colette (1989) *Les Partis Politiques sous La Ve République* (Paris: Montchrestien).

Ysmal, Colette (1990) *Le Comportement Electoral des Français*, 2nd edn (Paris: La Découverte).

Ysmal, Colette (1998) 'Le second tour: le prix de l'isolement de la droite moderée' in Pascal Perrineau and Colette Ysmal *Le Vote Surprise* (Paris: Presses de Sciences Po) pp. 285–302.

Index